ISLAND FISHING

History and Seascape of Marine Harvesting in the San Juan Islands amid the Salish Sea

Boyd C. Pratt

Mulno Cove Publishing
FRIDAY HARBOR

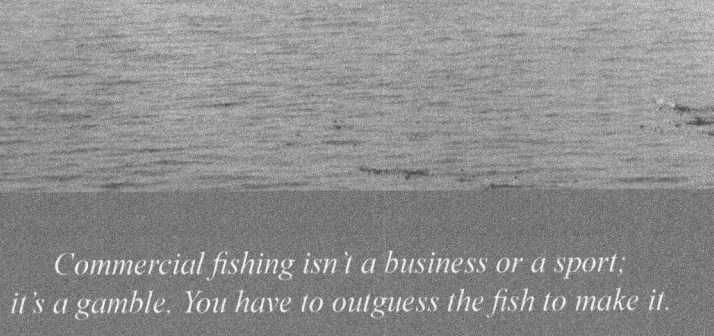

Commercial fishing isn't a business or a sport; it's a gamble. You have to outguess the fish to make it.
— Henry Cayou

ISLAND FISHING

History and Seascape of Marine Harvesting in the San Juan Islands amid the Salish Sea

by Boyd C. Pratt

Copyright ©2024 Boyd C. Pratt
2nd Edition
All rights reserved

No part of this publication may be reproduced or transmitted in English or in other languages, in any form or by any means, electronic or mechanical, including photocopying, digital scanning, recording, or any other informational storage or retrieval system, without the written permission of the author.

ISBN: 978-1-7342351-6-6

Published and Distributed by Mulno Cove Publishing
Printed in the United States of America

TABLE OF CONTENTS

Preface i
Introduction iii
The Salish Sea
    The San Juan Islands amid the Salish Sea 1
    Geology and Geography 2
    Island Coastlines, Sea Bottoms, Tides, and Currents 3
Natural History
    Ecosystem 9
    Seashore Zones 11
Indigenous Peoples
    History 13
    Fishing Villages 15
    Canoes 19
Indigenous Fishing Methods
    Shellfish and Other Tidal Zone Gathering 27
    Clam Gardening 28
    Eelgrass and Kelp Harvesting 29
    Spearing 30
    Raking 31
    Roe Gathering 32
    Gillnetting 34
    Reef Netting 35
    Weirs 41
    Trolling and Other Hook, Line, and Sinker Methods 41
    Sealing and Whaling 43
Indigenous Consumption, Preservation, and Trade 45
Europeans and Euro Americans
    Exploration and Survey 48
    Trade 50
    Boats and Ships 55

Fishing Methods after European and Euro American Contact
- Fish Trapping 60
- Reef Netting 81
- Weirs 86
- Beach Seining 87
- Purse Seining 88
- Gillnetting 102
- Trolling 107
- Setlines 112
- Bottom Trawling 113
- Sealing and Whaling 114
- Diving 117

Fish and Other Marine Harvests
- Salmon 118
- Herring and Smelt 122
- Halibut 129
- Rockfish 132
- Dogfish 134
- Shrimp 136
- Crab 137
- Lobster 138
- Kelp 138
- Nori 139
- Clams 139
- Oysters 142
- Shellfish Farming 147
- Scallops 150
- Abalone 150
- Octopus 151
- Sea Urchins 151
- Sea Cucumbers 153

Preservation and Marketing
- Salting and Smoking 154
- Canning 158
- Big Business 180
- Fresh and Frozen Fish 188

Fishers, Camps, Shoreline Structures, and Public Facilities
   Fishers 193
   Camps 197
   Shoreline Structures 204
   Public Facilities 206
Recreation
   Sport Fishing and Shellfish Harvesting............................ 208
   Hotels, Fishing Lodges, Resorts, and Marinas................ 214
   Derbies 217
Government
   National and State Fish Commissions 219
   Regulation... 220
Education, Research, and Advocacy 232
Current Regulations, Conditions, and Issues
   Regulation... 241
   Climate Change 242
   Piracy, Poaching, and Derelict Gear 244
   Finfish Net Pens... 245
   Southern Resident Killer Whales 248
Epilogue: And It All Comes Back to Salmon......................... 251
Acknowledgements 259
San Juan Islands Place Names... 260
Appendices
   Fish and Other Seafood 261
   Reef Nets 277
   Fish Traps.. 281
   Salting, Smoking, and Canning Operations................... 289
   Companies.. 296
   Boat and Ship Builders... 307
   Fishing Boats and Ships 311
   Island Fishers... 324
Glossary 342
Resources.. 352
Photo and Illustration Credits 371
Index 374

*Let us acknowledge that we reside on
the ancestral lands and waters of
the Coast Salish people,
who have called this place home
since time immemorial,
and let us honor and protect
inherent, aboriginal, and treaty rights
that have been passed down from
generation to generation.*

PREFACE

Growing up on islands, I have always been fascinated with the bounty of the Pacific Ocean and the inland waters of the Salish Sea. I am not a fisher. I have fished and gathered sea creatures, for pleasure, first in Hawaii, where my grandfather and several uncles were avid line and net fishers, and later on San Juan Island in Griffin Bay. But I have never fished for subsistence or a living, which is a significant difference from the people and the methods that I talk about in this book.

One thing that sparked my interest in fishing is the story of a place—Salmon Bank off the south shore of San Juan Island—as told by Julie Stein, a geoarchaeologist who holds a doctorate in anthropology and is the director of the Burke Museum. During the first two decades of the 2000s, Julie gave an annual outdoor talk for the National Park Service at Alaska Packers Rock on South Beach, part of the San Juan Island National Historical Park. She would begin by going back millennia to the geologic eras that created the San Juans, and then tell how the glaciations of the late Pleistocene carved and molded the landscape, the great weight of the ice pushing the islands down and then, retreating, leaving behind the glacial moraine that formed Salmon Bank and the stair-step-like evidence of varying shorelines that demonstrate the dynamic balance between the release of the weight and the addition of glacial ice melt to the seawater. Julie called our attention to the predominant southerly winds that swept the shore and prairie, helping indigenous peoples to dry and preserve their catch several thousand years ago at the Cattle Point site, the first systematically recorded archaeological site in San Juan County and Washington State. She would pull it all together by looking at that place through time, opening our senses to the dynamic interaction between sea and land and the peoples who fished and lived there.

In the 1960s, when I was a boy coming with my family to spend summers here, Friday Harbor was still a fishing village, and at night we could see the bright riding lights of the gillnetters and purse seiners anchored at Fish Creek. We would spend idyllic summer days digging clams in Mulno Cove and fishing for ling cod in the kelp beds off Dinner Island. My grandmother Ruth, armed with an oyster knife and wedges of lemon, almost single-handedly decimated the local oyster population. Back then, orcas were called killer whales and my brother and I were both awed and terrified when a pod surfaced around our 10-foot rowboat, so close we could feel the warm moisture of their exhalations on our faces. My kids grew up eating sockeye salmon we bought from a friend who reef netted off Stuart Island's Reid Harbor. All this, of course, is but a very small part of the 7,000-year history of fishing in the San Juan Islands and the Salish Sea.

This book is just one of the many histories that could be written about this subject. Its purpose is to offer a tribute to the fishers of the Salish Sea, and the San Juans in particular. It is neither my place nor intent to write about the central importance—both cultural and sacred—of fisheries to the Tribes and First Nations; I mean no disrespect by not emphasizing that in this book. Furthermore, I could not possibly mention all those who have benefited from the rich resources of the waters of the Salish Sea, even if I knew them or of them. My intent is to celebrate the rich and complex history of interaction among the varied fishing peoples of this unique place.

PREFACE TO THE SECOND EDITION

On this, the 50th anniversary of the Boldt Decision, I want to acknowledge its signal importance to the history of fishing here in the unceded waters of the Salish Sea.

INTRODUCTION

This book is a history of fishing in the Salish Sea in general and the San Juan Islands in particular. By fishing, I mean both the literal act of catching fish and the harvesting of sea animals and plants for all manner of use, along with all the related subjects such as transportation, processing, and marketing. Fishing, in this sense, includes mariculture, or the cultivation of marine organisms such as shellfish. The period covered by this history extends from the first human presence in the region to the present. According to some anthropologists, settlement in the region first occurred about 14,000 years ago; some Indigenous peoples aver that they have been here from time immemorial. I have not presumed to address the cultural, social, and spiritual importance of fishing to the Tribes and First Nations of the region, but instead concentrated on subsistence and commerce.

The Salish Sea is defined by: the western boundary is the entrance to Juan de Fuca Strait (a line between Cape Flattery and Carmanah Point); the southern boundary is the south end of Puget Sound; the northern boundary extends just beyond the Strait of Georgia to include those channels and waterways where the floodstream or tidal surge is from the south: Discovery Passage south of Seymour Narrows, Sutil Channel south of Penn Islands, Lewis Channel, Waddington Channel & Pendrell Sound, Desolation Sound, and the southern portion of Homfray Channel. This includes the waterways of the Strait of Juan de Fuca, the Strait of Georgia, Puget Sound, and all their connecting channels and adjoining waters, such as Haro Strait, Rosario Strait, Bellingham Bay, Hood Canal, and the waters around and between the San Juan Islands in the State of Washington, United States, and the Gulf Islands in British Columbia, Canada.

— Report of the Transboundary Georgia Basin-Puget Sound Environmental Indicators Working Group (2002)

The area of this study is the Salish Sea, with a focus on the San Juan Islands. Historically, this region, comprising Puget Sound, the Strait of Juan de Fuca, Boundary, Haro, and Rosario Passes, and Georgia Strait, was first called "Puget Sound" by the Euro American fishing industry and subsequently by the Washington State Department of Fisheries.

> *Strictly speaking, the name Puget Sound should be restricted to that long, narrow arm extending south from the Strait of Juan de Fuca, but a practice has developed, and is now common among fishermen and others, of designating all the great water area in the State of Washington comprising Puget Sound proper, Strait of Juan de Fuca, Canal de Haro, Rosario Strait, the Gulf of Georgia, and the smaller straits, bays, and sounds, as Puget Sound. ... This practice, for the sake of convenience, has been followed by this report.*
>
> — John N. Cobb, *Pacific Salmon Fisheries*, U.S. Bureau of Fisheries Report (1919)

The use of the name Salish Sea is of recent origin. It was initially proposed in 1989 by Western Washington University marine sciences professor Bert Webber; his proposal describes the inland marine waters of southwest British Columbia and northern Washington State as a single estuarine ecosystem and as such warranting an inclusive and descriptive name of its own. After the name was rejected because Webber was unable to demonstrate public use or familiarity with the name, he proposed it again in 2009. In August of that year, the British Columbia Geographical Names Office approved a resolution recommending that the Geographical Names Board of Canada adopt the name Salish Sea contingent on approval by the United States Board on Geographic Names. The name was endorsed by the Washington State Board on Geographic Names in late October; it was approved by the United States Board on Geographic Names in November and by the British Columbia

Geographical Names Office in February 2010. This book will predominantly use the term "Salish Sea" for the region, but the language in many of the historical resources will refer to Puget Sound in its broader use as a place name.

The importance of talking about the Salish Sea is based on its definition as a complete ecosystem that includes both the watershed and the marine environment. The area is largely defined by its signal species, the salmonids, and their habitat. Breeding in the many rivers and tributaries that surround the Salish Sea, salmon migrate to the open ocean and then return to their breeding grounds. Throughout historic time, salmon have been the principal catch in the region, so much so that various Coast Salish groups have called themselves "People of the Salmon." Later, with the introduction of Europeans and Euro Americans and their fishing technologies, salmon became the primary focus of their catch, processing, and marketing. Today, facing years of overharvesting and the impacts from a burgeoning human population, salmon remain the focus of restoration in the Salish Sea, with protection and restoration as the goal.

Several terms used in this book require explanation. As a general rule, the term "Indigenous peoples" refers to the inhabitants of the region prior to the arrival of Europeans, Euro Americans, and their descendants. In the Salish Sea, this refers to the Coast Salish—an anthropological term for groups of people who spoke similar languages—with the specific descriptive "Straits Salish" referring to the Coast Salish in the Salish Sea, related not only in their language but also in many cultural traits, such as reef netting. This includes the Lummi, Saanich, Samish, Semiahmoo, Songhees, and Sooke, with mutually intelligible dialects, as well as the Klallam of the Olympic Peninsula, a different language group.

The arrival of Europeans and Euro Americans complicated the naming of Indigenous peoples. Not only did the Spanish, English, and Americans overlay their own names on places in the Salish Sea, they assigned various peoples to various groupings that did not necessarily reflect how those peoples described themselves. When another system of control—government—was imposed, Indigenous groups were defined by recognition through treaties. In the newly formed Territory of Washington (1853), Governor Isaac Stevens negotiated 13 treaties with "Native Nations"; the Treaty of Point Elliott (1855) included "Tribes" of the Salish Sea. On Vancouver Island, James Douglas of the Hudson's Bay Company purchased, at the request of the British Crown, 14 parcels of First Nations land (now known as the "Douglas Treaties") in the period from 1850–1854. "Tribes" and "First Nations" then became "recognized" or "unrecognized" (i.e., defined by their political status in relation to the United States or Canadian governments).

The terms "European" and "Euro American" are used to define any non-Indigenous peoples. They include such ethnically diverse groups as English, Irish, Scots, and Welsh historically subsumed by the designation "English" and all sorts of immigrants classified as "Americans." Furthermore, the Hudson's Bay Company—at the forefront of European settlement in the region—employed, in addition to "Englishmen," a wide variety of ethnicities, including French Canadians, Hawaiians, Iroquois, Norwegians, and Metis (people of mixed French Canadian and upper Midwestern tribes). This terminology is compounded by the use of "Euro American" to describe ethnic groups such as the Japanese, Chinese, and Filipinos—clearly neither "European" nor "American" at the time.

In this book, I have tried to use (and explain the use of) the terms as they are found in original sources. For instance, the prevailing term for Hawaiians in the Pacific Northwest was "Kanakas," a designation that has been considered pejorative in the past but has recently been re-engaged by contemporary Hawaiians as a source of prideful identity. My intent is not to offend; my apologies for any whom I have put off by using language this way. Furthermore, in quoting from historic sources, there are expressed opinions or language that some may find offensive in light of our present experience and history; again, my intent is not to offend by doing so but to let the people speak for themselves within the context and language of their day.

Wherever possible, I have tried to include Indigenous group or place names in Straits Salish. These are rendered in Americanist Phonetic Notation or North American Phonetic Alphabet (NAPA), originally developed by European and American anthropologists for the phonetic transcription of Indigenous languages of the North America. For those who would like to hear how some of these names are spoken, I recommend the Samish Indian Nation's StoryMap "Coast Salish Place Names of the San Juan Islands," which includes links to recordings of the words being spoken.

The use of several technical terms can be confusing. The term "gear" is a common industry designation of the methods and materials used in catching or harvesting sea animals and plants. Because the Salish Sea covers a transboundary region with governments that have adopted different measurement systems—imperial/U.S. and metric—descriptions may differ, predominantly feet and tons but at times in meters and tonnes. Furthermore, the standard British and American marine measurement is the fathom (six feet), so in descriptions of depths of water or width of gear, the number will be in fathoms, not feet. But feet are used in other situations, such as the dimensions of a boat or building.

This book discusses island fishing by first describing the natural features of the Salish Sea and the creatures—flora, invertebrates, fish, and mammals—that inhabit it. (More detailed descriptions of individual species that were fished or harvested are contained in the appendices.) Because of the long history of occupation and use of the area by the Coast Salish, their canoes, fishing and harvesting methods, and preservation and trade are discussed as a unit. Once Europeans and Euro Americans arrived, Indigenous fishing did not cease, but it did change, and so becomes a part of the wider narrative. After the arrival of Europeans and Euro Americans, the book first discusses the change in boat and ship technology and then methods of fishing—"gear"— such as hook-and-line, spears, weirs, and nets, including encirclement, entrapment, and enmeshment. Then, specific catches are described by species: salmon being the central one, but also other types of finfish (herring and smelt and halibut and other ground fish), sharks, and invertebrates such as mollusks—clams, oysters, and mussels; crustaceans such as crabs, shrimp, and even lobsters; echinoderms such as sea urchins and sea cucumbers; and seaweeds. Once caught, seafood that was not immediately eaten was either shipped fresh or preserved: salted or smoked; canned; or frozen. The people who fished and where they worked come next, grouped principally by ethnicity and location. Recreational fishing, both for fish and shellfish harvesting, is a more recent phenomenon. Government involvement, often from establishment of Euro American political systems, first occurs in the areas of study and promotion, and then in intervention through legislation and regulation. Finally, issues of our contemporary world are discussed: current regulation; piracy, poaching, and derelict gear; finfish net pens; Southern Resident killer whales; and climate change (sea level rise, rising water temperatures, and ocean acidification). The epilogue, "And It All Comes Back to Salmon," attempts to bring the narrative full circle in order to understand our current situation in the light of history. Several appendices supplement the text: fish and other seafood; reef nets; fish traps; canneries; companies; boat and ship builders; fishing boats and ships; and, last but by no means least, island fishers. A thematic glossary is included to help with some of the more obscure terms. Because I find them distracting to the narrative, I have deliberately decided not to include either footnotes or endnotes, but there is a section, called "Resources," consisting of detailed suggestions for further reading, which indicate my sources. Because my intent is to let history speak for itself, through the words of historic peoples, I have cited the sources of any direct quotation.

A general theme articulated by Brian Fagan in his 2017 global history, *Fishing: How the Sea Fed Civilization*, is applicable to the post-contact era in the Salish Sea within the greater context of the Pacific Ocean: as a rule, fishers throughout history have overfished an area and then moved on. This has certainly been the case for the West Coast, with fishers moving from the Sacramento River (1850–1870) to the Columbia River (1860–1900), to Puget Sound (1890–1920), and then on to Alaska (1900–1960), the "Last Frontier." (Recent research, however, has shown that "Alaskan" salmonid populations largely originate in the Salish Sea.) It is tempting to view the history of fishing in the San Juan Islands solely within this context: the exploitation and then abandonment of a natural resource. But the history of these times is far more complex than that simple scenario. Taking the ecosystem approach as exemplified by the use of the name "Salish Sea," the interrelationships between natural and human groups paint a clearer picture of how the region works as a whole.

By looking at the finer grain, particularly through the lens of a common, everyday approach to history, one gets a better picture of the fishers of the islands of the Salish Sea. Ultimately, that is what this book is about: the people.

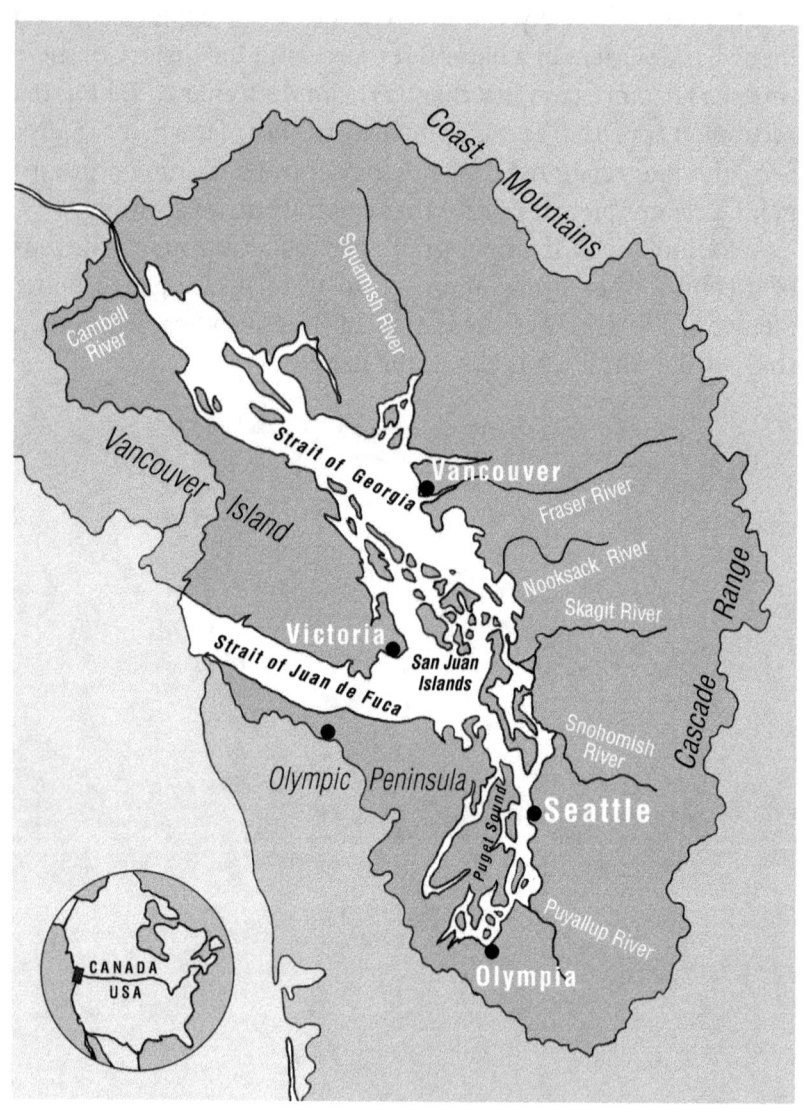

Map of the Salish Sea
(Marine Area in White and Watershed in Dark Grey)

THE SALISH SEA

The San Juan Islands amid the Salish Sea

This history focuses on the San Juan Islands, although by necessity it also includes aspects of the history of fishing in the surrounding Salish Sea. The Salish Sea, which is a recently (2009) designated region, consists of Puget Sound, the Strait of Juan de Fuca, and the Strait of Georgia. It can also be defined as the body of water surrounded by the landmasses of the Olympic Peninsula to the south, Vancouver Island to the west, and the Canadian and United States mainland to the north and east. This comprises a sea surface of 6,535 square miles and a coastline that is 4,642 miles long, and contains 419 islands, with a combined land area of 1,413 square miles. The San Juan Islands are bounded by Haro Strait to the west and northwest, the Strait of Georgia to the north and northeast, Rosario Strait to the east, and the Strait of Juan de Fuca and Puget Sound to the south. San Juan County—which encompasses most of the San Juan Archipelago and consists of over 128 named islands, reefs, and rocks at high tide—has about 175 square miles of land and more than 400 miles of marine shoreline.

Several river systems flow into the Salish Sea—mainly on the mainland to the north and east—the Nooksack, Skagit, Snohomish, and Duwamish—and the Olympic Peninsula to the south—the Skokomish, Quilcene, Dungeness, and Elwha. The main freshwater system is Canada's Fraser River, one of the major rivers of the North American continent and second in size only to the Columbia in the amount of water that it delivers to the Pacific Ocean. The Salish Sea, and the San Juan Islands in particular, can be considered as within the lower course of the Fraser. During its peak in late summer, the Fraser disgorges 2.6 million gallons of freshwater a second, and its plume, which forms a surface layer 6–33 feet thick, can easily be seen in aerial photographs reaching the Gulf Islands across from its mouth.

The physical features of the Salish Sea in general and the San Juan Islands in particular— geology and geography—have a signal effect upon local fishing.

Geology and Geography

The geology of the islands in the Salish Sea is extremely complex. In essence the islands comprise the highest points of a submerged mountain range, consisting of older base rock associated with the surrounding Cascade and Olympic Mountain ranges. During the late Pleistocene Era (occurring 50,000–12,000 years ago), a series of three great glaciations occurred, with the ice reaching as far south as modern-day Olympia, filling the depression known as the Puget Trough and leaving only the surrounding mountain ranges uncovered. Upon their recession, the glaciers not only scraped the existing rocky areas, but also left behind glacial till. One of the most important of these deposits is Salmon Bank off of South Beach on San Juan Island, a submerged shelf formed by glacial moraines. The mile-long Salmon Bank, which runs parallel to the shoreline a half mile offshore, averages about 10 fathoms in depth.

After the release of weight due to the melting of glacial ice, the islands gradually rose in a process called isostatic rebound. During the same period, the melting of the receding glaciers also caused a gradual rise in sea level, so that the result of these forces led to a series of shorelines that differed from the current one. At one point, the shoreline was 400 feet above what we find today. All or most of Beaverton, San Juan, and West Valleys and other lower areas on San Juan Island; Deer Harbor, Crow Valley, and Eastsound on Orcas Island; and major portions of Lopez Island were under water at one time.

The islands exhibit a wide degree of relief. There are numerous rocky knobs, including 15 mountains that rise 1,000 feet or more above sea level, with Mount Constitution on Orcas being the highest at 2,409 feet in elevation. The glacial scourings of the islands led to areas of low relief, such as glacial plains and gently rolling and basin-like areas, exemplified by San Juan Valley on San Juan, Crow Valley on Orcas, and several parts of Lopez.

Drainage mainly occurs by means of short, intermittent streams; only a few streams were probably capable of bearing fish spawning. Some estuarine tidal systems also occur, such as Fish Trap Creek, which drains into Cayou Lagoon near Deer Harbor on Orcas Island. The watersheds that recently or currently support marine fish such as salmonids are False Bay and Garrison Creeks on San Juan Island and Bayhead/Victoria, Fish Trap, Cascade, Crow Valley (West Sound), Doe Bay, and West Beach Creeks on Orcas Island.

Island Coastlines, Sea Bottoms, Tides, and Currents

The coastlines of the San Juan Islands are deeply indented with many sheltered coves and inlets, including several, such as East- and West Sounds on Orcas, which resemble fjords. This rugged and irregular shoreline is generally elevated and rocky, although there are stretches of gravelly and sandy beaches. The same physical forces that formed the exposed land also formed the sea bottom or ocean floor. The channels between the islands are generally narrow and U-shaped from glacial action and range from 16 to 100 fathoms deep. The large amount of water moving to and from the Strait of Juan de Fuca and the Strait of Georgia through the islands causes heavy riptides and eddies.

The situation of the islands also lends itself to several distinct marine habitats. Sheltered by Vancouver Island and the Olympic Peninsula from the direct waters of the Pacific Ocean, the Salish Sea has a wider range of salinity and temperature, which in turn requires a greater degree of tolerance by sea organisms. Average Salish Sea water temperatures vary from 45°F in the winter to 52°F in the summer. Water currents course through the islands with two ebb and two flood tides each day. Because of all the obstructions and constrictions in the inland waters, there is a large difference in tides: for instance, Victoria, on the southern tip of Vancouver Island, has tidal shifts 5 hours and 35 minutes later than Tofino, located on the west (Pacific) side of Vancouver Island. Tides in the islands can range up to 14 feet, with an extreme low of -4 feet and an extreme high of over 10.

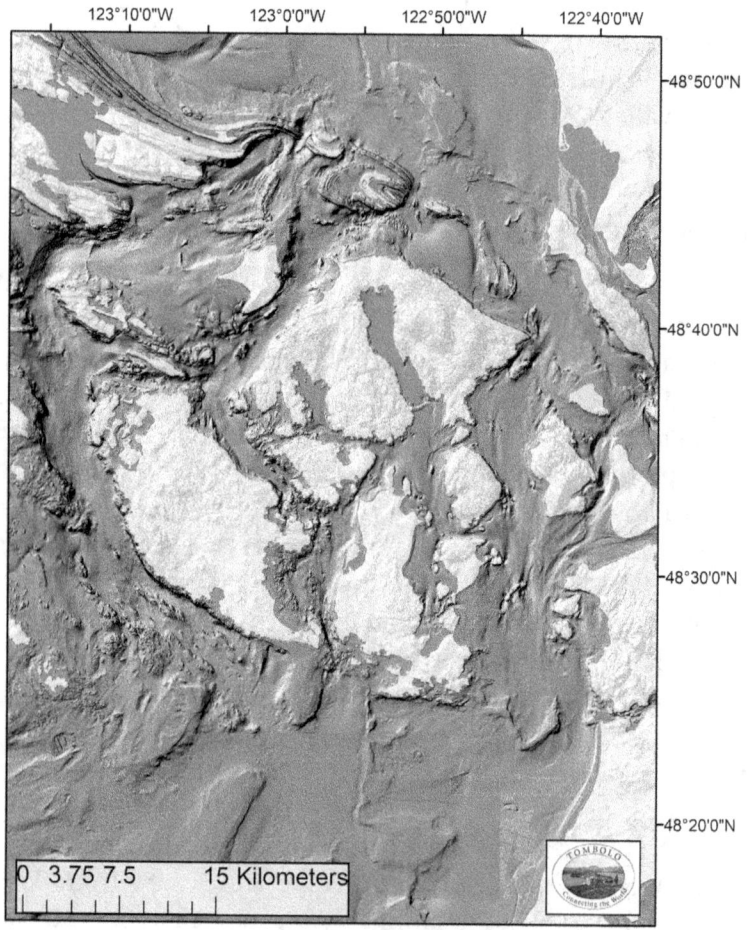

Map Developed by John Aschoff and Gary Greene
San Juan Archipelago in Central Salish Sea

*Bathymetry of the San Juan Islands
(courtesy of Tombolo Mapping Lab, Moss Landing Marine Labs Center
for Habitat Studies, Geologic Survey Canada, and NOAA)*

> The archipelago occupies an important position in its relation to the other parts of this region. Lying just north of the eastern end of the Straits of Fuca, through which the currents of Puget Sound, and perhaps also of the Gulf of Georgia, flow during the rise and fall of the tides, it obstructs the currents flowing to and from the Gulf of Georgia, giving them various courses of deflection, and often producing, in many places, tide-rips sufficiently extensive to endanger small craft.
>
> The islands are separated by narrow but very deep channels, so deep indeed that the largest class vessels can pass through almost any of them. This is the character of almost every narrow channel separating islands lying between the continent and Vancouver's Island, and has led many a sailor to compare these waters to the Straits of Magellan, where it is often difficult to find anchorage.
>
> — Geographical Memoir of the Islands
> between the Continent and Vancouver's Island
> in the Vicinity of the Forty Ninth Parallel of North Latitude (1860)

The overall system of circulation in the Salish Sea is complex and influenced by many variables. Because of the height of the Coast, Olympic, and Cascade Ranges, moisture-laden air coming in from the Pacific Ocean encounters the cool mountainous air and sheds most of its water, in the form of fog, rain, and snow, on the western slopes of the mountains. (An exception is the region defined by Victoria to the west, the Gulf Islands to the north, and Sequim on the Olympic Peninsula to the south, with the San Juans in the middle—the "Blue Hole," which, lying in a rain shadow, experiences drier, sunnier weather.) This precipitation feeds the rivers—mainly through the melting of the snow in late summer—and they in turn discharge their freshwater, laden with sediments, nutrients, and other organic matter, into the Salish Sea. Since freshwater is less dense than saltwater, it flows from the river's mouth and, in the case of the Fraser River, the main source, toward the Strait of Juan de Fuca and the Pacific Ocean, while the denser saltwater flows in from the ocean

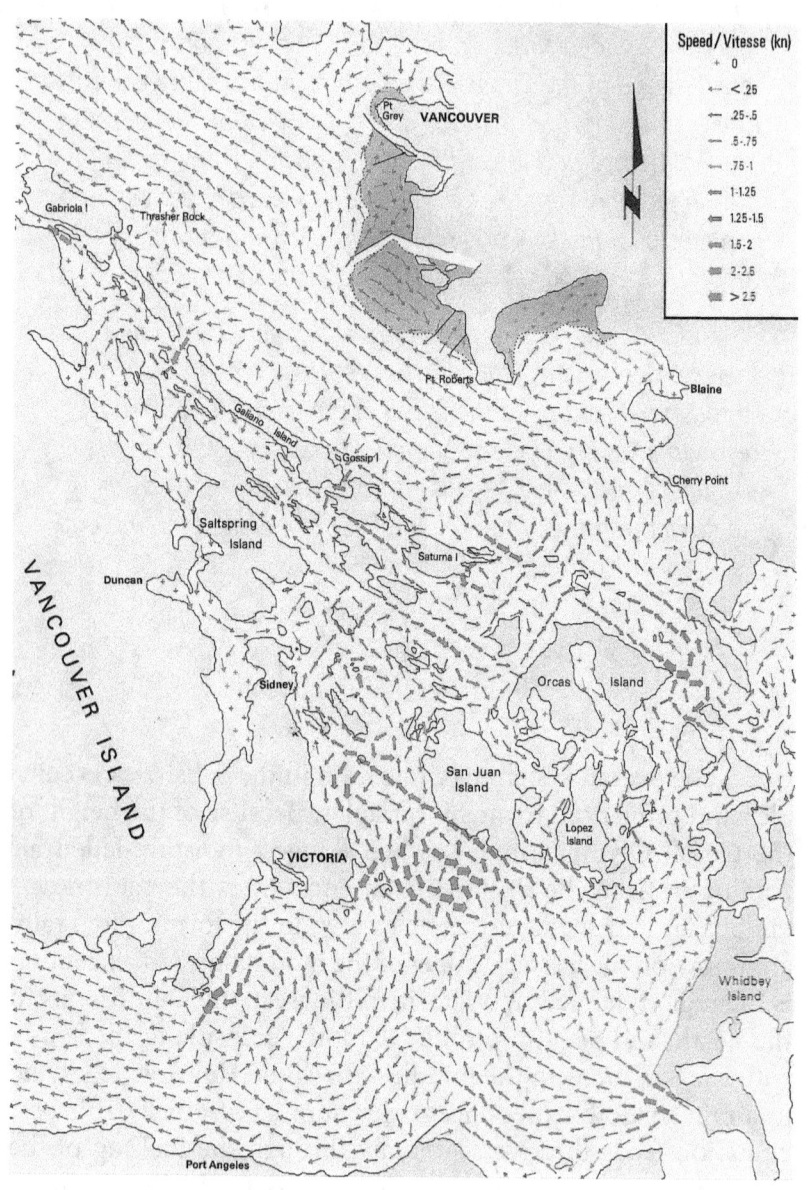

The Canadian Hydrographic Service,
Current Atlas Juan de Fuca Strait to Strait of Georgia, Chart 8

toward the islands and Strait of Georgia. Winds in the region, which are northerly in the winter, push the surface water off the coasts, which cause an upwelling of nutrient-rich but oxygen-poor water. These waters—outgoing estuarine surface water and incoming nutrient-rich ocean water—get mixed up when the currents encounter the sills of underwater mountains. Furthermore, tidal currents flow past protruding parts of land and cause eddies to the lee side of the land, bearing nutrients and microorganisms such as plankton to nearshore marine communities. This overall exchange of nutrients and other factors sustain the many unique habitats of the Salish Sea.

The Salish Sea, although an inland body of water, is affected by cyclical trends in the larger Pacific Ocean system. Three of these are the Pacific Decadal Oscillation, the El Niño-Southern Oscillation, and the North Pacific Gyre Oscillation. The Pacific Decadal Oscillation is an index of sea surface temperature, which shifts between warm (positive) and cool (negative) phases. In the positive phase, waters along the west coast of North America are warmer and winds tend to come from the south. The negative phase is the opposite: coastal waters are cooler, and winds tend to come from the north. Although the typical pattern is for the cycle (oscillation) to occur every 5–10 years, there have been longer periods of one mode predominating; in the late 1970s, for instance, a warm phase began after a 30-year period of cool conditions, affecting marine ecosystems throughout the Salish Sea. Since just prior to the turn of the present century, a cool phase has returned.

The El Niño-Southern Oscillation is a periodic fluctuation in the atmospheric sea level pressure measured between Tahiti in the central South Pacific and Darwin, Australia. The oscillation is negative when the measurement over Tahiti is lower than normal and that at Darwin is higher than normal; as a result, the normal easterly trade winds over the equatorial Pacific are diminished. The warm water mass that normally gets pushed to the western part of the Pacific Ocean shifts to the east, running along the coastlines of North and South America. This phenomenon, called El Niño, affects marine organisms through abnormal coastal sea levels, which suppress upwelling and reduce deepwater nutrient supply. The positive oscillation, La Niña, strengthens equatorial trade winds, resulting in colder waters along the west coasts. This oscillation can also affect storm systems in the region. The average storm events for the northwest coast—three in the period from October through December and four from January through March—can increase in a strong El Niño or moderate-to-strong La Niña year phase; they are less likely during neutral or moderate El Niño conditions.

The North Pacific Gyre Oscillation, which is determined by processes that control the height of the sea surface, has a strong influence on salinity and nutrients. It is a factor in the seasonal wind shift from southerlies in the winter to northerlies in the summer, which in turn affect upwelling, which brings deep, cold, salty, nutrient-rich, oxygen-poor waters to the surface. Upwelling is a direct factor in the production of phytoplankton, a major food source for the smaller marine organisms in the Salish Sea.

NATURAL HISTORY

Ecosystem

The Salish Sea offers a rich ecosystem for organisms, with thousands of species of marine invertebrates, hundreds of species of plants, more than 250 species of fish, almost 175 species of seabirds, and over 30 species of marine mammals. The physical nature of the region supports this vast array of wildlife, which comprises several interconnected and interdependent food webs. Two vital plant and algae species serve as habitat for many of the species in the area: eelgrass (*Zostera marina*) and bull kelp (*Nereocystis luetkeana*). The San Juan Islands have over 140 miles of eelgrass beds and a third of the bull kelp in the Puget Sound region. Eel grass—a grass, not a seaweed—is rooted by rhizomes into the sandy or muddy intertidal zones of bays, estuaries, and other nearshore areas, offering habitat for microorganisms such as phytoplankton and zooplankton and providing shelter and foraging areas for rockfish, salmon, and Dungeness crabs. Pacific herring lay their eggs on its strands. Bull kelp is a brown alga that forms forests along the nearshore environment and provides shelter for fish, invertebrates, and marine mammals such as otters, seals, sea lions, and whales. They attract many seabirds, specifically cormorants, gulls, terns, and great blue herons.

Local populations of forage fish, occupying the lower trophic level (i.e., near the "bottom" of the food chain) constitute a vital part of the Salish Sea food web. Consisting of about 10 principal species, of which Pacific herring, sand lance, and smelt (eulachon and surf and longfin smelt) are the principal species, forage fish feed on phytoplankton and zooplankton, converting nutrients to fatty tissues and in turn become prey to larger fish such as salmon, seabirds, and sea mammals. Habitat is particularly important: Pacific herring can only spawn in nearshore areas, laying their eggs on kelp, eelgrass, and other seaweeds; sand lance prefer fine-grain (sandy) beaches and underwater beds; and surf smelt need a particular texture of pebbly beach to lay their eggs. "Feeder bluffs," tall cliffs of clay and sand, gradually erode from wave action to form the substrate of beaches in coves and harbors, which in turn provide forage fish habitat.

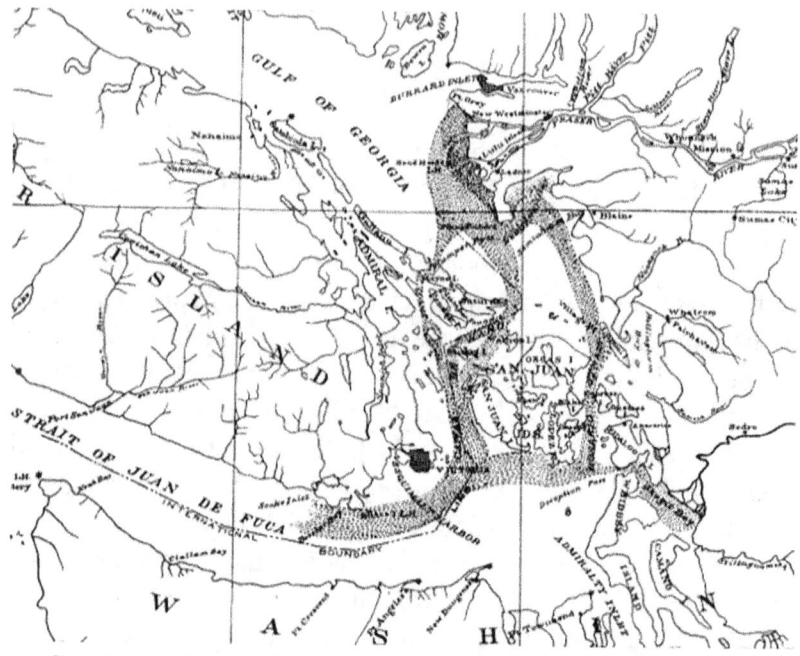

Sketch Map Showing the Approximate Route of the Sockeye Salmon in Approaching the Fraser River and Skagit River from the Strait of Juan de Fuca Richard Rathbun, A Review of the Fisheries in the Contiguous Waters of the State of Washington and British Columbia (1900)

Salmon, which are anadromous (live in both fresh- and saltwater), return as adults to their natal freshwater streams to lay their eggs in gravel beds and then die. The fry make their way down the river to saltwater as smolts and then spend several months to a year or two, depending on the species, in the nearshore environment, particularly around the San Juan Islands, to mature and then eventually migrate out to sea. The example of Chinook is instructive: 22 independent populations have been identified in the Salish Sea, and it is likely that they all occupy the San Juan Islands nearshore ecosystem at some point in their life cycles. Juvenile Chinook salmon found in the San Juans come from Whidbey Basin, Strait of Juan de Fuca, South Sound Fall and Hood Canal, Olympic Peninsula, and Nooksack River. Juvenile salmon from eight watersheds in British Columbia, Canada, also need the habitat found in the San Juans to survive. Canadian Chinook stocks found in the San Juans have been identified as coming from West Vancouver Island, Upper Fraser River, South Thompson River, North Thompson River, Mid Fraser River, Lower Thompson River, Lower Fraser River, and East Vancouver Island.

Seashore Zones

The seashore is divided into several zones according to the depth of water and the habitat that it creates. The intertidal zone, also known as the nearshore, is the area where the sea meets the land, within the tidal range: above water level at low tide and underwater at high tide. (Sometimes this is referred to as the littoral zone, although that can be defined as a wider region.) This area, depending on its exposure to air, can include several types of habitats with various species of life. The upper spray or splash zone, which is only submerged during exceptional high tides or storms, supports the hardiest species that are able to withstand its extreme desiccation and temperature range. The high intertidal zone features such species as periwinkles, limpets, and barnacles, which are able to conserve their water environment through shell closure or adherence to the rock substrate. The mid-tidal zone features a rich environment for bivalves such as mussels, clams, and oysters. The low-intertidal zone, which is exposed only at the lowest of tides, is perhaps the richest in marine organisms, such as sea stars, sea urchins, and many species of coral. Species also vary according to geologic features: rock shores feature crevices for anemones, urchins, crabs, and other crustaceans; sandy-gravel beaches offer important environments for forage fish eggs; and muddy-sandy shores featuring eelgrass beds are an important habitat for crabs as well as bivalves such as clams and for juvenile salmon and forage fish. Larger marine life—fish and mammals such as seals and sea lions—find foraging for food ideal at high tide in the intertidal zone.

The sublittoral consists of that part of the sea that is close to the shore and extends from the low tide mark of the intertidal zone to approximately 200 feet deep. In terms of marine organisms, this means the area whose depth does not exceed the reach of sunlight. This zone supports kelp forests as well as sea bottom environments for scallops, sea cucumbers, and sea urchins. Rocky or reef environments are good for oysters and other shellfish that adhere to rocks. Some sandy bottoms are perfect for sand lance beds. Free-swimming fish inhabit various parts of this zone: groundfish and rockfish, as their names indicate, are close to the mud and sand or reefs of the seabed, while others travel throughout the area.

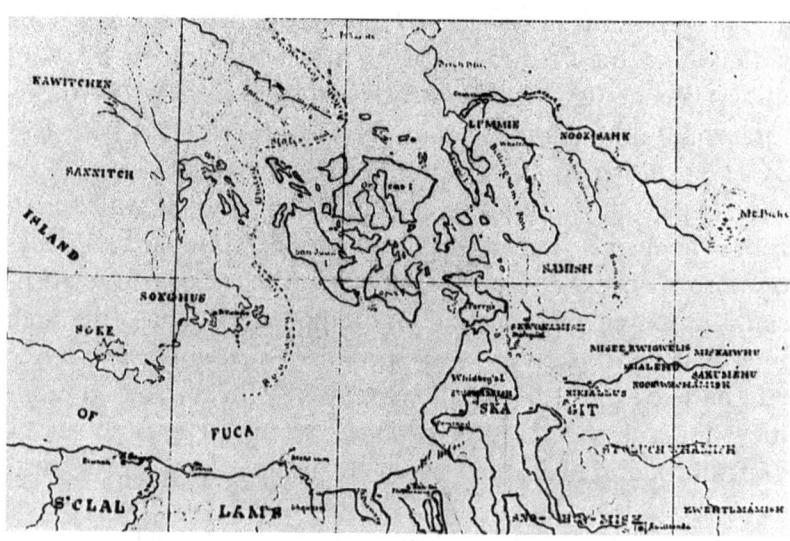

Map of the Indian Tribes and Lands Ceded by Treaty (George Gibbs 1855)

INDIGENOUS PEOPLES

Swe'tan was name of first man to land on what is now known as San Juan Island. He came from an unknown place in the sky, by Xa'als, the changer or creator. Xa'als tell him to make his home at the place now known as Pe'pl'ewelh (Mitchell's Bay), or in the neighborhood of English Camp, San Juan Island.

— Captain Jack, Yakship II, as told to him by his grandfather, Yakship

History

Indigenous peoples have been fishing in the Salish Sea for millennia. The Lhaq'temish (Lummi), W̱SÁNEĆ (Saanich), Samish, and Lekwungen (Songish or Songhees) claim that Open Bay (*Lhuh-lhee-ng'kwulh*) on Henry Island and Garrison (*Pe'pi'owelh*) and Mitchell (*Pqwéy7elwelh*) Bays on San Juan Island (*Lháqemesh*) are the point of origin of their peoples through their earliest ancestor, *sweh-tuhn*.

One way of identifying the Indigenous peoples of the Salish Sea is by language: the Coast Salish are grouped by their common Salishan languages, and local regional speakers have been called Northern Straits and are grouped with the speakers of Clallam, Nooksack, Halkomelem, and Squamish as Central Coast Salish. One of the defining features of the Straits Salish is the centrality the reef net for catching summer runs of sockeye salmon, returning to their natal streams in the Fraser River, holds in their economy and culture. At least two Northern Straits Salish groups had winter villages in the San Juans: the Klalákamish on San Juan Island and the Swallah on Orcas Island.

With the introduction of diseases by Euro Americans starting in the late eighteenth century, however, Indigenous populations throughout the region were decimated, and by the time Euro Americans began recording their presence in the islands, the various Straits Salish groups had relocated their winter villages to the surrounding areas: the Sooke (*T'Sou-ke*), Songish or Songhees (*LekwungƐn*), and Saanich (*Tsawout* and *Tsartlip*) on Vancouver Island; the Semiahmoo near Boundary Bay; the Lummi (*Lhaq'temish*, or People of the Sea) on Lummi Island and the Nooksack River; and the Samish around the Skagit River. All these groups continued to return to their traditional homeland in the San Juan Islands for fishing, gathering, and hunting during the spring, summer, and autumn months. They would either take their cedar planks, stretched between two canoes to form a catamaran, to village sites with posts and beams, where they would use them to clad their houses, or erect temporary structures made of woven rush mats.

Fishing salmon has been said to be the defining cultural trait of the Indigenous peoples of the Salish Sea, "The People of the Salmon," although it was also central to the culture and economy of other groups in the Pacific Northwest. The Coast Salish often named different times of the year according to the salmon available during that time; for example, the Saanich named the months of July, August, and September for the types of salmon harvested then: *hananƐ'n*, "humpbacked salmon"; *sowantan*, "coho salmon"; and *skeyƐ'n*, "sockeye salmon," according to Diamond Jenness (*The WSÁNEĆ and Their Neighbors*).

> *O Shwanaylets, our children this day eat the first of the fish that you have sent us. We thank you. We shall treat the fish carefully as we have always done.*
>
> — Diamond Jenness, *The WSÁNEĆ and Their Neighbors* (1935)

Because the Coast Salish, along with many groups that depended on salmon, believed that the salmon were like people who came to feed them with their flesh, they performed a First Salmon Ceremony, which, although it differed from group to group, had some essential features.

> *When the first sockeye is caught the little children sprinkle their hair with down, paint their faces and put on white blankets. They go out to the canoe and carry the fish on their arms as though they were carrying an infant. A woman cuts it with a mussel shell knife, after which the fish is boiled and given only to the children to eat. The sockeye is just like a person, they say; that is why they must be careful.*
>
> Erna Gunther, *Klallam Ethnology* (1927)

While reef netting, the first salmon caught would be brought by the crew to the beach, where the children were assembled. With white down in their hair and their faces colored with red ochre, they met the canoes, each child taking a single fish in their arms like a baby, steadying it by taking the dorsal fin in their mouths. Walking with a limp, they carried them to where the women waited by racks over long fire trenches. The women would then cut the fish, usually starting from the head facing away from them to the tail on one side, and then in the opposite direction on the other. The head, bones, guts, and tail would be separated from the flesh as a single unit. The flesh would be roasted on the rack over the fire and consumed by the children. Then they would ritually dispose of the offal, often by either placing it on rocks running into the sea or directly into the water. This would ensure that the fish would tell their relatives that it was safe to return to be caught by the reef netters.

Fishing Villages

Of the several permanent villages in the San Juan Islands, most, if not all, were used as bases for fishing operations. In modern place names, these included: Open Bay on Henry Island; Flat or Sandy Point, Lopez Village, Richardson, Sperry, and Watmough on Lopez Island; West Sound and Eastsound on Orcas Island; and Garrison and Mitchell Bays, Lonesome Cove, and possibly Fish Creek on San Juan Island.

There is a large amount of evidence of multiple locations of fishing camps throughout the islands. For instance, as part of

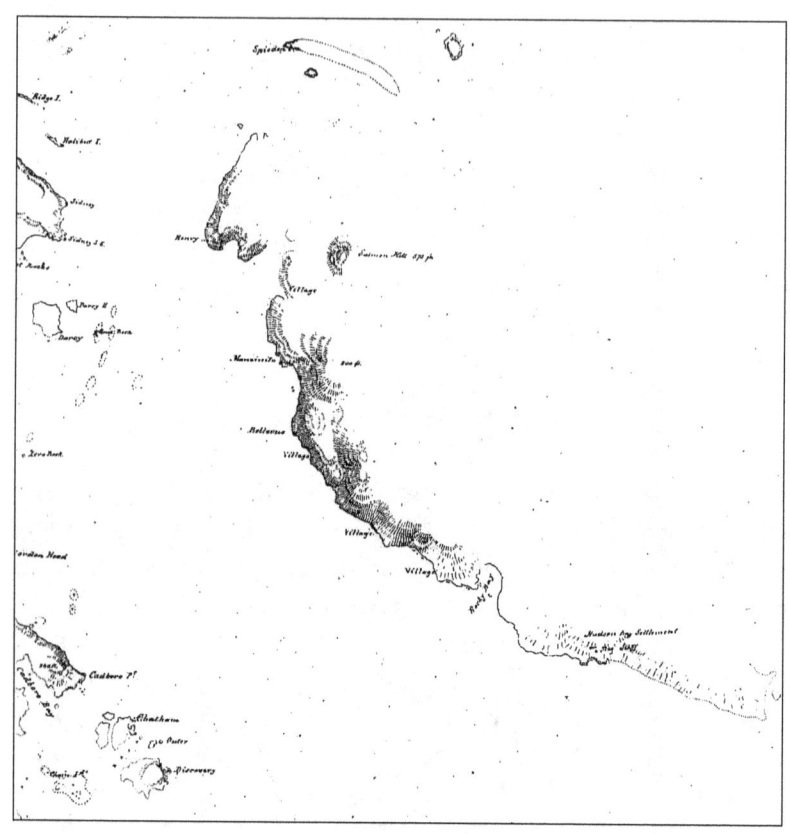

Triangulation of Rosario Strait and the Canal de Haro, George Davidson, United States Coast Survey, 1853–54

the 1854 Coast Survey, George Davidson, under the command of Captain James Alden, drew a chart of the west coast of San Juan Island that included four locations labeled as "village," which were probably fishing encampments. In the late 1920s hearings on traditional use areas in the federal court case of *Duwamish et al. v. United States*, several people giving testimony mentioned traditional villages and fishing camps around the San Juan Islands.

Indigenous place names also bear witness to the importance of fishing in Salish Sea economy: Cherry Point (*Nuxws7áx'wom*, place to always get butter clams) and Dakota Creek (*Kw'ol7óxwem*, place to get dog salmon) on the mainland; Decatur Island (*Sx'eméne7*, place of ratfish); Lopez Island (*Sx'wálech*, bottom of reef netting); Orcas Island (*Sx'wálex'*, scattered reef netting);

Patos Island (*Tl'x̓óy7ten*, place of harvesting oysters); Sucia Island (*Lhéwqemeng*, place of harvesting mussels); and Waldron Island (*Ch'x̓ení*, place of seaweed).

> **Question:** *What kind of houses did they have?*
> **Answer:** *...And they have a big place where they dry their fish, and split cedar and put the posts up like that, and they have long cedar posts, and they have that all filled up with fish, all kinds of salmon. I have seen fish so thick that the beach is all covered; you couldn't walk without stepping on the salmon of every kind. The richest country ever was, is this island....*
> **Question:** *What do you know about the fishing locations on these islands?*
> **Answer:** *Well, I know it was awful thick of them. I seen the Indians dry their fish, you know, and it would stand so high [illustrating], just like you would cut cordwood and cord it up, it was so thick. They just took what they wanted and just threw the others away, but of course there was no white folks around to get the fish, nothing of that kind. There was nothing but the Indians.*
> —Testimony of Caroline Ewing, March 12, 1927 *Duwamish et al. v. United States,* Court of Claims of the United States, No. F-275

With the initial settlement in the 1840s of indigenously populated areas of what was to become British Columbia, the British government, represented by James Douglas, negotiated the "Douglas Treaties" with a half dozen Coast Salish groups on southern Vancouver Island. These treaties, in exchange for access to First Nations lands, guaranteed them the right to hunt, fish, and forage "as formerly," which clearly included traditional fishing methods, catches, and areas. In the Territory of Washington, Governor Isaac Stevens negotiated a series of thirteen treaties with Indigenous groups; among these was the Treaty of Point Elliott (1855), which was signed by Indigenous groups in the Salish Sea region. It guaranteed "The right of taking fish at usual and accustomed grounds and stations is further secured to said Indians in common with all citizens of the Territory."

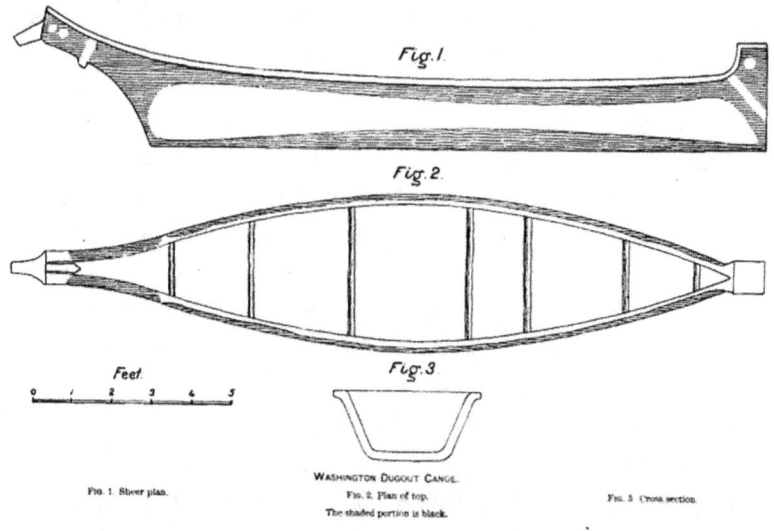

Washington Dugout Canoe ("Fishing Vessels of the Pacific Coast," Bulletin of the US Fish Commission 1890)

> The canoes of this region differ from anything we had seen on the voyage. They were made from a single trunk and have a shape that may be considered elegant, and which is preserved from change from stretching or warping by means of thwarts. The sides are exceedingly thin, seldom exceeding three-fourths of an inch, and they are preserved with great care, being never suffered to lie exposed to the sun for fear of rents and cracks. When these do occur, the canoe is mended in a very ingenious manner: holes are made in the sides, through which withes are passed and pegged in such a way that the strain will draw it tighter; the withe is then crossed and the end secured in the same manner. When the tying is finish, the whole is pitched with the gum of the pine. This is neatly done, and answers the purpose well.
>
> — Commander Charles Wilkes, Narrative of the United States Exploring Expedition (1844)

Canoes

The main means of transportation for the Indigenous peoples of the Salish Sea was by canoe. During the nineteenth century, when Euro Americans first began writing their observations of Indigenous canoes, the Coast Salish in the San Juans were using several types, differing by function, the styles of which varied through time. All early canoes were carved from trunks of trees native to the region, most commonly cedar (*Thuja plicata*), which has a grain that can easily be split and carved and contains a toxic oil (*thujaplicin*) that naturally preserves the wood against rot and insect attack. Within a common building tradition of cedar dugouts, what distinguished the styles of

> *They were trained in those days how to put up dwellings, their great big buildings, and how to make their fishing equipment, hunting equipment and build their canoes. They were the best canoe builders, well-trained. They would have a good supply of canoes so they could trade and sell to people who wanted to pay.*
>
> —Al Charles,
> quoted in Ann Nugent, *Lummi Elders Speak* (1982)

regional canoes were factors such as the lines of bow, stern, and gunwale and the section of the hull, all of which were influenced by the nature of the waters in which the canoes were used. The standard measures of the hull of a vessel are the length, beam (width at the widest point—usually the middle), and draw (depth). Canoe styles developed over time: from Salish (short and narrow, low prow)—for use in the calmer, inner waters—to Nootkan (larger, curved, pointed prow, and vertical stern)—for more stability, especially for reef netting—and finally the use by other tribes of the Northern style (largest, with vertical cutwater leading to angled prow and sloped stern with knob)—for long-distance freightage. Part of the reason for this change in style and size must have been reliance upon the larger cedar trees that were available on the west coast of Vancouver Island and Haida Gwaii (Queen Charlotte Islands).

Salish Canoes

The Salish canoe is long (20–30 feet, although it could reach up to 40 feet), narrow, and distinguished by an almost vertical cutwater with a long-angled prow and a steadily sloped stern that narrows to meet the rising gunwale. An important feature of the Salish canoe is the flare that is carved below the full length of the gunwales and is particularly pronounced at the bow and the stern. In the situation of either an approaching wave or a following sea, this feature effectively turns the force away and prevents the water from going over the gunwale to swamp the hull. With its rounded bottom, this early Salish canoe was particularly seaworthy in the inner waters of Puget Sound, the Islands, and the Gulf of Georgia, which can feature strong winds and currents and choppy waters but not the large swells and breaking waves of the outer Vancouver Island and Olympic Peninsula coast and ocean. While the lower prow cutwater slices through the waves, the upper portion flairs to resist boarding waves. Like most Indian canoes, these craft were beached with the bow facing water ward, both to deflect beach waves and for quick launching.

Both the Nootkan- and Northern-style canoes added material for the upper portions of the prow and stern, so that carvers were able to use only half of a large log, and not have to be too picky about selecting core wood that was intact and not fungal and spongy.

The lines of the canoe were carved with the eventual widening of the hull in mind. This widening was done by heating stones in a fire and then placing them in water in the hull, which was sometimes covered, to steam and soften the wooden hull fibers; thwarts were then placed to both widen the hull and raise the gunwale and stem line

West Coast or Nootka Canoes

The West Coast, or Nootka, style of canoe originated among the Nootkan (*Nuu-chah-nulth*) peoples of the west coast of Vancouver Island, but was adopted by tribes as far south as the Columbia River and as far north as Haida Gwaii (the Queen Charlotte Islands). This style of canoe was designed for the rougher waves of the Pacific Ocean. Unlike the Salish style, it features an angled cutwater that leads in one continuous, graceful curve to an animal head-like projection; below this, on the outside, is a knob that has been called, after Euro American contact, an "Adam's apple." The stern is almost vertical, with a knob at the top. The gunwale, which is close to horizontal, curves up to meet the prow, but essentially dies into the stern knob. The bottom is close to flat, lending stability when fishing or whaling. While whaling canoes, which carried a crew of eight (a helmsman, a harpooner, and six paddlers), ranged in length from 30–35 feet with a beam of 5 feet, those that were used in inland waters could range from 20–40 feet in length, although there were historically recorded instances of canoes that were 55 feet long and over 7 feet wide.

> [The canoe maker]…first softened the wood by filling…with water which he made to boil by putting red hot stones in it. The canoe was then partially spread and allowed to remain for a day.…The next morning after heating the water again with hot stones he built a slow fire of rotten wood and bark on the ground along the sides of the canoe to render the wood perfectly soft, or as he said, "to cook it", and then stretched the sides apart as far as was safe and kept them in position by means of stretchers or thwarts. I measured this canoe before he commenced to widen it and found that amidship, the opening was two feet eight inches wide, after he had finished the canoe I again measured it at the same place and found it was four feet nine inches…
>
> —James Swan, quoted in "Fishing Vessels of the Pacific Coast," Bulletin of the US Fish Commission (1890)

A fourth type of regional canoe—what has been called in English the spoon or shovel-nosed style—was well adapted to river use, and thus probably not used much, if at all, in the San Juan Islands—although it possibly served as a model for reef net canoes. Both the bow and the stern were symmetrically scooped, with flat ends and relatively shallow, flat bottoms. Ranging from 10–40 feet in length, a typical example from the Stillaguamish River measures 27' long but only 32" in the beam. These were designed to be poled through the rapid currents of the swift streams and rivers of the Nooksack, Upper Skagit, Sauk-Suiattle, Snohomish, Stillaguamish, Puyallup, Nisqually, Chehalis, Muckleshoot, and freshwater Duwamish.

Paddles varied among the various Indigenous groups within the region. Like paddles of other canoe-using groups, such as South Pacific islanders, Coast Salish paddles can be classified according to the various shapes used to describe leaves: cordate, deltoid, and elliptic; lanceolate; and oblong, obovate, oval, and ovate. Salish paddles were mostly oblanceolate, although some

Northern or Haida Canoes

The third major type of canoe is called the Northern or Haida style, named for the principal native group that produced it, although others, such as the Heiltsuk (formerly Bella Bella), Xa'islak'ala (formerly Haisla), Kwakwaka'wakw (formerly Kwakiutl), Tlingit, and Tsimshian not only used them but probably built them as well. The Haida peoples were particularly known for their canoe-making abilities, so that extensive trade in Haida canoes occurred throughout the region, leading to much confusion among Euro American observers as to the identity of the groups who were using Haida-style craft for transport. Northern canoes traded for goods ranging from 10 to 15 blankets to one slave. The Haida traveled easily in these canoes from their territory in Haida Gwaii 500 miles south to Puget Sound.

Like the smaller Salish canoes, which may have been the original inspiration for the style, the Northern canoe has both a vertical cutwater with a long, angled prow and a sloping stern. However, these vessels were on average larger and used several distinct pieces in their construction: one large log for the hull, with pieces added to the upper portions of the bow and stern. The hull section was rounded at the bottom and flared at the sides, leading to greater buoyancy and speed, and wash strakes—bands of wood—were sometimes added to the gunwales to provide extra height to prevent waves striking against the sides from washing into the canoe. Although the average size has been estimated at around 40 feet in length, 7 feet at the beam, and 3 feet deep, they could be as large as 64 feet in length, 8 feet at the beam, and 7'3" at the bow. These canoes were valued for their carrying capacity: some of the larger examples could hold up to 50 men and from six to eight tons of cargo.

were elliptic with a narrowing point. They were usually constructed of broad-leaf maple, with crutch-like handles carved out of the same piece of wood. Men's paddles differed from women's: they were longer and narrower, while the latter's were shorter and carved with a slightly fuller blade; the handle was sometimes broadened out at the end to include two thumb holes. It is interesting to note that in a photo of Kanaka Bay Camp, there are at least two men holding paddles, clearly in the Coast Salish style. (It is tempting to conjecture that there may have been a Hawaiian influence on local paddle design; outrigger paddles from the Hawaiian Islands at the time were rounded.)

> Now that is the sail of the ancient people before any white people came; to wit, short boards sewed together. The canoe-mast is short, for it just shows above the top edge of the board sail when it is standing up in the bow. The wind just blows against it and presses the board sail against the mast when the canoe is running before the wind.
>
> — Franz Boas, "Ethnology of the Kwakiutl," *Thirty-fifth Annual Report of the Bureau of American Ethnography, 1913-1914* (1921)

The Coast Salish sometimes used sails, which were made of rectangular mats woven of cedar bark, cattail, or rush. An older form of sail consisted of cedar boards thinly split and lashed together. Sails were rigged on a mast with two horizontal spars (top and bottom) and four lines. This could only be used to sail directly before the wind. After Euro American contact, sprit-rigged cloth sails were adopted. Within the canoe itself, there was a cedar-withe mat on the bottom with a sewed cattail mat on top of it, upon which the paddler knelt. Boating gear included a bailer made of folded cedar bark with a wooden handle and an anchor consisting of a rock about one foot in diameter with a hole through it and a cedar-withe ring, to which the anchor line was attached.

> The square stern is peculiar to the LkungEn fishing-boat. It seems that it was not made of one piece with the boat, but consisted of a board inserted into a groove, the joints being made water-tight by means of pitch.
>
> — Franz Boas, *The Lku'gEn* (1890)

The order of the paddlers in the canoe reflected that of the household, with the matriarch as steerer in the stern and paddlers arrayed according to family rank ahead of her. (This was also the order of living arrangement in the longhouse, and, in the case of reef net crews, the order of place in fish camps.) When the people moved from winter to summer villages, they would load the cedar boards that formed the siding of the longhouses and place them across two canoes, forming a catamaran platform that they could then load their belongings onto and paddle to their seasonal dwelling place.

One of the crucial transitions in canoe styles occurred in the construction and style of canoes used for reef netting. Originally, reef netters probably used a variant of the standard Salish canoe for their task. Wayne Suttles notes—and an illustration from Franz Boas's *The Lkuñ̃gEn* seems to confirm—that reef net canoes were high and pointed in the bow but low and flat in the stern, which was the part of the canoe where the captain of the crew watched for the incoming salmon. But other writers claim that by the mid-nineteenth century, reef netters had converted almost exclusively to the Nootkan canoe, because it offered greater stability in the smoother inner waters around the San Juans. Eventually, modern plank ("clinker built") boats replaced Nootkan canoes. However, when examined from a stylistic point of view, although the fundamental construction materials had changed, the form and details had not. Modern reef net boats still feature an almost vertical cutwater, a long projecting prow, flat bottoms with curved sides, and an upright stern.

Reef Net Canoes

Wayne Suttles conjectured that a modified form of the shovel-nose canoe was used by Salish groups for reef netting. Suttles' informants, who had not actually seen one, referred to the reef net canoe's wide bow and flat stern, which accords with Boas' description of the "large fishing-boat" of the Songish. Because reef net canoes were anchored with their sterns at the forward end of the net, the watchman was able to observe better from the sheared-off stern, while the rest of the crew lay in the bottom toward the bow, for stability. While the shovel-nose style of canoe was more appropriate to the calm waters of rivers and streams, and not the rougher waters of the Salish Sea, reef netting was usually deployed when the waters were calm.

INDIGENOUS FISHING METHODS

> *When the tide is out the table is set.*
> —Traditional saying

Shellfish and Other Tidal Zone Gathering

The Coast Salish harvested a variety of marine invertebrates throughout the Salish Sea, including mollusks, crustaceans, and echinoderms. Shell middens, ethnographic data, and tradition all indicate that Indigenous peoples have been harvesting shellfish in the Salish Sea for thousands of years. While occupying a harvesting or dwelling site, people deposited shells and other trash onto piles near their village or encampment; these refuse piles are called middens. The shell midden at English Camp, on the shores of Garrison Bay on San Juan Island, dating from around 1,000 years ago, is eight feet deep in some places, indicating an extensive period of use.

While it is a common assumption, based on modern-day recreational harvesting, that gathering along the shorelines and in the tidal zone is simple and straightforward, in fact it often requires an intimate knowledge of complex microenvironments: the occurrence of tides and the potential danger of currents and rogue waves, the specific location of shell beds and other resource areas, and in some cases the actual manipulation of the environment to foster certain organisms were all important factors. Shellfish could be gathered at any time, but the Coast Salish preferred summer. Harvesters—usually women—favored going to one location and processing large quantities of shellfish there, rather than moving around. Families often claimed ("owned") specific harvesting locations and handed down their use traditions through kinship lines.

Gathering was done either while walking along the shoreline at low tide or paddling in a canoe in shallow water. Shellfish harvested included barnacles, cockles, mussels, oysters, and scallops, as well as other marine organisms such as chitons, sea cucumbers, sea urchins, snails, and even whelks. Clam types included bent-nose, butter, geoduck, horse, little-neck (steamer), sand, and soft-shell. Clams were dug from sandy or gravelly flats, usually with a strong piece of wood called by the Lummi *skalax*. Cockles, mussels, oysters, and sea cucumbers were picked up directly from the exposed beds. Barnacles, chitons, sea urchins, and snails were picked or pried from rocks. All of these were washed in the saltwater and placed in an open-weave basket to allow for drainage while they were transported to the place for cooking.

> *My mother used to eat sea cucumbers but we didn't like them. Didn't like the looks of them. Too ugly. We also ate a seafood that looked like a little bootie. They were not mussels. They weren't Chinese hats. They stick on rocks. You pry them off. You don't cook them long. You bring them to a boil and take them right off. The shell is black and the meat is pinkish-white. I used to go with my mother and gather them. My mother used to eat sea urchins but I wouldn't. They used to eat them raw. I never did. I couldn't stand the looks of them. Anyway, I like my food cooked.*
>
> — Lucy Lane Handeyside,
> quoted in Ann Nugent, *Lummi Elders Speak* (1982)

Clam Gardening

There is a growing body of evidence of the practice of shellfish (specifically clam) "gardening" in the northern portions of the Salish Sea, such as near Quadra Island, as well as further north, to the Kwakwa̱ka̱'wakw Islands west of the mouths of Knight and Kingcome Inlets. The Coast Salish delineated the beds by taking the largest rocks and moving them out to extreme low-water marks, setting them in rows like a fence along the edge of the water. This allowed them to make the bed of the garden easier to dig in because only small pebbles and sand remained. It has also been suggested that harvesters transplanted favorite species of shellfish into the new beds for cultivation. The only known local example is of a family at West Sound on *Elelung* (Orcas) that cultivated a butter-clam bed.

> *They took the largest rocks that were in the clam bed and moved them out to extreme low water marks, setting them in rows like a fence along the edge of the water. This make clam digging very easy compared to what it had previously been because there are only small pebbles and sand to dig in.*
>
> — Bernhard J. Stern,
> *The Lummi Indians of Northwest Washington* (1934)

Eelgrass and Kelp Harvesting

Indigenous peoples harvested at least two types of Salish Sea marine plants and algae: eelgrass and kelp. The Straits Salish harvested eelgrass in canoes, taking long hemlock poles and winding the blades of the grass around until they could lift up the whole plant. They would then cut off the green leaves, retaining the rhizomes and leaf-bases, which they would either steam in a stew pot or eat raw, dipped in "grease" (eulachon oil). The Coast Salish also gathered herring roe from eelgrass beds, sometimes including the leaves rather than stripping off the roe.

Although northern First Peoples gathered kelp blades along with the herring roe that were deposited thereon, apparently the Coast Salish did not do so. But Indigenous peoples in the Salish Sea did harvest kelp for several non-food purposes. One of the most important was for use in fishing lines, nets, ropes, and harpoon lines made from bull kelp. The long stalks were cured by alternately soaking in freshwater and drying over a smoking fire; the lengths would then be spliced or plaited together. Because they would become brittle when dried, the lines had to be soaked to regain flexibility and strength. The floats or bulbs of the bull kelp were also used to store various liquids, such as grease, fish oil, and water. Indigenous fishers placed sticks of yew or split Douglas fir or western hemlock knots into kelp bulbs and buried them in hot ashes overnight to make them pliable for bending into halibut hooks.

"Sturgeon-Spearing on the Fraser," John Keats Lord, *The Naturalist in Vancouver Island and British Columbia* (1866)

Spearing

The Coast Salish used several different types of spears for catching different types of fish. They used two- and three-pronged spears to catch flounders from canoes, sometimes at night with torches. These were also used to spear dogfish in shallow water. Two-pronged spears, in combination with a long pole with a crook in the end, were used in catching octopus: paddling a canoe in shallow water, the fishers looked for an octopus' den, evident from the crab and clam shells around it; the pronged stick was used to force the octopus out into the open, where it was speared. Pitchfork-like spears, constructed with a shaft around eight feet long with a crosspiece of the same material with four-to six-inch-long prongs made of ironwood and set in a row, were used to spear flounders in the muddy waters at the mouth of a river at low tide. Either a leister spear—two flared prongs with backwards-pointing barbs flanking a shorter barb—or a simple two-pronged spear, with an inch-and-a-half-in-diameter, 15- to 20-foot-long shaft, was used to catch cod that had been lured to the surface by means of a wooden lure that was pushed down to the bottom and released; the lure would upend and revolve slowly as it floated up, imitating the cod's prey. The 8- to 12-inch-long lure was made like a shuttlecock in shape: a round head and body of cedar that was scorched black and smoothed, with three paddle-shaped vanes carved from the white wood of a Rocky Mountain maple and bound to the body with cherry bark.

According to Wayne Suttles' informants, the Semiahmoo used to harpoon sturgeon with "a 12-foot long fir shaft with a trident butt and two fore shafts of ironwood, each fitted onto a three-piece female head." Going out during the daytime at low tide, they would look for the sturgeon swimming seven to eight feet below the surface; at night, they could tell that sturgeon were present by the phosphorescent trails resulting from their swimming. Paddling alongside, the harpooner would thrust the harpoon in behind the head. The sturgeon would swim rapidly away, and the fisher would pay out an attached line and then ride it out until the fish tired, at which point the harpooner would pull the fish up and club it with a foot-and-a-half-long knotted yew club.

Raking

The principal means of catching herring and other small fish was by raking. A paddler in a canoe would sweep a rake—a 12-foot-long fir pole with hemlock, white fir, or bone (and later iron nail) teeth fastened at one-inch intervals into the three- to five-foot end cut flat—into a ball or school of herring and then deposit the impaled catch into the canoe.

> *I'll tell you how they fished for herring: they used this pole, kind of flat on one end; they used nails on it. I guess before that they used to use bones. They had a series of nails on the flat end of this pole. It was like a rake; they used to just swing this down in the water. Herring were so thick; put it down in the water and scoop the herring up. They would get caught on the end of those nails. They would bring them up and just shake them off and scoop them up again.*
>
> — Leo and Rose Senior, quoted in Ann Nugent, *Lummi Elders Speak* (1982)

Small fish like smelt were also shoveled with a paddle or stick from the shallows when they congregated near the shore. The importance of herring in the Northwest people's diet in the pre–Euro American contact period is evident from a 2013 analysis of archaeological sites along the Northwest Coast that date from 10,700 B.P. to the contact era (A.D. 1740–1860): of the 171 sites studied, 95 sites showed herring, as evidenced from bones mostly found in middens, as the single most numerous fish, and, in an additional 41 sites, it was the second most. All told, herring ranked among the three most abundant fish in 88% of the sites. This indicates that herring were not only an important food source but were consistently abundant enough during this long period to be the primary type of fish consumed. This is particularly true of archaeological sites in the Salish Sea, in comparison with sites in southeast Alaska, the northern British Columbia coast, and Haida Gwaii.

Roe Gathering

> *WEXES was the month that the herring came, sometime in the middle of that moon. The herring were the only fish that came to us automatically so our people took good advantage of it.*
>
> — *Saltwater People*, as told by Dave Elliott Sr. (1983)

During March and April, when the herring congregated to spawn in shallow waters where eelgrass grew, the Coast Salish would let down various materials such as kelp fronds and hemlock or cedar boughs, weighted with a stone and kept upright with a float, to catch the roe, which stuck to the surfaces. After several days the boughs would be removed and the roe dried, shaken off, and stored.

> Our people knew exactly when those herring were going to arrive. The old people would say, "They are not going to arrive on this tide." Our people didn't always tell the time by the day, or the moon or the sun. They knew the tide so well they would tell the time, exactly what time of year it was, by the tide that was coming and they would say those herring are going to arrive.
>
> The first herring that come in are not the real spawners. They're smaller fish and not as big as the mature herring. The spawners themselves are mature herring, females and males. The old people would tell us that first small ones arrive, they're the scouts, they come in to look the ground over. Our people didn't take them because they weren't of the same quality as the ones that come later.
>
> For two or three evenings these herring would arrive just at sundown in the shallow water. In the morning they'd be gone again. The next day the same thing would happen again, finally about the third day the real spawners would come in and then they would stay until the spawning cycle was finished.
>
> — *Saltwater People, as told by Dave Elliott Sr.* (1983)

> *In the old days spawning would last for as long as a month. That's how long they would stay, five weeks sometimes. Our people would take enough for their own use, not more, just enough that's all.*
>
> *They would put out cedar and balsam branches so the herring would spawn on the branches. They would then hang the branches up in the sun and the wind to dry. That's how they were preserved. When it was completely dry they would put it away for the winter.*
>
> — *Saltwater People,* as told by Dave Elliott Sr. (1983)

Gillnetting

The Coast Salish used gill nets to catch Chinook, coho, and pink salmon in the spring and summer whenever the fish were observed swimming close to shore. Gill nets were used on the Fraser River from the early historic period—the 1860s—by Indigenous peoples who sold the fish to Euro Americans. Gill nets are webbing with meshes that allow the fish's head to enter and get caught by its gills; the size of mesh varied according to the species of fish. (This is in contrast to a seine, which impounds the fish.) The top of the net was kept at the water's surface with wooden floats, which in most cases were upright three-foot cedar sticks, with half their length sticking out of the water, spaced three feet apart "like a picket fence," according to Wayne Suttles' Semiahmoo informant. The bottom was weighted with stones, sometimes wrapped in cattails and secured to the lower edge. There are two types of gill nets: stationary, which are anchored in place; and drift, which are allowed to float loose. Because they work best when the fish cannot see, and therefore avoid, the net, either muddy water conditions or night fishing is optimal.

Gill nets are measured by length in fathoms and width in the number of meshes. Gill net sizes varied according to the group using them, but a typical example given by Wayne Suttles was a Saanich net for Chinook, which had an eight-inch mesh and measured 10 fathoms long by 20 meshes (about 13 feet) wide. Another, Semiahmoo example had 5¾-inch meshes and was 40–50 fathoms long and 20–25 meshes wide.

Reef Netting

The specific technique of catching salmon by reef netting is probably the most distinctive cultural practice of the local Salish peoples. After a hiatus of several decades (1890–1935) when it was eclipsed by fish trapping, reef netting has continued to this day with modernized equipment. The method consists of forming an artificial reef such that the salmon, following the current, will be funneled into a net and caught. Reef net sites were chosen where salmon were naturally funneled over relatively shallow reefs with kelp, often near a promontory that caused the backward sweep of a current.

Reef Netting off Stuart Island
(courtesy of San Juan Historical Museum)

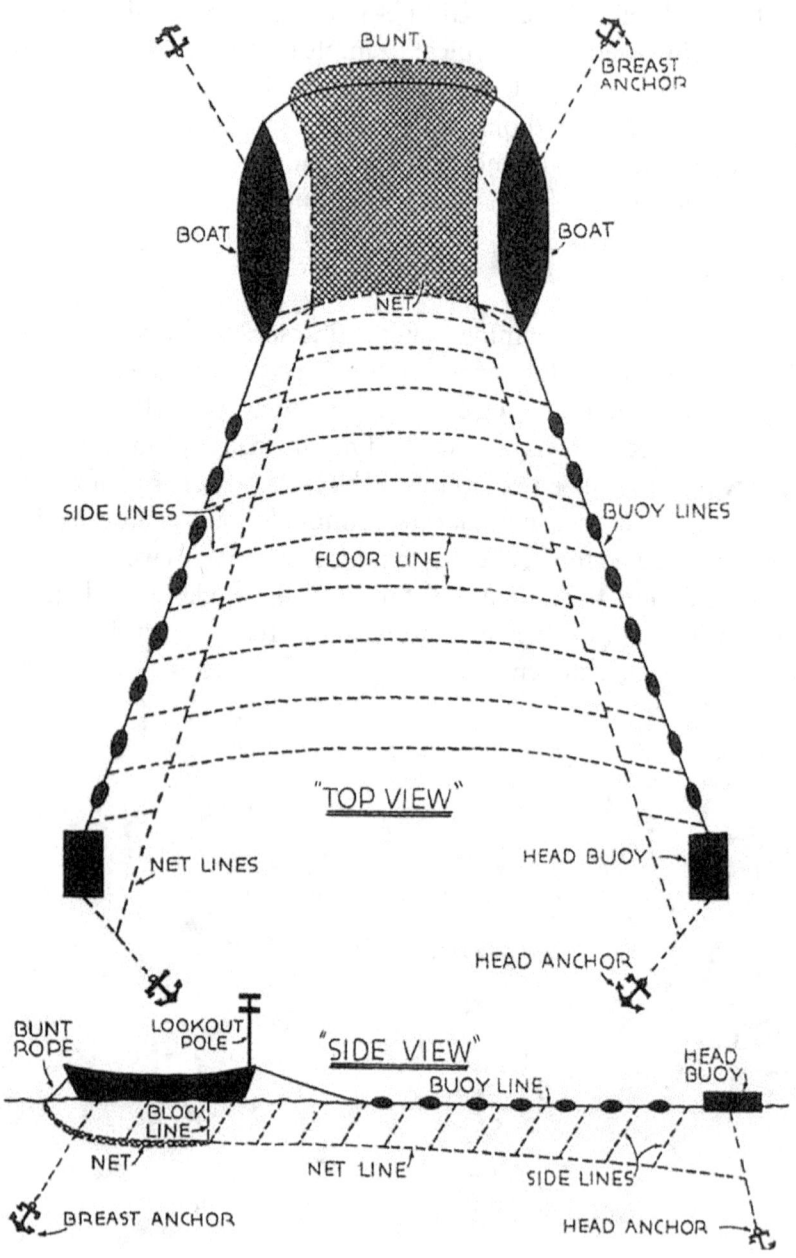

Diagram of a Reef-net (Pacific Fisherman June 1939)

The nets are made of Fraser river hemp, or fibre from the roots of the cedar; they are loaded at the bottom with round stones, about one pound weight, notched to prevent slipping, and buoyed at the top with blocks of cedar. This net is placed in the run of salmon, which either become entangled in the meshes, are drawn up and killed by a blow on the head with a stick, or speared by the Indian from his canoe whilst checked in their course by the net.

—Charles W. Wilson *Report on the Indian Tribes Inhabiting the Country in the Vicinity of the 49th Parallel of North Latitude* (1866)

In the traditional way of reef netting, two canoes, specially designed for the purpose, were anchored approximately 15–25 feet apart, with their sterns facing the current and the incoming salmon. No examples of historic reef net boats have been found; the only descriptions, from oral history accounts, suggest a low, wide bow and a vertical, notched stern that served as an observation platform. A net, made of dyed willow bark twine and approximately 20–30 feet wide and 30–40 feet long, was suspended in the water between the two canoes. If there was kelp, a channel was cut in the bed. If not, an artificial channel was created by laying out a funnel from each canoe toward the current. This funnel, consisting of side and floor lines attached to a top, buoyed lead line and a bottom, anchored net line, sometimes with beach rye grass tied to them to serve the illusion of being eel grass at the bottom of a channel, through which the salmon had to pass. Captains of the reef net crew, or their designees, stood at the stern of each boat and watched for the salmon entering the net, at which point ropes holding the boats apart would be slackened and the two canoes would swing together, capturing the fish in the net, which was then emptied into the shoreward canoe and paddled to the fishing camp. The Salish reef netted both for the subsistence of their tribes and trade with other groups.

> When fish are running in good numbers ten to fifteen Indians form a crew for a reef net, and a haul can be made every minute or two if necessary. Some of the Indians are very expert at this kind of fishing, and have taken as many as 2,000 salmon in a day. In such cases the clutchmen ["klootchmen" or women] come out with canoes and boat the fish ashore so that the operations of those engaged in fishing will not be interrupted.
>
> — J. W. Collins, "Report on the Fisheries of the Pacific Coast of the United States," *United States Commission on Fish and Fisheries Report for 1888* (1892)

In the mid to late summer fishing camps were established near reef net sites throughout the islands. They were located on a southeast- or southwest-facing promontory, either directly on shore or across the bay from a net site. Because the camp was used for drying the fish, exposure to both sun and wind was important; hence the south-facing directions. The camp itself consisted of a U-shaped arrangement of structures, arranged around a fish-drying scaffold and open to the shore where the canoes were pulled up on the beach. Suttles notes that the name that Boas recorded for the scaffold— *squlaā'utq*—is the same as the name one of his informants used for the whole camp— *sxwalaq'utxw*—which literally means "reef-net house." The own-

> And they had shelters where they made their equipment, like lumber, rope, fishing equipment. Near where they built their canoes, their mutual fishing locations were well known. Each family had their reef netting location. Each location had a name. It dates way back. They just didn't go and step on somebody's toes.
>
> —Al Charles, quoted in Ann Nugent, *Lummi Elders Speak* (1982)

er's house could be of regular longhouse construction, with the posts and beams left for the winter and then either walled with planks or mats taken from the winter villages, or it could be a more impermanent structure of posts and beams with mat walls. Furthermore, just as the spatial arrangement of family members within the longhouse reflected the paddling order in their canoe, so also did the spatial arrangement of the fishing camp reflect the order of owner/captain and two canoe crews. Caroline Ewing, one of the elders who gave depositions in the petition *Duwamish et al. v. United States* (1927), described "a big place where they dry their fish, and split cedar and put the posts up like that, and they have long cedar posts, and they have that all filled up with fish, all kinds of salmon."

> The fishing village is arranged in the following way. The centre is formed by the scaffold for drying salmon (squla'utq). It consists of two pairs of uprights carrying a cross-beam each, which support the long heavy beams on which the salmon are dried. These are cut off close to their supports nearest the sea, while at the other end their length is different according to the size of trees which were used in the construction. The house of the owner of the fishing-ground stands behind the scaffold. On both sides of the latter there are a number of huts. The crew of one boat lives on one side, that of the other on the other side.
>
> — Franz Boas, *The Lku'ñgEn* (1890)

At the end of the fishing season, the camps were dismantled, and the fishers traveled back to their winter villages. Diamond Jenness documented a leaving ceremony, in which the fishers cleaned up the camp site and burned the debris in a festive manner. This may explain why during the archaeological excavation of these sites there is often found a layer of ash and burned material.

> Women and children, under the supervision of the priest, gathered up all the loose sticks and refuse on the beach and piled them in a heap. Then toward midnight everyone rose, lit the bonfire, and threw into the air balls of mixed deer-fat, camas, and bird's down, yelling the names of the places they fished and saying "I feed you this." Then they scattered their fire, threw the burning brands in play at one another, and yelled and danced until daylight, when they packed up their belongings and return to the Saanich Peninsula.
>
> — Diamond Jenness, The W̱SÁNEĆ and Their Neighbors (1935)

Estimations for daily catch vary, but 2,000 fish seemed to be an average. Richard Rathbun noted in 1900 that "There is a small but productive reef inside Iceberg Point at the southern end of Lopez Island, on which a few nets are used, and where daily catches of 3,000 to 4,000 salmon are sometimes made."

> Our course was inland, up a good-sized river, thickly shrouded with almost tropical vegetation. Presently we came to an Indian salmon weir, a high framework of poles reaching across the stream, and serving also as a light foot-bridge. At intervals, wicker-work shields are suspended in the water, and just against them, baskets like a lobster pot; the salmon, rushing up the stream, is met by the shield, and turning, falls into the pot. The fishery belonged to one of my men, and as we came, an Indian was just taking a noble salmon out.
>
> — Theodore Winthrop, By Canoe and Saddle (1913)

Weirs

One of the principal methods of capturing salmon in the rivers of the region was by means of a weir, a framework of poles that supported a walkway with barriers and pots for catching the fish. Because there are few perennial streams—and no rivers—in the San Juans, this type of weir was not used, but a modification may have been. There is a reference to an old weir at the entrance to a stream on Orcas Island (such that the locals called it "Fish Trap Creek"), but it was not known when it had been used.

> *Although this bay [Fish Trap Creek, which drains into Cayou Lagoon and then Deer Harbor on Orcas Island] is a prominent feature it has no existence on the chart of the U.S. Survey and the inhabitants in the absence of any other name call it "Fish Trap", because at the mouth of the stream emptying into it there is an old weir in which the natives have been in the habit of taking salmon.*
>
> — *Report of Dr. C. B. R. Kennerly of a Reconnaissance of the Haro Archipelago* (1860)

Later fish trap maps show "brush weirs" used offshore in several locations in the islands: Open Bay off Henry Island; Andrews Bay off San Juan Island; and south of Goose Island off Lopez Island.

Trolling and Other Hook, Line, and Sinker Methods

A traditional means of fishing all over the world is by means of a hook, attached to a line, and weighted down with a sinker. The Coast Salish used several materials to construct their fishing lines. Bull kelp stipes were dried and then soaked in freshwater, stretched, and twisted for greater strength. They were then tied end to end with what is today called a "fisherman's knot": two overhand knots, each tied around the standing part of the other. Because of the length of the original stipes—up to 80 feet—these lines could be used for deepwater fishing. Nettle fiber was also used for lines, as was the inner bark of the cedar tree. The latter, stripped from split lengths and twisted into a three-strand rope, was particularly useful for halibut fishing. Sinkers were made from stones that were either wrapped with cherry bark straps, grooved for lashing with lines, or perforated for a rope to pass through.

The form of the hook depended on the catch. One of the most intricate was a halibut hook. The halibut, a right-eyed groundfish, swims horizontally and its jaws hinge sideways. A halibut hook was commonly made of yew wood (although balsam, fir, hemlock, and spruce knotwood were also used), steam-bent to form a U-shape, with a sharp barb, lashed to the shank, pointing inward from one of the ends of the bent hook, and the line on the other part of the shank. The halibut takes in the full hook and then, unable to swallow it, tries to eject it, resulting in the angled barb penetrating the mouth. Baited with either strips of octopus or a small fish impaled on the barb, two of these hooks were rigged to a spreader that hung several feet above where the line was anchored with sinkers to the sea bottom; the line was held up with a small, submerged bladder float and indicated with a larger bladder buoy riding on the surface.

The Coast Salish trolled for salmon in canoes with the line attached to their hand or the paddle so that it jerked forward with each stroke (imitating a bait fish); a small sinker stone attached partway back from the hook kept the line at a certain depth. Hooks were made of wood, with a bone or shell barb lashed to face backward and baited with herring.

Baited throat gorges were also used to catch bottom-feeding fish. The gorge, a slender bone sharpened at both ends, was firmly lashed in the middle to leaders attached to lines. The fish would swallow the bait and the gorge would toggle or turn sideways, causing it to lodge in the throat.

An distinctive method of using bait fish for cod was practiced by some Coast Salish. A small greenling or "tommycod" was attracted by crushed sea urchins and speared. The fisher would then put a rock in its stomach, cut away from one side to make it uneven, and tie a line around it. This bait was lowered to the bottom and then rapidly pulled to the surface, making it spin or wobble. A lingcod, rising for the bait, could either be speared or, if it swallowed the greenling, pulled to the surface and speared.

Sealing and Whaling

The Coast Salish hunted seals and porpoises, but probably—according to Wayne Suttles and other anthropologists—did little whaling, except for taking advantage of a dead whale when washed up on the shore.

> *Will Jakle thinks that the big bone mentioned in the Islander last week as coming from the Katz place is a fragment of a skeleton of a whale which was stranded at the south end of the island many years ago. Jas. Scribner says that the carcass of an immense whale, which he thinks was as much as eighty feet long, was towed ashore at Mitchell bay by Indians seventeen years ago. It was cut up on the beach and bones of the great skeleton were strewn along the shore for a long time.*
>
> —The San Juan Islander, June 2, 1911

Harbor seals were speared with a harpoon with two fore-shafts, each of which had a three-piece female head. The harpoon shafts were made of fir; the fore-shafts of ironwood. The head was made of two spurs of elk bone fitted on either side of a blade made of antler, bone, or mussel shell, with a single barb, lashed together with nettle fiber and sealed with pitch. Porpoises were harpooned in the same manner as seals.

Seals were also caught by net, made of willow bark twine and formed into a 10-inch mesh. Anchored by large stones at the ends and held up with cedar floats at the top, the net was set at night around a rock where the seals were known to sleep. The Songish and Samish would drive the seals into the net and then club them. The Saanich would lay the net around the rock at high tide, allowing the seals to swim in over it; in the morning, at low tide, the seals would get caught in the net when they tried to swim out. Seals were also clubbed, on the nose, as they slept on the beach.

Hunters would steam the meat of porpoises and seals in a pit, often near where they were captured. Sometimes the meat was saved by drying. Oil from both types of animals was saved in seal bladders and served in shells with meat or dried fish. Seal intestines were used as buoys.

INDIGENOUS CONSUMPTION, PRESERVATION, AND TRADE

The Coast Salish used a variety of methods for preparing and cooking shellfish for eating. Many seafoods were eaten raw or cooked near the place of harvest. Sea urchins, as well as some varieties of clams, were eaten raw. Other varieties of clams were steamed on a bed of hot rocks in a pit. Some varieties were first steamed open, and then strung on a stick that was then placed next to a fire for roasting. They were then strung on cedar bark line and placed in a sheltered location to dry. Strings of dried clams could be used for food later in the year or for trade for other items.

> In the early part of the preserving season, the people would go out and get clams and they would shell them out there, bring them back in in baskets, build a great big fire pit, and cook them. After they were cooked, they'd string them up on cedar strips and hang them up to dry. They preserved from about June right through the winter.
> — Al Charles, quoted in Ann Nugent, *Lummi Elders Speak* (1982)

In reef net camps, the salmon were dried for later consumption and trade. Women gutted and then filleted the salmon by removing the head, tail, and spine, leaving two halves of flesh that could be kept splayed open with wooden splints. In some instances, the head and tail, still connected by the spine, were dried or smoked and stored to be used later as flavoring in stews and other meals. Long trenches were dug in the ground and a structure of upright posts with horizontal racks was erected. Depending on the location, such as near South Beach on San Juan Island, the prevailing winds were sufficient for drying the salmon fillets; often this was supplemented by smoky fires in the trenches, which helped dry out the flesh and kept insects from laying eggs on them. Julie Stein and others have conjectured that if located in a windy situation, the poles and racks were kept upright with clay footings and guy cords secured to anchor stones.

> *They catch lingcod and split them in half. Take each half right off the backbone. You take that backbone right out and throw it away. And you take a pole and hang one half of one on one side and other half you hang on the other side so the backs aren't touching together. That's the way you hang them up to dry. They hang them up single too. They bust that up and make soup, the belly part. They take salmon and split it like your were going to hang it up to smoke, and you smoke it about a day and half or two days and you take it down and cut it right in half down the middle, split it again. Then you hang it up where it'll really be as dry as a board.*
>
> — Herman Olsen,
> quoted in Ann Nugent, *Lummi Elders Speak* (1982)

Meat from shellfish such as clams, cockles, and oysters could be eaten raw, steamed, or dried or smoked. Most of the cooking was by steaming: a pit measuring about two feet by four feet was dug, sticks were laid down, and then cobble-sized rocks were placed upon them and the fire burned. When it had burned down, the ashes were removed, and the clams were placed upon the level bed of stones and covered with kelp blades or white fir boughs. After several minutes, the clam meat would be removed from the shells, which had opened, and eaten. In some species, such as butter clams, the meat would be removed from the shell and spitted on a sharpened ironwood stick, and these sticks would be leaned near a fire for drying and smoking. Other shellfish, such as cockles and rock clams, were roasted without being steamed. The dried meat was removed from the sticks and strung on a cedar bark line; these could then be stored in a plank shed or a smokehouse at the winter village.

Anthropologist Gordon Hewes has estimated that the per capita annual intake of salmon in the precontact period was as high as six hundred pounds. The Indigenous peoples of the Salish Sea often traded the bounty of their harvest with other groups, such as peoples of the mainland plateau region. Strings of thirty or so clams, or about two feet long, were traded in this manner. When the Salish Sea peoples began going south to work in the hop fields, they would sell these strings to locals for two or three dollars each.

EUROPEANS AND EURO AMERICANS

Exploration and Survey

European exploration of the region began with the Spanish: in 1790, the sloop *Princesas Real*, under the command of Ensign Manuel Quimper and Pilot Gonzalo Lopez de Haro, got as far as present-day Victoria. The next year Francisco Eliza sent First Pilot Juan Pantoja y Arriaga, commanding the schooner *Santa Saturnina*, to explore (and name) Haro and Rosario Straits. In 1792, Captain George Vancouver, looking for the Northwest Passage, ordered his lieutenant, William Broughton, to reconnoiter the San Juan Islands while he explored Puget Sound. Broughton sailed between San Juan and Lopez Islands, exploring both Upright and San Juan channels. Charles Wilkes of the United States Exploring Expedition arrived in 1841 and spent several months surveying the Salish Sea, producing the first accurate charts of the San Juan Islands.

Starting in 1850, the United States Coast Survey charted the islands under the command of James Alden, U.S.N., with the side-wheeled steamer *Goldhunter* and later the U.S. Surveying Steamer *Active*; they produced a Coast Survey map in 1858 entitled "Reconnaissance of Washington Sound and Approaches." From 1857 to 1861, English Captain G. H. Richards, commander of *H.M.S. Plumper*, and his crew surveyed the islands as part of the general effort to chart the west coast of Canada.

> *Salmon abound in great quantities at certain seasons of the year, when the water in every direction seems to be filled with them. We caught large quantities of red fish averaging 12 pounds each, some Cod, closely resembling those on the Atlantic side and a few fine Halibut.*
>
> —James Alden, LT. Com. U.S. Navy,
> Assistant to the U.S. Coast Survey, to Prof. A. D. Bache,
> Superintendent of the U.S. Coast Survey, October 31, 1853

> In the vicinity of the southern end of the island [San Juan] are perhaps the best fishing grounds on Puget Sound. Great quantities of halibut, codfish, and salmon are taken by the numerous tribes of Indians who at the proper season resort to this vicinity for the purpose of fishing. The Hudson's Bay Company were formerly in the habit of putting up at this place from two to three thousand barrels of salmon alone which were bought from the natives. Persons supplied with the proper appliances for carrying on a fishery might find it a profitable occupation.
>
> On its eastern and southern sides [of Lopez Island] there are quite good fishing grounds where the natives yearly take great numbers of salmon and halibut.
>
> — Geographical Memoir, Appendix E
Report of Dr. C. B. R. Kennerly
of a Reconnaissance of the Haro Archipelago,
addressed to Archibald Campbell, Esq.,
U. S. Comm. N. W. Boundary Survey, February 20, 1860

Because of the dispute concerning the location in the Salish Sea of the boundary between Great Britain and the United States, the United States Boundary Commission spent two substantial sojourns in the San Juans, surveying the islands and assessing their economic value. George Clinton Gardner oversaw a field party of 14, which included William J. Warren as secretary; George Gibbs, a linguist as well as geologist and ethnologist; Joseph Smith Harris, assistant surgeon and naturalist; Henry Custer, topographer; and Dr. C. B. R. Kennerly, a surgeon and naturalist. Their reports described the islands in general and each major island in particular, noting physical features and speculating on economic potential. Special mention is made of the rich fishing grounds at Salmon Bank off San Juan Island and off the south end of Lopez Island.

Kennerly sampled Olympia oysters, which he retrieved from Griffin Bay, calling them in his journal entry of February 26, 1859, "miserable little things…but of better quality than the oysters of this coast generally." In February of 1860 Warren, on Orcas Island, noted "an Indian fishery about a half a mile south of Point Doughty", which was "only occupied during the salmon season. From the size of the lodge erected a large body of Indians must resort to this spot, and the immense quantities of salmon heads that were strewed around gave evidence that the last season's fishing must have been eminently successful."

After the settlement of the boundary dispute in 1872, the islands were surveyed and divided into townships and sections according to the United States Public Land System. The General Land Office hired three surveyors—T. M. Reed, James Tilton Sheets, and John M. Whitworth—who began work in the autumn of 1874 and continued through the 1880s; some areas were not completed until the 1920s. Included in their cadastral maps as well as their field notes are the various meanders of the shoreline; sometimes these include names of persons who had settled there—often fishers—and the structures they occupied.

From 1888 to 1898, the United States Coast and Geodetic Survey, under the direction of Coast Survey Superintendent Alexander Dallas Bache, mapped and charted the San Juan Islands and their surrounding waters. The Hydrographic Survey was charted by Lt. J. N. Jordan in the steamer *Earnest*. The topographical maps, called T-sheets, were prepared by Captain John J. Gilbert, using three vessels: steamer *Gedney* for supplies and steam launches *Fuca* and *Tarry Not*. The T-sheets as well as the field notes and photographs that accompany them contain a great deal of information about maritime activities in the islands.

Trade

With the merging of the North West Company with the Hudson's Bay Company ("the Company") in 1821, the latter became the principal trader in the Pacific Northwest, establishing its headquarters at Fort Vancouver on the Columbia River in 1825. Two years later the Company founded Fort Langley on the Fraser River, which became the center for trade with Indigenous peoples in that region. They began buying salmon from them, for their own use as well as for trade, and salmon soon became the most important trade item for the Company in the region.

> *These islands are exceedingly valuable, not only on account of their relative position to Vancouver Island, but also from the fact that their shores and inlets abound with salmon and other fish which form a productive export and an inexhaustible form of great wealth.*
>
> — *Chief Factor James Douglas to Sir John Pakington, Duke of Newcastle, British Foreign Office, November 24, 1853*

It was the presence of the Straits Salish peoples fishing the seasonal runs of salmon that first attracted the Company to establish an outpost on San Juan Island. The initial Company operations on San Juan Island were seasonal fishing stations: encampments where items such as blankets were traded for salmon. The fish were packed in salt brine in large wood barrels. Governor James Douglas wrote to Company Secretary Archibald Barclay in a letter of June 25, 1851, that a Company boat was "now taking in salt and barrels for a fishery which we propose establishing in the Island of San Juan." (The Company not only approved of the fishery but said "it always affords us great satisfaction to learn that exertions are made to explore and turn to account the resources of the Colony.") That season the crew put up only 60 barrels of salted salmon.

> *In the month of June [1851] I was sent to San Juan Island to establish a salmon fishery, starting in a canoe, with an Indian crew, Joseph W. McKay as pilot and locator of a site, and four French Canadian workmen. We selected a small sheltered bay, erected a rough shed for salting, packing and curing of salmon, not known at that time, afterwards to become such an extensive and remunerative industry.*
>
> — *William John Macdonald undated manuscript, Royal British Columbia Archives, Victoria, B.C.*

Salmon had become an important export for the Company, surpassing fur in overall value at Fort Langley by the late 1840s. It was shipped primarily to San Francisco and the Sandwich Islands (Hawaii), although markets as far away as Australia and London were also attempted. The salmon, which were obtained by trading with Indigenous peoples (at a rate of 60 fish for a blanket worth $4), were placed in wooden barrels and packed in brine made with salt shipped as ballast from the Sandwich Islands. Each of these Company barrels, which contained 40 to 50 salmon and weighed 180 pounds, could fetch from $8 to $14. In addition to Belle Vue, as the Company called San Juan Island, fisheries were established at Fort Hope, Nanaimo, and Fort Victoria. The Company established a trading post in Honolulu as early as 1834, where they sold salted salmon among other goods. This was then used by industries in Hawaii—particularly sugar cane raising—to feed their workers. In one of the ironies of history, young Hawaiian men who had once enjoyed the fruit of the land and the fish of the sea were inducted into the global capitalist market, where they became "free agents," and then had to turn to salted salmon from thousands of miles away for sustenance.

> Salted salmon, delivered in barrels to the plantation store, provided the fish that Hawaiians could no longer provide on their own during the work week.
>
> — *Pacific Commercial Advertiser*, October 26, 1867

This was not dissimilar to the use of preserved fish (salted cod) for slaves in the sugar industries of the West Indies. However, Hawaiians adopted it into their diet to the extent that "Lomi Lomi Salmon" (from the Hawaiian word for kneading or massaging—*lomi*), which incorporated other ingredients introduced to the islands such as onions and tomatoes, became a standard dish in traditional Hawaiian luaus.

SALMON LOMI (12 servings)

2 lbs. salt salmon
6 large tomatoes
2 bunches green onions tops

Scale salmon, place in pan, pour boiling water over it and drain. Repeat 3 times. Pick the salmon into small pieces, removing all bones and skin. Cut onion tops into 1-inch pieces, peel and quarter tomatoes. Knead all together thoroughly. Chill and serve in small bowls.

— *The Helen Alexander Hawaiian Cook Book* (1938)

One of the reasons for the establishment of the Belle Vue fishery was the failure of the Fraser River salmon run in 1851. What the precise yields were subsequent to the first season are not known, although Douglas wrote in early September of 1852 that about 290 barrels had already been put up and the catch was still in process. W. J. Macdonald reminisced that the annual output was between two and three thousand barrels.

One of the principal sources of profit for the Hudson's Bay Company is their fishery here. According to the statement of Mr. Griffin, over 2000 barrels, each containing from 40 to 45 salmon, have been collected heretofore during the year. Halibut and cod fish are also taken in large numbers in the vicinity of the island, and are said to be unsurpassed in quality.

— *Report of Henry Custer, Assistant, of a Reconnaissance of San Juan Island, and the Saturna Group* (1859)

According to another observer, by the mid-1850s the Belle Vue fishery was producing around 300 barrels annually. Trading for or catching the salmon, salting it down, and packing it were certainly still going concerns in 1856, when Douglas wrote to Post Trader Charles Griffin regarding the availability of barrels for the operations.

> ...A cooper is now sent with Napoleon, to put up casks in order, and if the fish yield at all well, you may keep him at San Juan to put up as many fish as you can possibly cure, an additional number of casks and a quantity of salt will be sent over if required. Fish are very scarce in this quarter, and we shall be delighted if you succeed in curing 2 or 300 barrels.
>
> — Governor James Douglas to Post Trader Charles John Griffin, August 8, 1856

In the *Belle Vue Sheep Farm Post Journal*, Griffin mentions fishing in late August/early September of 1858, but apparently the fish were not biting. A year later, George Gibbs mentions that in former times the operation had put up 1,500 to 3,000 barrels a year (although, based on other sources, a tenth of which is probably more likely) but he confirms that there was no catch in 1858. Entries in Griffin's *Post Journal* in subsequent years (September 2, 1859, and July 12, 1860) mention the cleaning and repair of salmon barrels and cauldrons, but no catch.

> Let out net this morning at 9 am:- & left it until 8 pm:- in the water without the smallest success – although salmon were jumping all round it & even over it!
>
> — Charles John Griffin, *Belle Vue Sheep Farm Post Journal*, September 1, 1858

Boats and Ships

At first Euro Americans used Indigenous canoes for transportation throughout the Salish Sea. Within a short time, however, they imported new boat-building techniques. In contrast to traditional Indigenous boats, which were carved out of tree trunks, Euro American boats were primarily constructed of wooden planks that were fastened together to form a hull. Of "clinker-built" or "lapstrake" construction, these consisted of long boards that were attached to a framework such that each course overlaps the one below. Although dugout canoes persisted through the 1920s—and American and English settlers used them throughout the late nineteenth century—the Coast Salish gradually adapted to clinker-built boats, largely small 14- to 16-feet-long oar-powered skiffs that were easily built or cheaply purchased. When reef netting was revived in the 1930s, clinker-built reef net boats were built; several boat-building families provided most of the Lummi fleet for the industry.

Euro American clinker-built boats ranged in size from small craft—dinghies, dories, and long or whale boats, to larger sailing craft such as sloops, schooners, brigs, and barques. Boats and ships are classified by their motive power: oars or paddles, sails, or steam (and later gasoline) engines. Sailing craft were most often classified by how they were rigged, with spars or poles forming a mast, yard, boom, or gaffs, as well as the ropes that secured the spars and sails. These classifications included the number of masts as well as the number, position, and type of the sails.

During the nineteenth century, most new boats were brought to the Salish Sea from elsewhere. Some of the larger ships, such as multi-masted sailboats and steamers, were built at shipyards on the East Coast and sailed around the Horn to the West Coast. Shipwrights began building boats and ships in the region as early as the 1850s; one of them was Charles Brown, who came to Lopez Island in 1869. In the 1850s and 1860s, Brown had built several schooners and sloops in Port Ludlow, Port Townsend, and Scow Bay. In the late 1890s and early 1900s, local boatwrights and shipwrights began working on vessels for San Juan waters, and shipyards sprang up on all the major islands. In the 1900 federal census, there are a half a dozen men listed as either "boat builder" or "shipwright," and this does not include those who were only part-time builders. Perhaps the first were William Crook, and his son James, who homesteaded the site of English Camp after its abandonment by the Royal Marines in 1874; from the evidence of half-hull models found at their place as well as William's background as a shipwright in England, they probably built several boats at Garrison Bay. After purchasing the steamer *Buckeye* for a government mail contract, Andrew Newhall established a shipyard in Cascade Bay, Orcas Island, where he built the steamer *S.S. Islander* and steam launch *Loretta*. At Olga, R. C. Willis, a shipwright from Liverpool, England, together with his son Bruce built fishing vessels, including a boat as well as several skiffs for the Haines Oyster Company's shrimp operations. On Shaw Island, Delbert "Del" Hoffman constructed several boats, including the tug/tender *Arthur G.*, the sloop *Reliance*, the tug/fish tender *Bermuda*, and the fishing boat *Klatawa*. William and Joseph Reed and brother-in-law Henry T. Cayou founded Cayou & Reed on Decatur Island and built their first boat, the *Mary C.* (named after Cayou's wife Mary, the sister of William and Joseph) in 1903. Eventually they built over 40 boats there.

Several other boat-building operations were run by extended families. At Friday Harbor on San Juan Island, brothers Albert, Frank, Joseph ("Joe"), and Peter ("Pete") Jensen, together with Joseph ("Joe") Groll, established the Friday Harbor Lumber and Manufacturing Company on the waterfront at the base of West Street in 1904; in addition to milling and planing, they built ships there. In 1910, Albert Jensen left to establish a shipyard on the south side of Friday Harbor that eventually became the Albert Jensen & Son Shipyard. One of the first boats he constructed was the *Nereid*, which served as a tender for the Friday Harbor Packing Company. Eventually Albert and his son Nourdine built 150 boats at their yard. (The Jensen Shipyard was recently bought by the Port of Friday Harbor and continues in operation today.)

Several shipyards on Lopez were established by two (possibly three) brothers and their sons, with an interesting immigration story. According to family lore, when they came to the

Fishing Boat for Henry Cayou, Reed Shipyard, Decatur Island, 1903; Alphonse Meyer second from left (courtesy of Lopez Island Historical Society)

United States in the late 1880s from Norway, the Jorgensen family were not able to keep their patronymic (their father was Steffen Jorgensen), so they adopted different names: Peder (Peter) Martinus took the last name Schruder, and Mekal (Michael) adopted Norman. Michael Norman and his son Arthur established a shipyard on the northeast shore of Mud Bay and built the *Uno* (1894) and launch *Outlook* (1913). In 1902 Peter Schruder bought property at Otis, at the head of Mud Bay; there he and son Louis ("Louie") established a shipyard, as well as a sawmill, and over the next few years built fishing as well as other boats, including the *Alpha* (1901) and the *Hope* (1902). A third Jorgensen brother (or possibly a first cousin), known variously as Alphonse Meyer (Meir), Johan Meier Larsen, or Johan Jorgensen, was also a fisherman who built his own boat to sail to the gold rush in Alaska. Because many in the family worked on the boats, sometimes it is unclear who built what. For example, the *Outlook*, which was supposedly built by Peter and Louie Schruder, is credited in *The San Juan Islander* newspaper to "Meyer's boat shop."

Another set of immigrant brothers—Wilhelm ("William") Christian and Christian ("Chris") Sebelin—ran a shipyard on the shores of Fisherman Bay in the early twentieth century. In 1918 they built the *Dora* for themselves at Mackaye Harbor near Richardson and purse seined in the 1920s and 1930s. By 1940, they were listed as oar makers and according to local lore had designed a machine for making oars. They both remained bachelors.

> To get money I used to build a V-bottom double-ender rowboat for a dollar a foot. That was a lot of money at the time. My father taught me how to build 'em... We'd go out and pick up drift logs. There were lots of nice cedars drifting around in those days. Booms would break up and the logs would go adrift. We'd take them to the sawmill to be made into boards, then plane them with a hand plane.
>
> We used galvanized nails for boat work because they wouldn't rust. They were all square cut at that time.
>
> We'd mix our own paint out of white lead and linseed oil and give them one coat. There was no filler or dyer or anything in it. Lots of boats never got painted because people didn't have the paint.
>
> Dad hardly ever used oarlocks because a set cost twenty-five cents. He would put pins like they have in the Navy and save the twenty-five cents. Then we'd shape our oars out of a piece of cedar with a drawknife.
>
> —Al Coffelt, quoted in Ron Strickland, *River Pigs and Cayuses: Oral Histories from the Pacific Northwest* (2001)

Shipyards also were established in the greater Salish Sea region. One of the most influential for the San Juan Islands fleet was the Skansie Shipyard in Gig Harbor. In the early 1900s,

> ...around 1902 we made Power boat and inlarge[sic] 30 foot oar boat. Saw it in two and added in center 8 feet longer and installed 7 horse power Standard Gas Engine. It never failed to go and we made good season. At same time, right after everybody made power boats, us brothers start building little cabins on our boats and others boats and little by little start build or repair small boats.
>
> —Peter Skansie, *Autobiographical Sketch*
> (Gig Harbor Historical Society website)

brothers Peter, Mitchell, Joe, and Andrew Skansie, who had immigrated from the island of Brac, Dalmatia (currently part of Croatia), began to modify purse seiners, which had been rowed by oar with a crew of eight men, to power boats by installing gasoline engines, increasing the length of the hull, and adding cabins. Peter and Joe returned to fishing, but Mitchell and Andrew continued the business, building much of the Croatian Gig Harbor purse seine fleet that fished the San Juan Islands, among other places in the Salish Sea.

FISHING METHODS AFTER EUROPEAN AND EURO AMERICAN CONTACT

Fish Trapping

> ### Fish Traps
>
> Fish traps consisted of four parts: lead, heart, pot, and spiller. The lead consisted of up to 150-foot-long log pilings steam-driven into the seabed 10–15 feet apart in a straight line diagonal to the prevailing tidal flow. Galvanized metal wire netting that extended from the bottom to the high-water mark was stapled to the pilings. This diverted the salmon in their migration and led them into the heart, a funnel that was 10 feet on the outside and narrowed to the pot. The pot consisted of a large, tarred cotton-web pen, 40'-square and deep enough to hold up to 70,000 salmon. From the pot the salmon were turned into the spiller, a bag similar to but smaller than the pot. (Spillers were added to traps with just a pot to handle larger catches that could not be loaded right away; some traps located at high-yield sites had two spillers, one on each side of the pot.) Inside was an apron-shaped brailer that was powered by a trap tender, a tug-like vessel that had a crew of 8–10 men. These men would brail the salmon into scows, which were then towed to the canneries.

Fish traps were introduced to the Salish Sea from the Columbia River area, the first being located at Point Roberts in 1880. At first the Coast Salish, mainly Lummi, tolerated the imposition of this new type of fishing in their traditional fishing grounds. However, the Euro American owners soon began placing their traps so as to intercept the fish before travelling into the reef nets, as well as forcing the Lummi from their nearby fish camps. While the epicenter of this conflict was the rich fishing grounds near Point Roberts, which directly intercepted the sockeye runs to the Fraser River, fish traps were built on other prime reef net sites in the San Juan Islands, including Open Bay off Henry Island and Andrews Bay and Pile Point off San Juan Island. This eventually led to a formal protest in 1894 on the part of the Lummi Tribe—unfortunately, to no avail. (It wouldn't be until the 1970s that their treaty rights were recognized and reaffirmed with the Boldt Decision.)

The first trap in the islands was built by Henry Cayou, off Eagle Point on San Juan Island in 1888. He signed a contract with Alaska Packers Association to supply salmon at six cents each to their canneries at Blaine and Point Roberts. Fish traps grew steadily in numbers, until about 168 were located in the region, with three to nine at Salmon Bank alone. The number of fish traps ranged from a low of 13 in 1898 to a high of 168

> *Living as we do on the shores of Puget Sound our principal means of subsistence, especially during certain seasons of the year, is fishing our best grounds situated near the reef of Point Roberts of this state. Several years ago white men began to encroach on our ground. We were willing to have them share with us the right to fish but not satisfied with equal rights they have yearly made additional obstructions to prevent our catching fish, by setting traps, and placing piling around the grounds. They have driven us from our old camping ground on the beach and have so treated us that we feel we must now appeal to you for assistance. In our treaty with the government we were given the first right to hunt and fish on our old grounds and we know too well that the good government that has so far protected our rights will not permit us to be trodden upon simply because we are Indians. We the Indians of this reservation do therefore earnestly pray that you will call upon the U. S. District Attorney of Seattle to prosecute those who are robbing us of our lawful rights.*
>
> — *Petition to the Commissioner of Indian Affairs, Lummi Tribal Archives (1894)*

in 1913 in the "Puget Sound" region, defined as north of Sandy Point (Point Roberts and Boundary and Birch Bays), south of Sandy Point and north of Deception Pass (Rosario Strait, Salmon Banks, Haro Strait, and including Lummi Island), along West Beach, Ebeys Landing, and the south side of the Strait of Juan de Fuca, east of Whidbey Island (mainly the Hope Island area), and south of Point Wilson (Admiralty Bay and Hood Canal). (This does not include traps in the British Columbia portion of the Salish Sea; the first one was placed in 1894, with the highest number being 17 in 1905, and about eight on average.)

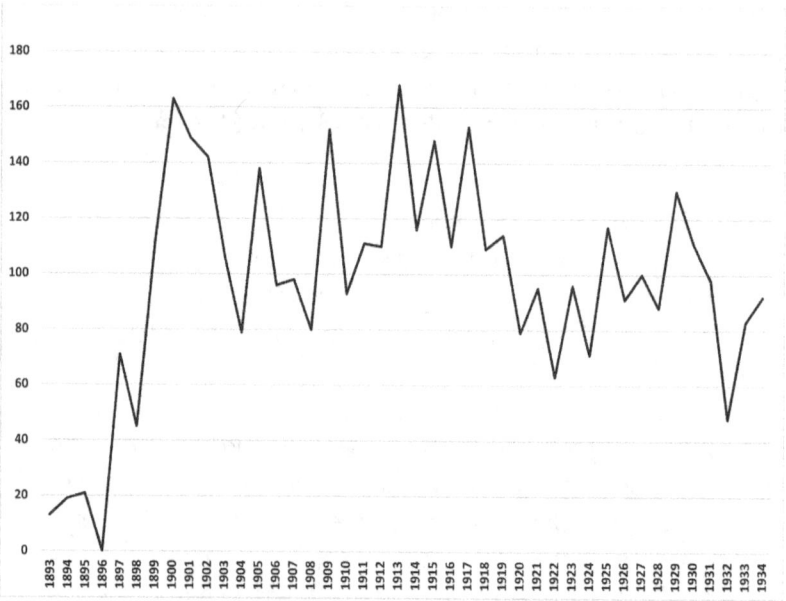

Fish Traps in Puget Sound, 1893–1934

In 1901, *The San Juan Islander* reported that there were around 40 traps in San Juan County alone, employing about 300 men just working on the traps, with an average wage of $50 per month including board. Fish traps were very efficient at catching salmon—usually 15,000–20,000 a night—but eventually they were banned by passage of state Initiative 77 in 1934. It is estimated that from 1873–1934, about 37% of the sockeye were caught by this method in this region.

Salmon Bank and South Beach, US Coast & Geodetic Survey T Sheet, 1897

Various laws regulated the design, size, and layout of the fish traps. Starting in 1892, Washington State law required that fish traps be removed from the water during a part of each year; this meant that engineers had to survey the exact location of the pilings prior to removal in order that they could be placed

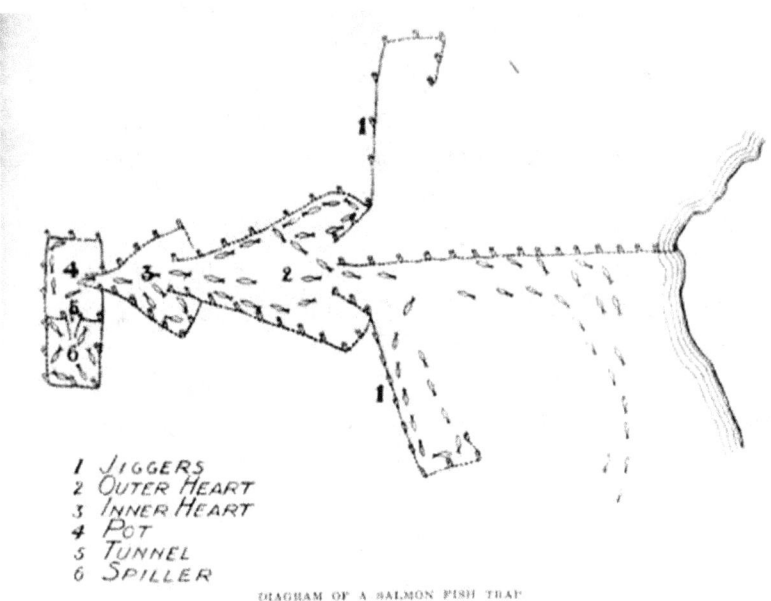

Diagram of Fish Trap (Pacific Fisherman January 1904)

in their licensed positions in spring of the next year. In 1897, statutes required that the lead had to be shorter than 2,500 feet, and the mesh had to be greater than three inches. Between the nets, the end passageway had to be at least 600 feet, and the later passage at least 2,400 feet, so that nets would not run in a continuous, connected series. Another law was passed in 1897 that prohibited traps from operating in water over 65 feet in depth.

> *A salmon trap is stationery and consists of webbing or part wire netting, held in place and position by driven piles. This piling is held together above water by a continuous line of wood stringers, also used to fasten webbing to or walk on if necessary.*
>
> *First, the lead, running at right angles with shore or 35 degrees, as the case may be; this consists of webbing or wire netting, hung from top of high water or a little higher to the bottom, making a straight solid wall; the salmon, generally in schools, running along the shore and striking this obstruction, as a rule follow it and with very little hesitancy go straight where lead and into the corral or "pot,"...which is at the end of the lead, the entrance to some being cone-shaped, with smaller end running into the pot in a horizontal position... This "tunnel" is made of web and held in place by ropes and rods, gradually decreasing in circumference until only a small opening is left for the fish to go through. Below this on the outside is what is termed the "apron," a sheet of web stretched from bottom upward, to lead fish into tunnel, when swimming low in the water.*
>
> *At a distance of about two thirds of lead from shore begins what is called the "hearts." These are V-shaped and turned toward the lead, beginning at a distance of thirty to forty feet on either side of same, running parallel with it; the "big*

heart," or outer heart, first; the inner heart relieving the first being smaller; the lead and hearts terminating in nearly the same place, where the tunnel begins leading into pot.

Some traps have a "jigger," an extension of outer heart on a hook-shape, in addition to the hearts, another safeguard, to turn the fish in the "right" direction.

The "pot" is placed at right angles with lead, where it ends, and immediately adjoining same; it is a square corral with web walls and bottom, connected in the shape of a large, square sack, with piling on all sides to which it is fastened. This web sack is hauled up and down by means of ropes and tackles, either by hand or as is most popular, by steam, when the steamer arrives.

The "spiller" appears directly adjoining the pot in either end, and is simply a container for fish. Where a spiller is used, the fish are generally lifted from there and the pot left down.

— Chris H. Richardson, "Trap Fishing,"
Pacific Fisherman vol. 1, no. 1 (1904)

To establish a fish trap, the location was surveyed and filed with the county and the state, and a state license—usually relatively cheap compared to the wealth the trap would generate ($125 in the early 1900s)—was purchased. The county assessed the sites, and the property taxes were relatively low at first; when Progressives gained control of county offices in the early twentieth century, they raised taxes, causing the companies to protest. In 1927, Stephen B. Gross testified in *Duwamish et al. v. United States* that it cost from $5,000 to $30,000 to put in a trap and operate it during a season. According to August C. Radke's analysis of the operations from 1904–1919 of the Deep Sea Fish Company, which owned three traps off Cherry Point in Whatcom County, about half of the $5,000–$10,000 annual expenses on each of its traps was spent on installation and half on operation. Traps had to be used at least once in four years, so in some cases dummy traps, consisting of skeletal piles and random nets, were set up in order to secure a site through a season when it was not needed. Men like John Troxell monitored the ownership of trap locations in the islands, and if they were not used, they would "jump" the claim.

Pile Driving a Fish Trap (courtesy of Lopez Island Historical Society)

Fish trap operators needed pile drivers with rigging, scows (both "pot" and "deck"), tugboats, and yards and sheds for winter storage. (John Wade says that Web Street is where Friday Harbor Packing Company stored theirs.) Wire netting and tarred webbing were prepared during the late winter/early spring, surveying and pile driving began in early spring, and the season, usually beginning in May, lasted through October, when the traps were dismantled and towed home.

In March, the fish trap crew would lay out the rolls of five-foot-wide, 100-foot-long wire, with an aperture of no less than three inches, for the leads. A roll was laid on top of another and the selvages connected with metal hog rings, so that the layers unfolded in an accordion pattern to the depth of the water, which had been carefully calculated by the trap operator. Next, the cotton webbing for the spiller—a forty-foot square box with a bottom—was cut and bound by hand with web needles, like a weaver's shuttle formed as a tatting bobbin. The webbing was tarred by dipping with a winch in a trough and then spread out to dry. The piles, which could be up to 100' long (for the maximum depth of 65' at low water), were driven by steam-powered drivers with 80-foot gins and three-ton drop hammers at 10 feet apart.

> Now came the pile driver and for days on end, when the water was smooth enough we'd hear the rhythmic zzzz-thump-punk-punk sound as the hammer was hoisted and allowed to drop from the top of the gins; falling onto an up-ended pile with such force that it bounced a couple of times. Again the zzing as the hammer was raised, and the thump-thunk-thunk, raising, falling, bouncing until that pile was solidly driven into the ocean bottom; move the pile driver along ten feet and repeat.
>
> — Beryl Troxell Mason, *John Franklin Troxell, Fish Trap Man* (1991)

Although local forests often provided trees for piles, some wood came from as far away as Hood Canal. In 1899, the tug Puritan towed 350 85-100-foot-long piles to Shultz and Gross' trap near Mitchell Bay; six years later, the steamer Doctor brought another boom to their Andrews Bay trap for a cost of $5.00 to $5.50 each, depending on length. Pile drivers charged from $50 a day in the early 1900s to $100 a day after World War I.

Tarring Webs for the Oceanic Canning Company (courtesy of Lopez Island Historical Society)

*Diver Jumping off Scow to set fish trap webs
(courtesy of Lopez Island Historical Society)*

After the piles were driven, the capping scow and crew attached horizontal pilings six feet above the high water. The netting was secured to the capping piles with 2½-inch staples and then unfolded like an accordion. Workers then fastened it with "shove-downs"—3"-diameter sapling poles that were shoved down through cable nooses to hold the wire snug against the pilings. After building a capping consisting of two-by-twelve-inch planks, the spiller was rigged so that one side could be lowered to allow a pot scow to enter. The spiller web was controlled with winches and cleats at the corners.

The last structure was a watchman's cabin, six-foot square, placed on the corner capping nearest the tunnel, allowing for a clear view of the tunnel, with the adjusting cleats near the watchman's left hand. Finally, a diver went to the sea bottom to examine the full length of the lead, the hearts, the pot, and the spiller, to make sure the salmon could not find a hole to escape through.

The times of year when salmon ran depended on the species: pinks started in late June and continued through August; sockeyes began in late July and continued through late August; and coho came in the fall. Traps were "lifted"—the fish removed

At fishing time a large deck scow is lined up alongside of the spiller and beyond it a trap steamer furnished with a brailer operated by steam. Within the spiller is a stationary scow upon which fishermen stand, seven or eight in number, and raise by hauling the large dip net, about forty feet square. The brailer, which is a dip net on a smaller scale, being 12x12 feet in size, dipping over into the net thus raised, takes up hundreds of fish at a time and by means of steam-operated tackle dumps them on the deck of the scow.

Brailing goes on until the spiller is emptied of thousands of fish, possibly. The large scow is capable of holding 12,000 Sockeyes. It is towed by the trap steamer to the next trap where like proceedings are had, as above.

— *The Shield: Official Publication of the Employees of Pacific American Fisheries and Allied Companies vol. 1, no. 8* (December 1918)

Watchman on Fish Trap (courtesy of Lopez Island Historical Society)

by brailing—about twice a week early in the season and every other day during the heavy runs. The tug would tow a pot scow—a 30-foot-long, 10-foot-wide boat without a deck that held three tons of fish—to the trap and maneuver it into the spiller. A web brail—a three-foot-diameter iron-ringed dip net—was used to brail the fish into the pot scow. Boards were put onto the pot scow to protect the fish from the sun, and the scow was towed to the next trap. In some cases, there were so many salmon that they couldn't get the pot scow into the trap, and the operator had to request a steam-brailing outfit, capable of taking a ton of fish with one scoop. The brailer lay alongside the trap and dipped into the spiller from over the capping. The fish had to be processed within 72 hours of being taken out of the water, so it was important to get them to the cannery quickly. When the scows were taken to the company's deck scow (a completely decked barge with four bins constructed above board, which could hold seven tons), a person with

Men Brailing Salmon from Shultz and Gross Fish Trap into the Michigan (courtesy of Northwest Room, Tacoma Public Library)

*Loading Scows at Shultz and Gross Fish Trap;
Note the Salish Canoe in the Foreground
(courtesy of Northwest Room, Tacoma Public Library)*

a tally-counter in each hand—one for sockeyes, the other for humpbacks—would tally the count as men pitched fish from the pot scow's hold into the company's container. The salmon were again tallied when they were taken to the cannery, and theoretically the two numbers were supposed to agree, although the trap operators often thought the cannery men were shorting them.

Fish traps were subject to both natural disasters and predators. In August of 1911, "a heavy tide, unusually high and unusually swift, amounting, in fact practically to a tidal wave" hit several fish traps, causing significant physical and financial damages. Occasionally orcas, sometimes called killer whales or blackfish, were caught in the traps, causing substantial damage and usually culminating in the killing of the animals. Fish trap watchmen were given the task of keeping an eye out for both seals and sea lions, who could do great damage in a short amount of time if they entered the pot. They also had to remove clumps of kelp and other drifting seaweed as well as fending off driftwood, often in the form of very large logs.

And then there were the fish pirates. Because of the value of the catch held at fish traps, piracy became a serious problem. Fish pirates would come in quietly in the middle of the night and, either in collusion with the watchmen, who were some of the lowest paid in the industry, or sometimes beating them up and throwing them in the water, would help themselves to the catch. Giving themselves names like "Owl Eye Joe," "Nosey Hermann," "Sleepy Eye Charlie," and "Shifty Sam," some became folk heroes because they were stealing from company traps. Some were lionized because of their skill: Bert "Spider" Jones of Anacortes, for instance, could navigate his double-ended 42-foot boat through the dark and fog, guided by compass, the flight of "skags" (cormorants, which perched atop the piles), and intuition.

FISH PIRACY ON WEST COAST
Two Young Men Guilty of Stealing Salmon

Last Sunday night various fish camps along the west coast of San Juan island were visited by "fish pirates," who stole salmon wherever they could find them—whether in the canoes of the Indians, who have been catching barely enough fish to enable them to buy the necessities of life, or at the comfortable camps of well know citizens at Ziegler's beach and vicinity. Two young men well known on the island were suspected and Tuesday evening they were arrested by Sheriff McCrary. They are John Kelly, Jr., and Joe Fleming, eldest son of Jas. M. Fleming, one of the oldest settlers and best known farmers on the island. As only a few fish were taken at any one place the charge filed against them was petit larceny. Young Fleming, evidently sorry for his part in the affair, turned state's evidence and told the story of the thievery. He said that 171 fish were taken and that they were sold the following morning to the buyer of the little steamer "Hoosier Boy," of Anacortes, for fifteen cents each.

—*The San Juan Islander,* October 8, 1902

I run without lights altogether. I wouldn't run onto no rock because I knew where to go. That was the easiest part. I'd look up in the sky. Or to get to a trap on the reef way out in the middle out there I used to follow the skags [cormorants]. The skags'd fly straight out to the fish trap. No matter how foggy it was, all I'd do was follow the skags. Nothing to it. Big black birds. I had lots of tricks.

I'd keep hid during the day and come out during the evening after the patrol boats had all left. The nighttime was when I done my work, and they done theirs in the daytime. Gosh, I used to travel all over. Oh, the fish traps was thick. God, they were thick. Every night I used to get a load of fish.

— Bert "Spider" Jones, quoted in
Ron Strickland, *River Pigs and Cayuses:
Oral Histories from the Pacific Northwest* (2001)

One of the places where Jones probably hung out was Fish Creek on San Juan Island ("the patrol boats couldn't see me because I was laying up on the bank under the trees and brush"); the watchman for one of the traps on Salmon Bank would obligingly walk over the ridge and tell Jones when he could come get the fish.

The Washington Fish Commission set up a Fish Patrol in 1899, but they could not guard against the many middle-of-the-night piracies. The trap owners even went to the extent of deploying fast-moving boats with officers aboard "armed to the teeth with rifles and other firearms," but the thievery continued. According to a 1902 Whatcom dispatch to the *Seattle Times*, some arrested pirates made an unusual claim in their defense: "that the fish are not in possession of the trap men until they are taken from the sea and loaded into scows; that so long as they remain in the trap the game law that is old as man applies; that the fish are not taken in any sense of the word when they enter the trap, as the place where they enter remains open, and they can go out whenever they choose."

> Henry Cayou...is one of the few residents of this county who has "struck it rich" this year in the fishing business. He owns a half interest in two traps at the south end of the Lopez island which have been paying their owners about $1,000 a day since the big sockeye run began. They have a contract with the Northwest Packing Company, of Blaine, for 6,000 fish a day at 12 cents each, and the company has been taking about 8,000 a day at that price. The traps have been full continuously since the run began and have had to be kept closed a considerable part to the time to avoid breakage by overcrowding.
> —The San Juan Islander, August 8, 1901

In San Juan County, fish traps were originally owned by locals such as Henry Cayou, Shultz and Gross, and John Troxell. Henry T. Cayou was born in Deer Harbor, Orcas Island, to Louis Cayou and his second wife, Mary Ann Sulwham, who was part of the Mitchell Bay Band, with parents who were Lummi and Saanich. After Louis' death, Mary Ann married the chief fisherman of the San Juan (Mitchell Bay) Tribe, Pe-el (Harry Seawalton Sturgeon), and Henry claimed later in life that he learned how to fish from his stepfather starting at age nine. At one time, he was thought to have caught a million salmon in his lifetime. In 1901, *The San Juan Islander* reported that Cayou, in association with J. P. Nelson, had trapped upwards of 500,000 sockeyes in their two traps off Watmough Head, Lopez Island, selling 203,070 to the Northwest Packing Company in Blaine. A year later, Cayou sold the traps for $20,000 to C. R. Hadley and H. C. Griffith, of Whatcom, who, together with Nelson, incorporated the Watmough Fish Company, with capitalization of $50,000. In 1909, *The San Juan Islander* reported that he planned five fish traps in the islands: near Decatur; off Long Island at the south end of Lopez; two outside Deception Pass; and one near Kellet Ledge between Lopez and Decatur Islands. He later built a fish trap at Dot Island, off Decatur Island, which subsequently belonged to the George

& Barker Company, of Point Roberts. Cayou also chartered his fish boat, built in 1911 at the Reed Shipyard on Decatur Island and named after his first wife, the *Helen T.*, to George & Barker. William Shultz, born in Delphi, Indiana, moved to Tacoma in 1889, and then a year later to Roche Harbor, where he started as bookkeeper of the Tacoma and Roche Harbor Lime Company, rising to become general manager, superintendent, and eventually vice president. In 1896, along with Samuel Gross, P. S. Cook, Dr. I. M. Harrison, and E. W. Harrison, he incorporated the Andrews Bay Fishing Company. Samuel H. Gross, born in Ellsworth, Maine, had moved to California in his twenties and then, like many early American pioneers in the islands, north to the Fraser River Gold Rush. In 1868 he filed for a homestead on San Juan Island and farmed, but eventually fell into debt and almost lost his farm. In 1896 Shultz and Gross purchased tide lands near Mitchell Bay and two years later they built a fish trap off the south end of Henry Island, near the entrance to Mosquito Pass and Mitchell Bay. This proved to be a major fish producer, and they sold the catch under contract to the Aberdeen Packing Corporation in Fairhaven (sockeyes) and the Great Northern Fish Company of Seattle (humpbacks) for a handsome profit. When the Pacific American Fisheries Company was formed in 1899, Shultz and Gross sold this trap—including the estimated value of that season's catch—for a substantial sum (*The San Juan Islander* first reported that it was $30,000 total; later they corrected that to $40,000). They then set up another trap south of the former at Smallpox Bay (then called Brann's Bay), which also proved to be profitable. In 1903, the operations of the new canning conglomerate, the Pacific Packing and Navigation Company (PP&N), were curtailed, and most traps in the region were closed; however, the September 17 issue of *The San Juan Islander* reported that "in the midst of the general disaster which has overtaken the fishing industry this season," the Shultz and Gross trap had caught over 329,000 fish and "the run of silver salmon is only just beginning." Around 1904 they sold this trap and, on December 23, 1905, dissolved the partnership. By the time Gross died in 1907, he had made a considerable amount of money.

> ...*One of the most successful traps constructed and operated in San Juan County is that of*
>
> ### Shultz & Gross
>
> *located on the south end of Andrews Bay, near Roche Harbor, San Juan Island. Over 400,000 fish were here caught this year in this trap, of which over 200,000 were of the sockeye variety. This trap is constructed with a pound net and has three pots. It has double hearts—three on one side of the lead and two on the other. The individual members of this firm are Wm. Shultz and Samuel Gross, of Roche Harbor.*
>
> — Supplement to *The San Juan Islander,* 1901

After quitting at Roche Harbor and dissolving the partnership with Gross in 1905, Shultz worked with Captain George J. Willey operating the Blaine Packing Company (1906) and the Crest Canning Company in Anacortes (1907). In 1909 he, along with Willey and W. E. Persell, formed the Friday Harbor Packing Company and the Mitchell Bay Fish Company. William Shultz continued as manager of both companies until his death in 1925, and his obituary read "Pioneer Puget Sound Canneryman Summoned by Death."

John Franklin Troxell was born to Frank and Kitty Troxell, who had come from Pennsylvania and homesteaded on the north end of the Lopez Island in 1885. He got his first job as a helper on a pile-driving crew and then worked on building fish traps with Ernest Davis and his brothers Rowland ("Rolly") and Arthur, sons of James and Amelia Davis, who had homesteaded on the south end of Lopez Island in 1869. John Troxell and Ernest Davis put in a fish trap at Aleck Bay and fished it for the years 1901 and 1902; they then sold it for $50,000 and split the proceeds. Ernest had previously married John's sister Maybelle; after the sale, John married Eunice Davis, Ernest's sister. The new owners of the trap could not find the pile holes, so Troxell was called back to manage the trap for several years (and eventually claimed it again in the 1910s). In 1909 he worked at Sperry's Lagoon, putting in fish traps for the Pacific American Fish Com-

On and around the edges of the level meadow facing Richardson and sloping to a no-bank beach in the harbor all the buildings and facilities for living and operating the business were eventually constructed. Our house stood about seventy-five feet from the shore at the south west corner of this meadow. The vegetable garden stretched north from the house yard and parallel to the beach. Across the garden on the northeast corner was a lane between the cook house steps and the garden fence; the lane that ended at the dock and from which, later, the rolls of made-up wire were to be loaded onto the scows. On an east-west line along the base of the chicken yard hill stood first the cookhouse, next, a cabin for Hans Floe and his Norwegian bride when Hans was first our crew foreman. Beyond the cabin was built the crew's bunkhouse, and finally on the east shore stood the net house constructed out onto a dock in the bay.

On the south line of this level area going east from our house you'd come first to the well. This was a dug well with a five hundred gallon fish tierce on a tower over it. That tank was filled by hand pump and the water flowed from it by gravity to faucets at the back steps of the house, and to the cookhouse. Beyond the well stood the barn and tool shop. Along the inner harbor shore were built the purse seine boat ways, the skids on which to haul out the piles for winter storage, and then over toward the tar tank and the net house more ways for hauling out and servicing the scows. Farthest from the house, but easiest to be built was the float-dock with a small storage building housing rope, cable, oars, pics, pike poles, tubs and barrels, etc., and even contained bins for the summer ice storage. We got to this float by way of a foot path at the end of the high bank from beyond the net house, out onto a gang plank on the tip of that rocky point. Eventually, several dolphins were driven in the bay for tying up scows and boats during the fishing season.

—Beryl Troxell Mason, *John Franklin Troxell, Fish Trap Man* (1991) pany in Anacortes. In the 1911 and 1912 seasons he made a deal with Dan Campbell of the Astoria Puget Sound Canning Company at Chuckanut that if he successfully operated the Long Island trap off Lopez, the company would finance his operations through a partnership. Troxell went on to own and operate several other traps off Lopez: Aleck Bay and Iceberg Point, and for a few years off Woody and Hall Islands, as well as at Huggins Bay in big years. At first, he hired Norwegian crews, with foreman Hans Floe in charge, but later he hired locals, and family and relatives, including the Middletons: Aunt Lois, cooking for the crew, and Uncle Elbert, who served in several capacities, including carpenter and watchman. Relatives Carl and Edna Mueller had a cabin on "the Rock"—a high rocky island 150 yards off the north arm of Aleck Bay—from which Carl would row to watch over the Aleck Bay trap.

A TRUE FISH STORY

Articles of incorporation of the Lopez Island, Bellingham Bay, Orcas Island, Lummi Island and San Juan Fishing Companies, ostensibly five separate concerns, have recently been filed at Olympia, the incorporators of each being F. I. Lord, W. J. Goode and H. A. Fairchild and the aggregate capital stock only $5,000. And thereby hangs a tale—a fish tale. Mr. Lord is a son-in-law of Mr. Ladner, one of the wealthiest and most extensive cannerymen on the Fraser river and vice-president of the company which proposes to build a cannery at Richardson. ... What is of more interest to the people of this county, however, is that we have learned from unquestioned authority that the sole object of these various incorporations is to acquire possession of all the desirable fish trap locations in this and Whatcom counties, which are now available, so as to enable them to control the big end of the salmon run each year and take the fish to the Fraser river to be packed in the canneries there.

— *San Juan Islander*, December 19, 1895

Putting in the fish traps involved large amounts of capital and labor, so it is little wonder that most of them were owned by the large cannery syndicates, such as Pacific American Fisheries (PAF) and Alaska Packers Association (APA). In the late 1890s, as large companies began consolidating the fishtrap industry, Washington State passed a law (Section 3349) decreeing that no one person or corporation could own more than three trap sites. The APA and PAF got around this by forming subsidiary fish trap corporations. For instance, when Ed Deming took control of the PAF in 1904, he reorganized the Deep Sea Fish Company, which owned three traps off Cherry Point, with 700 shares, 698 of which were owned by himself, one by his brother A. W., and the other by D. M. Brosseau, PAF's auditor. From 1904 through 1914, the Deep Sea Fish Company declared five dividends for a total of $131,445. Canning companies like the PAF were known to buy other, smaller cannery companies just to obtain their fish trap locations and operations, often shuttering the cannery after the purchase.

A typical seasonal fish trap catch can be seen from data compiled by Jackilee Wray in her 2003 ethnographic study of Salmon Bank: in the years from 1917 to 1924, the catch at the Pacific American Fisheries (Friday Harbor Packing Company) Trap No. 557 ranged from a high of 77,079 salmon in 1918 to a low of 5,343 in 1923, for a seasonal average of 27,000.

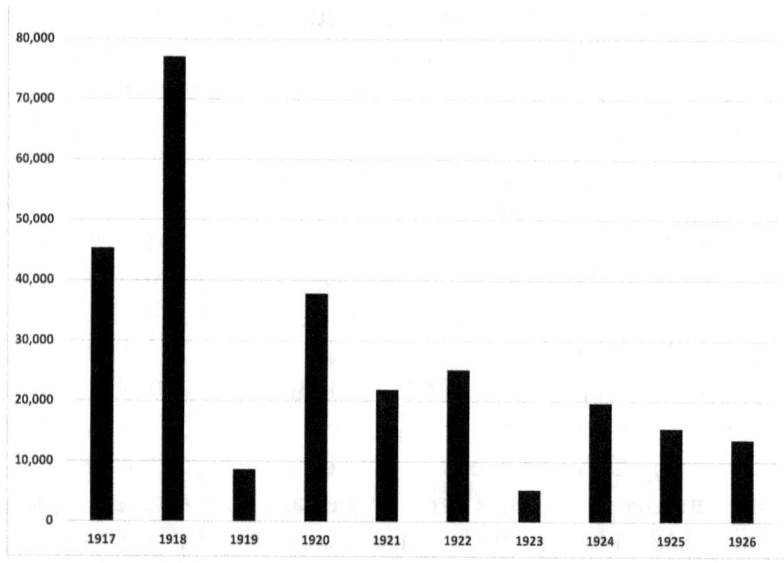

Seasonal Catch at Pacific American Fisheries Trap # 557, 1917–1926

A good day's "lift" was 15,000 fish, but there were some spectacular daily catches: on July 29, 1917, for instance, Pacific American Fisheries Trap No. 549 at Salmon Bank caught 28,000 sockeye in that day's lift, and a staggering 40,000 were recorded at one of John Troxell's locations.

> *When we went out there and put in those reef nets, we caught fish right off starting the first day and the white fishermen never had one to eat. They didn't know how to catch them. They didn't know how to use a reef net. Every night when we'd go home, you could go down and sit on the beach and see them out there measuring our reef net and copying it. They'd wait until it was nighttime before they'd go and copy our reef net. Measure all the lines then they'd go back and try to fix theirs the same way.*
>
> — Herman Olsen,
> quoted in Ann Nugent, *Lummi Elders Speak* (1982)

Reef Netting

There must have been a considerable number of reef nets in the late nineteenth century, but the advent of fish traps forced them from their traditional spots or thwarted their catch by being placed in the way to block salmon from entering. Some 15–20 (16 in 1889) nets were set in the Point Roberts area alone, and in 1894 there were 25 in Whatcom County and 14 in San Juan County; in 1901, about half (15) of the 27 reef nets total were licensed to Lummis and the others to residents of the San Juans. Based on an 1895 interview by Richard Rathbun with reef netters Joe Cagey and Dick Edwards, who had eight gears off Iceberg Point

> *Each gear has four anchors, one inshore from the inside boat, one outside the outer boat, and one 100 to 200 ft. from the bow of each boat. Log buoys mark the head anchor cables and also the far end of each buoy line, which leads to the bow of its corresponding boat; the two forming a funnel on the surface of the water. This "funnel" is marked by three-foot wooden buoys, some crude and some carefully whittled. These buoy lines converge from the approximately 200-ft. gap at the head buoys to the two open boats between which the net is spread. Boats and nets are comparable to the tube of the funnel, a tube that averages 40 ft. in width.*
>
> *Two ropes fastened from 25 to 35 ft. down the head anchor cables slant upward to the front of the weighted net. These are the "net lines." From each buoy to the net line under it are tied six-thread "sidelines" at intervals of about a fathom. Across the funnel from net line to net line are spread from ten to thirty "floorlines" at the same intervals. Every three feet or so in the ply of the sidelines and floorlines the crew inserts stalks of silvery marsh grass (replaced anew every few weeks), and so they create the appearance of a reef.*
>
> — Beatrice "Reef Net Betty" Annette Lowman,
> "Reef Nets Come Back in Puget Sound Salmon Fishery,"
> Pacific Fisherman, June 1939

on Lopez Island, Russel Barsh has calculated the productivity of these gear: they were netting 3,000–4,000 sockeye during each outgoing tide, which, at 10 cents a pound, may have earned about $2,000 per day—a huge sum for the time. However, the number of gear continued to fall, and less than a dozen were set in the period leading up to 1934, the year that fish traps were outlawed. In response to the impact of fish traps on salmon numbers, Canada banned the use of reef nets in 1916. After the passage of Initiative 77, which banned the use of fixed nets in the State of Washington, there was some debate about whether reef nets were included in the law, but this was eventually resolved to allow for this gear.

Although following the same traditional design and methods, the technology of reef netting changed; cement anchors (and sometimes even car frames weighted with boulders!) replaced stone; cotton twine (and eventually nylon, in 1950s) was used instead of willow bark for the netting, manufactured rope replaced willow fiber lines, and plastic strips replaced silvery marsh grass as reef imitation. Polarized glasses helped to spot the fish. The boats themselves, although maintaining the general dimensions and form of the canoes, were clinker-built, and wooden, and later steel pipe "poles" or towers were added for easier observation. Most boats were double ended, ranging in length from 25 to 40 feet and a beam under six feet, with fore-and-aft planked bottoms. Although some boats were self-propelled, they were usually towed to the reef net site and then tended by flat-bottomed skiffs. The work of hauling in the nets, originally done by hand, became easier with hand-operated and, after World War II, battery-powered winches. With improvements to the gear came the rise in cost for the outfits, while crew sizes fell from ten to twelve fishermen to two to six.

Modern reef net crews occupied cabins near the fishing sites. There were several located at the point to the south of Reid Harbor, Stuart Island, and on Kellett Bluff, which forms the west part of Open Bay, Henry Island. These structures were of simple wood-frame, often "box," construction: vertical 1x12 boards nailed at the bottom to a sill and at the top to a plate, left exposed or clad with shingles. They had simple gabled roofs that were either shingled or covered in tar paper. Because fishing was in the late spring, summer, and fall, the weather was not too cold, and food could be kept cool in pantries on the north sides. Beds were metal-and-wire cots with mattresses; cooking was done on small woodstoves.

> On the bow of each boat are look-out poles or stands on which fisherman cling through storms and good weather, peering into the water for flash, fin, bubble, or quiver of salmon. Others in the crew sit quietly, fearful of frightening the fish more than they already frightened from being pursued by seine boats all the way in from the ocean. The customary shout at the sight of fish in the net is "Give 'em Hell!" and the motionless crew snaps into action.
>
> The strip of dark net suspended between the boats is commonly 42 by 49 ft., of 3¾ in. mesh. As the forward corners of the net, sunk to 20 ft. or more by heavy lead sinkers, are block lines by which the rib-lined front of the net is hand-lifted. Bunt lines at the back corners restrain the net as the tide running against it causes it to bag or purse where the web is gathered to the bunt line. Middle lines also help in hauling the net and pocketing the salmon.
>
> With the fish definitely confined, breast anchor lines are slacked off and the boats move together as fishermen pull against each other at the net. As quickly as the salmon, untouched by any pugh, are dumped into one of the boats, the net is loosened and lowered and the boats are pulled back to their original position. If reef net fish are pughed at all it is in making the transfer to the cannery tender. For fresh fish dealers each salmon is lifted into boxes by hand or packed to the trucks by a grip under the gill covers.
>
> —Beatrice "Reef Net Betty" Annette Lowman,
> "Reef Nets Come Back in Puget Sound Salmon Fishery,"
> Pacific Fisherman, June 1939

Bill and Alfred, Bill's and Alfred's sons, all Chevaliers, are fishing this year and General and old Isaac, the rain maker, and General's sons and Johnny Sam and Louie Smith. On three locations, 15 men are employed. Norman Mills, a son-in-law, is on his own boat, the Aloma, buying fish. Caroline, his wife, and little Wilma Jean are living in a little house taken off a PAF barge and planted on Stuart beach. Lizzie Chev, from Waldron, is there with her menfolk and Adelaide Chev lives on Stuart. Sarah and Katherine, the Indian women, cook for their men and so all the crew gets fed. Reef net fishing time is a time of work and picnic and camping and nobody would miss it for the world!

— June Burn, "70: Reef Netting, Oldest Way of Fishing,"
100 Days in the San Juans (1946)

Modern Reef Netters off Stuart Island
(courtesy of San Juan Historical Museum)

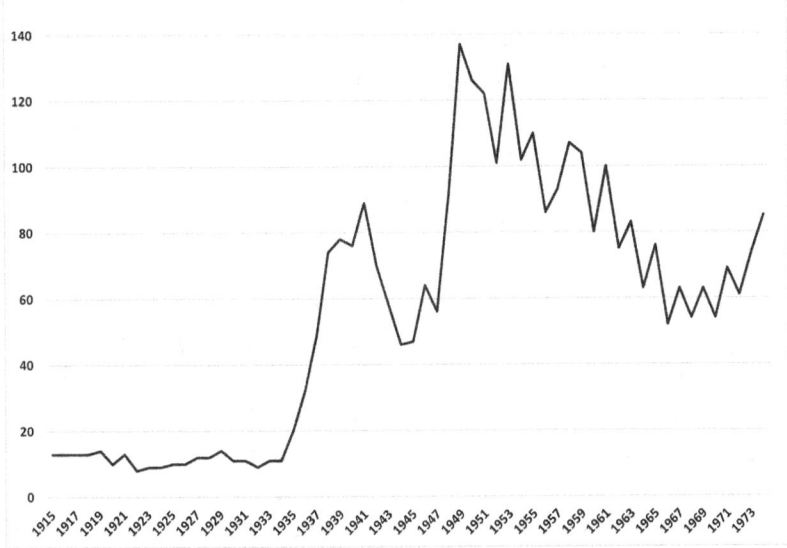

Reef Net Licenses, 1915–1973

From the evidence of license numbers, reef netting had continued during the period of competition with fish traps, but mainly in the San Juan Islands where the traps had not closed off all of the good sites as they had in the Boundary Bay/Point Roberts/Lummi Island areas. From 1915–1934, the annual number of licenses remained low, from 8–13, but after the passage of Initiative 77 it jumped to 20 and by the late 1940s numbered above 100. Except perhaps for the case of the revived Lummi fishery and some notable exceptions in the San Juans (the Chevalier family at Reid Harbor, Stuart Island, and Open Bay, Henry Island, as well as Herman Olsen on San Juan Island), ownership of the reef net sites passed into the hands of Euro American fishers. In contrast to the precontact-period reef netting, which was largely for subsistence or trade, modern reef netting is done for commercial purposes.

"Reef Net Betty" (Beatrice Annette Lowman), in her 1939 article about the revival of reef nets, noted contemporary rig owners in the San Juan Islands: Henry Cayou, Bill Norton, E.

Kimple, and Bruce Boddington on Orcas Island; Ed Chevalier and Barney Mordhorst off Stuart Island; Jesse Coffelt, Walter Anderson, and the Fagerholm brothers off Lopez; Chester Coffelt, Spencer, and Troxell off Shaw Island; and Bruce Boddington and Rod Wells on Henry Island. Another owner at Open Bay on Henry and two more at Smallpox Bay are mentioned but their names are not given. Together, these make up the fifteen legal locations officially delineated by state law in the San Juan Islands (RCW 77.50.050 *Reef net salmon fishing gear—Reef net areas specified*). In *The Fishermen and The Fisheries of the San Juan Islands*, reef netter Ralph Lillie listed many of the owners and gear work from 1941–1955 at Battleship Island; Open Bay, Henry Island; Fisherman Bay, Flatpoint, and Iceberg Point, Lopez Island (Gear No.1); Gear No. 1 and 2, Neck Point, and Squaw Bay, Shaw Island; Stuart Island, Gear No. 1, 2, and 3; and Andrews Bay and Mitchell Bay Reef, San Juan Island. Lillie retired from reef netting in 1998 and, along with about 30 others, sold his license in a government buy-back program. By the 1980s, there were only 21 gears in the San Juans, six of which were owned by Indigenous peoples. Today there are only three gears in the San Juans: Jack Giard at Fisherman Bay (Lopez Island); Brendan Flynn at Reef Net Bay (Shaw Island); and the Chevalier family at Reid Harbor (Stuart Island).

During Reef Net Betty's time, Farwest Fishermen collected the fish from island rigs for the canneries. Reef-netted fish, because they were not bruised ("unpughed"), were valued as fresh fish and therefore fetched a higher price, so most of the Chinook, coho, and chums went to urban markets such as Seattle.

Weirs

Weirs are barriers, usually made of brush or stakes that have matting adding, which block the passage of fish and divert them into a pot or some sort of trap. Evidence of weirs in the San Juan Islands is scant; most historical records indicate that weirs were primarily used on rivers by the Lummi (Nooksack) and Samish (Samish). There is a reference to an old weir at the entrance to a stream on Orcas Island (such that the locals called it

"Fish Trap"), but it was not known when it had been used. There are also several maps of "Brush Weirs": one near Open Bay on Henry Island; another near Goose Island, north of Iceberg Point, off Lopez Island; and near Andrews Bay on San Juan Island. The Goose Island one is the only that is labeled with a catch, which is herring.

Beach Seining

Beach seining is conducted with a seine net from 100 to 400 fathoms long and about 35 meshes deep at the shallow end and 400 meshes at the deep end. A dory with the shallow end attached was rowed toward the beach from a larger boat, which pays out the seine against the current in a large semicircle. When it is fully paid out, the line attached to the deep end is rowed ashore and hauled in with horses (or men) to capture the enclosed fish. When Henry Cayou seined at South Beach on San Juan Island, he used 7-8 men to set the net and 4-5 horses to haul it.

Historically, beach seining is associated with the shallow bars and beaches near the mouth of the Columbia River. However, there is evidence of several local efforts: Henry T. Cayou beach seining with horses on South Beach on San Juan Island and Flat Point on Lopez Island and Edouard Graignic fishing for herring with his family by lighting a fire on the beach at night and rowing a net around the fish that were attracted by the light. Reef-netter Harry LeMaister of Lopez Island also beach seined with horses.

Purse Seining

Purse Seining

Originally, purse seining was conducted with "scow seines," composed of a skiff and a scow. The four- or six-oared skiff was flat bottomed with a turned-up stern, 7 feet in the beam and 25 feet in length, the latter 8 feet of which was decked for stowing the seine. The 20-foot long, 8-foot wide scow had hand winches on each end. The rowers in the skiff towed the scow from sheltered anchorages (such as Kanaka Bay on the west side of San Juan and Richardson on the south end of Lopez) out to the fishing grounds and then back again at night. (Later, steam-powered tow boats were used to take the scows to and fro.) The seines were about 200 fathoms long and 25 fathoms deep, with 3¾" mesh. The purse line, made of 1½" hemp, was threaded through 5" galvanized iron rings; it was hauled in by means of a hand winch on the scow.

Purse Seiners, Aleck Bay, Lopez Island
(courtesy of Lopez Island Historical Society)

Purse Seiner with Net Displayed, Kanaka Bay, San Juan Island (courtesy of San Juan Historical Museum)

Purse seining is done with a large boat accompanied by a large skiff. The skiff lets out the net from the boat in a circle, which ends up at the mother boat, hopefully enclosing a school of salmon. This "purse" is then drawn closed, and the net drawn into the boat. Purse seiners fish from daybreak to sunset on open commercial fishing days.

Seining was first introduced into the region around 1886; John Cobb attributed this method to Chinese fishermen, but it has been conjectured that these gear may have been beach or drag seines. Purse seines—where the bottom of the seine is drawn together to form a "purse"—were probably introduced in the 1890s by Scandinavians and "Slavonians" (Yugoslavs—most likely Croatians) and became common around the islands in the first decades of the twentieth century. Many boats, skippered by Croatians, came out of nearby harbors: Bellingham, Anacortes, Everett, Gig Harbor, and Tacoma. According to George A. Rounsefell and George B. Kelez, purse seining in the San Juan Islands "received considerable impetus from the location of a cannery at Friday Harbor in 1894 and three at Anacortes in 1896," in addition, of course, to those at Bellingham.

The boats used in the salmon fishery are about 25 feet long and 7 feet wide, the greatest width being at the stern, which is square. The bottom is flat, but turns up slightly at the stern. These boats have three thwarts adapted for two men rowing at each. About 8 feet of the after part of the boat is decked over and upon this deck the seine is stowed. ... The salmon seine being thrown over the stern of the boat, it has to be stowed fore and aft instead of athwartship. The corks are placed on the port side, the twine on the starboard side. The twine is thrown in a heap, not arranged neatly in "flakes" and "bits" as upon a mackerel boat, because the man that throws it is not particular to have it clear the stern so as not to retard the speed of the boat in going around a school. The result is that the oarsmen have an extra amount of work to perform.

The scow, upon which most of the work is done, and which is considered indispensable in setting the seine, is 20 feet long by 8 wide, and at each end of it is an iron winch. These winches are used for the pursing up, the seine being pursed from the scow. There is a wooden purse davit which is stepped into the side of the scow and to which are attached two 3-inch wooden blocks, the purse line leading from therein to the winches at either end. Eleven to fourteen men are required to set the seine, six at the oars, two at the seine, and two on the scow. Of those at the seine, one throws the corks, the other the twine. The cost of a salmon seine boat and scow is from $1,200 to $1,300.

— Captain Turner, *Explorations of the fishing grounds of Alaska, Washington Territory, and Oregon during 1888 by the U.S. Fish Commission Steamer Albatross* (1890)

Drawing the Seine Closed
(courtesy Northwest Room, Tacoma Public Library)

The seines themselves were long and deep.

These seines are 200 fathoms long, 25 fathoms deep in the bunt, and 20 fathoms in the wings; they have a 3-inch mesh. The twine used in their construction is of three sizes, Nos. 12, 15, and 18, No. 12 being used in the bunt, No. 15 at each side of the bunt, and No. 18 in the wings. The foot line is heavily leaded, and the bridles are about 10 feet long. One and one-half inch Russian hemp is used for the purse line. The rings through [which] the purse line is rove measure about 5 inches in diameter, and are made of small-sized galvanized iron.

— Captain Turner, *Explorations of the fishing grounds
of Alaska, Washington Territory, and Oregon during 1888
by the U.S. Fish Commission Steamer Albatross* (1890)

Starting upon a fishing trip, the boat, with its scow in tow, is rowed to a favorable locality where salmon are likely to occur, and, having anchored the scow, a lookout is kept for fish. As soon as a school is sighted the boat is shoved off, leaving one end of the seine attached to the scow. A circle is made around the fish, the boat returning again to the scow, when all hands jump aboard of it and commence to haul in on the twine and corks, two men standing at the winches and slowly taking in the slack on the purse line. It is not, however, until half the length of the seine has been pulled in that they begin to purse up in earnest. At this time the anchor rope is slacked off, and, all hands laying hold of the purse line, purse the scow into the middle of the seine...

During the slow process of pursing a man stands at the davit with a long pole, having a block of wood called a "plunger" fastened to it. This is kept working up and down between the purse lines, for the purpose of frightening the fish away from the center of the net; and it is, no doubt, very effective in saving the school, as the bottom of the seine is left open from 25 to 40 minutes, which is ample time for a salmon to find its way out.

From an hour and a half to two hours are required for setting, pursing up, and stowing the seine ready for another trial. On two occasions, when the operations were timed, they consumed on an average 1 hour and 45 minutes.

— Captain Turner, *Explorations of the fishing grounds of Alaska, Washington Territory, and Oregon during 1888* by the U.S. Fish Commission Steamer Albatross (1890)

A typical local operation was the Westcott Bay Fish Company, incorporated by James Holden, president, M. Robinson, vice president, John Reisinger, secretary, E. Wold, treasurer, and

H. Ingham in the spring of 1899. They had a steam tug, the *Hector*, as well as a new scow, a seine boat, and seines. Unfortunately, it did not seem very successful, due to a "lack of skilled hands," but when Holden sold out two years later, he listed the equipment as "A first-class outfit for salmon or herring fishing, including the steamer 'Hector,' 7.97 gross tons; two scows and one seine boat, all nearly new; one salmon seine, 900x80 feet; one herring seine, 500x33 feet."

> *In no branch of the fisheries has the introduction of the gas engine made more noticeable changes than in purse seining. When sails were the motive power broad, flat, scow-like boats were used, and these were propelled by either oars or sails, or by both. In 1903 the first gasoline-powered seine boat appeared on the salmon fishing grounds of Puget Sound. The vessel was named the Pioneer and she was equipped with a 5 h.p. Standard engine. The first season she easily demonstrated her vast superiority over the other purse seiners in the quickness with which she could reach a school of fish after it was sighted and in surrounding it with her seine. The next year there were a few more built or so equipped, and the number has steadily increased until at present there are about one thousand operating in Puget Sound, Alaska, and British Columbia.*
>
> — *Pacific Fisherman Yearbook* (1919)

Prior to the fishing season, there was a lot of work to be done on the purse seine boats and gear. The boats were repaired, scraped, and painted. Special care had to be taken of the nets.

> ...in those days we used cotton linen nets. They, periodically, because of their short life, if not properly cared for, they would deteriorate so we would have to tar the nets and that is you put them into a huge vat of hot tar and you pull them through the tar, stretch them out in the fields and let them dry. Messy, messy, messy job. If the net was brand new it needs to be tarred immediate before usage. ...On many occasions though we had to re-tar a net. Now that was more difficult because it was wirier, harder to control, harder to handle, and very hard on the hands. It was like chicken wire, that tar would dry and be very stiff and cut your hands to pieces the first number of sets that you take.
>
> — Mike Milat, "Purse Seine Gear,"
> Bret Lunsford, *Croatian Fishing Families of Anacortes* (2011)

The lead lines were made of four-strand manila with barrel-shaped pieces of lead with holes in them so they could be slipped on the line and secured. During this early period, the floats were made of Spanish cork.

> Well these corks needed to be waxed periodically because if they weren't they would sponge up, gather up water and not float well. We had big vats filled full of paraffin with fire under them until all that melted, then dipped the corks, put them on a big long line of string, of fifteen, twenty, thirty corks on the string and stuff them down into that wax, pick them out, and let them dry.
>
> — Mike Milat, "Purse Seine Gear,"
> Bret Lunsford, *Croatian Fishing Families of Anacortes* (2011)

The nets also had to be periodically mended. Some fishers were known for their prowess knitting with a net "needle," which was actually a thin, flat piece of wood about six inches long, with two points at one end, a single point at the other, and small shaft within a hole in the piece; the twine was spooled around this shaft and the groove between the two end points.

Power engines, introduced in the early 1900s, provided more mobility for the purse seiners to go where the fish were. The most popular engine was the 40 and 50 hp Frisco Standard, built in San Francisco. With the increase in size and engine capacity, seiners no longer needed land-based camps, and the crew slept aboard. In addition to Friday Harbor, the anchorage in Griffin Bay near Fish Creek on the south end of San Juan Island became an important location.

> At Kanaka bay, on the southwestern shore of San Juan island, we put in. There twenty-two canneries maintain scows permanently during the fishing season. Each cannery is represented by a buyer who lives aboard a scow in the harbor and takes the fish as the purse seine boats bring them in. Each day a tender from the cannery represented arrives and tows away the loaded scow. The system obviates the necessity of the seine boats making the long trip into the canneries when they are full. Often they get all they can carry early in the day, put into Kanaka bay, unload on the buyer's scows, and are enable to get out and fish for the rest of the day.
>
> —William Slavens McNutt,
> "A Day with a Fish Buyer," Anacortes American, August 14, 1913

During the catch, tenders—boats that were designed to transport the catch—took the fish from the fishing boats and transported them to the canneries. Several of the companies that operated the canneries also owned the tenders, but they were sold off starting in the 1950s.

Modern Purse Seiners

The first (5 hp) gasoline-powered purse-seine boat appeared in the region as early as 1898 and in local waters around 1903; most had been converted by 1907. Typically, these early boats were about 30 feet in length. Soon the horsepower increased to 45–75, and the length of the boats correspondingly grew to 45–55 feet. From 1910–1920, boat length increased to up to 68 feet long. The Territory of Alaska, whose fisheries were administered by the federal government, restricted purse seine boat length to 58 feet, so many of the Puget Sound boats that also went north to fish in Alaska waters conformed to that standard. Built with rounded sterns, these boats featured an elevated section where a movable platform (turntable), set on a pivot, had a long roller. The turntable swung around when hauling the net aboard, and the roller was powered, which assisted the crew in pulling the net aboard by hand. From there the seine was paid out and hauled in by means of winches that were powered off the motors. With a total crew of eight to nine, the net was first hoisted into the boat with a boom equipped with pulleys and later hoisted with a power block or reeled in with a large drum attached to the stern. The fish are then removed and placed in the hold.

Purse seine boat building began to increase in the 1910s. In his research for *The Link between the Two Harbors*, John Wade found that there were 41 boats built in the region from 1912 to 1920, the biggest year being 1917, with 14 new boats. From 1925 to 1930, another 45 were built, but once the Depression had hit boat building ceased. This is corroborated by the rise in purse seine licenses: in 1908, there were only 69 purse seiners licensed in Puget Sound; in five years' time, that had increased to 252, reaching an all-time peak of 420 in 1917. The purse seiners' share in the crop rose concurrently: in 1913, it was only one-third of the Puget Sound catch (compared to 61% taken by fish trap); two years later, the percentage had risen to 57%.

Purse Seine Licenses, 1897–1935

As the Washington State Fish Commissioner said in his 1919 report, "Use of the purse seine stole upon us like a thing in the night," giving as his reason: "Their greatly increasing use occurred during the world war and for that reason did not attract the notice or excite the comment they would have under ordinary conditions." The rise in purse seiners was also fueled by the wartime economy, with its emphasis on providing canned salmon to the war effort (particularly the U.S. Army and the English market). Salmon prices rose from 12.8 cents per fish in 1913 to 53.9 in 1917, peaking at 71.2 the next year. The same 1919 report noted: "Stimulated by the high prices which they received for their catch, the fishermen are building larger boats so as to enable them to go farther out to sea, making use of larger nets, while the ranks of the fishermen are steadily augmented by persons attracted from other occupations." The depression of 1921 and the decline in fish prices led to a smaller fishing industry, particularly purse seiners. As the 1923 *Washington State Fishery Report* noted, "The drop in the run of fish, and greatly increased cost of operating due to the war, together with the low selling value of the fish, made the industry unprofitable for the purse seiners, and many of them removed to California or Alaska with their vessels." However, by 1923 the fish industry was beginning to recover, and purse seine licenses rose from 133 in that year to 251 in 1931.

> ...there has undoubtedly been an increase in number and efficiency of purse seines during the last few years. But it is also a fact that the increase in the number and efficiency of purse seines reduces the efficiency of the pound nets and traps in the taking of fish for the reason—among others—that the prevalence of purse seines in the vicinity of fish traps scatters and diverts the schools of fish and causes them to pass out into deep water beyond the traps, and we think that it can be safely asserted that while the total number of appliances and gear may have been increased in recent years, the efficiency in the catching of fish has not been much, if any, increased.
>
> —Washington State Fish Commissioner, *Fishery Report* (1913)

It was estimated that in the 1930s a purse seine boat cost $30,000, with the nets adding another $3,000 at least. Since this was such a large capital investment, unaffordable for most individual fishers, many of the purse seine operations were financed by the canneries. This led to a system in which the owner, captain, and crew of the boat, as well as the boat itself and its equipment, received shares of the money from the catch. Daniel Boxberger gives an example of a typical division for a Lummi purse seine outfit with 12–14 shares: skipper 1, crew 1 each, boat 2, net 1½, and skiff 1½, with the understanding that the actual allocation of the boat and equipment shares was at the discretion of the owner (usually the skipper). After the passage of Initiative 77 banned fish traps, construction of purse seine boats rose dramatically. June Burn, in her 1946 *100 Days in the San Juans*, describes a typical nine-person purse seine crew of the boat *Veteran*: Peter Skansie, owner; his eldest son Vincent, co-owner and skipper; his youngest son Antone, engineer; Paul Zanchi, net man; Mike Jerisich, skiff man; Tony Janovich, deck man; Alfred Goldman, brother-in-law of Vincent Skansie, second skiff man; Fritz Haberecht, cook (and extra hand); Tony Lovrovich, another deck man; and Antone Cosulich, "pelican hook man" (the pelican hook holds the release of the net back until ready). Their shares were divided 13 ways: 2 for the boat; 2 for the owner, and 1 for each of the nine members of the crew.

Purse Seiner Home 2
(courtesy of San Juan Historical Museum)

World War II brought many technological advances to purse seining (as well as gillnetting). Sonar, radar, echo sounders, and the radio phone helped locate fish and communicate their location. Furthermore, the addition of power to net skiffs improved productivity in purse seining. As the 1946 *Pacific Fisherman Yearbook* noted, "The fishing vessels of 1945, class-for-class, carried power far-and-away beyond the concept of earlier years. They gave evidence, too, of the departures in instrumentation, equipment, materials and methods which seem certain to mark construction in 1946, and into the years beyond." In 1953, drum seines—which spooled the net, purse line, and cork line onto a seven-foot-in-diameter reel on the stern of the boat, replacing turntables—were introduced in the Point Roberts area from the British Columbia fisheries. That year, 10 boats adopted the drum seine; within a few years the fleet was almost totally converted. In 1953, the power block was invented by a Croatian fisherman named Mario Puratic and patented that year; it soon became known as the Puretic (Puratic's named spelled in English) power block. Mounted on a boom, the power block hoists the net to pile it on the deck. Because many Puget Sound purse seiners also operated in Alaska, where they did not allow drums, the power block became the predominant net-handling system. Both purse seiners and gillnetters also adopted nylon nets in the 1950s; not only were they less visible than the old cotton-twine systems, but they lasted for five to six years—as opposed to one to two years—with less maintenance. By 1960, a fully equipped boat averaged about $245,000 to build.

Before Initiative 77 banned fish traps, purse seining predominated for schooling salmon—sockeye and pink—and gillnetting for Chinook and coho. From 1934 to 1950, purse seiners dominated for all types of salmon catch, except for Chinook. Improvements in the productivity of purse seining by means of gear efficiency as well as time spent fishing reduced crew size from eight to ten fishermen to four to five, which in turn shifted the fishing labor force toward gillnetting. In the 1970s and 1980s, due to the higher cost of boats and gear and the reduced size of the crew, shares were readjusted. For example, the vessel and gear might get 6 shares, the skipper 2, and the four crew members 1 each, for a total of 12 shares.

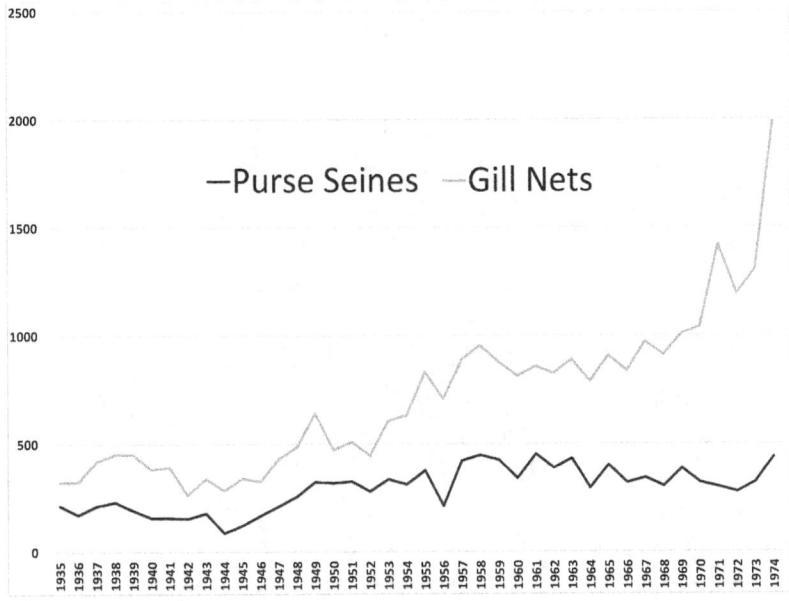

Purse Seine v. Gill Net Licenses, 1935–1974

Gillnetting

Columbia River Salmon Boat

Gillnetters used one of the more common boats to be seen in Salish Sea waters, particularly in the last quarter of the nineteenth century: the double-ended Columbia River Salmon Boat. Howard Chapelle, in his classic *American Small Sailing Craft*, attributes its origin to J. J. Griffin, who built a craft of this design in San Francisco in 1868 for a fisherman on the Sacramento River. This was followed the next year by a similar boat built for Columbia River gillnetting, and the type subsequently proliferated. It was soon mass-produced as a stock model, and as a result prices became relatively inexpensive ($220 in 1872). The Columbia River Salmon Boat has double ends. Although early boats were 22–23 feet long, 8 feet wide, 4 feet deep, and open, by the late 1870s they were lengthened to 28 feet, and washboards and end-decks were added. They were built with steam-bent frames and planking of Douglas fir. The boats were rigged with a single mast with spritsail and sometimes a jib. The crew of two to three fishermen who sailed and rowed them often had to stay out for several nights, so they used the boom and the sail to form a cockpit tent and cooked on an oil stove. Designed for heavy use by the gillnetters who rented them from canneries, they were solidly designed and built to last 10–15 years. Historic photographs of Kanaka Bay and Victoria Harbor reveal myriads of Columbia River boats, probably sailed by Mitchell Bay, Saanich, Songhees, and other Coast Salish gillnetters. Boats were equipped with power engines as early as the 1890s; most had been converted by 1914.

Boats Moored at Kanaka Bay; note the Columbia River Gillnetters as well as Salish and Nootkan Canoes (courtesy of San Juan Historical Museum)

According to George A. Rounsefell and George B. Kelez's 1938 study, gillnetting was the first method that Euro Americans used for fishing salmon in the region; however, it was not used as commonly as other types of gear. Two types of nets were used: drift and set. Drift nets were handled by two or three men, one or two rowing with a man letting out the net to drift and then taking it in after the fish were caught. Set nets were anchored, usually near the mouth of rivers and streams such as Skagit Bay and Skagit River, the estuary of the Snohomish River, and off the mouths of the Nooksack and Samish Rivers. They were used in some locations in the San Juans, such as Open Bay on Henry Is-

Gillnetters Waiting the Turn of the Tide (courtesy of Lopez Island Historical Society)

land, Andrews Bay on San Juan Island, and along the northwest shore of Orcas Island. Gillnetting was originally done at night, best when there was a bright moon in a clear sky so that the fish could not see the cotton-twine (at the time very visible) net.

> *Prior to the past two seasons, the fish traps were the main reliance of the canners, although gillnetters did a profitable business. For the past two years the boats used in the salmon fisheries have steadily grown in size and have gone further out in the straits after the fish. Last season there were more fish taken from large boats out in the strait than were taken at the traps, reversing the old order of things.*
>
> *Where the flat-bottom Columbia river boat was the type in use formerly, last season saw large sized power boats, carrying very much larger nets than in previous use—boats fit for any sea or any weather; boats, moreover, which could be used in other fisheries after the salmon season is over.*
>
> —*The San Juan Islander*, January 12, 1912

Rounsefell and Kelez noted that of the drift nets licensed by the State of Washington Fisheries Department in 1899, only five were from the San Juan Islands; in 1901, 63 drift net licenses were from the San Juans and nearby Boundary Bay, while 15 (of 369) set net licenses were from the San Juans and none from Boundary Bay. Gill nets mainly caught coho and Chinook salmon. On occasion, fish trap operators would set a gill net at a trap location instead of driving the trap, because the license fee was 4–10 times less expensive. Washington State banned set gill nets in freshwaters (i.e., rivers and streams) in 1921; consequently, the number of set licenses during the 1920s fell drastically to a tenth of their number before that time, while drift net licenses dipped slightly and then rose again in the 1920s and 1930s.

After high school I looked around and saw 3 choices, farming, logging or fishing, to me the decision was easy. My mother made me promise if I chose fishing, I would first get an education. I became a school teacher with my summers off to fish. I learned a trade from a Gig Harbor skipper and after a number of seasons, I acquired my own boat. I fished each year after 1954 and sold my boats after the 2003 season and retired.

—Wally Botsford, The *Fishermen and Fisheries of the San Juan Islands* (n.d.)

Modern gillnetting, which can be done by a single fisherman, requires less investment in capital and labor. While gillnetting occurred sporadically in the islands during the later nineteenth century and first half of the twentieth century, one of the first groups to gillnet on Salmon Bank, starting in the early 1940s, was the Croatian Bajocich family from West Seattle: father John and sons John Jr., Martin, and Albert. They used linen nets, 65 meshes deep and 300 fathoms long, with wooden corks, pulled by hand, and fished from Columbia River–model bowpickers. The boom in gillnetting really came after WWII with the return

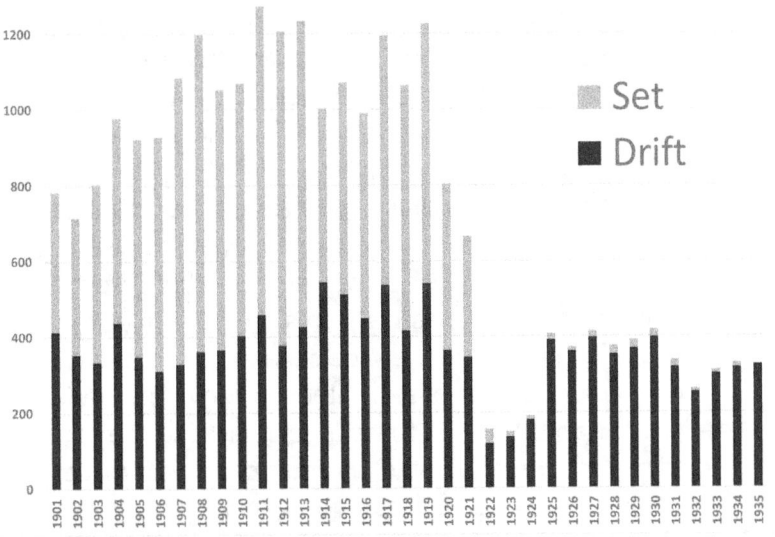

Gill Net Licenses, 1901–1935

of servicemen and military industrial workers—Boeing, for instance, laid off thousands of workers after the war—as well as the reduction in crew size of purse seiners. Furthermore, because gillnetting could be a seasonal occupation, workers in occupations that occurred out of season, such as teachers, could spend summers gillnetting. All this contributed to a dramatic rise in the number of fishers gillnetting: in the period from 1951 to 1974, Puget Sound gill net licenses increased 300%.

Modern Gill Netters

With the advent of power engines in the early 1900s, gill net boats and their nets increased in size; technological advances such as the power reel as well as the echo sounder and radio phone aided in the speed of the set and location of the fish. The main advantage, however, was the speed with which the boat could move to an area where the fish were. In comparison with purse seining, which requires a captain and crew of seven to eight, modern gillnetters may be operated by a single fisherman, who sets a long (around 300 fathoms) line of net, 200 to 250 meshes deep, with cork on top, lead on the bottom, and lanterns at the ends, to drift near the shore. The size of the mesh in the net determines what type of fish get caught by its gills—smaller fish swim through and larger fish turn away. After a while, the fisherman reels in the net, releasing the salmon that are caught by their gills in the mesh of the net and putting them in the hold. At first, the net was brought in by hand; later, a mechanized reel (drum) at the stern of the boat controlled by a foot pedal was used, until it in turn was replaced by power blocks hung from a boom or davit. With modern systems, the net can be let out in 5–10 minutes and then reeled in as quickly, allowing for a larger number of sets. Although early nets, made of dyed cotton twine, had to be used at night so the fish would not see them, with the introduction of nets made from newer synthetics such as nylon, gillnetting could be done in the daylight as well as nighttime.

Ross's Trolling/Gill Net Boat

A combination trolling–gill net boat, designed in 1933 by the British Columbia marine architect D. A. G. Ross, offers a clear example of a mid-twentieth-century trolling craft. Double-ended, it was 28' in length with a beam of 8'3" and a draft of 2'9". The boat cost $825 to build without the engine; a 7 hp gas engine would add $250 or so to the cost. There is a semi-circular cabin slightly forward to midship, where the fisher could take shelter, and an ample "killing hold" for the fish just forward of the stern. Historic photos of local harbors and docks show many of this type of boat moored to wharves or even "rafted"—aligned next to each other.

Trolling

Until 1900, most trolling—trailing baited hooks or lures on lines—in the San Juans was conducted by the Coast Salish, although some Euro Americans trolled from rowboats, using one or two lines. J. W. Collins in his 1892 *Fisheries* annual report, while not including trolling as a means of commercial fishing, said that "the Indians employ trolling hooks and spears in the Sound and small streams tributary thereto, and parties fishing for pleasure also use spoon hooks and trolling lines." (This is an early mention of what would become a major component of the region's modern fishing scene: recreational or sport fishing.) Until 1905, trolling was conducted almost exclusively by Indigenous fishers in dugout canoes. With the advent of canneries, trollers fished the waters in the San Juans—particularly off the west coast (Kanaka and Mitchell Bays) and south end (Salmon Bank) of San Juan Island and around northeast Orcas Island, in the areas of Doe Bay, Olga, and Point Lawrence. Traditionally, Indigenous peoples used herring or perch bait, attached to a hook on the end of a single strand of stretched and dried kelp. In the 1880s, 50–100 fish were the average daily catch.

*Fishing Boats Rafted at San Juan Canning Company
(courtesy of San Juan Historical Museum)*

> *The line fishing or trolling is carried on mainly during November, December, January, and February by both Indians and whites. The principle localities brought to our attention were... off Victoria, Becher Bay, among the San Juan islands;... At Victoria winter fishing is carried on to a distance of 8 or 10 miles from shore, chiefly from December to February inclusive, the Indians going out whenever the weather is suitable... The San Juan Islands afford good winter grounds, and Quinnat [Chinooks] are also taken among those islands in April and May.*
> — Richard Rathbun, *"A Review of the Fisheries in the Contiguous Waters of the State of Washington and British Columbia," Report of the Commissioner of Fish and Fisheries* (1897)

The San Juan Islander noted that Indigenous peoples and Euro Americans were mutually trolling at Kanaka Bay, with a "spoon hook," in the 1890s and 1900s. In the 1900s and 1910s, the paper reported on large groups of "British Columbia Indians" who camped along the north shore and trolled for coho. In September 1909, the paper noted that "There are 75 trollers, principally Indian women, engaged in catching silvers [coho] for the Friday Harbor Packing Company." The price of fish varied from year to year, often depending on the size of concurrent runs of other salmon species: in 1907 buyers were paying 15 cents per fish but only 14 cents a year later; in 1911, trollers were "making good wages at 25 cents for silvers [coho]," but then two years later it was down to 15 cents again. The main catch was coho, and the trollers sold these fish to the canneries or to fresh-fish buyers who would pick them up as soon as possible and send them on ice to the mainland, where they were packed and shipped by rail across the nation.

Trollers Are Making Big Money

The fishing banks are now paying larger dividends than any of the other banks in the county and the fishermen are swarming there like bees around a bee hive. Catches of 20 to 40 a day and even more are reported. At 35 cents each, it looks like easy money. But it's not so easy. There are some hardships connected with it. It's a cold, wet job. The sea is sometimes rough, and roughing it in a tent or a smelly greasy boat is far from a life of ease. The pay is good however, and that is about everything. The whole town is enthusiastic about the fishing and all who can are preparing to go. Mayor Murray is going. Also Congressman Humphrey is going as an equal partner of the mayor's. Fishing pays better than these little political jobs. ... Other leading citizens will be pulling and chugging about the banks before the month is up. The most successful trollers use a small launch and put out from three to five lines. The lines are fastened to poles running out from each side of the boat. It's lively work when two or three fish are hooked at the same time. The fun should last for a month longer. Better go while the fishing is good.

— The San Juan Islander, September 22, 1911

Modern Trolling

The adoption of motor power aided in the spread of trolling in the beginning of the twentieth century. The boats, only 20–30' long and worked by a single fisher, could troll from two to six lines of one to three hooks each, held out from the hull by "outrigger poles" perpendicular to the fore-and-aft line of the boat. Around 1918, with the invention of the power gurdie—motorized winches that help haul in the lines that are strung from outrigger poles—trolling became even more efficient. In his U. S. Bureau of Fisheries 1921 *Pacific Salmon Fisheries* report, John N. Cobb says that "the outer lines are attached to fish poles 15 to 18 feet long, rigged on either side. Those poles are usually hinged at the foot of a short mast and lowered outboard by a halyard running through a block at the masthead, with the additional brace of a forward guy, which, with the drag of the lines aft, holds them in position." Power gurdies were first developed for cotton lines; later, metal lines made of copper and then stainless steel increased the ability for faster trolling but also increased drag (and therefore demand for more powerful engines). Cobb describes a wide variety of spoons, most with single hooks: "ordinary Siwash pattern"; brass or silver wobblers, Nos. 4 and 5 in size; and copper, copper and silver, or brass spinners, two to three inches long, of the "Siwash and Victoria patterns." When bait was used—invariably herring—it was hooked so as to stretch the herring out as if it were alive and swimming. Outside lines were 60 feet long; inside ones 40, with heavy line material from the pole to the sinker (two to three pounds for a power boat; one for a rowboat), then a lighter line followed by a piece of wire and the spoon.

In the late 1800s, most trolling was conducted from a canoe or rowboat, with handlines attached to a paddle or a fisherman's leg when rowing. The basic gear consisted of several fathoms of "cuttyhunk"—twisted linen line—with a length of piano wire for a lead and hooks with several spinners or spoons, a gaff, and a fish knife. The fishers would often bring along their own rake to secure herring for bait. Areas close to shore were preferred, particularly kelp beds. The introduction of bamboo poles and walnut reels, as well as cotton line, made the fishing easier. Handlining—pulling in the line without a pole or reel—was tough on the hands themselves, and devices such as "nippers"—pieces of inner tube with a hole cut out for the thumb—helped prevent too much rubbing on the palms.

Fishing by hook and line gradually increased in the early decades of the twentieth century: George A. Rounsefell and George B. Kelez stated that "We may assume that the troll fishery was of little importance prior to about 1910, and that the number of boats increased thereafter to a maximum [1,032 licenses] in 1919" (unfortunately, there is no solid data on this, because licenses were not required until 1917). In addition to fishing grounds off the bar of the Columbia River and Swiftsure Banks (off Cape Flattery), John N. Cobb, in his 1921 *Pacific Salmon Fisheries*, noted that young coho salmon, called "Blue backs," started coming through the Strait of Juan de Fuca north to the Gulf of Georgia, and quickly increased in size from two pounds to four to six, which offered an important fishery for trollers for the fresh-fish market.

> *One of the most amazing developments of the fishing industry of this state during the last four years has been fishing for our salmon with hook and line... [T]his period of time witnessed the building up of the great fleets for operation off our Pacific Coast line from the Columbia river to Cape Flattery... It was the hook and line fisherman or the troller who first started the intensive offshore fishing for immature salmon.*
>
> —Washington State Fish Commissioner, *Fishery Report* (1919)

Trolling Licenses, 1917–1935

Beginning in 1907, the State of Washington increasingly restricted many fishing areas to only hook and line. This allowed trollers to fish in areas where gillnetting, purse seining, and traps were not allowed. Although some troll fishermen sold to the canneries, their main customers were the fresh-fish markets; with their smaller catch and powerful boats, they could deliver quickly to buyers. According to Daniel L. Boxberger, "In 1928, when the Trolling Vessels Owners' Association was chartered in the State of Washington, it was estimated that over 2,000 trollers were operating in the North Pacific Coast salmon fishery and that 672 of these were licensed for Puget Sound." However, the trolling industry gradually moved out from the Puget Sound region to catch immature salmon along the outer coast, from the mouth of the Columbia to the Strait of Juan de Fuca.

Setlines

A setline, or, as it is also known, longline, is a method of fishing in which a very long line with shorter, hooked and baited lines attached is either set in one place or allowed to drift.

The basic unit of the setline is a "skate": a 50-or-so-fathom-long groundline made of sisal or hemp (or nylon in more recent times) with loops of twine known as "beckets" to which are attached five-foot-long lines with baited hooks set at intervals of 5, 9, 13, 18, 21, 26, or even up to 42 feet. These set intervals, "snoods" or "gangions" (also spelled "ganyons," "gangens," or called "ganging lines") allow for coiling up the line neatly when it is hauled in and made ready for baiting and resetting: the fisher coils the groundline and lines up each becket on top of each other in the center of the coil. Two or more skates are joined up to form a "string." Strings are anchored at each end, with a buoy line, buoy, and an attached cork buoy with a pole and flag, kept upright with a weight. The setting is made over the stern of a motorboat, but the haul is taken over the side with a small power winch, with the boat slowly motoring ahead so as not to put a strain on the line.

Setlines were principally used for halibut, although in the Strait of Georgia in Canada they were also used for rockfish and dogfish.

Bottom Trawling

Trawling, or "dragging," refers to the method of dragging a net along the ocean bottom to take in bottom fish. There are two types of trawl nets: beam and otter. The beam trawl, as the name implies, is a net whose mouth is kept open by a metal beam across the top; it is attached on either end to a trawl head, which has a main bridle connecting to the warp, which is hauled by the boat. The net forms a pocket that narrows into the "cod end," where the fish are collected. The more recent otter trawl, introduced to the area around 1910, has a similar net, but it is kept open by flanking otter boards, connected by travel warps to the ship, that flare outward with the drag, opening the wings. The bottom opening of the net—the ground rope—has rollers, while the top or headline has floats. The belly of the net funnels into the cod end.

Because of the weight and drag of the net, trawlers used steamers 50–75 feet in length, which were more powerful than the common fishing steamers. The trawl was let out on the starboard side; after a period of half an hour to three hours, the net would be hauled in—at first, by hand, later by hydraulic drum—over the rail, and the catch dumped on the deck. Because a trawl net is indiscriminate in its catch—any fish caught in its sweep will be funneled into the cod end—the crew of three to five would jump in and sort through the various types of fish, discarding small and unwanted fish. The main catch was bottom fish: halibut, sole, flounder, hake, and varieties of cod. During World War II, the price of dogfish livers rose, so trawlers focused on that catch.

The Canadian government regulated the trawl industry first by prohibiting catching halibut by trawl (only lining was allowed) and then in 1931 closing the season during the winter—at first January and February and later including December. Later, both size and area limitations were imposed.

Sealing and Whaling

According to Wayne Suttles, in the latter part of the nineteenth century there was an Indigenous man who lived on the north shore of San Juan Island and specialized in hunting porpoises and seals, both with rifle and harpoon. After rendering the oil, he would sell it to Euro Americans for $1.50 for five gallons.

In the 1860s, Euro Americans hunted whales, first in the Saanich Inlet and then expanding to Haro Strait and the Strait of Georgia. Scotsman James Dawson lanced but lost three whales in the Saanich Inlet in 1866. Abel Douglas arrived in Victoria in 1868 and began whaling with Dawson's British Columbia Whaling Company in the 47-ton schooner *Kate* in the Inlet; they killed eight whales that year. They then retrofitted the scow-schooner *Industry* with four 250-gallon tanks and were able to bring to Dickson, Campbell & Company's wharf in Victoria 19 casks (about 100 barrels) of humpback oil. The next year Douglas separated from Dawson and went into partnership with James Strachan; using the *Industry*, they moved their operation to the Gulf Islands, first setting up a processing camp at Whaletown, Cortes,

Island where they flensed (cut up) and rendered (boiled down in try pots) some 20,000 gallons of oil, and then Hornby Island. In 1871, Douglas had the 40-foot schooner *Triumph* built and set up camp on Pasley Island, off the mainland coast of British Columbia; later he processed his catch on a beach near Marble Bay on Texada Island, which would become known as Blubber Bay. The American Captain Thomas Roys, who in a year's whaling in the Strait killed many humpbacks with the cannon-fired harpoon he had invented, formed the Victoria Whaling Adventures Company but set his sights on the outer coast of Vancouver Island. He returned later to the Strait of Georgia, but with little success. Whaler Elijah Fader based himself in Blubber Bay but used a steamer to haul his catch to Mitlenatch Island.

> *They had a big shed where they had the iron pots, you know, where they boil the blubber, the fat, and they had the harpoon on the whale's head. And then they hauled it up to the shed. They had a big thing [a windlass] right on the shore; edge of the water, and two men kept going around and around, walking around the big thing. And the rope was coming in, bringing the whale up; it was a slow job. And then they cut the whale up with a great big knife, ready to boil; all the fat. It was all chopped up in squares and the fat was that [about 12 inches] thick; it was all fat; just excepting the ribs; very fat.*
> — Reminiscences of Elizabeth Silvey, as recounted in Jean Barman, *Maria Mahoi of the Islands* (2004)

In the early 1900s, whaling—this time by means of steamers—became popular in British Columbia, particularly on the west coast of Vancouver Island and the northern mainland coast, as well as north into Alaska. In 1905 Captains Sprott Balcom and William Grant formed the Victoria Whaling Company, which hunted blue, humpback, fin, sei, and sperm whales. They first established whaling stations at Sechart and Kyuquot on Vancouver Island and then at Rose (1909) and Naden (1911) Harbours near the northern B.C. coast. For two winters in 1907, they did hunt in the Strait of Georgia, processing at Pages (Pipers) Lagoon near Nanaimo and as a result extirpated humpbacks from the Strait: in the last season they reported killing 96. In 1915 the company's assets were purchased by William Schupp of the Seattle-based American Pacific Whaling Company, but the operation was managed, as the Consolidated Whaling Corporation Ltd., from their headquarters at Point Ellice, Victoria. Whaling continued off the coast of British Columbia until the 1960s.

There is little to no evidence of historic whaling in the San Juan Islands or the Salish Sea, except for occasionally taking advantage of stranded whales. Such an event occurred in May of 1906, when a 32-foot humpback whale stranded itself on Minnesota Reef, near Brown Island in Friday Harbor. Bruce Willis, who discovered it, took some of the blubber and rendered it down to 40 gallons of oil, which, according to Willis, would have been more if the whale had been in better shape. The tail was saved for the local school museum and the carcass left for Professor Joubert of the Marine Laboratories to reduce to a skeleton.

Whales—particularly orcas—posed a threat to fish traps, where they could get caught in the nets and damage the gear before being killed and removed. Until the late 1950s, there was systematic slaughter of killer whales because fishermen considered them a threat to salmon (bounty programs on seals were also implemented, for the same reasons). In June of 1961 the Canadian Department of Fisheries mounted a .50-caliber machine gun overlooking Seymour Narrows, north of Campbell River, to kill passing orcas; although it was never used, and removed a few months later, it is indicative of the attitude toward killer whales. A more recent phenomenon was the live capture of orcas for display at aquariums; about 80 were captured and transported in the period from 1962 to 1973. For instance, Sk'aliCh'elh-tenaut otherwise known as "Lolita" at the Miami Seaquarium, or Tokitae, was captured on August 8, 1970, at Penn Cove, Whidbey Island, when she was about five years old and still remains in captivity.

Diving

The most recent fishing gear is diving. Self-contained underwater breathing apparatus, or scuba, gear was developed in the 1960s, followed in the 1970s by surface-supplied air systems consisting of a compressor on a boat with an air-supply line ("hookah") connected to the diver below. Diving allowed fishers to harvest northern abalone, geoduck and horse clams, pink and spiny scallops, sea urchins, sea cucumbers, and octopus from the seabed. This led to overharvesting in some species, such as the northern abalone, which were rapidly reduced in numbers by divers—commercial, recreational, and poaching—using scuba gear. All abalone fisheries were closed in British Columbia in 1990, and in 1999 abalone became the first invertebrate to be listed as Threatened by the Canadian Committee on the Status of Endangered Wildlife. As a result of this and other overharvesting, various species fished by both commercial and recreational divers are now regulated by both the American and Canadian governments.

FISH AND OTHER MARINE HARVESTS

Salmon

In order to understand the signal importance of salmon in the fisheries of the Salish Sea, it is important to grasp their sheer abundance in the past as well as the relentless harvesting that led to their decimation. The historic population of salmon in the Salish Sea is hard to measure. One can get at the figures by approximately gauging the catch and how it varied over time.

Sockeye salmon, which run annually, exhibited a pronounced quadrennial cycle in the first part of the twentieth century, particularly in the years 1901, 1905, 1909, and 1913, prior to the Hell's Gate blockage of the Fraser River. In 1901, the run was so large that Henry Newton on his way back from Salmon Bank reported in the August 16 issue of *Fairhaven Weekly World Herald* that the salmon were so thick off Iceberg Point on Lopez Island "that they frequently got into the screw of the steamer and were cut and mangled." In the Puget Sound region, the years 1905 and 1909—both sockeye salmon quadrennial runs—yielded staggering cannery pack numbers: 203,000 cases in 1905 and 255,500 four years later. The year 1909, which coincided with the Alaska-Yukon-Pacific Exhibition in Seattle, saw not only one of the largest runs but was also advertised as such. Visitors at the Expo were encouraged to visit the Pacific American Fisheries cannery and fish traps near Bellingham. Daily catches that year ranged from a low of 50,000 to a high of 224,000 sockeyes.

Pink salmon, or humpies, less desirable for the canneries, run only in odd-numbered years and were often used to take up the deficit of sockeyes in their "off" years. In 1907, a "light" year for sockeyes, the PAF opened one trap to let out 75,000 pink salmon because they were unable to can them; 75,000 had already been brought to the cannery that evening and an additional 40,000 the next morning.

> Said S. H. Gross, the well known trap man, to the editor of the ISLANDER a few days ago:
>
> You know about as much about salmon as I do (he doesn't though, as a matter of fact) and I know as much as you do. There are many things about the fish and their habits that none of us know. We know little about "whence they come and whither they goest," what they feed upon and why the annual "runs" of the various species vary so enormously in size. Take our trap, for instance (the Shultz and Gross trap at Brann's bay). Four years ago we caught 177,000 sockeyes. This year we caught 98,000, but we caught 50,000 more in July this year than we did in July 1901. This year we caught 54,000 humpbacks while two years ago we caught 277,000. Some schools went past all the San Juan traps this year and the largest run ever known, which found its way into the Fraser river after the Canadian season has closed, didn't touch the San Juan banks at all. I don't know why, you don't and nobody does. It is my theory that they simply went astray, as some people do, and got lost.
>
> The San Juan Islander, October 21, 1905

In the 1910s, fish numbers in the region defined as Puget Sound began to decline, and by 1914 the PAF's Alaska cannery was outproducing its Bellingham facility; this disparity grew such that in 1922 the Alaskan pack was 10 times that of Puget Sound. Subsequently it never dropped below a factor of three. Part of this was due to the 1914 Hell's Gate rockslide on the Fraser River. Contractors for the Canadian National Railway began construction in the Fraser River Canyon in 1911, blasting a right-of-way and boring tunnels, which resulted in large amounts of debris falling into the river. In February 1914, a huge rockslide occurred at Hell's Gate in the middle of the canyon, blocking the river and obstructing the salmon from returning to their spawning grounds. Although this obstacle was removed by 1915, its effects, along with the other work in the canyon, had a huge impact

> **Question:** Did they use to waste great quantities of fish here at the canneries by catching more than they could use?
> **Answer:** Well, yes, the seiners, of course they had no use— they claimed the humpbacks was not a good food fish, and the sockeyes and the humpies run the same time, the same season, you know, and they would take in sockeye salmon, take them out, throw them in their boat, when they were seining, you see, and then they would throw the humpies overboard.
> **Question:** Would they be dead or alive as they threw them overboard?
> **Answer:** Well, by the time they stuck a pick through them they would die. There would not any of them live.
>
> —Testimony of Stephen B. Gross, March 12, 1927
> *Duwamish et al. v. United States,*
> Court of Claims of the United States, No. F-275

on the subsequent years' salmon run. The extremely low 1917 salmon catch and pack indicated the continuing decline of the salmon population in the region.

> Forget the sockeye. If we can forget the sockeye, I think there is a chance of building up the salmon industry with the cheaper fish. Of course there won't be as much profit in them as in the sockeyes, but, the payrolls will be the same, and that is what counts most.
>
> — E. B. Deming, PAF Manager, *Bellingham Herald,* August 14, 1924

Salmon numbers fell further in the 1920s. The depression of 1921 and the decline in fish prices led to a smaller number of fishers, particularly purse seiners. As the 1923 *Washington State Fishery Report* noted, "The drop in the run of fish, and greatly increased cost of operating due to the war, together with the low selling value of the fish, made the industry unprofitable for the purse seiners, and many of them removed to California or Alaska

> You can't have your salmon and waste it too. Several years ago the United States regarded as almost inexhaustible the supplies of salmon on our coasts. Now Secretary Hoover comes forward with word that the supplies along the Atlantic Coast have been exhausted. Add to that the story of the Pacific shores, where wasteful exploitation has reduced the quantity available by 50%. Terrible toll has been taken of salmon as they come up the rivers and streams to spawn. Robbed of a chance to reproduce its kind the salmon is passing out of the picture.
> — L. H. Darwin, Washington State Fish Commissioner, "The Lesson of Salmon," *Bellingham American*, November 10, 1926

with their vessels." In 1925, a private utility, Puget Sound Energy, built a dam at Concrete on the Baker River, near where it joined the Skagit River. Although they constructed fish ladders to accommodate the salmon returning upriver to spawn, it was later determined that there was up to a 50% mortality rate among the fingerlings encountering the dam spills and turbines. (This was exacerbated by the construction of an Upper Baker River Dam in 1959, which inundated the natural Baker Lake and its surrounding valley and spawning grounds.)

> **Question:** Do you know the fishing conditions here in the San Juan Islands?
> **Answer:** Yes, I do. I know there is lots of fish traps here, lots of fish been caught—caught by the millions.
> **Question:** As far back as you can remember, how did the quantity or number of fish at that time compare with the quantity or number of fish now available?
> **Answer:** There is one now where there was billions of them in them days, 20 years ago, or 50, 40 years ago.
> —Testimony of William Rosler, March 14, 1927
> *Duwamish et al. v. United States,*
> Court of Claims of the United States, No. F-275

Herring and Smelt

Herring fishing in the region began with the Hudson's Bay Company, with commercial catches first reported in the Strait of Georgia in 1877. Fishers first caught herring with drag or beach seine nets; by 1905 gill nets were also used. With the advent of power boats, purse seines were used, which efficiently raised the catch from 130–650 tonnes before to 30,000 after. Most of the Canadian catch was exported to Asia, reaching a peak of 45,000 tonnes in 1928; the decline in this demand led to a reduced catch (13,000 tonnes) and transition to the fish meal or oil industry.

In the San Juans, commercial Euro American herring fishing began with the Graignic family on Waldron Island. Edouard Graignic, a Frenchman who had moved there in the late 1870s, fished for herring with his family by lighting a fire on the beach at night and rowing a net around the fish that were attracted by the light, a method called beach seining. The whole family was involved in cleaning, smoking, and packing—20 to a box—the catch. Graignic sailed to Victoria to market the pack in his sloop, *City of Paris*.

Graignic Family in the City of Paris
(courtesy of San Juan Historical Museum)

Waldron Herring Fisheries

In an interview with A. W. Thomas, of Thomas Bros. & Co., of Waldron, we learn that this season's pack of herring has been unusually large, and although coming late in the season has more than taxed the capacity of their extensive fishery. They have established trade with parties in Victoria, and, besides supplying the market with fresh fish, they have packed some 21,000 boxes and pickled upwards of a hundred barrels. They contemplate enlarging the plant—just doubling its capacity,--in the spring. Graham Bros. and Capt. Edw. Graignic will also increase their facilities before next seasons pack. The fishing industry of the county is now well established and assuming proportions which will place it in the fore ranks, not only of this county but the entire Puget Sound country.

—The Islander, December 27, 1894

    In the 1880s, Bernhardt Mordhorst and Frederick Hay, both originally from Schleswig-Holstein, Germany, operated a herring fishery at Reid Harbor on Stuart Island. They not only supplied fresh herring for bait to halibut schooners going north to Alaska, but also had a saltery on the harbor and a smoking house on a small cove just outside. According to Stuart Island historian James Bergquist, they would steward the herring by cutting boughs and putting them in the harbor for the female herring to lay their roe, thus encouraging larger schools. Mordhorst continued his herring operations after his partner's death in 1887.

    Ellery and Ashton Thomas established a herring smokery on Fishery Point on Waldron Island in the 1890s. They built two 60-foot-long smokehouses and sent the packed fish by boat throughout the region. On March 28, 1895, *The Islander* reported that they had shipped 25 tons of smoked herring, packed in 10-pound boxes, to Getz Brothers, San Francisco, via the steamer *Walla Walla*. The Thomas brothers put in a herring trap off Waldron in 1895.

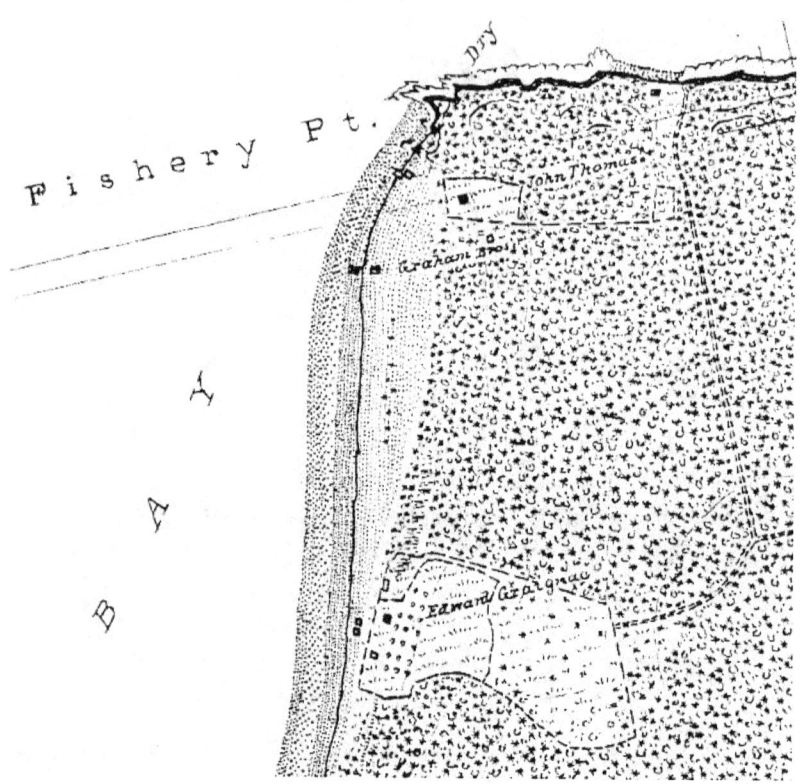

Fishery Point, Waldron Island, US Coast & Geodetic Survey, 1894 (note: Edward [Edouard] Graignic, Graham Brothers, and John Thomas)

    In 1899 the Red Cross Fish Company herring packing plant was established at Mitchell Bay on San Juan Island, and Max Johnson, who had worked for years in fisheries off the coast of Norway, was hired as the manager. In addition to smoking the herring, packers also pickled them with salt in 50-gallon wooden barrels. Often women, called "chokers," were the ones who prepared the herring by gutting them. On March 12, 1900, the packing and smokehouse burned. Although Johnson said that he in-

> *Mr. Mordhorst is preparing for herring fishing. He is an experienced fisherman, and puts up the finest smoked herring and salmon on the coast.*
>
>   The Islander, August 30, 1894

> THE ISLANDER *acknowledges receipt of and returns thanks to the Red Cross Fishing Company, operating at Mitchell bay, for a box of "fresh smoked 'Kipper' herrings." Mr. Johnson, manager of the company, says: "These are the first of their kind put up on the Pacific coast. In England they are considered a treat by rich and poor and seldom is a breakfast table of the queen without them. It is my opinion and my aim to soonest possible start a cannery for canning these fish. Every can now sold in the States comes from England or Scotland. This is a shame when they can be put up here. The herring on this coast are equal if not superior to the European fish..."*
>
> —*The San Juan Islander*, February 8, 1900

tended to rebuild—in fireproof brick or stone—on the tide lands fronting the old location, the newspapers soon reported that he had become the manager of the Pacific American Fisheries salting department, and a new plant was erected in Port Townsend in 1904, employing some 20 men and packing 25,000 boxes of smoked herring per season.

Herring was also used as bait fish, particularly for halibut. The April 28, 1898, edition of *The San Juan Islander* noted that "Eduard Graignic, of Waldron, was in port Tuesday on his way to Mitchell Bay for herring for halibut fishing." In the 1910s, several of the Alaskan halibut fishery schooners would anchor in Reid Harbor on Stuart Island in order to get herring for bait.

Another product of herring was fish oil, which was used for greasing skins in tanneries and skid grease in logging camps (to be replaced later by dogfish oil). Herring was steamed in wood boxes and then pressed for oil. One barrel, typically 200 pounds, would render 1.5 gallons of oil. According to one fisherman in Puget Sound, a nightly catch of 200–300 barrels could produce 30 gallons of oil, which sold at the time (late 1880s) for 35–45 cents per gallon.

Commercial herring fishing in the Salish Sea collapsed, due to decreasing stock, soon after World War I. After that time, the principal means of herring fishing was by means of traps, which were located near spawning grounds (i.e., not in the San Juan Islands), and the harvest was mainly used as bait for commercial halibut, crab, and shark fisheries. Annual catches ranged from a high of 1,311 tons in 1926 to a low of 36 tons in 1942. In the 1950s the use of the herring catch shifted to recreational salmon fisheries. In 1957, the State allowed the reduction of herring to oil and meal as well as some use for crab bait. The main fishery area was in Bellingham Bay, where annual landings ranged from 1,500–3,500 tons; this was phased out in the early 1980s due to concerns about the reduction in stock, particularly in the Cherry Point spawning area. However, in 1972, the Cherry Point herring stock were caught for sac-roe; two years later landings reached a peak of 4,000 tons. Declining stock led to region-wide closure in the mid-1980s. In 1988, non-tribal spawn-on-kelp and treaty sac-roe resumed at Cherry Point; this was closed in the mid-1990s and remains so until a minimum spawning mass of 3,200 tons is reached.

Meanwhile the Canadian catch in the Strait of Georgia, used in the reduction market, reached a peak of 77,000 tonnes in 1963, and then collapsed and was closed in 1967. In 1972, similar to the American industries, roe harvest began, capturing spawning herring near the shore with seines or gill nets and extracting the roe. The main market was Japan, and it became so lucrative that competition again led to population collapse, such that the government implemented a fixed-quota system in 1983. After another collapse in 1986, leading to closure of the Strait to herring fishing, stock levels have risen again, and there is now limited fishing north of the border. Annual average catch in the Strait of Georgia is about 27,000 tonnes, with spikes of 35,000 tonnes. Recently conservation groups on Hornby Island have been objecting to the currently allowed commercial catch in Baynes Sound, which usually happens in a narrow window of a few days in late February or early March—and most of the harvest takes place in a 24-hour period. The allowed catch is 20%, based on the current projection of median spawning biomass of 90,250 tonnes for the Gulf of Georgia.

On the American side of the border, commercial fishing for herring is currently allowed in central and south Puget Sound waters (not the San Juans, which are closed all year round) using a lampara seine—a net the shape of a spoon with a short leadline under a longer floatline—or dip bag net with area and timing restrictions. Lampara nets cannot exceed 200 feet and cannot contain meshes less than ½ inch; logbooks must be filled out for every set and submitted monthly. Annual landings for the period 2003–2012 averaged 335 tons; in 2012, licenses included seven lamparas, six dip bags, and two drag seines. The catch is almost wholly used for bait for the sport fishery.

In 1893 James G. Swan published the paper "On the Sardine Fishery of Puget Sound" in the *Bulletin of the United States Fish Commission*, arguing that there was a great prospect for the canning of the California anchovy, which was called a sardine but is distinct from the California sardine.

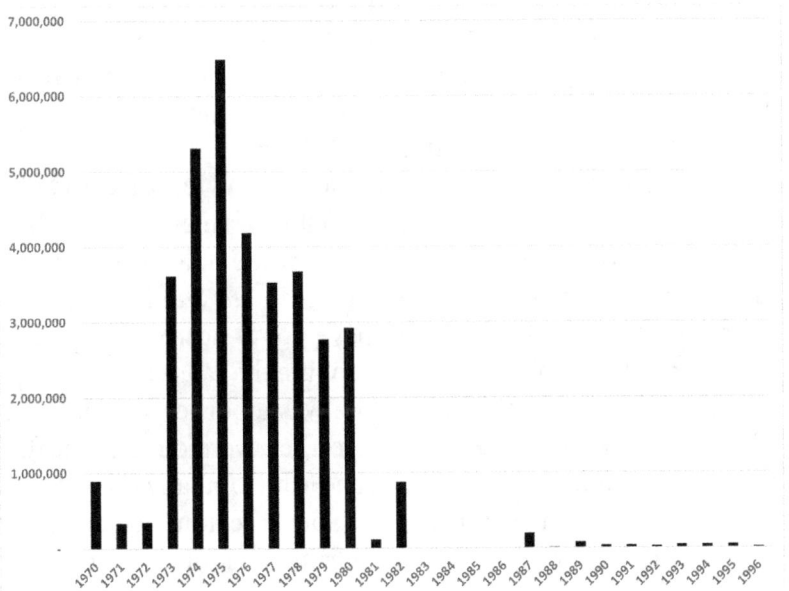

Herring Catch (in pounds), San Juan Islands, 1970–1996

> When taken in Monterey or San Diego bays, it is only fit for bait; but in Puget Sound, which is its northern limit, it is in perfection, and is one of the fattest and most delicious flavored of the small fish, and is considered by experts to be far superior, in point of flavor and richness, to the best Mediterranean sardine. Some Norwegian and Russian fisherman here have put them up, in limited quantities, in vinegar and spice, and they are delicious and sell readily; but the men who attempted the enterprise were without capital, and there has been no one with executive ability to push the business forward to success.
> — James G. Swan, "On the Sardine Fishery of Puget Sound," 13th Bulletin of the United States Fish Commission (1893)

Swan noted that unlike herring, which hug the shore and can easily be caught with beach seines, anchovies keep to the deep water, so they must be caught with purse seines with a small mesh. In 1904 *The San Juan Islander* reported that a "party of Scandinavians had encountered millions of anchovy fish near Anacortes and speculated on the potential for this "North sea delicacy." However, there is little evidence of anchovy ever becoming a marketable catch in the Salish Sea.

Although as late as July of 1907 it was reported that "A. D. Davis and P. Schruder caught 150 lbs. of smelt in Mud Bay," local harvest of smelt also suffered a considerable decline in the early 1900s. A February 15, 1908, article in *The San Juan Islander* remarked that "Smelt are said to have pretty nearly disappeared from our waters," and went on to attribute the cause to the dumping of sawdust by a mill "before the waste burner was built" in West Sound, where "a few years ago they were quite plentiful." Around the same time, the San Juan Fish Company of Seattle, a major salmon handler in the Puget Sound region, turned to the Quinault River for adequate and reliable quantities of smelt for their cold storage processing.

Halibut

Euro Americans fished with hook and line for halibut in the same areas where the Coast Salish had fished (and continued to do so). Canadians fished in the Strait of Georgia, and Halibut Bank, only 15 kilometers from Vancouver, became a favored fishing ground. By 1898, the Fisheries of British Columbia reported that 850 tonnes of halibut were being brought into Vancouver. In the northern portion of the San Juans—Mitchell Bay on San Juan Island, Stuart Island, and Waldron Island—local fishermen trolled for and caught halibut throughout the 1890s–1910s. As local areas got fished out—in 1908 the Canadian Inspector of Fisheries had already warned about declining stocks—the action moved outward to Cape Flattery, the banks off the coast, and then up into Alaska. According to the boat historian Howard Chapelle, a form of sharpie—"a double-ended gaff-schooner... heavily built and ballasted and not intended for great speed"—was used by local fishermen to work the Strait of Juan de Fuca as well as the islands' waters. In the 1910s, several of the Alaskan halibut fishery schooners would anchor in Reid Harbor on Stuart Island in order to get herring for bait. They would return there on the way back: the schooner *San Jose* was there in late August 1912 with 90,000 pounds of halibut, which would fetch a price of 5½ cents per pound in Seattle.

> The halibut fishery during these yeas [1900–1920] was largely a process of depleting the Puget Sound banks. In 1892 halibut banks extended from Cape Flattery through the Strait of Juan de Fuca to the south end of Whidbey Island in the sound. As late as 1905 a considerable quantity of large habitat was landed at Bellingham from nearby water. By 1910 practically all of the banks in the sound had been discovered and fished out.
>
> — Lloyd Spencer and Lancaster Pollard, *History of the State of Washington* vol. 2 (1937)

Historically, Flattery Bank, an area of about 1,100 square miles with a minimum depth of 27 fathoms, just a dozen miles off the Cape Flattery lighthouse, was fished by the Makah as part of their traditional use area. They would set out from Neah Bay in large cedar canoes and fish with many-fathom-long cedar, sinew, or kelp lines with multiple hooks designed for a halibut's mouth. In 1888, Gloucester Captain Sol Jacobs brought three halibut schooners from Massachusetts around Cape Horn and began camping near Neah Bay and fishing the Flattery Banks. Each of the boats—the *Oscar and Hattie*, *Mollie Adams*, and *Edward E. Webster*—carried six dories each, from which two-man crews would fish with long lines. They would then sail the catch, on ice, to Tacoma, where it would be placed on the Northern Pacific Railroad cars for shipment to Boston and other cities on the East Coast. By 1915, the Puget Sound–based halibut fishery had grown to a fleet of 97 vessels, most owned by corporations. The regional halibut fisheries had collapsed just five years later, and trollers were going from Puget Sound and the San Juan Islands out the Strait of Juan de Fuca to Cape Flattery, up the coast of Vancouver Island, and on to Alaska.

In the late 1910s, fishermen and fish processors pressured the Canadian and United States governments to intervene. Although negotiations failed in 1919, four years later the Convention for the Preservation of the Halibut Fishery of the North Pacific was signed, establishing the International Pacific Halibut Commission. With regulation, both the halibut population and catch rose until the 1970s, when a larger and more efficient fleet emerged. In the 1990s, "derby-style" fishing—where everyone competes for a season of a few days—was replaced with quota systems, where individual boats were awarded a percentage of the catch and the captain could decide when to fish.

Small-scale halibut fishing continued in the San Juans into the second half of the twentieth century. June Burn, in her *100 Days in the San Juans* (1946), mentions that there was a halibut bank between Waldron and Skipjack Islands where locals Bill Chevalier, John Taylor, and Ab Severson fished commercially. Halibut is currently fished recreationally in the Salish Sea; both

For the purpose of developing the stocks of halibut of the Northern Pacific Ocean and Bering Sea to levels which will permit the optimum yield from that fishery, and of maintaining the stocks at those levels, the Commission, with the approval of the Parties and consistent with the Annex to this Convention, may, after investigation has indicated such action to be necessary, with respect to the nationals and fishing vessels of, and fishing vessels licensed by, the United States or Canada, and with respect to halibut:

- *Divide the Convention waters into areas;*
- *Establish one or more open or closed seasons as to each area;*
- *Limit the size of the fish and the quantity of the catch to be taken from each area within any season during which fishing is allowed;*
- *During both open and closed seasons, permit, limit, regulate or prohibit the incidental catch of Pacific halibut that may be taken, retained, possessed, or landed from each area or portion of an area, by vessels fishing for other species of fish;*
- *Fix the size and character of Pacific halibut fishing appliances to be used in any area;*
- *Make such regulations for the licensing of vessels and for the collection of statistics on the catch of Pacific halibut as it shall find necessary to determine the condition and trend of the Pacific halibut fishery and to carry out the other provisions of this Convention;*
- *Close to all taking of Pacific halibut any area or portion of an area that the Commission finds to be populated by small, immature Pacific halibut and designates as nursery grounds.*

— International Pacific Halibut Convention, *Protocol, article III, section 3* (1979)

British Columbia and Washington State issue sport fishing licenses for halibut, with restrictions on location, season, and size (to ensure reproduction by mature adults).

Rockfish

The name "rockfish" encompasses a wide variety of species, but only a few of them were fished commercially. Principal among these is lingcod, which is the largest local greenling; it can grow up to five feet in length and weigh over 80 pounds.

> ### The Lone Fisherman
>
> *There is a lone fisherman camping on the beach near Pt. Lawrence, Orcas Island, who makes a specialty of cod fishing, and makes a good living at it too. He gathers in an average of 75 pounds of rock cod, lin[g] cod and kelp cod from his set lines every day and gets six cents a pound for them.*
>
> *The business requires no capital, the expenses are light, and there are no hardships in connection with it in the summer time.*
>
> —The San Juan Islander, September 1, 1911

Although historic Canadian catch statistics lumped together "cod-like" species, it is estimated that 90% of the catch was lingcod. Most of these were fished by handliners; over 200 boats fished the Strait of Georgia, with a record catch of 3,000 tonnes in 1936. On a local scale, *The San Juan Islander* reported on May 20, 1910, that "Peter Stuhr and Otto Nelson are having good luck fishing for rock cod and black bass off the west coast of San Juan. They caught 600 pounds of bass at one haul one day last week and 400 pounds at another time." Like halibut, however, cod was probably commercially fished out in the San Juan Islands to a large extent by 1900. From the evidence of an 1895 newspaper piece that talked about a business plan to invest in a schooner with the proper equipment for fishing and curing to be sailed to Alaska for fishing, cod fishermen were already looking north for better fishing grounds.

A PROPOSED INDUSTRY

A number of the substantial business men of Friday Harbor and vicinity are talking of organizing a company to go into the cod fishing business. It is proposed to organize a company with a capital stock of $10,000; purchase a schooner and fit her up with all the necessary paraphernalia for cod fishing and send her to the fishing grounds of Alaska. The curing and packing establishment is to be located in Friday Harbor, and the headquarters of the company is to be here. The scheme is not merely talk but is backed by old Gloucester fishermen, and other men who have money, and at present bids fair to develop into a reality in the near future.

— The Islander, January 10, 1895

In the Gulf of Georgia, however, trawlers soon became the main source of the rockfish catch. The catch—mainly red snapper (yelloweye rockfish)—ballooned in the 1920s, from 44 tonnes at the beginning of the decade to 1,000 tonnes in 1926, and then declined to an average of 253 tonnes per year. With the growing demand for fresh fillets in the 1940s, there was another boom, but catches fell rapidly, to just a few tonnes a year, in the 1950s. As a result of declining populations, in the mid-1980s new restrictions were put in place, leading to total bottom-trawl closures. Fisheries and Oceans Canada has subsequently instituted commercial quotas, which are about 30 tonnes a year. In Washington State the Department of Fish and Wildlife has imposed strong restrictions on commercial rockfish harvesting. In response to the recreational overharvesting of rockfish in San Juan County, the Marine Resources Committee recommended eight voluntary no-fish zones in the late 1990s. Although there has been some recovery in populations of groundfish, the Puget Sound/Georgia Basin distinct population segment in Washington State is currently listed as threatened under the Endangered Species Act.

Dogfish

The Coast Salish had traditionally caught and used dogfish for several purposes, principally their livers for oil and their skin as sandpaper. When a demand for oil for lumber skids came with the arrival of the Euro Americans, Indigenous peoples caught dogfish and then processed their livers. The women would cut out the livers, boil them, and then put them in sacks into a canoe and trod on them to extract the oil, which was then put into cans and sold to the lumber operations.

> *Dog fishing seems to be a fine industry around here. It is reported that Mr. J. W. Modie caught 800 at one haul. He is a professional fisherman and everybody knows it.*
>
> —The Islander, October 31, 1895

In general, though, dogfish were generally considered a pest by Euro Americans because they were caught up in nets along with target species such as salmon or while trawling for bottom fish.

However, some islanders fished for dogfish and rendered them for their oil, which was used both as a fertilizer and to grease the logs that made up the "skid roads" in logging operations. June Burn, in her *100 Days in the San Juans*, relates that dogfish livers were first processed for their oil by the Fox brothers, of Bellingham, on Blind Island in Blind Bay, Shaw Island. In 1897, W. F. Robinson, president of the Seattle firm of Robinson & Colt Company, explored the area with a view toward establishing a plant for manufacturing commercial fertilizers, utilizing dogfish oil. This did not come to pass due to a lack of sufficient supply. Edouard Graignic of Waldron Island, Bruce Willis of Olga on Orcas Island, G. T. Peterson of Mitchell Bay on San Juan Island, and E. T. Erickson and Jens Johnson near Prevost Bay on Stuart Island all fished for dogfish and sold the oil. In 1906, Willis

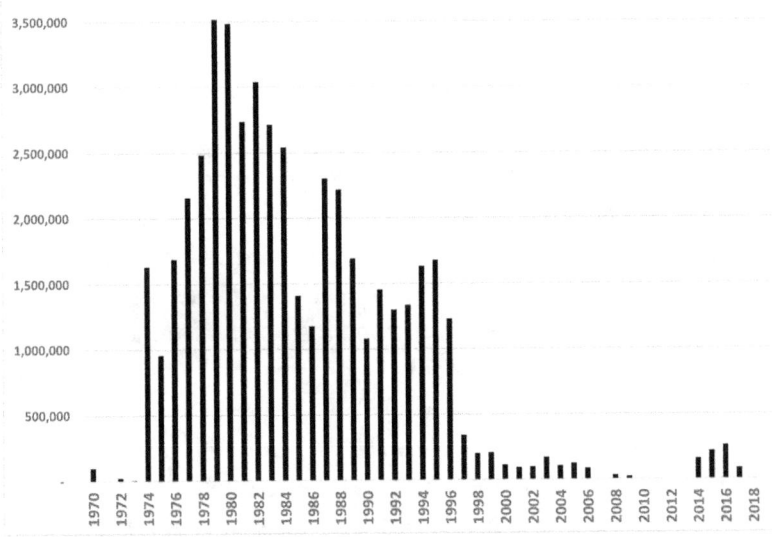

Spiny Dogfish Catch, San Juan Islands, 1970–2018

sold 30 gallons in Friday Harbor for 25 cents a gallon—although he claimed he could get 10 cents more in Anacortes. A national article titled "What Shall Be Done with Dogfish" picked up by *The San Juan Islander* that year talked about a congressional appropriation to study dogfish, both in terms of its elimination and its use for fertilizer and oil.

During World War II, because of the shortage of North Atlantic cod liver oil, dogfish oil fetched good prices. The liver of a dogfish can be up to a third of its body mass, so fishermen, upon catching it, would quickly extract the liver and throw the rest of the body back into the water (often to find them filling their subsequent net sets). June Burn, in her *100 Days in the San Juans*, mentions that Ralph Wood and Ethan Allen on Waldron caught dogfish with setlines during the war, but that they, along with Ralph and Ab Severson, although still catching some, had switched over to ling cod, for their livers. In 1950, however, a synthetic Vitamin A—the beneficial part of the liver—was developed, and the dogfish-liver-oil market collapsed.

Shrimp

> About a ton of shrimp is shipped from Orcas daily. They are caught in deep water, their home and feeding place being on the bottom. At Orcas they are found at a depth of from 20 to 30 fathoms, or 120 to 180 feet, respectively. They are caught by means of a trawl or box seine which is lowered to the bottom of the water by heavy chains and weights and the shrimp are scooped into it and then hauled to the top and dumped into a scow or boat.
>
> Two steamers are used in trawling with the shrimp seine. The steamers are placed quite a distance apart and a rope attached to the box seine is fastened to each steamer. It is dragged along the bottom in this manner for a distance of several hundred feet. The seine is raised and the wriggling creatures are dumped into a boat and are quickly made ready for shipment to the various markets. When just taken from the water the shrimp are brown, but when placed in boiling hot water turn pink or red.
>
> — *Bellingham Herald*, quoted in *The San Juan Islander*, January 28, 1904

In the 1890s a new industry of shrimp began in the Puget Sound region. Shrimping had been done in the waters near San Francisco since the 1870s; before the turn of the century, they were discovered in Puget Sound. After shrimping extensively in the Hood Canal area, H. L. Haines of the Haines Oyster Company of Seattle discovered them in Harney Channel near Orcas Island in 1903, deploying several steamers to trawl for them. Other beds included Birch Bay, Point Roberts, and around Waldron Island. During the early 1900s, local beds were discovered near Flat Point, Lopez Island, in San Juan Channel, and off Blakely Island. When the Haines Oyster Company secured a contract to furnish a large quantity of shrimp to a San Francisco firm in 1905, Haines moved with his family to Friday Harbor. Haines skippered the steamers *Zebeitka* (named after his sister) and *Alta*. Captain Bert Hale had the *G. Vasa*; Captain Blackman, with the Seattle Oyster and Fish Company, had the *Crescent*; and R. C. Willis and his son Bruce, of Olga, used the ketch-rigged *Ailsa*. All soon went farther afield, first to Hood Canal and later the Anacortes area and near Tulalip. Catches could be as much as 700 pounds a day and sold in 1904 for 15 cents per pound.

Crab

Individual (recreational) harvesting of crabs, particularly Dungeness, must have occurred in the islands throughout the nineteenth century. A 1911 article in *The San Juan Islander* mentions that "Crabbing is the favorite amusement now. Large numbers of fine large crabs are being caught." Whether there was a large commercial catch then is not known. In 1907 the paper did mention that Bruce Willis of Olga was planning on fishing for "crab and other things," and the first crab cannery "on the North Pacific Coast" was built in Blaine in 1902. The Washington State Fish Commissioner report for 1905 listed a catch of 35,000 dozen crabs statewide; some of this must have come from the San Juans.

Crabbing is done with traps or "pots." These are rope or wire-mesh devices, in the form of either a box or a cylinder, averaging in size about 3' x 3' x 2' high or 3' in diameter and 2' high. The bait—fish heads and other carrion—are placed in a mesh box in the middle of the trap; the crabs crawl into the trap through one-way wire "doors" and cannot be get back out.

Lobster

In 1906 the Washington State Fish Commission made arrangements to introduce eastern lobsters from Maine to Puget Sound. Under the headlines "HUNDREDS OF LOBSTERS PLACED IN OUR WATERS," the November 23, 1907, edition of *The San Juan Islander* reported that "The nucleus of what may prove to be a very important industry in this county was started Thursday when hundreds of eastern lobsters were 'planted' at various points in our waters by an agent of the government, under instructions from the fish commission." A year later, several specimens, probably from that batch, were found near Decatur Island by Dr. R. M. Gordon, who was monitoring the project. In 1909, the paper's report of the finding of a small lobster on Center Island prompted hope that in fact the transplanted lobsters may have bred. However, there was no more discussion until 1914, when State Fish Commissioner L. H. Davis proposed establishing a "Lobster Station" in San Juan County, saying (erroneously) that "this is the first attempt to propagate lobsters in Puget Sound." There is no further evidence of lobster cultivation in the Salish Sea.

Kelp

For a brief period, kelp was commercially harvested in the San Juan Islands. Founded at Port Stanley, Lopez Island, in 1913 by a Mr. Schwablin, the Puget Sound Potash and Kelp Fertilizer Company built a plant in 1917 to manufacture three products: potash, used for gunpowder in World War I; kelp fertilizer; and iodine. The steam driven plant, built on a bulkhead at the shore, housed a boiler, engines, kiln, conveyors, hoppers, and blowers. A conveyor moved the kelp from the harvester at the pier to the building, where it was "dewatered" in centrifugal extractors and dried in a cylindrical kiln. The product was then screened, sacked, and stored for further processing. Many Lopez Islanders worked at the plant, including Ray Spencer, who was living on Blakely Island at the time and was rowed over and back each day by his wife Kate. The barge *Harvester King* was used to harvest the kelp: it had a 16-foot cutter bar, which could be raised or lowered depending on the cutting conditions; upon being cut the kelp was moved to a large open hopper amidships. The plant closed in the 1920s due to lack of business. After the company shut down operations the *Harvester King* was used as a ferry for one year and then converted to a freight boat.

Nori

In the 1970s several groups looked into the feasibility of nori (seaweed used for food) cultivation in the Pacific Northwest. A formal study conducted in the 1980s concluded that the San Juan Islands provided the best area for nori aquaculture in the Salish Sea.

As a result, New Channel Nori farmed the red alga *Porphyra yezoensis* at two sites near Stuart Island in the winter of 1988-1989, resulting in the production of an estimated 500,000 sheets, processed by Canada West Nori.

> *These results, combined with later results from private companies, have shown that the best results are from the San Juan Islands area because of the dramatic mixing of oceanic waters and freshwater runoff from the Fraser River.*
>
> —Thomas F. Mumford, Jr.,
> *"Nori Cultivation in North America: Growth of an Industry,"*
> S. C. Lindstrom and P.W. Gabrielson,
> *Thirteenth International Seaweed Symposium* (1990)

Clams

Harvesting of clams from their native beds in the San Juan Islands has occurred for thousands of years. With developing markets in the Puget Sound region in the 1890s, canning clams became an important industry. The first firm to can clams in the islands was established by J. Broder in 1901; in 1903 he went into partnership with George Mead, of Seattle, and they expanded operations with an 18 by 24–foot, two-story addition to the cannery. In 1905 this firm was reorganized as the Island Packing Company, a joint-stock company, with Broder as president, Mead as secretary, L. B. Carter as treasurer, and E. H. Nash as general manager. They doubled the capacity of the facility to 500 cases a day and expanded into canning salmon, so they could run throughout the year. Throughout the first decade of 1900s this operation produced thousands of cases of canned clams and clam "nectar" yearly. A case consisted of either 24 two-lb. or 48 one-lb. cans. Each case required a little over one sack, or two bushels, of clams (a sack weighed approximately 125 pounds). In 1902, a sack of clams cost about $1. Harvest and production numbers (in cases) gleaned from *The San Juan Islander* tell the story: 1905—"Twelve boat loads of clams, about 400 sacks in all…this week"; 1906—"400 cases last week"; 1907—"500 sacks …past three weeks"; 1908—3,000 cases "this winter"; and 1910—"200 sacks…dug by Indians who are camped at White Beach, Orcas Island."

> Unless the state legislature takes some action soon with a view to protecting the clam beds and checking the inroads that are now beginning made upon them it will only be a question of time, and not a very long time either, when clams will be a rarity on Puget Sound and the native Indians will be deprived of one of their chief sources of sustenance. The law at present recognizes no property rights in a clam bed, as it does in an oyster bed, and there is no provision for their protection for the benefit of the public.
> —*The San Juan Islander*, April 3, 1902

As early as 1902, Broder warned of diminishing stock from the local beds and suggested that the State institute regulations to limit exploitation by adopting property rights to clam beds in the same manner that they had for oyster beds. That year, he had got many of his clams locally from Charles Williams of Peavine Pass, off Orcas. But the *Fairhaven Times*, in reaction to *The San Juan Islander* advocating for state restrictions, countered that the years 1894–1896 had been particularly heavy on the local clam beds. Most of the newspaper reports in the first decade of the 1900s were of Indigenous peoples coming from British Columbia to sell their clams: "The largest fleet of Indian fishing boats seen in the harbor this year was here the first of the week. They brought many hundreds of sacks of clams for the Island Packing Company and took away with the large quantities of provisions and other supplies" (*The San Juan Islander*, December 19, 1908). In 1907 S. M. Bugge, who had taken over the Island Packing Company, established the Tuana Packing Company on Lopez Island; there they packed clams from British Columbia's Indigenous peoples as well as from Port Townsend. (Bugge went on to establish a clam cannery in Port Townsend.)

Herbert "Bert" Coffin, working at the clam cannery in 1906 for $.15 an hour (he soon got a nickel raise), wrote in the Monday, March 6th entry in his journal that "This is good work except that it is hard on the fingers. When I finished Thursday night my fingernails were all worn down to the quick as if I had eaten them off and every finger was sore from cuts caused by broken clamshells."

During the latter half of the twentieth century, harvest of geoduck clams in the Salish Sea began to grow in economic importance. Washington State began annual scuba surveys of geoduck resources, and in 1970 the State Legislature established a commercial geoduck clam fishery, which is administered by the Department of Fisheries (later merged into the Department of Wildlife). In 1976, Washington State divers introduced surface-supplied air systems and mechanical harvesting by means of water hoses and hydraulic "stingers" (water jets) to loosen the substrate to harvest burrowing geoduck and horse clams in the Canadian part of the Salish Sea. This method creates a hole 1½–2 feet in diameter and exposes all clams in the hole regardless of size or species. Today the wild geoduck clam industry, which is year-round, generates about $22 million revenue for the State through a competitive bid process and sale of the rights to harvest shares of annually set quota on discrete geoduck "tracts."

Oysters

The Chinook and Chehalis, whose villages were on Shoalwater (later named Willapa) Bay, harvested native oysters, which formed an important part of their diet. In 1851 Charles J. W. Russell first harvested these native oysters for shipment to the San Francisco market, employing Indigenous peoples to harvest them and then transporting them overland to Astoria, whence he shipped them to San Francisco. The trade was very profitable: a basket of oysters harvested at Shoalwater Bay for $1 could be sold in the city for $30. With the importation of Eastern oysters to California in the late 1800s, export declined, but the development of the native-oyster industry in Washington expanded, particularly in the Olympia region. The establishment of Olympia as the Washington State capital is said to have been due to marketing of native oysters alongside lobbying for the location.

In nearby Victoria, as early as 1859 native oysters harvested from Sooke were offered at Rudolph's Oyster Saloon. An editorial in Victoria's *British Colonist* decried the fact that Indigenous women monopolized the sale of oysters in town, earning the relatively handsome sum of $4–5 per day. Experiments in planting oyster beds at Gorge, Esquimalt, and Oyster (later Ladysmith) Harbours began as early as the mid-1860s, in order to compete with the importation of Olympia oysters from Washington State across the boundary. In 1866, large beds of native oysters, which were said to be three times as large as those in the vicinity of Vancouver, were discovered at Comox (Baynes Sound). The British Columbia Inspector for Fisheries mentioned the first oyster lease at Mud Bay on the south shore of Victoria West in 1882, and the next year the lessee, the Mud Bay Oyster Company, planned to import and seed Eastern oysters there. Cultivation never really took off, however, and in subsequent years, native oysters were harvested from nine designated sub-districts in British Columbia: Nanaimo, Cowichan, Victoria, Clayoquot, Alberni, Alert Bay, Quathiaska, Comox, and the adjacent mainland. By 1900, 1,600 barrels (one barrel contained 250 pounds of oysters) valued at $8,000 were harvested in British Columbia. Those from Comox became a major source of native oysters: in the years 1907–1911 the yields were 160, 140, 150, and 80 sacks, or, at 118 oysters per pound, approximately two million oysters each year. The area soon became overharvested, so much so that few native oysters are found in any of these areas today.

OYSTER CULTURE

Its Beginning in the County

Prior to 1860—he [Captain Warbass] has no idea for how long a period—there were a great many native oysters in a small lagoon near the site of the American military camp on San Juan Island and also a great many in a small bay on the north end of Lopez Island, long since filled up. The winter of 1860–61 was so cold that these shallow lagoons froze to the bottom and the oysters were all killed. During the summer of '61 Capt. Warbass sent some Indians to the Samish flats to get a supply of seed oysters and they brought over two or more sacks which were planted in the large lagoon in Griffin bay, about four miles from Argyle. The experiment was successful and for many years native oysters have been plentiful there and large quantities of them have been taken away by the Indians and sold.

— The San Juan Islander, June 5, 1902

Meanwhile, in Washington State the Olympia industry expanded, providing the impetus for the State Legislature in 1895 to pass the Bush and Callow Acts, allowing for the purchase and sale of tide lands for the purpose of raising oysters. In the early 1900s, these tide lands were worth $1,000–$1,500 per acre (and assessed at $1,000 per acre). According to newspaper accounts, Edward Warbass had planted oysters brought over by Indigenous peoples from Samish flats in 1861 in either Old Town or First Lagoon. In 1902, the State Fish Commission began introducing Eastern oyster seeds for planting in Puget Sound beds. These were first sown in the Samish Flats, with operations like the Bellingham Oyster Company (700 acres) and the Samish

Oyster Company (800 acres), as well as the Oyster Creek Oyster Company, growing the Eastern oysters on their beds. The Fish Commissioner, T. R. Kershaw, visited the "lagoon...at the head of North Bay" (Jackson's Lagoon on San Juan Island) and reported: "It covers about ten or twelve acres and has a very narrow entrance which could very easily be closed by a dyke and gate to regulate the depth of water and prevent any injury to oyster ova from tidal currents."

Tidelands Ownership in San Juan County

The State process of "Application to Purchase Tide Lands" (later changed to "Application to Purchase Tide Lands for Oyster Planting and Cultivation") under the Bush and Callow Acts in San Juan County began in 1896 with No. 2474 (which indicates how many others had been purchased elsewhere in the State) by James M. Coleman of Seattle for tide lands on Waldron Island. The big rush came in 1897, when there were 40 applicants, slowing to 9 in 1898, 5 in 1899, and then tapering off to 1 in 1900; 2 in 1903, 1904, and 1908; 1 in 1909; and two more in 1910. Many of these early applications appear to be simply means of securing ownership of prize sites for waterfront lands used for canneries or fish trap operations. For instance, the fish trap operation of Shultz and Gross, either through principals William Shultz and Samuel Gross or through the latter's sons George and Stephen, applied for several locations at Open Bay on Henry Island and Andrews Bay and Roche Harbor on San Juan Island. At Friday Harbor on San Juan Island there were at least half a dozen applications, principally by the Island Packing Company but also by San Juan County itself. On Lopez Island, both the Oceanic Canning Company and its manager, R. C. Kinleyside, secured prime waterfront at Richardson, while others, like William Graham, got adjacent tide lands, and there were several applicants vying for areas around Deer Harbor, Eastsound, and West Sound on Orcas. Other notable applicants included Irene Weeks for Lopez Village and Ben Lichtenberg at his farm on Lopez Island; E. V. Cowell at Lime Kiln and Eliza Jakle, who secured rights near her land on the south end of San Juan Island; Henry T. Cayou on Decatur Island; and Bernhardt Mordhorst for Reid Harbor on Stuart Island. Of the individual applicants who were from outside of the county, several were from Coupeville (nearest Samish Bay), Fairhaven and New Whatcom (which would join to become the City of Bellingham), and Port Townsend.

In contrast to the early push to obtain title to tide lands for purposes of securing favorable waterfront landings and operations, many applicants in the early 1900s actually sought to produce shellfish on their tide lands. Former county auditor William O. Clark (then of Olympia) filed for tide lands at Fisherman Bay,

Lopez Island, and both Clarence M. Tucker and John L. Murray obtained the potentially rich tide lands at North Bay, near what is now called Jackson Beach, on San Juan Island. *The San Juan Islander* reported regularly on the subject, noting on April 16, 1905, that "City Engineer Gerhard, of Fairhaven, went to Lopez Tuesday to survey an oyster location in Fisherman's bay" and, on June 10 of the same year, "Wm. O. Clark…came down from Olympia with a large quantity of seed oysters with which to stock his location in this county." In 1909 the newspaper report that "H. A. Armstrong found a large eastern oyster on his tideflats near Argyle," and surmised that it may have been a survivor from the government's efforts at planting from several years back. In 1914 an oyster bed had been started on Lopez Island. All of these operations did not last, however, and it would not be until the latter half of the twentieth century that oyster farming in the islands became viable.

University of Washington zoology professor Trevor Kincaid, who was instrumental in establishing the Marine Laboratories at Friday Harbor, is also well known for his advocacy for and introduction of Pacific oysters from Japan. In 1912 Kincaid arranged for the shipment of 600,000 seed oysters. Later, Olympia oyster farmers J. Emy Tsukimoto and Joe Miyagi bought 600 acres in Samish Bay for their Pearl Oyster Company and had 400 cases of oyster seed shipped to them from Japan; unfortunately, most of them died, but after being dumped into the water it turned out that the spat on the shells had survived, leading to the propagation of millions of oysters in the bay. Pacific oyster culture was restricted to Samish Bay until the late 1920s, when it was introduced to Willapa Bay and Grays Harbor, among other locations in Washington. Operations such as the Rockpoint Oyster Company, first established by E. N. Steele and J. C. Barnes, survived the Great Depression by building a restaurant, run by Zenzabaro Maekawa, on the newly constructed and scenic Chuckanut Drive. (Sadly, the Maekawa family was interned during World War II; after the war the restaurant passed into other hands.)

Shellfish Farming

In the early 1960s Bill and Doree Webb started a summer camp at their property on Westcott Bay on San Juan Island. Westcott Bay and the adjacent Garrison Bay are fairly shallow, with a narrow entrance from Mosquito Pass, allowing the water to warm up in the spring and nutrients from seasonal streams to be trapped in the bay. Warmer water and nutrients, which support the growth of algae, make the area ideal for shellfish aquaculture. In the 1970s several researchers from the University of Washington conducted experiments with clams and oysters in the bay. This endeavor gave some other islanders the idea to start a shellfish farm. When their plans did not work out, Bill Webb pursued the idea and by the late 1970s he began buying oyster and clam seed and suspending it in the bay in some homemade trays. In 1980 the first harvest was well received by a local restaurant, and with the establishment of a shellfish hatchery on the site, the sea farm began to expand, with the goal of producing a consistent supply of high-quality shellfish and offering them directly to restaurants. Westcott Bay Sea Farms raised and sold clams, mussels, and oysters until around 2005. In 2013, Erik and Andrea Anderson bought the property from the Webb Estate and built up the operation once again. Today, the farm not only produces and sells oysters, clams, and mussels but also has a restaurant and rental space for events.

In the 1980s, several aquaculture projects began on Lopez Island. In 1980, James Bill, David Bill, and James Bergdahl installed an experimental 25' by 16' float 150' offshore of Hunter Bay to raise mussels on ropes. Learning from both their operation as well as one on Penn Cove on Whidbey Island, in 1982 Scott McCullough started the Lopez Mussel Company at Shoal Bay with an 8' by 10' raft with ropes hanging from it on which to grow the mussels. He expanded his operation to Hunter Bay in 1985 and the operation lasted into the 1990s.

The McKay family's Crescent Beach Oyster Farm had been raising oysters on Crescent Beach since the 1970s. Judd Cove Shellfish was formed by Bill Bawden in the early 1990s. In 1993, he got the first new aquaculture permit since San Juan County

Growing Oysters at Westcott Bay

The shellfish are spawned in the Westcott Bay hatchery and cultivated in lantern nets suspended in deep water for optimal growth and safety. When the oyster seed is about 2–4mm in size it can be moved to a floating raft system called an upweller. The high flow in the upweller is created by a submersible motor, which moves hundreds of gallons of algae-rich seawater through the barrels of small shellfish. Easily accessible in barrels with mesh on the bottom, millions of tiny shellfish can be cared for until they reach about 12mm, when they can be moved to the nursery trays. The 12mm oysters from the upweller are loaded in plastic trays, which are assembled into stacks and held together with ropes. The stacks are then taken by raft out to longlines (3/4" poly rope) that stretch east to west across the lease area. This is referred to as suspension culture, with the shellfish contained in equipment suspended above the bottom. This means that the shellfish are protected from predators and are underwater, feeding and growing constantly. The stacks of trays are brought in after about 6–9 months, when the shellfish are large enough to be transferred to the lantern nets.

The final stage of the operation involves Japanese lantern nets. Each net has ten tiers. Oysters from the nursery trays are loaded at 750 per tier and the opening is sewn shut and the nets can be taken out to the longlines. The large mesh size of the nets allows ideal flow for water and food and the oysters are usually at harvest size within six months. The floating longline system is easily accessed with the work raft and oysters are brought in to the dock, cleaned, sorted and shipped to order each week. The harvested shellfish are cleaned to table-ready condition, sold at the farm, or chilled and hand-packed for sale to fine restaurants across the country.

—Description of Webb's operation at Westcott Bay, promotional material (2000) imposed a moratorium on aquaculture in 1986; he farmed on Crescent Beach tide lands leased from a private owner. At first with "line oysters" (oysters raised from seed with several on one shell and then transferred to lines) and later with bags on racks, which produce a better half-shell presentation oyster.

> Each bag-and-rack platform will be half the size of a 4-foot-by-eight-foot plywood sheet. Uncoated metal rebar racks will support plastic mesh bags for up to 100 oysters each and will sit 12 inches off the reef bottom. The racks will begin as close as 100 feet from the road right-of-way and extend up to 600 feet south.
>
> *The Journal of the San Juan Islands* April 14, 1993

After the death of Bawden and his wife Char (Charlene) in 2017, Geddes Martin, Mike O'Connell, and Pete Steverson purchased the operation. Currently, under Martin and Steverson, they produce about a million oysters a year, catering to the Orcas Island community and restaurants as well as shipping produce to as far away as New York and Las Vegas.

Jones Family Farms has a shellfish operation, originally called Sweetwater Shellfish Farm, on the north end of Lopez Island at Shoal Bay. The site, which they purchased in 2004, is ringed by shell middens that bear witness to past harvests; it consists of a three-acre tidal lagoon with a freshwater spring and three acres of tide lands. The lagoon, which had been a marsh that was enlarged and deepened with machinery, was once separated from the bay by a tidal gate. With an environmental restoration grant, the gate was removed so that the waters could once again circulate. Both European Flat and Olympia oysters are raised entirely in the lagoon; Pacific oysters are started there and finished in the tide lands. The Joneses ship their oysters throughout the United States.

Mark and Toni Sawyer opened Buck Bay Shellfish Farm in 2008, on Mark's family farm on Orcas Island. The farm produces oysters and clams, which you can buy raw, and serves these and Dungeness crab and local caught fish at their bayside bistro.

The shellfish industry is heavily regulated by agencies such as the U.S. Army Corps of Engineers and the Food and Drug Administration; the Washington State Departments of Health, Natural Resources, and Ecology, Fish and Wildlife; and the San Juan County Health Department. The Washington State Health Department tests the shellfish each week and the growing waters bimonthly for Paralytic Seafood Poisoning (PSP) from "Red Tide," a discoloration of seawater caused by a bloom of toxic red algae.

Scallops

Both pink and spiny scallops were first commercially harvested by divers in the Salish Sea from 1982 to 1998. Due to overharvesting, the season was closed by the Washington State Department of Fish and Wildlife until 2016, when they restarted it. In Washington State, nearly all commercially harvested scallops are taken in the San Juan Islands. While the 2020–2021 season is currently closed, the quota for the last season recorded (2018–2019) was set at 4,524 pounds.

Abalone

Indigenous peoples harvest abalone both for consumption and use of the shells for jewelry. Although pinto abalone have historically never been recognized as a commercial fishery by Washington State, in modern times scuba divers have harvested them in the Salish Sea, particularly in the San Juans, the Strait of Juan de Fuca, and the Strait of Georgia. The Washington State Department of Fish and Wildlife set a bag limit of five per diver, but some 40,000 were harvested annually from 1980 to 1992. At that point, because of declining numbers, the bag limit was dropped to three, but the population continued to decline, prompting the State to declare it an endangered species in 2019. Part of the problem was poachers, one of whom admitted to harvesting between 25,000 and 40,000 pintos alone. In Canada, all abalone fisheries were closed in British Columbia in 1990, and in 1999 abalone became the first invertebrate to be listed as Threatened by the Canadian Committee on the Status of Endangered

Wildlife. Today the pinto abalone is functionally extinct in the San Juans, in that it does not have a sufficient population to naturally reproduce.

Octopus

There are several accounts of fishermen encountering octopus, or "devil fish" as fishermen called them prior to modern times, either in their traps and nets or just near where they were fishing. Beryl Troxell Mason, in her reminiscences of her father, John Franklin Troxell, has some photos of devil fish taken from near their dock on Lopez, saying that they "were far too old and tough to make good eating—and no one but purse seiners from Trieste or Croatians from Anacortes would eat octopus." The March 31, 1906, *The San Juan Islander*, reported that Bruce Willis had caught a 50-pound devil fish, adding that "They are the most unappetizing looking creatures but the meat is really a delicacy. Wholesale fish dealers in Seattle pay two cents a pound for them." About the same time three years later, the paper noted that one had been caught in the net of a shrimp steamer. After making similar disparaging comments about its appearance, the paper went on to say that "devil fish find ready sale in the Seattle markets at six cents a pound, Chinese and Japanese being the principal purchasers. The tissue, while quite tough in the raw state, is said to be very palatable when properly cooked." It appears that fishermen did not go out of their way to fish for them.

Sea Urchins

Non-tidal zone harvest of sea urchins for *uni*, their reproductive organs, which are highly prized in the restaurant market, is a fairly recent phenomenon—red sea urchins since 1978 and green sea urchins since 1986—resulting from the invention of modern diving equipment. Most divers use surface-supplied air systems: "hookah" air lines connected to compressors aboard their boats. While the diver scours an urchin bed, fighting strong currents, the crew member on board manages the air pump and struggles to keep the boat from hitting rocks or the shore. The harvest is hauled up in a 200-pound net by power winch and

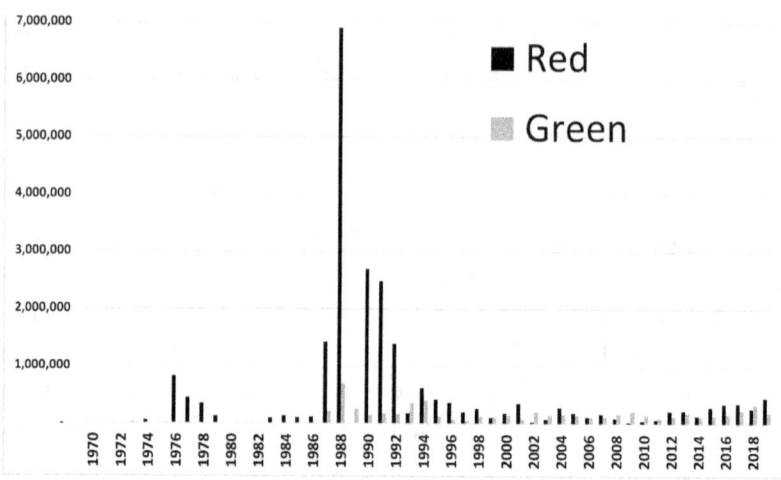

Red and Green Sea Urchin Catch (in pounds), San Juan Islands, 1970–2019

covered from exposure to rain, because freshwater will spoil the urchins. A typical daily catch can be around 1,200 pounds. The Washington Department of Fish and Wildlife has established Marine Protection Areas for non-tribal recreational and commercial fishermen (with most of the treaty tribes accepting this limitation) for both sea urchins and sea cucumbers in three areas in the San Juan Islands: a portion of Haro Strait from Lime Kiln to Cattle Point; San Juan and Upright Channels, from Jones Island to the north to Friday Harbor; and Turn Island to the south. The Department sets the harvest at 4% of the estimated biomass, and good divers are careful not to overharvest their beds. The San Juan Islands' harvest is the largest in Washington State, and most of it is shipped directly to Japan. With the exception of a huge spike in the period from 1987–1992, the annual Salish Sea commercial harvest has ranged from 230,000–650,000 pounds. Current 2020–2021 Washington Department of Fish and Wildlife District 1 (San Juan Island Area) quotas, subject to minimum size limits, are 175,000 pounds for green and 151,000 for red sea urchins.

Sea Cucumbers

The non-tidal zone harvest of sea cucumbers is also a product of modern diving equipment. The principal market for *hoisam* is China, where the skin and muscles are used in cooking and medicine. Wild harvest in Alaska and the Pacific Northwest fetches good prices because the Asian region is largely overfished, and aquaculture is the main source of sea cucumbers in China. Annual commercial sea cucumber harvest in the San Juans, relatively non-existent prior to a huge spike in 1991–1993, has leveled out to a range of 200,000–640,000 pounds, or an average of 480,000. The 2020–2021 Washington Department of Fish and Wildlife sea cucumber quota for District 1 (San Juan Island Area), which is now closed, was 114,000 pounds.

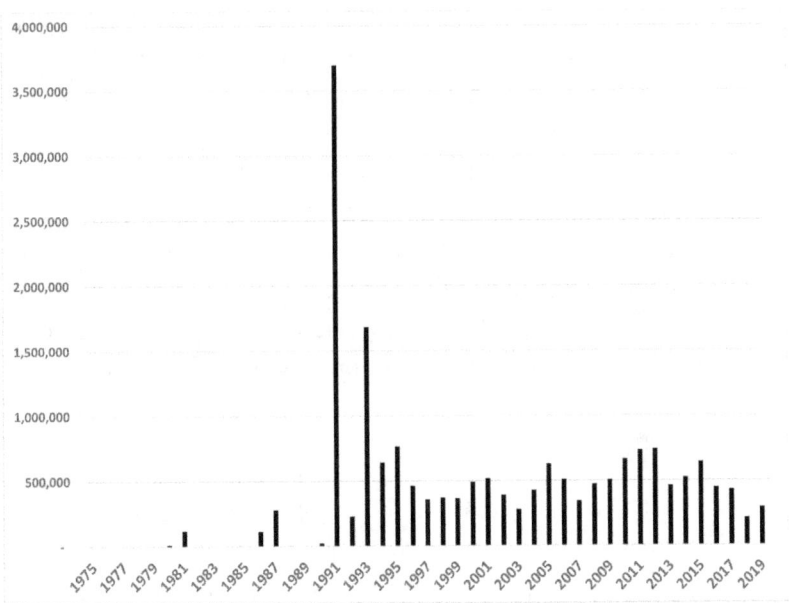

Sea Cucumber Catch (in pounds), San Juan Islands, 1975–2019

PRESERVATION AND MARKETING

Salting and Smoking

Prior to the 1890s, when canneries were established in the Salish Sea region, pickling (salting) or smoking were the principal means of preserving fish and other seafood. The main method was to remove the head, tail, and viscera of the fish and, after soaking it in saltwater, packing it with salt in a barrel. The number of salmon per barrel varied by species: 10–14 for Chinook, 25–30 for chum, 25–35 for coho, 40–52 for sockeye, and 70–80 for humpback.

> In dressing salmon for pickling the heads are removed, the fish split along the belly, the cut ending with a downward curve at the tail. The viscera and two thirds of the backbone are removed, and the blood gurry, and black stomach membrane scraped away. The fish are then scrubbed and washed in cold water. They are next placed in pickling butts with about 15 pounds of salt for every 100 pounds of fish. The fish remain here for about one week, when they are removed, rubbed clean with a scrub brush and repacked in market barrels, one sack of salt being used for every three barrels of 200 pounds each.
>
> — John N. Cobb, *The Salmon Fisheries of the Pacific Coast* (1911)

Barreling was the ordinary shipping method for preserved food at the time. Standard barrel sizes derive from the British measurement system based on the tun, which contained 210 imperial gallons or 252 U.S. gallons. A butt is a half tun (130 U.S. gallons), a tercian or puncheon a third tun (84 U.S. gallons), a hogshead a quarter tun (63 U.S. gallons), a tierce a sixth tun (42 U.S. gallons), and a barrel an eighth tun (32 U.S. gallons).

Many accounts of local salting operations mention shipment of empty barrels from cooperages in regional cities. In 1911 N. E. Churchill advertised that he had "fish barrels" in 200-, 100-, and 50-pound sizes for sale at his Friday Harbor store. (Some salting facilities packed their mild salmon in tierces that weighed 300 pounds.)

The Hudson's Bay Company began pickling salmon locally; they first traded for fish caught by Coast Salish in the seasons of 1851 and 1852 and continued to do so after the establishment of Belle Vue Sheep Farm in 1853 on San Juan Island. At the Great Northern Fish Company, of Seattle, William H. Thompson, manager, salted down and barreled salmon at both Mitchell Bay on San Juan Island and Richardson on Lopez Island, starting in 1898. A year later the Great Northern Fish Company built a new wharf at Mitchell Bay, and operations continued through 1900.

In the early 1900s, Captain R. E. Davis salted barrels of the salmon that he had caught with traps; newspaper articles note his extensive production (440 barrels) at Richardson on Lopez Island during August of 1901. Richardson also seems to have been the site of a smoking operation established by Graham and Hodgson around the turn of the last century.

There were two types of smoked salmon: mild and hard. Both types entailed a continuation of the process of pickling. The fish were taken out of the pickling barrels and soaked to remove as much of the salt as possible. They were then attached on the skin side to a "bacon hanger"—a framework of wires that had "six or more points bent at right angles to the frame, terminating at the top in a hook." Each of these was hung from a round stick in the smoker. When the smoker was fully loaded, a small fire of non-resinous wood was built underneath. The fire was then maintained so as to provide more smoke and less heat, so that the fish was cured with the smoke rather than cooked by the heat. "Mild" smoking lasted about 8–10 hours.

Hard smoking was used when the product took more time to market. Following the process above, the pieces of salmon are kept longer over the fire in order to dry them thoroughly; this usually took about two days. They were then cured with a dense smoke produced by smothering the fire with sawdust, with the ventilator partially closed; this gave the pieces a dark color. As with mild cured salmon, the pieces were removed from the hangers, wrapped in oiled paper, and packed in wooden boxes holding 30 pounds each.

Salmon, particularly Chinook, were also kippered. This light-colored fish was cut into one-pound pieces—about six inches long and three inches wide—and soaked in a vegetable dye to give it a reddish appearance—a concession to public expectation. The pieces were placed on trays of ½" wire mesh; these trays were placed on racks that could be wheeled into the smokers. They were smoked for 16–18 hours over a medium fire and then, the fire having been fed, they were back for 25–35 minutes at 250–275°F. The product was perishable, so it had to be refrigerated if kept for a long time.

Individuals also smoked salmon (along with other meats such as beef and pork) for personal use. On old farmsteads throughout the San Juan Islands one can still see tall (too tall to be an outhouse), narrow wood structures with vents in their roofs.

Here, Tommy, is how to build a smokehouse…

Build a tight little house about 2 by 3 by 6 feet high. It will hold six trays of inch [1" mesh] chicken wire. The door should fit tightly. Hinge it at the top.

Now build a fire tube underground about four feet long. At the entrance, set in a flue lining for the firebox—Mr. Raney's is about 8 by 10. He used a terra cotta tile section about 3 feet long from the firebox to the house through which the smoke goes. Now build your fire of green alder, keep it going low and steady for 10 hours to kipper your salmon, lower still for two days to smoke it. When the house is built, all you have to do is catch the salmon to fill it.

—June Burn, "29: How to Build a Salmon-Kippering House," *100 Days in the San Juans* (1946)

There were several commercial smokeries in the San Juan Islands. The Thomas brothers established a herring smokery consisting of two 60-foot-long smokehouses on Fishery Point on Waldron Island in the 1890s. In 1899 the Red Cross Fish Company built a herring packing plant at Mitchell Bay on San Juan Island. The manager, Max Johnson, also kippered herring and salmon there, claiming that this was first time it had been done on the Pacific Coast. Unfortunately, on March 12, 1900, the packing and smokehouse burned.

Early in 1909, *The San Juan Islander* noted that the Friday Harbor Canning Company was going to use the plant of the Island Packing Company in Friday Harbor for the "salting and shipping of fresh fish," under the supervision of George McIllroy. For supplies, the company had placed an order for 1,000 barrels and was receiving 100 tons of salt from San Francisco via the *Archer*.

One of the principal Seattle buyers of fresh salmon for smoking was the Chlopeck Fish Company, founded by brothers Con (Conrad) and Ed (Edward). They would buy fresh local salmon, ship them to their plant in Seattle, and then salt them. In a September 28 article in *The San Juan Islander* reviewing their 1907 season, the paper noted that the Chlopeck Fish Company had put up 750 tierces of mild cured salmon and 2,500 barrels of humpbacks. It noted that they were packed in refrigerator cars and shipped directly to the East.

On September 26, *The San Juan Islander* published the *Pacific Fisherman*'s review of 1913, entitled "Light Season for Mild Cure on Sound": "Taken altogether the Puget Sound mild cure pack will not total 3500 tierces this year." The *Fisherman* mentioned five main firms putting up mild salmon—the San Juan Fishing and Packing Company, the Chlopeck Fish Company, Everett Fish Company, Eggers Fish Company (Tacoma), and the Pacific American Fisheries in Bellingham—as well as two individuals—John Emmo and J. Foss. The fish were "Obtained from the San Juan Islands, on the South Shore to the Strait from Port Townsend out."

Salmon on the Friday Harbor Packing Company Floor with "Iron Chink" (courtesy of San Juan Historical Museum)

Canning

Canning became the principal method of preserving seafood during the last quarter of the nineteenth century. Canning seafood began on the West Coast in 1864 when brothers William and George Hume, together with tinsmith Andrew Hapgood—all from Maine—started a cannery on the Sacramento River. After depletion of the runs there, in 1866 they moved north to Washington Territory, where they established a small cannery on a scow on the Columbia River, near Eagle Cliff in eastern Wahkiakum County. Soon the Columbia River became the foremost salmon canning center on the West Coast. In 1877, George T. Myers constructed a small cannery in Mukilteo; he later moved the operation to Samish and then to the foot of Blanchard Street on the Seattle waterfront. He finally moved to the foot of Dearborn Street, where he operated as G. T. Myers and Company until his death in 1933. Only a few canneries—mainly in the southern portion of Puget Sound—operated in the Salish Sea region prior to 1890. With the success of fish traps in the Port Roberts area, a cannery was built at Semiahmoo in 1891, followed by another at Point Roberts two years later. By 1900 there were 19 in the region, six of which were in Anacortes and 11 in Whatcom County, another at Point Roberts, three each at Blaine and Fairhaven, and one each at Chuckanut and Lummi Island. Five years later, the *Pacific Fisherman* noted that there were 139 canneries in Alaska and Puget Sound.

*Women Working on the Packing Line
(courtesy of San Juan Historical Museum)*

Prior to 1900, most of the process of canning was done by hand. Workers would arrive in early spring to start manufacturing cans, which were cut, shaped, and soldered together in a separate facility. Salmon came in seasonal runs; when they were running, the canneries operated at full capacity, with fish literally piled several feet deep on the floor awaiting processing. The salmon, after being delivered, were slimed (the fins, viscera, and blood removed), and then sent to the butchers, who removed their heads and tails and gutted them. A row of "gang knives" cut the fish into proper sizes and passed them along to the workers who packed the cans. These rows formed "lines" in the cannery, so canneries were classified by their number of lines.

*Salmon Cans Stacked in Warehouse
(courtesy of San Juan Historical Museum)*

> The tin plate being squared in the square shears, was then cut into proper sized pieces for can bodies, and eight of these pieces in a bunch were passed through the can forming machine (consisting of three steel rollers) and rolled into shape. Eight of these rolls were taken at time by each Chinaman working at the seamer bench, and by him one tine at a time placed on the seamer cylinder (each Chinaman having a set of two each cylinders at his bench) in a way so that the two edges of the tin would come tightly together, and be held under the edge of a thick piece of slate, held in a frame over the cylinder, and raised off of the cylinder by a spring.
>
> A drop of solder and a particle of rosin being placed on the seam next to the slate was evenly distributed over the seam by a hot seaming copper made for that purpose… The can was then seamed on the inside by a man or boy having a pointed copper, and from him it went to the bottom table. The bottom edge of the tin being dipped into a dish or vessel contain a piece of netting or waste saturated with acid, then the bottom was placed on it, and a cut drop of solder dripped into the can, then it was ready for the floater, as the man was termed whose work it was to solder on the bottoms. The floating was done by inserting a specially made copper into the can. The copper was flared at the end so that it was semi-circular at its edge, and it enabled the floater to perform his work very quickly. As soon as the cans were made they were taken to the reamer to have the top edge reamed out and then piled up ready for use.
>
> —T. E. P. Keegan, "Old and Modern Ways of Canning Salmon," *Pacific Fisherman* vol.1, no.1 (1904)

The cans were wiped clean and the tops sealed; after being tested for leaks in the "bathroom," the cans were conveyed to kettles where they were boiled for several hours. Workers stamped a small hole in each can to vent the air, and then they were boiled in another kettle for two hours. Removed from this, they were washed with caustic soda and allowed to cool and then lacquered and labeled. The standard case of canned salmon—usually wooden boxes called "shooks"—contained 48 one-pound cans, and it took about 10–12 six-pound fish to fill a case. In 1902, a case sold for about $3.50.

> From there the fish would flop on their back and slide into the Iron Chink...and were grabbed by a pointed set of spears at the tail and dragged through a series of knives and brushes that did about 85% of the cleaning of the fish.
>
> This was the machine I ran for a few consecutive summers. It was a loud circular crashing and clanging machine that spluttered and tossed fish guts in a hollow for 10 feet around it. This means that the entire time the machine was on, I in my rain gear was being splattered by the evisceration of thousands of fish. I used to laugh to myself when I thought of what my parents would say if they saw me. All those years of worry and money put toward educating me and here I was spending 18 hour days covered in fish guts for some $3.50 an hour.
>
> — Jim Lawrence, *Callused Hands Hungry Heart: Memoir of a Fisherman-Farmer* (2011)

In the early 1900s, various aspects of the canning process became mechanized. In 1903, Edmund A. Smith, along with John W. Haubner, invented a machine that could gut and clean salmon at a rate of 110 fish per minute, as compared to an experienced worker's two per minute. Because the invention took the place of the many Chinese who were willing to do this work that white workers shunned at a far lower wage, Smith called it the "Iron Chink." Machines that produced the cans soon followed. The fish, after passing through the Iron Chink, went to a mechanized set of gang knives that cut up the salmon into proper sizes. Machines then placed the fish pieces in the cans and soldered on covers.

After testing, six coolers were placed on a car, which was wheeled by track into a steam box that did the first cooking. After being tested for hot leaks, the coolers were again placed on cars and rolled into steam retorts, where they underwent the second

Advertisement for "The Iron Chink"
(Pacific Fisherman)

> *Near the door, trays of shining cans were fed empty, one by one, into the bottom of a machine which received from a conveyor belt at the top, the cleaned, beheaded, betailed, befinned salmon. Within this machine, the filler, a razor-sharp cutting blade sliced the fish to fit the cans. The cuts of salmon were moved along on a revolving belt, as were the cans on another belt simultaneously, until they met and fish fitted into can mechanically. Full cans passed then through a closing machine and onto great trays to be conducted, stacked carefully so they would heat evenly, into the steam retort for cooking.*
>
> — Caroline Reed,
> Underpinning: A Vivid Recollection of Life in Washington State in the Early Part of This Century (1989)

cooking. Both the cleaning with caustic soda and subsequent lacquering were done in large vats, the latter handling 1,500 cases a day. Labeling machines could handle up to 1,000 cases a day. Adoption of the "sanitary can," entirely made by machine with one-piece lids that only had to be crimped, came later, around 1913. All this mechanization saved considerable labor power.

Labor for the canneries came from Indigenous peoples and immigrant groups who could be hired at the lowest wages: first Chinese, then Japanese, and later Filipinos. On March 23, 1906,

> *As hot cans came from the retorts, a gob of solder dropped over each tiny steam vent to form a vacuum in the cooling process, and the trays were lifted upstairs to cool. There the expert Chinese testers bent swiftly over each, tapping and listening. Their little chopstick-like testing rods fluttered like birds' wings as, with a minimum of movement, they fussed over hot cans rapping and listening with their specially trained sense, here and there tossing out a can.*
>
> — Caroline Reed,
> Underpinning: A Vivid Recollection of Life in Washington State in the Early Part of This Century (1989)

Loading the Retorts
(courtesy of San Juan Historical Museum)

Bert Coffin, who canned clams alongside them, commented in his journal, "These Indians are good workers, having worked in salmon canneries for several seasons on the British side."

Before the Island Packing Company was established in 1894, permission was sought from the "white" citizens of Friday Harbor to allow "Celestials" to work there—but only seasonally. Nevertheless, the Chinese paid taxes, worked on road crews, and even participated in local events such as the Fourth of July celebrations. At the time the Pacific American Fisheries bought the Island Packing Company in 1899, there were 80 Chinese and Japanese and 70 white workers. Chun Ching (also called Chin Chun or Chin Ching) Hock was the first labor contractor for Chinese workers in the islands. Arriving in San Francisco when he was 16, Chun came to Seattle and first worked for the Yesler Mill but soon established his own mercantile store, the Wa Chong Company. Chun was paid in cash or with real estate for each worker and in the early 1900s owned land to the north of Friday Harbor, which he eventually sold to J. A. Gould, a cannery owner and founder of the San Juan County Bank. The Salmon Bank Can-

> The butchering and sliming of the fish -- work repugnant to the white man -- may now be done by machinery. The first machine, the Iron Chink, has displaced a considerable percentage of labor. The name of the machine is obvious and indicates the character of its work. It slits the fish, cuts off the fins and removes the entrails. Operated by four men it can butcher enough fish in one day of ten hours for 1,600 cases of forty-eight cans each, or an increase of fifty to seventy-five per cent for each man over the hand method, at the same time making the work much easier....
>
> —Special Report on the Salmon Canning Industry of the State of Washington as Relating to the Employment of White Labor, Made by the State Commissioner of Labor (1915)

ning Company at Richardson on Lopez Island contracted with the Wa Chong Company for Chinese workers, guaranteeing two months of labor for $70–$140 per month.

After Pacific American Fisheries Manager E. B. Deming met Seattle businessman Goon Dip at the Alaska-Yukon-Pacific Exposition on China Day (September 13, 1909), Goon became the sole labor contractor for the PAF, at first with Chinese workers. Later Goon Dip contracted with Japanese workers, designating some as subcontractors and foremen in order to bridge the language gap. Tension developed between the Chinese and Japanese, particularly when the latter had to serve under the former. After 1910, Japanese workers in the Salish Sea region began to break away from the Chinese-dominated contractor system and organize for themselves. San Juan Island resident Koheiji "Jack" Saoka, who first came to the island in 1917 and worked at the Island Packing Company, eventually became a supervisor because of his language skill, and even established a florist business on the side with his wife Yuki in Friday Harbor. (They were relocated to an internment camp on the mainland in 1942.) During the 1920s and 1930s, immigrants from the Philippines—"Alaskeros"—con-

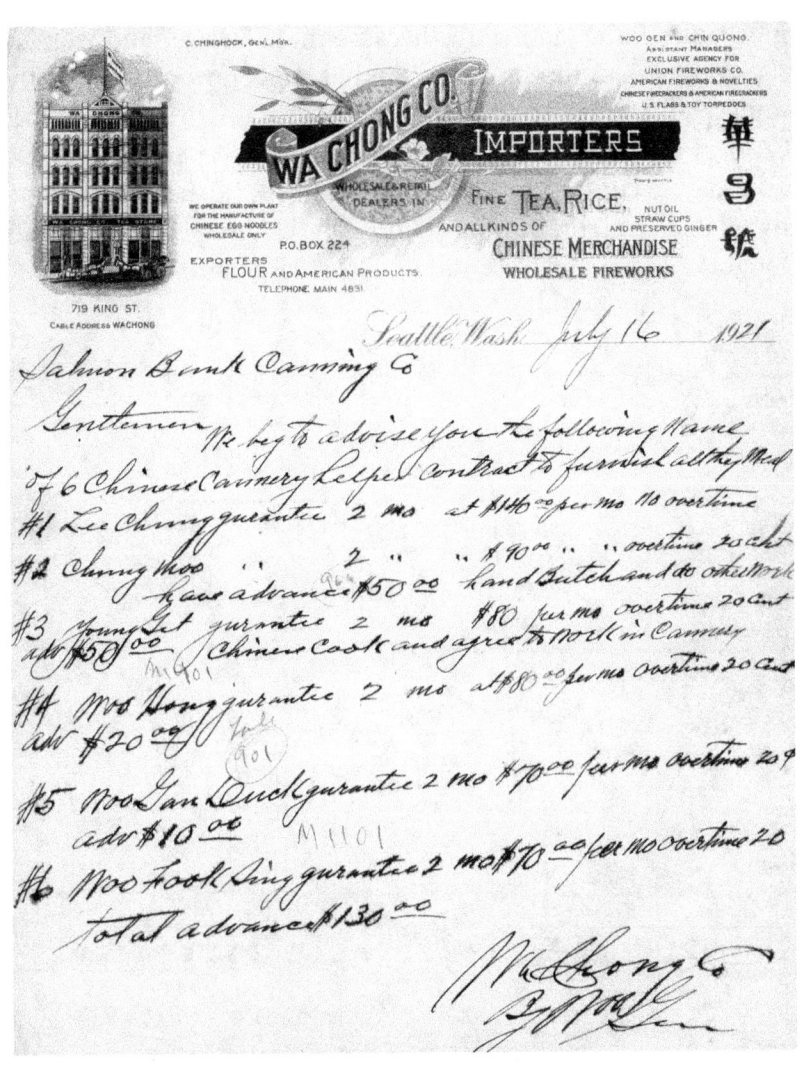

*Wa Chong Company Labor Invoice
(courtesy of Lopez Island Historical Society)*

tracted out to canneries, mainly in Alaska, where most of the Pacific salmon industry had shifted. After the building of Jackson Cannery in the 1950s, some of the workers there were Filipino.

Early on, in most canneries the Chinese did the hard and messy work of cutting off the tails and heads, gutting the fish, and operating the machines, while local Euro American women hand-packed the salmon in cans. As canning became more mechanized, the labor force became more "white" and women took on more of the jobs. Despite this, women were consistently underpaid compared to men: for instance, in 1910 at the PAF cannery in Bellingham, women were paid $1.50 per day for a 10-hour day, in contrast to $2.50 for men. In 1911, Washington State mandated an eight-hour day (which the canning companies had fought), but women were still underpaid well into the 1970s.

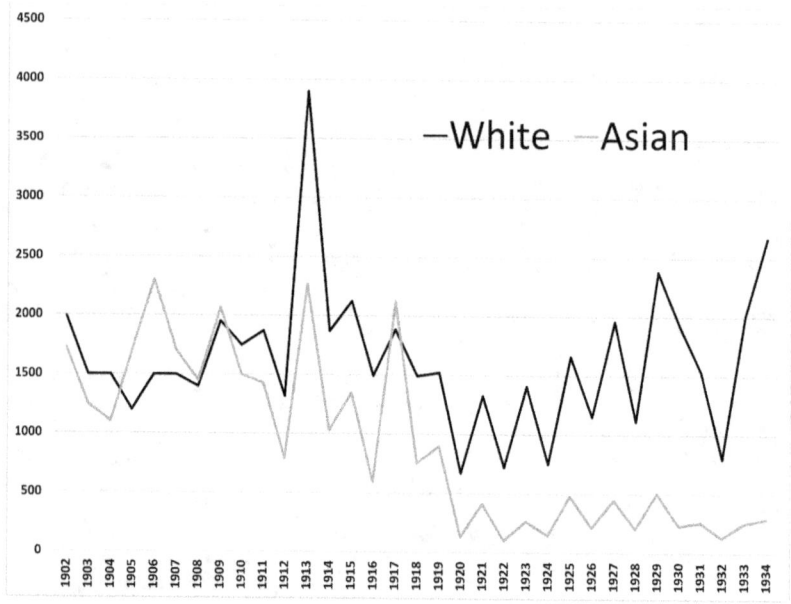

Ethnicity of Cannery Workers in Washington State, 1902–1935

Cannery workers often stayed at dormitories or boarding houses near the canneries. "Foreign" workers, such as the Chinese and Japanese, had their own, segregated dormitories: there was a "Chinese Boarding House" on the shore to the south of the main Island Packing Company cannery in Friday Harbor and a "China House" on Davis Head near Richardson, Lopez Island. Later, a large "Jap House" is indicated on the 1930 Sanborn Insurance Company map of the Friday Harbor Packing Company, on the slope above the main cannery facility. In Deer Harbor, Henry

Women Cannery Workers, Wander Inn, Richardson, Lopez Island
(courtesy of Lopez Island Historical Society)

Cayou's cannery allegedly had a bunk house/cook house for the Chinese, Filipinos, and even Hawaiians who worked there. While some rations were provided by their labor brokers—during the 1899 packing season, the commissary Goo Shung advertised for "little pigs" in *The San Juan Islander*—to supplement their diet, Chinese would often establish gardens to grow vegetables near the boarding house or on leased land. Women who worked as packers either camped near the canneries or stayed at boarding houses like the "Wander Inn" near Richardson.

The first cannery in the islands was the Island Packing Company (IPC), established in 1894 near the current ferry dock in Friday Harbor. After improvements in 1896 and 1898, the Pacific American Fisheries Company bought the IPC, renaming it the Friday Harbor Packing Company (FHPC), and built a new cannery building 50 by 100 feet and two stories high.

OUR SALMON CANNERY

Messrs. [John] Develin and [F. W.] Keene first came to the Sound some time in April on their way to Stuarts island, having heard that the salmon passed that island on their way to the Fraser river. By chance they met Sheriff Thomas, who induced them to stop at Friday Harbor. After looking the ground over they decided that our county seat was a suitable place to locate. But the question arose "will the citizens of San Juan island allow us to bring chinamen to work in the canne[r]y which we propose to build?" A meeting was called at the court house hall, to get the sentiment of the people on this question, and it was found that the people of Friday Harbor and vicinity were almost unanimously in favor of allowing the cannery—chinamen and all, provided, that, the company would pledge themselves that the mongolians would leave just as soon as the canning season was over. ...If we let the pig-tailed celestials get a foothold in San Juan County, we will have no body but ourselves to blame.

—The Islander, July 5, 1894

In 1908, William Shultz, George J. Willey, and W. E. Persell incorporated the FHPC and leased the facility from the PAF. Four years later, the FHPC rebuilt the cannery into a huge, 300' x 250' structure. Meanwhile, in 1910 they had purchased the adjoining wharf and warehouse from local merchant N. E. Churchill. William Shultz ran the cannery until his death in 1925; George Willey took over as principal owner and manager until his retirement in 1935. Closed intermittently in the 1950s, it was used for canning peas and strawberries during late 1950s and early 1960s; it closed permanently in 1964.

On October 23, 1895, R. C. Kinleyside, J. A. Gould, and C. A. Phelps filed for articles for incorporation for the Oceanic Canning Company, proposing to build a cannery at Richardson, Lopez Island. At first, Charles A. Phelps was the general manager; eventually, Thomas E. Ladner, with canneries at Ladner's

Landing, B.C., became the general manager. Construction began in November of 1895 to prepare for the 1896 season. The buildings included a 40-by-100-foot house for storing the nets, a 30-by-60-foot mess house, and a wharf that measured 50 by 200 feet. Netting and twine were ordered from the American Net and Twine Company of Boston, six scows were built for the operations, and the steamer *San Juan*, steered by Captain Hanson,

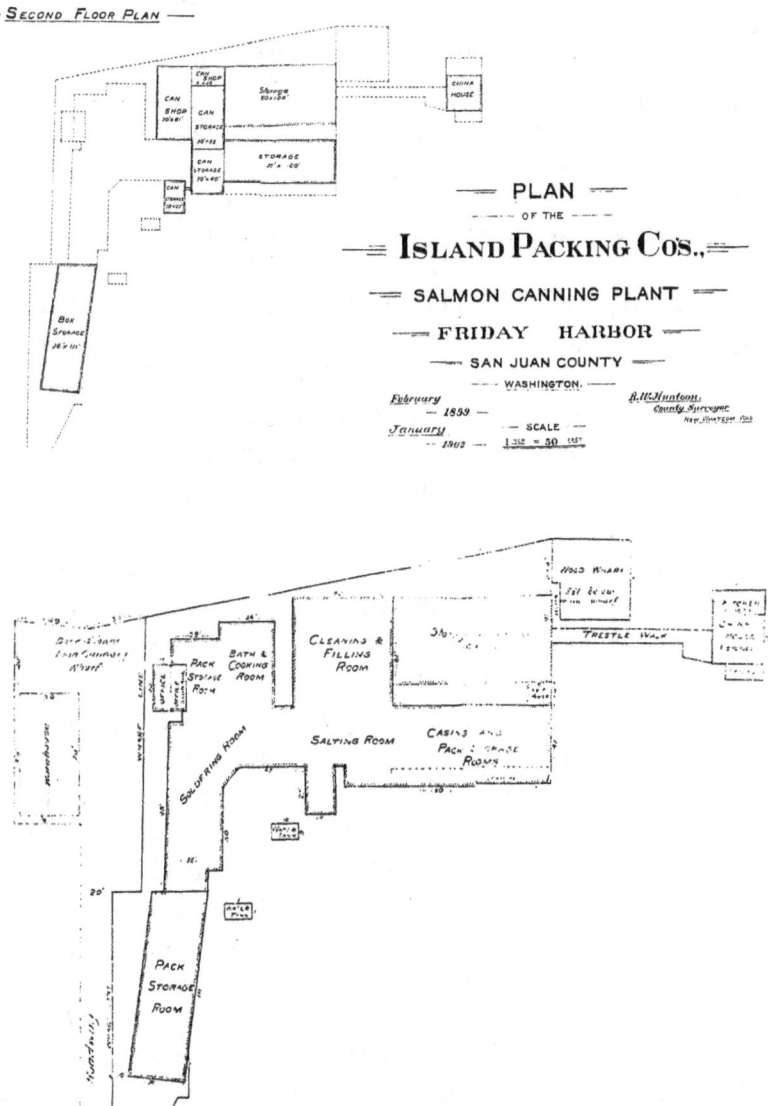

Friday Harbor Packing Company with Fishing Boats and Nereid
(courtesy of San Juan Historical Museum)

was brought up from Seattle. Just a few years later (1898) the newspapers noted the sale of the company's pile driver as well as the relocation of their scows to Canada. It also reported that "three scows, three seine boats, three purse seiners and some other fishing gear" were being brought from Canada for fishing near Lummi Island.

John Broder, who had established a creamery on the Friday Harbor waterfront in 1901, sold a half interest to George Mead in 1903, and they built a cannery for clams and fruit on the waterfront at the base of West Street. In 1905, their Island Packing Company was reorganized as a joint-stock company, with Broder as president, Mead as secretary, L. B. Carter as treasurer, and E. H. Nash as general manager. They built a large addition to accommodate a salmon-canning plant and extended the wharf by 40 feet. In late 1912 the *Journal* noted that articles of incorporation had been filed for the San Juan Canning Company, whose officers were Joseph S. Groll, president and manager, John Haubner, vice president, and E. H. Nash, secretary and treasurer, to be located on the Friday Harbor waterfront. Then, *The San Juan Islander* stated that Groll was in Seattle arranging for machinery and contracting for "oriental labor" for a new "San Juan Packing Company," and in February of the following year it was being erected. Anticipating its imminent opening, *The Islander* described it as a two liner with a projected capacity of 1,600 cases per day; the main floor space was 80 by 172 feet, with a smaller

> *San Juan county promises soon to lead all the counties of the state in the number of salmon canneries and the amount and value of the product. It is understood that the capacity of the Island Packing Co.'s plant here is to be considerably increased in the spring; the work of driving piles for the foundation of the Oceanic Canning Co.'s plant at Richardson is well under way, and it is reported that ground had been purchased upon which a large cannery will be erected near Roche Harbor. Let the good work go on. There is plenty of room and there are myriads of fishes in the briny deep to supply the canneries.*
>
> —*The Islander*, December 12, 1895

(30-by-110-foot) space used for office and storeroom. Later in the year (July 4) the paper mentioned that the plant was up and running. This cannery processed salmon until the 1920s, when it canned peas; it was torn down in the 1940s.

Several more canneries were built on Lopez Island about the same time. In 1901, Irene Weeks sold land to "Anacortes parties" for a 40-by-75-foot cannery, principally for fruit, but also clams and crab. In 1907, S. M. Bugge, who had taken over the Island Packing Company in Friday Harbor, organized and incorporated the Tuana Packing Company on Lopez in 1907 (according to Bugge, Tuana was the name of an Indigenous tribe in Jefferson County). The principal pack were clams, which were obtained from the surplus brought to Friday Harbor by Indigenous peoples from British Columbia, as well as from Port Townsend.

Two other canneries—the Hodgson-Graham and the Hidden Inlet Cannery—were built at Richardson, Lopez Island, in 1913. The Hodgson-Graham Cannery, also called the Salmon Bank Cannery, was built in time for the fishing season that year; Angus McGuire was the president. A two-line cannery with a capacity of 1,400 cans a day, the main building was 80 by 100 feet with an adjacent building measuring 40 by 66 feet; there was also a boarding house for workers. In 1916, N. P. Hodgson sold the cannery to Ira Lundy. It burned down in February 1922. The Hidden Inlet Cannery, owned by a company of Englishmen and managed by F. J. Comeau, was built in the summer of 1913. The cannery itself, constructed on rock, was 30 by 150 feet, and ran two lines (although in 1914 the May 14 edition of The San Juan Islander noted that it would only operate one line that season). Apparently, it shut down in 1922, soon after the Hodgson-Graham Cannery burned down.

During the 1910s other canneries were built in the islands. In April of 1912, the Shaw Island Canning Company was incorporated by businessmen from Bellingham for the "business of fishing and canning all sea animals and…also…fruits and vegetables." A cannery was constructed on Blind Bay and the next year (1913) packed 5,400 cases of salmon.

Canneries at Richardson, Lopez Island
(courtesy of Lopez Island Historical Society)

Hodgson-Graham Cannery, Richardson, Lopez Island
(courtesy of Lopez Island Historical Society)

Hidden Inlet Cannery with Fishing Boats
(courtesy of Lopez Island Historical Society)

*Salmon Canneries of the George W. Hume Co.
and Deer Harbor Fisheries Co., 1919
(John N. Cobb photographer)*

Around 1914 Henry Cayou built a facility on the west shore of Deer Harbor, called the "Red Cannery." The cannery was first operated under the name of The Orcas Island Canning Company; later it became known as the Deer Harbor Packing Company and the Orcas Packing Company. In the 1940s there were several liens upon the cannery for equipment and materials; eventually the mortgage company foreclosed on Joseph N. Dion and Sidney Blutreich, co-partners of Deer Harbor Packing Company, and the property, then owned by Sigmund Einstoss and the Orcas Packing Company, was sold in a sheriff's auction.

William J. Norton and Northern Pacific Fisheries built a cannery around 1917 on the east shore of Deer Harbor for the George W. Hume Company, subsequently called the "White Cannery." The Deer Harbor Fisheries Company was packing salmon there in 1919. In 1918 Northern Pacific Fisheries Company built a cannery on land purchased from William Norton and Henry Cayou at West Sound. Western Fisheries was operating his cannery when it burned down in August 1920; the next year, Western Fisheries leased the Deer Harbor Fisheries cannery. The cannery must have closed down and been demolished several years later.

In 1930 Norton established a floating cannery in Deer Harbor; it is not clear how long this lasted.

CANNERY BUILDING

1 Engine, steam, complete for front end operation

1 Engine, steam, complete for back end operation

5 wooden tables for hand packers

150 cooker trays

2 only hand trucks for retorts

4 only retorts

1 iron chink

1 small motor with direct connection to Main Line Power

1 ½# line packing machine complete

1 1# tall full line packing machine complete

(the last two items belong to Continental Can Co.)

OFFICE
BLACKSMITH SHOP
BOILER ROOM

BUILDINGS

1 Supt. Bldg., complete with running water

1 cook house

1 large rooming house

— Purchaser's Assignment of Real Estate Contract, Orcas Packing Company and Joseph N. Dion, June 1, 1953

A truckload of fish can come down the sandy road along the spit, unload at the big door, or a boat can come to the beach on the other side. From the first bin, the fish go to the cleaning and washing tables where they are also boned. From here to the brine tank overnight—it is the just-right salting that tells whether you're a good smoker or not. ...A hay fork covered with wire netting lifts the pieces of fish out of the brine onto racks on trucks. These are rolled into the smokehouse, stacked up in front of a big fan which distributes the smoke evenly around all the trays, and dries the salmon sufficiently as it smokes.

Outside this smokeroom, with a funnel leading into it, there is a common, everyday stove with stacks of dry alder, madrona, willow or maple—they do not like the tongue-bite of fish smoked with green wood of any sort and here again is an important point.

— June Burn, "90: Smoked Salmon for Your Lunch!"
100 Days in the San Juans (1946)

In 1948, John Jackson built a smokehouse for kippering and hand-packing salmon on what was known as Little Island, connected to Argyle Spit on San Juan Island at low tide. Two years later, he built Jackson Cannery and improved the road to Little Island. The 40–50 workers were mostly women (at a 3:1 ratio) and they did all of the hand-packing and were paid per can. In 1953, the Cannery bought three partially complete propeller-driven gill net boats from Instos Cannery at Deer Harbor, as well as parts for five more. The latter were converted into jet boats, which use a jet of water as propulsion, and used for gillnetting. After slowing down due to competition from fresh frozen salmon, Jackson Cannery was sold in the late 1970s.

The summer passed into fall and work at the cannery was all consuming when the wild sockeye salmon were running. Large vessels known as tenders swaggered, with their sterns dragging low, into the cannery at any hour of day or night bulging with fish. These boats were hired by the cannery to buy fish in the sheltered waters of the fish grounds and deliver them to the cannery, when full, where they were unloaded into brailer bags or conveyor belts and sluiced into the caverns of the canning facility.

There were concrete bulk headed rooms that were filled to capacity measuring 4 feet high and 30 feet by 30 feet where workers waist deep in fish pushed them with rakes toward gated troughs. Thousands of pounds of fish lay in these rooms waiting to be processed, their vacant eyes staring at the ceiling, life and spirit left in the ocean.

Sledded through a sluiceway onto a table known as an indexer, the fish were one by one conveyored side by side toward a revolving propeller-like blade that would decapitate each just behind the gill plate. This ghoulish invention would and could cut any finger or body part with relentless precision.

The fish were then dropped on to a table where they were grabbed by any of a dozen workers, known as slimers, and with knives they would clean the fish for the final trip toward cutters that segmented the fish to specific sizes so they would fit into either quarter pound or half pound tin cans.

Lids slid down log tracks and flipped face down onto the fully packed and slated cans of raw fish. The lids were sealed and the cans dropped into large wagon baskets that were wheeled on train tracks into enormous retorts or pressure cookers where they were subjected to extreme heat and cooked through. This process was loud, wet, messy and exhausting and we had shifts that lasted until the fish were all in cans.

There were no breaks except lunch and dinner, no overtime and I think my top wage was in the $4 an hour range. I remember a shift of 32 hours on the clock and many 18 and 20 hour days.

— Jim Lawrence, *Callused Hands Hungry Heart: Memoir of a Fisherman-Farmer* (2011)

Big Business

At the turn of the last century, the fishing industry in the Salish Sea began to coalesce into several large firms and tend toward monopoly conditions.

The Alaska Packers Association (APA) was consolidated in 1891 from 31 canneries, mainly to control the salmon-packing industry in Alaska. Henry Frederick Fortmann, owner of the Arctic Packing Company, one of the original member companies, served as APA president from its inception until 1922. In 1916, the APA merged with several principally Californian companies to become California Packing Corporation (CalPack), which was eventually reorganized as Del Monte. The APA was known for its "Star Fleet"—the last fleet of commercial sailing vessels on the West Coast. Although ostensibly rivals, the Pacific American Fisheries and the APA often worked in conjunction; for instance, one of the fish traps at Salmon Bank off San Juan Island was run by the APA, and the prominent feature on South Beach was known as "Alaska Packers Rock."

> At that time many critics who knew little of the value of the claims staked out in the watery Klondike of this matchless archipelago, declared that the Chicago capitalists had been fooled into paying most extravagant prices for their trap locations. One hears very little of that sort of talk now. If there are any who are still inclined to think that the shrewd Chicago packers who have made many millions in meat listened guilelessly to a fairy tale and recklessly invested their money upon the scaly basis of an ordinary fish story, they might perhaps be convinced of their error if they were able to make a bona fide offer of twice the amount which the company paid for the fishing rights that it acquired.
>
> —*The San Juan Islander*, September 7, 1899

Pacific American Fisheries (PAF) was incorporated in 1899 and soon became the largest trust operating fish traps and canneries in Washington State. The PAF was formed to take over the bankrupt Franco-American North Pacific Canning Company, which had been established by the entrepreneur (and schemer) Roland Onffroy in 1898. The company was incorporated in New Jersey with a capital of $5,000,000; the officers were a wholesale grocer, meatpacker, attorney, and several financiers—all from Chicago—and thus became known as the "Chicago Syndicate."

THE BIG FISH COMPANY

The Deal Closed and Work to Begin at Once in Earnest

The Pacific American Fisheries Company made the final payments on the traps, canneries, etc. and the property was turned over to the company Friday. By the terms of the sale Alsop Bros. received $90,000 for their traps, Wright Bros. $110,000, L. Pike $45,000, Shultz & Gross $30,000, Kildall Bros. $35,000 and the Island Packing Company $125,000. Of the foregoing San Juan County is particularly interested in Shultz & Gross and the Island Packing Company, both being residents of our county. Shultz & Gross operate their traps this year and receive the profits therefrom. The Island Packing Company, which is owned solely by F. W. Keen and J. A. Gould, will go out of business. It speaks well for our county that of the eighteen canneries on Puget Sound the Island Packing Company's cannery at Friday Harbor is the only one taken by the new company. There is no question but this plant has been the most successful in Washington and that owing to the personal supervision of Messrs. Keen and Gould it will also make large profits...

This is the largest deal ever consummated in this county and its final result means much more to us than anyone has yet dared to anticipate. It is estimated by those who are in a position to know, that at least $75,000 will be paid out for wages to men employed on the traps alone, say nothing of the thousands that will be paid to operatives in the cannery here and their general expenses...

— *The San Juan Islander*, April 6, 1899

The PAF not only bought the cannery in Bellingham and within a year doubled its size, it also purchased the Island Packing Company in Friday Harbor and then most of the fish traps in the Salish Sea. In this manner they were able to secure a monopoly of the salmon-canning market by expanding both horizontally and vertically: owning or controlling the canneries and ensuring the supply of fish from what were heretofore unreliable sources by controlling and owning the fish traps, as well as even supplying boats and gear to fishers.

> Up to the middle of last week the five traps of the Pacific American Fisheries Company on the salmon banks had caught, in round numbers, 867,000 fish, and now the number is doubtless considerably in excess of 1,000,000. At the same time the Anacortes Packing Company's big trap on the banks had caught over 250,000, and 300,000 would doubtless be a low estimate of its output up to date. In the big double trap at the south entrance to Mosquito pass, which Shultz & Gross sold last spring to the Pacific American Fisheries Company, reserving the fishing rights for this season, over 100,000 sockeyes and more than 300,000 humpbacks have been caught, and the catch for the entire season will undoubtedly exceed half a million, and that of all the eight traps mentioned at least 2,000,000.
>
> —*The San Juan Islander*, September 7, 1899

Because of their Chicago mercantile origins, company executives were also well familiar with food-distribution systems. The food brokerage firm of Deming and Gould, which had originated in St. Louis with Frank L. Deming, E. B. Deming, and William Gould and had expanded to Chicago, had originally handled the marketing for Onffroy's business; this led to the Chicago financial connection. E. B. "Ed" Deming became the PAF director in 1900 but was forced out of that role with Onffroy's reorganization of the business.

THE RECORD BROKEN

The Local Sockeye Pack Exceeds That of Any Other Year

30,000 CASES WORTH $135,000

Some Figures of Approximate Cost and Profit to Cannerymen This Year

...An idea of the profit derived from the operation of a cannery as favorably located and well equipped as the one here, when there is a big run of sockeyes, may be easily obtained. In the first place it is estimated that the actual cost of the fish, when taken from the traps equipped with "spillers," does not exceed 2½ cents each. Counting a dozen sockeyes to a case of forty-eight cans, the cost of the "raw material," per case, is only 30 cents. The canning process costs about 50 cents, and 80 cents more will cover cost of cans, cases and shipping, while 40 cents is probably a liberal estimate for taxes, insurance, repairs and incidentals. So it would seem that in an exceptional year like the present the total cost of salmon per case, where the supply is taken from traps numbered among the big producers, does not exceed $2, and the wholesale selling price does not vary much from $4.50... Stockholders in the big "combine," however, cannot reasonably expect to get dividends on the basis of such figures as those above given for the reason that the property acquired is capitalized for millions more than the original cost and princely salaries are paid to chief officials and heads of departments, the president's salary being equal to that of the president of the United States.

—The San Juan Islander, August 22, 1901

In 1901, Onffroy worked to establish an all-encompassing Alaskan and Pacific Northwest salmon trust, which included the PAF. On July 19, the Pacific Packing and Navigation Company (PP&N) was incorporated in New Jersey with $25,000,000 from eastern capital and local Bellingham bank loans. Despite his extensive efforts, the new corporation was not able to get control of the APA, which continued to produce canned salmon, principally in Alaska but also in the Puget Sound region. In 1902, the APA inaugurated a "Salmon War," when they underpriced their lower-grade salmon (but not their higher-grade red salmon), eventually forcing the PP&N, as well as the PAF, into receivership. Ed Deming, biding his time, bought up several canneries and fish traps and, when the PAF was auctioned off, made an offer to the winning bidder, which was unable to capitalize the bid, for the company on behalf of many of the original Chicago backers. Pacific American Fisheries was reincorporated in Portland, Maine, on Christmas Eve, 1904, with a capitalization of $1,500,000. Deming became the director and effectively ran the company, despite some challenging periods, until his death in 1942. In 1928, Pacific American Fisheries was reincorporated under the laws of Delaware as the Pacific American Company, a publicly held corporation with a capitalization of $7,500,000. This newly infused capital allowed for further expansion into Alaska, but also led to a change in approach to management, "in line with present-day ideas of business and finance." A year later the name was changed to Pacific American Fisheries, Inc., and was only changed back in 1961, five years before its demise.

The APA and the PAF proceeded to dominate the fish pack in the region referred to as "Puget Sound" (mainly the Salish Sea) and Alaska. In the period from 1905–1912, the PAF alone packed an annual average of 23% of the canned salmon in the Puget Sound region. Even though the PAF started expanding into Alaska, with its first cannery established at Chilkat in 1906, the APA and the PAF had what can only be termed a compatible competition, with their directors and presidents often consulting with each other, even to the point of price-fixing.

> ...see if you can get the A.P.A. to enter into such an agreement as they did last year, to wit: that we would name our prices [of sockeye salmon] together and neither one nor the other intimate the price futures until we had an opportunity to talk over the situation. ...This does not mean necessarily that we should both name the same price, but if we hang together as we did last year and before naming prices consult each other it will undoubtedly be to the interest of all concerned.
> — Frank Deming, correspondence with his brother Ed, 1906

Both firms expanded their monopolies vertically, from control of the fish supply by purchasing fish traps to buying can-manufacturing and wooden-case-making subsidiaries, to warehousing, shipping, and distributing concerns. At the same time, they expanded their canning operations throughout the Salish Sea and Alaska.

Several trade and professional organizations were founded in the early twentieth century to aid with the salmon-packing industry, such as the Puget Sound Packers Association and the Association of Pacific Fisheries. The National Canners Association was originally formed in 1907; in modern times, it has become the National Food Processors Association (1978) and then the National Food Products Association (2005). During this time the food industry—and particularly salmon canners—has relied on these associations for government and regulatory affairs representation, scientific research, technical assistance, education, communications, and crisis management.

> The past year [1899] has marked the greatest development in the salmon industry of the Sound in the history of the state of Washington. The Sound now produces about one third of the output of the world. The Columbia River, Alaska waters and Russian and English rivers add to the output, but Puget Sound is easily first. In proof of this figures are given by packers and canners on the Sound which show that the pack up to October 31st last was nearly 500,000 cases larger than it was last year and its value will reach the enormous sum of nearly $3,500,000. It is no wonder, then, that Eastern capital should look with eager eyes toward the Sound. Much of this capital has found investment here during the past season and as a result new canneries, new traps and new methods of treating the fish were introduced and this made it possible to increase the output so largely. Hundreds of additional men found employment, there was more freight for the railroads and express companies and for vessels plying the Sound and every city on its banks benefited. How great are the possibilities for this industry cannot be estimated, for the waters of the great inland sea seem to fairly swarm with fish.
>
> — "Salmon Canning on Puget Sound,"
> The Wave, November 11, 1899

The packing companies also worked to grow the market for their products. Before the emergence of the Columbia River fisheries, canned salmon was popular in Australia, Great Britain, and other non-domestic markets as a nutritious, inexpensive food for working families. As output increased, companies began efforts to convince Americans to eat canned salmon. The APA, for instance, published several how-to books, starting with the Karluk Packing Company's 36-page cookbook *Horse Shoe Red Salmon Cook Book, How To Eat Canned Salmon*, which included a section titled "How to Open the Can." In 1904 the APA published a 64-page "St. Louis World's Fair Edition," entitled *How to Eat Canned Salmon, Choicest Recipes*. A year later, the APA rebranded some of their product as "Argo Red Salmon," with a corresponding cookbook. The domestic taste for canned salmon grew steadily.

San Juan Canning Company Fortune Brand Label
(courtesy of San Juan Historical Museum)

With their vertical monopolistic structure, ranging from supply (fishing) through processing (canning) to marketing (branding and wholesaling), the companies could market canned salmon in several ways: with distributer's brands, with cannery labels, or with cannery labels and brands. For example, the John F. Lalla Company of Chicago adopted the label "Atlas" for red sockeye, while the Joseph Travers, Ltd. of London and Liverpool labeled their sockeye as "Alpha." Deming and Gould, the selling agents for PAF, established brands such as "Auk" and "Virginius." For labels identifying both the packers and the selling agent, they used names such as "Autumn" or "Uwanta" or distinctive company logos. In the 1910s, trade associations such as the Puget Sound Salmon Packers and the Association of Pacific Fisheries began a major advertising campaign to market canned salmon, including designating a Friday in March as "National Canned Salmon Day."

The industry also generated trade journals. *Pacific Fisherman Journal*, "The Only Journal Devoted Exclusively to the Fishing Industry of the Pacific Coast," was founded in 1903. The January 1904 (volume 2, number 1) edition is particularly instructive, containing articles by David Starr Jordan ("The Salmon of the Pacific"), Chris H. Buschmann ("Trap Fishing"), Barton W. Evermann ("The United States Bureau of Fisheries"), and T. E. P. Keegan ("Old and Modern Ways of Canning Salmon"). After 1911 the *Journal* became the annual *Pacific Fisherman Yearbook*, which also published under the titles *Pacific Fisherman Year Book*, *Pacific Fisherman International Yearbook*, or simply *Pacific Fisherman*. The *Yearbook* published annual statistics on production in the Pacific Northwest and Alaska as well as articles on various aspects of the trade, such as gear and methods, regulation, and current research. It was absorbed by the East Coast publication *National Fisherman* in 1966.

Fresh and Frozen Fish

In addition to smoking, salting, and canning, fish were packed with ice to keep them fresh for short periods of time. Fresh fish from reef nets, traps, and trolling were sold to mainland markets starting the 1890s. An 1898 item in *The Islander* noted that "The *Michigan* brought in about 400 spring salmon from the Island Packing Company's trap on the salmon banks last Tuesday, all of which were shipped fresh to Seattle fish dealers." In 1899, the *Whatcom Reveille* reported that the PAF was shipping from Fairhaven, on average, 6,000 pounds of fresh silver salmon to eastern markets per day. The fish were shipped two ways: west of Chicago, consumers demanded that the salmon be dressed (which, weighing less, cost less to ship), while East Coast consumers demanded that they be whole. (At the time, an interesting state statute required that the words "Puget Sound Salmon" be prominently displayed on the boxes.) Beryl Troxell Mason wrote that her father had ice houses at their place on Mackaye Harbor on Lopez Island, so that they could put the freshly caught fish, particularly Chinook salmon, on ice in the boats for quick shipping to the mainland. One of the main fish buyers was the Chlopeck Fish Company of Seattle, which bought salmon for both the fresh and salted markets; their wharf and plant at the foot of Wall Street occupied a principal location on the Seattle waterfront.

In 1888, methods of successfully freezing fish were developed in the Sacramento and Columbia Rivers regions and were introduced into the Puget Sound region in 1892. Railroad refrigerator cars ("reefers") with ice and heavy insulation had been initially developed in the 1860s; by the time preserving fish by freezing had been introduced to the Pacific Northwest, connections could be made to national markets by means of the extensive railroad networks (the Northern Pacific reached Tacoma in 1888 and the Great Northern reached Seattle in 1890). The best method had three principal features: getting fish fresh; freezing them; and coating them with a thin glaze of ice. The best salmon for freezing were coho and chum, with other species used, except for sockeye, which were too oily. John N. Cobb, in his 1921 Bureau of Fisheries publication *Pacific Salmon Fisheries*, described the freezers, which were kept at about 10° below zero. Each freezer was piped with two feet of 1¼-inch pipe per cubic foot of freezing space. The freezers consisted of two bunkers, nine pipes wide, spaced 10 inches apart. A 3½-foot passage ran through each freezer; the salmon, laid on metal sheets, were placed on the tiers of pipes. The salmon, when frozen, were taken to a glazing room kept at 20°F, where they were dipped in water to form a thin glaze of ice, to ensure that the fish were not exposed to air. Each fish was then covered with oiled paper or parchment, wrapped with heavy brown paper, and packed in boxes of 250 pounds each, which were placed onto the refrigerator cars and shipped.

In 1900 the *Fairhaven Herald* reported that Roland Onffroy, the entrepreneur who put together the North American Fisheries Company, was installing liquid-air machinery on the company's steamers for freezing fish as soon as they were caught. After freezing, they were transported to cold storage on land (such as a facility in Fairhaven), glazed with ice, and then loaded onto railroad refrigerator cars for transportation to markets throughout the United States and, having been transferred to cold storage ships on the Atlantic seaboard, Europe. In 1907 *The San Juan Islander* reported that the San Juan Fish Company was buying salmon from the traps in the San Juan Islands, placing them in ice in boxes on board their steamers, and shipping them to Seattle, where company workers cleaned and froze them.

> *The importance of the fishing interests on the Pacific coast of the establishment of properly constructed freezing-houses can hardly be overestimated. The demand for fresh fish in all parts of the country is a growing one, and apparently increase more rapidly than the population. This demand should be met and all legitimate means should be employed to increase it. Among the methods so far adopted for the preservation and distribution of fishery products, none perhaps has met with greater or more deserved favor than that of artificially freezing many species of fish which can be satisfactory kept in this manner and distributed through the means of refrigerator cars over an enormous extent of territory. In the matter of supplying the demand for salmon, the Pacific region unquestionably has an advantage, and one that it is believed will be maintained if all available resources are utilized. It will doubtless be found that a greater amount of money will be realized if a larger percentage of the products of the salmon fishery can be disposed of in a fresh condition instead of being canned. And this additional advantage will accrue: that the quantity of salmon consumed will be much larger than heretofore, which must manifestly be to the profit of the producer.*
>
> — J. W. Collins,
> "Report on the Fisheries of the Pacific Coast of the United States,"
> United States Commission on Fish and Fisheries Report for 1888 (1892)

The main market for Salish Sea salmon caught by trolling was for fresh fish in local urban centers. John N. Cobb, in his *Pacific Salmon Fisheries* (1921), reported on a relatively new marketing method: shipping fresh fish. Beginning in Tacoma in 1914, fresh salmon was shipped to any express office in the United States, with a rate dependent on location: $1.50 east and $1.25 west of the Mississippi River. (Subsequently—by the time of his report—the western region shipping rate had been raised to $2.50.) Each individual fish was packed with 20 pounds of ice; ice was added every 15–20 hours, depending on the weather. The main market was the Midwest, with little access to fresh fish.

As air transport became more affordable and widespread, fresh salmon were flown, on ice, to urban markets. The improvement of freezing methods in the 1930s also bolstered the market for frozen salmon. After World War II, while markets for these two products increased, Americans began to lose their taste for canned salmon. As commercial production of ice became more common, fishers loaded their boats' holds with ice in order to preserve their catch until they could reach shore or a tender. Some trollers also added freezing equipment on board their boats. This catch, called "clipper caught," consists of perfectly dressed and frozen fish with no broken fins, cuts, missing scales, blood in the body cavity, or presence of sea lice. The freshly caught salmon (except for sockeye) were headed and cleaned and washed in circulating sea water. After being chilled at -15°F over a three-to-four-hour period, they were dipped several times in a solution of corn sugar and freshwater/seawater, until they had a heavy, clear glaze. Each fish was then placed individually in a heavy-gauge plastic bag. This supplied a premium product that was then air shipped throughout the world.

> *The San Juan [Fish] company, although it does little canning, claims to handle more salmon in the course of a year than any other company operating on Puget Sound, not even excepting the P.A. F. The salmon which they take from their traps or buy during the summer are packed in ice in boxes on board their steamer and taken to Seattle where they are cleaned and placed in cold storage rooms where the temperature is close to zero and often below. After being frozen they are dipped in water and given a thin coating of ice and when shipped are rolled in sheets of oiled paper and packed in boxes in refrigerator cars. The company makes large shipments of frozen salmon to Germany, France, and other European countries.*
> — The San Juan Islander, August 3, 1907

Today, while consumers can still buy cans, the principal markets for salmon are either fresh or frozen. Most canneries in the Salish Sea area had closed by the end of the 1920s. During the interwar period (1918–1941), the PAF packed a record 158,260 cases of Puget Sound salmon in 1927, but ended in 1938 with only 19,609, and did not pack any fish from 1939 to 1948. After it resumed packing, a high of 83,589 cases was reached in 1950, but this was an exception—many years there were only 10,000 to 30,000, and the year before the PAF was sold, 1965, case count was only 1,253—in contrast to the Alaska canneries, which were consistently packing 200,000–400,000 cases each season during that period. The Friday Harbor Packing Company, which had stopped canning salmon in the 1950s, was used for canning and freezing other products and closed permanently in 1964.

> After a while the [Friday Harbor] cannery closed down. It was a little union problem. The employees had been promised, according to the union contract, that they would get five cents an hour bonus for every hour they worked over 200 hours in the summer time. The owner, a guy named Einstoss, wasn't too happy to pay that five cents an hour. The last year that the cannery operated the cannery was all ready to go, the fish buyers were practically on their way to buy fish, and the union decided to push for this five cent overtime that all of us who worked there were entitled to. He said he'd write out a check for $2000 and that the Union could divide that among all the employees. Some of the employees who had been working there were a little hard-headed, and they said "We want every nickel that's coming to us," and Einstoss says, "Take the 2000 bucks or I shut her down." And they said, "Okay, shut her down." And that's what he did. They disbanded the cannery, dismantled the machinery, sent it to Seattle or somewhere else, and started shipping to La Conner.
>
> — Calvin McLachlan, interviewed by Didier Gincig, November 4, 1996

FISHERS, CAMPS, SHORELINE STRUCTURES, AND PUBLIC FACILITIES

Fishers

Indigenous peoples have been fishing in the Salish Sea for millennia. During the late nineteenth century, they were forced from ownership of their traditional fishing grounds in the San Juan Islands, but fishers came from villages on Vancouver Island and the mainland to the islands and then returned for residence during the winter. Many Mitchell Bay Band, Sooke, Songhees, Saanich, Semiahmoo, Lummi, and Samish family members had married Euro Americans, and ownership of island fishing sites were kept among relatives. It is difficult to estimate how many Indigenous peoples were fishing in local waters, but in the historic record there are many accounts of fishers coming from British Columbia to catch salmon and other fish and harvest shellfish.

J. W. Collins, dispatched by the U.S. Commissioner of Fish and Fisheries to report on the Pacific Coast in 1899, said that 40% of commercial fishermen in Washington State were "Native." In William A. Wilcox's 1892 report, in Puget Sound and the Strait of Juan de Fuca 43% of boat fishers were "Indians," 20% Scandinavian, 19% Caucasians of North American birth, and 17% from southern Europe.

Beginning in 1860, the United States federal government began enumerating the population of the San Juan Islands, noting names, relations, ages, country of origin, and occupation. The number of men (and they were exclusively men) who claimed "fisherman" as their occupation in the census rose from 1 in 1860 to 4 in 1870 (2, both Danes, on Lopez, and 2 on San Juan, both probably at Mitchell Bay) and then to 16 in 1880: 6 on San Juan (most of whom were near Mitchell Bay); 1 on Lopez; 3 on Orcas; 3 on Waldron; and 1 each on Blakely, Decatur, and Shaw. The 1887 territorial census lists 5 on San Juan and 3 on Lopez. The 1889 territorial census documents a large group—11—fishing on Waldron.

These numbers change radically in the 1900 federal census, revealing the rise in corporate fishing and how it was distributed geographically through the islands. On Orcas, only 6 were enumerated as "fisherman," but the smaller islands had a disproportionate number: 4 on Blakely (which covered Decatur), including Henry Cayou and R. W. Davis, both owners of traps; 4 on Stuart; and 14 on Waldron—plus a group of 8 that included a boss, partner, 7 employees, and a Japanese cook—possibly a fish trap operation. On Lopez, there were 29 enumerated but only 2 in Precinct 1, the north half of the island, because most were concentrated in the Richardson area at the south end of the island. Among these were several groups associated with pile driving operations: these crews ranged in size from 6 to 13 (including several engineers), and several had a cook, suggesting an encampment. The census taker for San Juan Island, C. M. Tucker, was more specific in distinguishing between net fishermen (8) and trap fishermen (4, with a "Trap Foreman" and a "Watchman Fish Trap"). He also enumerated several other groups associated

*Indigenous Fishers Bringing Their Catch to Sell
(courtesy of San Juan Historical Museum)*

The Fisheries of San Juan

There are within the limits of this county thirty-one traps, employing in the aggregate about 200 men, and representing an annual outlay for construction of approximately $100,000, and an expense for wages and board during the fishing season of about $12,000 a month. This for the traps only, and not taking into account the wages of the crews of attending steamers or any of the other expenses of steamboat operation.

In the Pacific American Fisheries Company's cannery at Friday Harbor, seventy-four white persons and eighty Chinese and Japanese are employed. If we add the number employed by the Great Northern Fish Company in salting fish at Richardson, Mitchell bay and Stuart island, and those engaged in independent fishing with gill nets, reef nets and purse seines, we have at least 500 persons who find employment in this great industry for several months in the year in this county only.

—*The San Juan Islander*, September 7, 1899

with the fish industry: an engineer with 6 Chinese and 3 white "day laborers" (possibly a pile driver operation); the fish cannery with its supervisor, James Burke, a "Salmon Cannery Boss," Sing Lee, and 46 laborers and 1 "Can Tester," all Chinese; 2 (women) listed as "Filling Salmon Cans"; and a group of 12 Japanese "Day Laborers" and a Japanese "Servant House," all of whom may have been associated with the cannery in Friday Harbor. Ethnically, the largest groups of non-Indigenous peoples working in the fish industry were the Chinese and Japanese, associated with the canneries. Although there are several references to Japanese purse seiners in San Juan waters, Japanese workers constituted a far greater portion of the Fraser River fishery north of the border: in 1896, 452 of the 3,533 provincial licenses were held by Japanese fishers; five years later (1901), they held 1,985 of a total of 4,722. By 1915, the British Columbian government had issued licenses for the Fraser River fishery to 1,320 Japanese, 962 Euro Americans, and 295 "Indians."

There were several nationalities represented among the Euro American fishermen in the San Juans. Several Danes (Peter Asplant, Alfred Flint, Peter Lawson, and Rasmuth Yansen), Finns (Ole Hogan, Charles Johnson, and John Kertula), and Norwegians (Chris Olson) stand out, as well as some Frenchmen (Edouard Graignic on Waldron and Peter Lami on San Juan).

Often ethnicities specialized in and monopolized specific fishing jobs or gear. Coast Salish fishers, with their traditional knowledge of salmonid behavior and migrations, continued to supply salmon to the local canneries well into the twentieth century, despite the loss of traditional reef net sites to fish traps. They also composed the largest group of fishers trolling for coho and Chinook, particularly off the west coast of San Juan Island. (North of the border, between 1881, when the Canadian government first required fishing licenses, and 1887, 600 of the 700 licenses were issued to "Natives.") Coast Salish, mainly from across the border with British Columbia, brought clams to Friday Harbor and Lopez Island canneries.

"Slavonians" or "Slovenians" (also called "Austrians" in the U.S. census)—immigrants from Austria, the Dalmatian Coast, and Croatia—dominated the purse seine industry. Many of these settled in communities such as Tacoma, Gig Harbor, Everett, Anacortes, and Bellingham. An example is John Ross Sr. and his family. Born to the Jadrošić family on Premuda, an island in the Adriatic Sea that is now part of Croatia, John married Johanna (Eva or Iva) there and they came to the United States in 1887. Changing their family name to Ross and settling in Gig Harbor, they raised a family of ten, including sons John Jr., Emmett, and Adam, who helped their father fish and then continued the business after John Sr. died in 1928. During the fishing season, the Rosses camped on the beach below Peter Lawson's farm on Eagle Cove. The Ross' daughter, Winifred Andreana, married Crijack "Jack" Domemick Bujajich, who was also from Premuda, and the

Bujajich family fished alongside the Rosses. In nearby Anacortes, there are many Croatians who purse seined in the Salish Sea, and names such as Andrijic, Barbarovich, Bozanich, Dragocich, Gugich, Maricich, Peticsh, Suryan, and Voolich, among others, are common.

> *Talking about speaking in Croatian, when I fished with Rudolph literally the whole crew spoke it all the time, all during the day, at meals and everything. English was, even though most of us all knew English, it was a given thing that you spoke to each other on the boat and commands and everything else were given in Croatian. Once in a while there would be some American people on board and they of course couldn't speak it so they had to learn what ortza (breast line) meant, and they did. They would pick up on that. But for their benefit we told them in English what was going on and what they need to do.*
> —Mike Milat, *"Purse Seine Gear,"*
> Bret Lunsford, *Croatian Fishing Families of Anacortes* (2011)

Norwegians, although constituting a small percentage of purse seiners, soon composed a major portion of the fish trap and gill net operators: Sverre Arestad, in his 1943 article "Norwegians in Pacific Coast Fisheries," claimed that "at least 23.5 percent to 35 percent, possibly 50 percent" of trap fishermen—in Alaska at that time—and 25% of gillnetters were Norwegian.

Camps

Fishers usually located their camps close to where they were fishing. A chart produced by the 1853–1854 U.S. Coast Survey indicates four locations on the west side of San Juan Island marked "Village"—most likely Indigenous peoples' fish camps, including, from south to north, at a bay north of Pile Point, a bay north of that, Lime Kiln, and Mitchell Bay. In 1858, when G.

John Ross, Sr. Family Encampment at John Lawson Farm (courtesy of San Juan Historical Museum)

H. Richards, captain of the *HMS Pumper*, charted the waters off San Juan Island, including the south end, he marked an "Indian Village" below the Hudson's Bay Company establishment, above what is now called Grandma's Cove. Another Richards chart, of Roche Harbor and its vicinity, dated 1865, indicated a "Salmon Fishery" on the south shore of Mitchell Bay. This may have been the "Songas [Songhees] Village" that Charles Griffin mentions several times in his *Belle Vue Sheep Farm Post Journal*; for example, on October 5, 1854, he recorded an expedition there to trade for dry salmon. The American North West Boundary Commission, on its exploration of the San Juan Islands, recorded several fishing villages. Visiting Stuart Island in February 1860 Dr. C. B. R. Kennerly described two villages, "one of immense size," and concluded that "The fishing grounds of this vicinity must be extensive and of much value to induce to many native to visit them yearly for their supplies."

> About a half mile south of Point Doughty [on Orcas Island]... The fishing station near our camp is only occupied during the salmon season. From the size of the lodge erected a large body of Indians must resort to this spot, and the immense quantities of salmon heads that were strewed around gave evidence that the last season's fishing must have been eminently successful.
>
> — Journal of Wm. J. Warren, Sec'y N.W. Boundary Commission of an Expedition in Company with C. B. R. Kennerly Surgeon and Naturalist, to the Haro Archipelago (1860)

This custom of Indigenous peoples camping on the west side of San Juan Island near prime fishing grounds continued into the twentieth century. A 1904 article in *The San Juan Islander* noted the temporary camps of the fishing families, with shelters made out of driftwood or sail tents.

> ...There are hundreds of canoes drawn up along the shore or gracefully riding on the waters, guided by the dexterous hands of the natives trolling for the silver salmon. All along the coast from Eagle cove to Mosquito pass smoke curls upward from the camp fires of scores of Indian families, huddled close together in rudely constructed driftwood huts or under the scant shelter of canoe sails close to the water's edge.... The Indians are nearly all from British Columbia and most of them from Vancouver Island...
>
> "Along San Juan's Western Shore Hundreds of Indians Fishing For Silver Salmon," *The San Juan Islander*, September 24, 1904

The mainly Euro American fishing crews that tended the fish traps also camped on land near their locations. Crews numbered from 20 to 30 men, including drivers, cappers, spillers, roustabouts, cooks, and watchmen. They camped in tents and huts along the shore nearby, at places like Lovejoy Point on Lopez Island and Kanaka Bay and South Beach on San Juan Island. In some cases, facilities were built by the fish trap company for housing the workers. In 1896, contractor James L. Farnsworth, who had been instrumental in constructing the cannery building and wharves of the Friday Harbor Packing Company, built a bunk and mess house for the crew that was overseeing the trap at Open Bay on Henry Island; later that year he built a "new fish house" for Joseph Sweeney and others at Kanaka Bay. Watchmen, however, usually spent the whole season in a small shack atop the trap, moving kelp and drift logs away from the nets, warding off seals and sea lions, and (theoretically) guarding against fish pirates.

The men on shore were joined by the crews of purse seine boats. A 1901 article in *The San Juan Islander* reported that more than 400 men fished at Richardson that season and were camped nearby. In 1910 it reported that over 400 were camped at the Fleming Place near Kanaka Bay, San Juan Island, and "a consid-

Camping Tents of Fishers at Lovejoy Point, Richardson, Lopez Island
(courtesy of Lopez Island Historical Society)

> The ranch of Mr. James M. Fleming occupies a charming location on Kanaka bay and especial interest attaches to it because throughout the months of July, August and September of each year it is the camping ground for a large number of fishermen.
>
> ...The strait of Juan de Fuca is one of the great fishing places of Puget Sound and during the season several scores of men engaged in this industry make Kanaka bay their headquarters and Mr. Fleming's ranch their temporary home. Seine boats leave this point twice each day with a compliment of six to nine men to each seine and each of these boats has its own cook who is responsible for the management of all commissarial matters.
>
> In the purchase of provisions, these men make enormous demands upon the products of Mr. Fleming's ranch, buying all the meat, eggs and farm products raised thereon throughout the fishing season.
>
> —Islands of San Juan County, Washington, supplement to the Everett Morning Tribune, 1908

erable number" further south at Eagle Cove and at Richardson, Lopez Island. In the 1890s, Edgar J. Ziegler, who had married homesteader James M. Hannah's widow Minerva, operated a store at False Bay. Later, James Fleming allowed a tent city of fishermen on his place, and mercantilists N. E. Churchill and John L. Murray opened a tent store there in 1905. In 1909 Fleming and his wife Janet drew up a lease with the George & Barker Company of Point Roberts for use of the entire waterfront of his place, including the right to drill a well, while reserving the "right and privilege to sell or furnish to the fishermen locating on the premises herein leased, any or all supplies said fisherman may desire to obtain."

Purse Seiners Arriving

J. M. Fleming hauled out a big load of merchandise yesterday for this summer store at Kanaka bay. There are already thirteen purse seine crews at his place, numbering nearly 100 men, and more than twice as many more are expected. The camp sites at all the big camps of purse seiners have been leased this year to the George & Barker Company, of Blaine, who, it is said, have assigned the leases to the canners' association, of which A. Lowman, of Anacortes, is president. The Fleming and Lawson camps, on San Juan, and the Barlows' bay camp, near Richardson, are the principal ones under lease. The fleet of seiners will be larger than ever before this year, forty new boats having been built since last season.

—The San Juan Islander, July 1, 1910

Photos—some taken by noted local photographer James McCormick in 1911—of the shore and fields above the Kanaka Bay bank show an extensive settlement, with tents arrayed on two sides of a central drive and what appear to be larger tents that may have been used as cafeterias. In 1905, the encampment was large enough to merit a separate column in *The San Juan Islander*, reporting the news from "Fleming's Beach": visitors,

*Camping Tents of Fishers at Peter Lawson Farm, ca 1905
(courtesy of San Juan Historical Museum)*

parties, and entertainment, including a traveling show of four "letter carriers from the Seattle post office"—a "banjo specialist," "mandolin artist," comedian, and baritone, who performed in Murray's tent store. In 1913, William Slavens McNutt published an impressionist report on "THE PURSE SEINERS" in *The San Juan Islander*, describing not only the extent of the fishing operations but the social life at the camp. Arthur Clement, son of Janet Fleming by a former marriage, inherited the 500-plus-acre farm, where he traded for fish or sold goods such as chickens, eggs, rabbits, and garden vegetables to the mainly Croatian fishermen from Gig Harbor and Tacoma.

> *Each man of every crew brings to the banks with him his barrel of wine. Some of the men live aboard the boat and many in tents ashore at Kanaka Bay where there is a veritable canvas city during the short season of the big run. The purse seiner's Sunday begins at four o'clock Friday afternoon and lasts until four o'clock Sunday morning. Where the fish are running and everyone is making big money this is the time of much joy and more wine ashore. The fishermen gather on the beach, sing their native songs, dance, drink, stage wrestling bouts and cockfights and hold big carnival generally. Be it said to the credit of these newcomers to our shores that in all the time I spent among them at Kanaka Bay on San Juan island, where upward to a thousand gather I saw not one fight and the only horrible example of bestial drunkenness was furnished by a nondescript beach comber who made me feel like changing my name by claiming he was Irish.*
>
> — Will Slavens McNutt,
> "The Purse Seiners," *The San Juan Islander*, August 8, 1913

On South Beach on San Juan Island, off which there were at least five fish traps run by the Alaska Packers Association, Pacific American Fisheries, Friday Harbor Packing Company, San Juan Fish Company, and John Troxell, there was a camp with wooden shacks and a cook house for the men. Water, bought from Eliza Jakle, who owned most of the land, was obtained from the springs there.

Shoreline Structures

The variegated shoreline of the San Juan Islands, with its coves, bays, and harbors, offered many places for sheltered anchorage for fishers and their boats and ships. The 1893 report of the U.S. Coast and Geodetic Survey of a portion of Orcas, San Juan, and Shaw Islands (T-sheet 2230) noted that "Grindstone Harbor [on Orcas Island] is a snug and safe harbor for small craft and is a favorite rendezvous for fishing sloops." Other favored locations for fishing boats to anchor in the San Juans included: Mackaye and Richardson on Lopez; Deer Harbor, East Sound, and West Sound on Orcas; Blind and Parks Bays on Shaw; Reid and Prevost Harbors on Stuart; Andrews, Deadman, Garrison, Kanaka, and Mitchell Bays and Friday and Roche Harbors on San Juan; and Cowlitz Bay on Waldron.

> Let's get acquainted with Mackaye Harbor, a protected deep water harbor almost encircled by a barbed-hook shaped rocky peninsula, a place chosen for a home site but also sufficient elbow room to maintain and operate the equipment of a half dozen fish traps. Here was the business that kept six to twenty men working winter and summer. This place is, by definition a peninsula because all that held this one hundred acre parcel onto Lopez Island was the narrow neck of land extending from the west end of Agate Beach to the south end of Barlow's Bay, perhaps a quarter of a mile on a north-south line. After that the definition breaks down, for once through the outside gate into the harbor it was home and safe. We never knew a hurricane. We never had a flood. The bay never went dry. To dredge was unnecessary...
>
> — Beryl Troxell Mason,
> *John Franklin Troxell, Fish Trap Man* (1991)

Many of the natural advantages of their sheltered anchorages were soon enhanced by the construction of docks, landings, piers, and wharves. All the canning companies, in addition to erecting the canneries themselves, built wharves for loading fish trap piling and net gear and unloading the catch. Major ports like Friday Harbor and Richardson bristled with shoreline structures. Soon, smaller bays attracted entrepreneurial groups that strove to make their communities the best place for basing fishing operations and docking for supplies.

ACTIVITY AT OTIS

The road surveyed by Mr. Vaughn... leads from the main county road to the water front of lot 1, section 17, range 1, west, where our people have decided to immediately erect a suitable wharf and thus supply a long felt want in this part of Lopez Island. To give shape to their matured plans, almost to a man the enterprising citizens of this vicinity turned out on the morning of the 18th. It was soon evident that all had come to act, not merely to talk, as is too often the case. The first thing in order was to organize the wharf company. This was effected by making Thomas Graham chairman and C. Carrothers secretary of the meeting. The following named persons were then elected as officers of the company, viz: President, C. A. Anderson; secretary, C. Carrothers; treasurer, Thomas Graham; trustees, C. A. Anderson, Thomas Graham and H. L. Dikeman. As foreman of the work of constructing the wharf our efficient ship-carpenter, Mr. P. Schruder, was unanimously elected. The next thing in order was to proceed at once to the getting out of the needed piles. Many willing hands made short work of this. The pile-driver is on the ground, but our piles will not be driven for a month or so yet. In order to reach water of the required depth the wharf will be long, but the work of construction will not be difficult. Our bay being so well protected there can be no delay in handling freight here. There will be a safe slip made for the shipping and landing of live stock. Upon the whole it is believed that the wharf here will be a benefit to all citizens of the south half of Lopez.

— *The San Juan Islander,* January 31, 1901

Structures were built out from the water's edge for the purpose of tying up and loading and unloading boats and ships. Although the terms dock, pier, quay, and wharf seem synonymous, distinctions can be drawn between them. A dock is a structure built specifically for loading and unloading cargo and passengers from boats and ships. A wharf is a complex of several docks and a quay is usually a publicly owned dock. Piers are longer structures that connect a dock or wharf to the land and are considered mainly pedestrian in use. Early construction consisted of gabions that were filled with stones (piers) to above the high tide, with a wooden superstructure that formed the dock; there are remains of these at both American Camp, where the Hudson's Bay Company built a pier out into Griffin Bay, and English Camp, where the British built wharves for boats and ships. In the mid-1800s, the steam hammer was invented; this machine used steam to raise a heavy hammer that would then be released to drive pilings into the ground or seabed. Pilings consisted of long logs or poles that were coated with preservatives—usually creosote. Modern construction is with steel beams. If the wooden docks were not secured directly to the piers, docks were designed to float in order to allow for tidal changes.

Public Facilities

San Juan County, consisting solely of islands, has from its establishment supported marine traffic. Many of the county roads were laid out so that they ended at the shoreline, which allowed for public access to and from the water. Today the County maintains 14 public docks: four on Orcas Island, three on Lopez Island, two on San Juan and Stuart Islands; and one each on Decatur, Shaw, and Waldron Islands. Moorings other than docks or wharves are usually buoy tie-ups. Buoys are flotation devices that are attached by means of a cable, chain, or rope to a weighted sinker that rests on the seabed.

In 1911, Washington State passed legislation enabling local voters to create publicly owned and managed port districts. There are three official (special taxing districts governed by a board of publicly elected officials) ports in the San Juan Islands:

Lopez, Orcas, and Friday Harbor. Both the Port of Orcas and the Port of Lopez are principally concerned with airport operations. The Port of Friday Harbor was established in 1950; eight years later a small pier and floats were installed to offer tie-ups for fishing boats. In 1968, the main pier—the Port's largest—was built. In 1972 the Port installed 172 permanent slips and began to lease land in the harbor area to businesses. In the early 1960s George Williamson, an outboard motor expert from Oregon, constructed a one-story building at the north part of the harbor for a sales-and-repair shop; the Port purchased the Williamson building and pier in 1977, and the San Juan Yacht Club was constructed on top of the existing building in 1986. In 1982, the Port purchased all the land on the north side of Front Street from Spring Street to the Williamson Building. During the next two years, the Corps of Engineers designed, built, and installed a floating breakwater, and 300 more slips were added to the Port. Final extensions to the breakwater were completed around 1985. The Port reacquired the San Juan Marina lease in 1994 and rebuilt the pier and a passenger terminal at the base of Spring Street (Spring Street Landing, 1995–1997). Recently (2018) the Port acquired Albert Jensen & Son Boatyard and Marina Shipyard as part of its mission to support local maritime business.

RECREATION

Sport Fishing and Shellfish Harvesting

> [John Gordon, captain of the British frigate HMS America] was preparing his rod to fish for salmon with the fly, when I told him the salmon would not take the fly but were fished with bait. I then prepared tackle with bait for him and he went in a boat to the mouth of the [Victoria] harbour, where he caught several fine salmon with the bait. His exclamation on his return was, "What a country, where the salmon will not take a fly."
>
> —The Honorable Roderick Finlayson, *Diary*, summer 1845

Although sport fishing in the Salish Sea began almost as soon as Euro Americans arrived in the region, during the nineteenth century it was largely confined to members of the English leisure class. A testament to this is the book *Fishing in British Columbia*, written and published in 1907 by Thomas Wilson Lambert, which dealt exclusively with the potential for recreational fishing in the province. During the twentieth century the influence of sport fishing on the regulation of fish stocks in the Salish Sea became more pronounced. This is exemplified by the Canadian Department of Marine and Fisheries' 1925 closure to all but sport fishing on the Capilano River, which emptied into Burrard Inlet in British Columbia, allowing officials to fine Dominic Charlie, a Squamish hereditary chief whose people had been granted a reserve for their right to fish in that area of the river, for using non–sport fishing gear. The case *Rex v. Charlie*, at first overturned, was decided in favor of Fisheries Canada and reinforced their ability to restrict a First Nations fishery to all but sport fishers.

Sports fishing in British Columbia was largely unregulated from the arrival of Euro Americans to the middle of the twentieth century. As the sport fish catch—particularly of salmon—began to rival commercial operations, Fisheries and Oceans Canada began to realize the importance of monitoring and regulation. In 1951, a daily bag limit of 10 salmon of a minimum size of 8 inches was established; in 1963 the number was reduced to 4 and the size increased to 12 inches. Competition between the commercial and recreational fisheries led to the creation of the Advisory Committee on Salt Water Sport Fishing (1964) to represent the sport fishing interest; this was renamed the Sport Fishing Advisory Board in 1974. By the 1980s, the sport Chinook and coho catch, which prior to that time had been less than half that of the commercial share, grew to three times that of the latter. In 1980 alone, recreational fishers caught more than a million salmon in half a million boat trips. In 1981, Fisheries and Oceans Canada introduced a new tidal-water fishing license for sport fishers, reducing the salmon limit to 2 of a minimum length of 18 inches.

> *Recreational and commercial salmon fisheries operate very differently. The recreational fishery accounts for a relatively small portion of the total annual harvest of salmon. It is primarily concerned with the quality of the angling experience and the opportunity to fish throughout the year. In contrast, the commercial fishery, which takes place mainly from July to November, accounts for the vast majority of the total salmon harvest and is primarily concerned with the quantity and value of the catch.*
>
> — Fisheries and Oceans Canada, *An Allocation Policy for Pacific Salmon*, October 1999

The Pearse Commission, appointed to study the situation, issued a report in 1982 that recommended "maximizing the available catch between the sport fishery and other fisheries in proportions that will generate the greatest value." The number of tidal fishing licenses increased from 282,000 that year to 453,000 by 1993. In 1998, Fisheries and Oceans Canada—which had been reorganized as the Department of Fisheries and Oceans in 1976—established a salmon allocation policy that "provides the recreational sector priority access to Chinook and coho during periods of low abundance," as well as offering sport fisheries access to pink, sockeye, and chum after conservation needs are addressed and First Nations needs are met. In 2006, it was determined that although recreational fishers represented only 3% of the total annual salmon catch, they caught 35% of the Chinook and 30% of the coho and represented 40% of the economy of fishing and aquaculture in British Columbia.

> ...a new industry has sprung up in the past 10 years, that of sport fishing in Puget Sound, providing **employment** to thousands and **enjoyment** to thousands more. That industry is entitled to protection and encouragement.
>
> — Unnamed Seattle journalist, quoted in *No Fish Traps* (1934)

In Washington State, sport fishing became increasingly popular during the twentieth century. Sports fishermen had a major influence on the passage of Initiative 77, the 1934 ban on fish traps. They were instrumental in forming the Salmon Conservation League of Washington, with the slogan "Save Our Salmon" (S.O.S.), which helped emphasize the toll of commercial fishing on salmon populations captured by fish traps, while ignoring the growing impact of purse seining and gillnetting—and even sport fishing—on these same stocks. A major sport fishing advocacy group, the Puget Sound Anglers, was formed in the mid-1980s by disgruntled regional chapters of Trout Unlimited, led by a group in the Renton area. They affiliated with a regional publication called *The Reel News*, which still offers "News and Voice for the Outdoor Sportsman."

Washington State did not keep statistics on sport fishing prior to 1939, when an estimated 252,571 salmon were caught by recreational fishers. This amount had more than doubled to 544,700 by 1963. In 1958 minimum size restrictions (20 inches) were imposed, and the catch gradually declined. The first

Washington State Sport Catch Report was published in 1967, based on estimates from catch-record cards, which are used by license holders to document their catch. In 1975, marine sport harvest estimates were added to the annual reports, and a year later shellfish were added. Steelhead were added in 1994. Today, catch-record-card data are collected for salmon, steelhead, sturgeon, halibut, and Dungeness crab.

The Annual Sport Salmon Catch has been summarized for the period from 1971–2018 (the most recent reported year); Area 7, the "San Juan Islands" (an area which ranges from the international border to the north to Smith Island to the south, and extends from Haro Strait on the west to the mainland on the east), ranged from a high of 55,396 to a low of 3,428 in 2004 in 1976 but has exhibited a gradual decline in numbers in recent years—with exceptions such as 40,107 in 2015, when there was a strong run of Chinook.

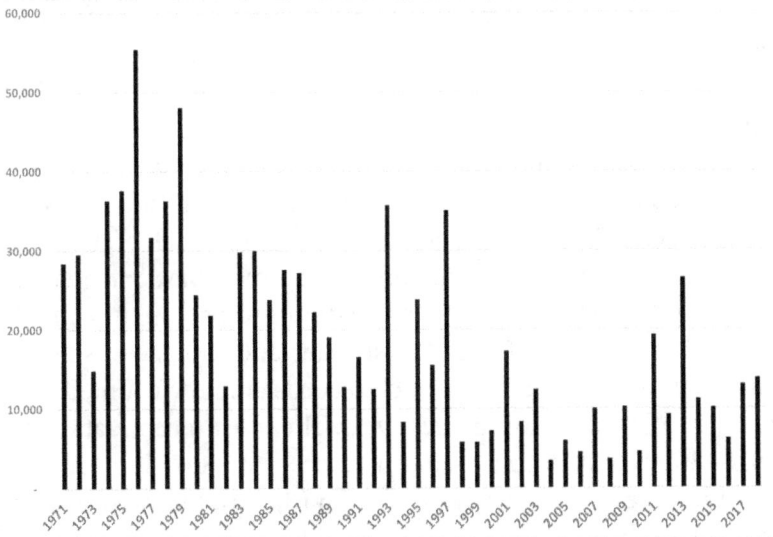

Sport Salmon Catch (in numbers), San Juan Islands, 1971–2018

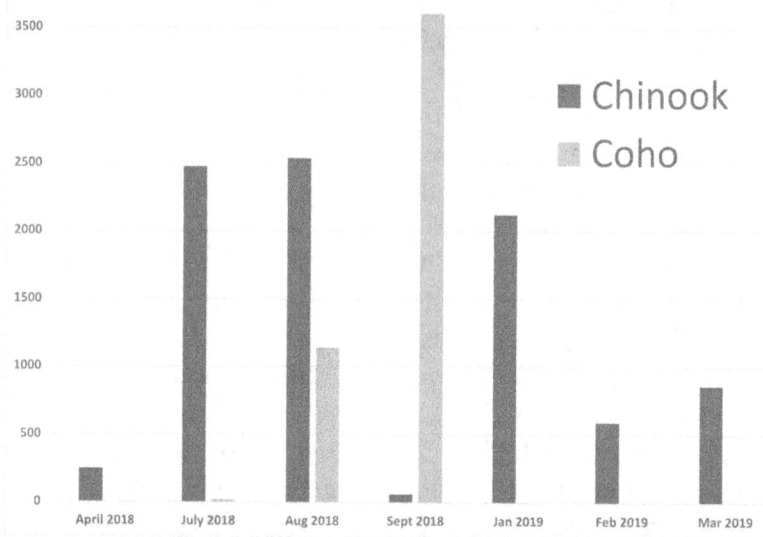

Sport Salmon Catch (in numbers), San Juan Islands, 2018–2019

Currently, Washington State requires licenses for "Saltwater," with catch cards required for salmon, steelhead, sturgeon, and halibut, as well as licenses for "Shellfish/Seaweed" for harvest of clams, mussels, oysters, shrimp, crab, squid, other shellfish, and seaweed. A Puget Sound endorsement and catch-record card is required for Dungeness crab in certain Marine Areas, including Area 7 (the Salish Sea including Gulf of Georgia, north of San Juan Islands, Bellingham Bay, Samish Bay, San Juan Islands, and Anacortes). A "Combination License" allows anglers to fish in both saltwater and freshwater and to harvest shellfish and seaweed. Salmon sport catch records are now counted from April 1 to March 31 of the next year. The most recent data, from 2018–2019, with a total salmon catch of 13,867, indicate that Chinook are the most common catch (8,900), followed by coho (4,764), with only a handful of pink (5), 198 sockeye, and no chum. This occurred through 32,272 angler trips, for an average of 4.3 salmon per trip.

Dungeness crab have two seasons: summer (July–September; opening and closing varies) and fall/winter (varies), usually Thursday–Monday, with a catch limited to five 6.25" minimum-size crabs per day per license. The latest recorded season, 2018,

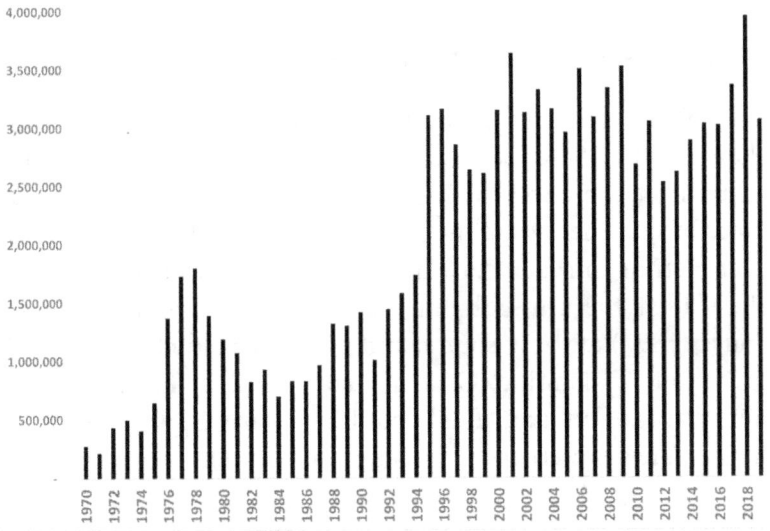

Dungeness Crab Catch (in numbers), San Juan Islands, 1970–2019

noted 428,012 pounds of recreational catch during the summer and 78,775 pounds during the fall/winter, in Area 7. Spot shrimp netted in Area 7 during May–July included 52,304 pounds in 10,298 angler trips, for an average of about five pounds per trip.

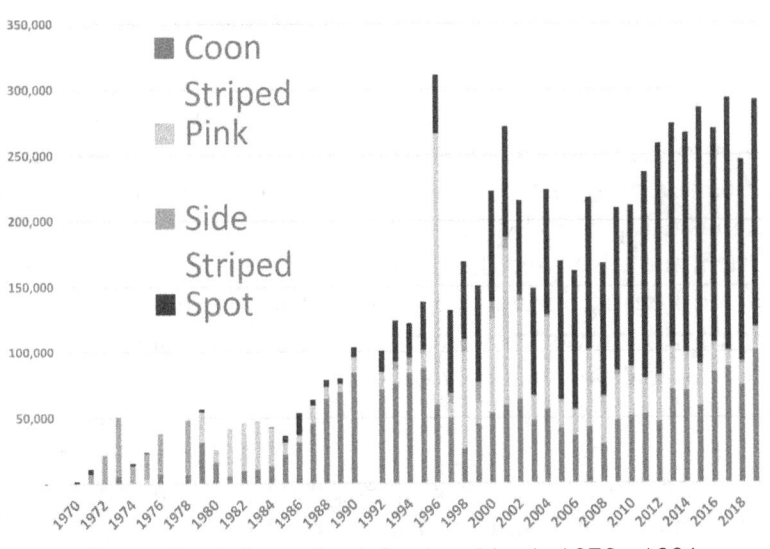

Shrimp Catch (in numbers), San Juan Islands, 1970 - 1996

Hotels, Fishing Lodges, Resorts, and Marinas

The first hotels were built on all three of the major San Juan Islands in the 1880s, 1890s, and early 1900s. On Lopez Island at Richardson, there was the Richardson (Ridley) Hotel (1890). On Orcas Island, there were the Norton Hotel (1891, later called the Deer Harbor Inn) at Deer Harbor, the East Sound House (1891, later called the Outlook Inn) at Eastsound, the West Sound House (1897) at West Sound, and the Orcas Hotel (1900–1904) near the ferry landing. On San Juan Island, at Friday Harbor, there was the San Juan Hotel (late 1870s–early 1880s, later called the Bay View Hotel) and Tourists Hotel (1891).

> *Some Bellingham tenderfeet, who are camping at the Willis farm on Orcas island, were trolling for salmon in the Pass the other day. A kid was holding the line, and the man at the oars was pulling hard and perspiring copiously without making much headway. He suggested an investigation of the trouble, when it was discovered that there was a big salmon on the spoon. The monster was dragged into the boat and tipped the scales at 38 pounds.*
> — The San Juan Islander, July 28, 1911

While these early hotels probably entertained guests who came to the islands for sport fishing, in the 1910s, 1920s, and 1930s several resorts and lodges, mainly on Orcas Island, were established specifically for the tourist trade, including sport fishermen, and advertised themselves as such. At first some of these offered housing in tent-cabins—wood floors and partial walls roofed with canvas tents; later, guests preferred more permanent accommodations such as wood cabins. Typical of these later establishments was the fishing resort near Eastsound called Cramer & Kertis, built by Mr. and Mrs. A. J. Cramer in 1938; it featured 10 cabins that could be rented furnished or unfurnished, as well as shower and laundry facilities in a boathouse.

Fishers and their Catch, Buckhorn Lodge, Orcas Island, Washington, August 1928 (courtesy of Orcas Island Historical Society)

The Buckhorn Lodge (1934), located on 300 acres at the foot of Buck Mountain near Moran State Park, billed itself as "The Fisherman's Paradise" and boasted a lodge that could accommodate 100 guests and seat 75 diners, as well as 16 cottages, and boats to rent for both salt- and freshwater fishing. The Salmon Bight (later renamed the "Casa Mar Silva"), featuring four rooms, a dining room, and a boathouse, opened in the 1930s on Cormorant Bay near Deer Harbor. In 1935, the Culver family built the Point Lawrence Lodge (later billed as the "First Fishing Resort" on Orcas Island) and boathouse, which along with 10 cabins offered lodging for fishermen who had previously boated to the island and camped on the beach. Proprietor E. J. Hilbert would send prize salmon catches to sporting goods stores in Seattle to lure sport fishermen (including Eddie Bauer) to the resort. Local newspapers used to post the catches of the various lodges to advertise the island's tourist fishing industry.

Rates for Board and Room

Two Persons In Room, $20.00 per week each.
One Person In Room, $24.00 per week.
Day Rate, $3.00 to $4.00.
Monthly Rate, $75.00 to $90.00.
Children Under 12, $12.00 to $18.00 per week.
Special Rates for Parties.

◊

• Salmon Bight Lodge is located on Orcas Island's west coast, facing President Channel and the sunset. . . . Take auto ferry from Anacortes, Chuckanut Bay (near Bellingham), or Sydney, B. C., to Orcas Island. Stage to Island points, or follow Deer Harbor and Salmon Bight signs to large S. B. L. sign between West Sound and Deer Harbor.

◊

MR. AND MRS. FRED M. McCREARY, Props.

ROLAND McCREARY,
Fishing Guide, Excursions, Archery

For Reservations, Write or Phone

Salmon Bight Lodge

Deer Harbor, Wash.   Phone 5X

SALMON BIGHT LODGE

ORCAS ISLAND

"Vacation Land Complete"

SAN JUAN ISLANDS . . . WASHINGTON

Salmon, Guests and Guide Return to Lodge Dock

Home of the Magic Sunset

A Secluded Retreat In Primitive
Seaside Setting

◊

Homelike, Pleasing Atmosphere

*Salmon Bight Lodge Brochure
(courtesy of Orcas Island Historical Society)*

In the 1950s and 1960s, several large resorts constructed marinas for visiting boaters (and fishers). Roche Harbor Resort, begun in 1956 when the Tarte family established a "boatel" at the old lime company's town, soon expanded its docks to eventually offer slippage to accommodate 377 boats. Rosario Resort was established in 1960 at the property on Cascade Bay where Robert

The Fisherman's Paradise

Eighteen large sixteen and eighteen foot newly-built Martin boats, with or without new motors. Guides furnished. Only ten minutes to lake fishing, where cutthroat and Eastern brook trout abound.

— Buckhorn Lodge brochure, *Finest Beach on Orcas Island* (1940s)

Moran had retired in 1904 and built a mansion and boatyard; it offers 30 slips and eight mooring buoys. Smaller marinas were established at several convenient anchorages in the islands: on Lopez Island, Lopez Islander Resort Marina and Spencer's Landing, run by Tanbark Marine, Inc., with 110 permanent moorage slips; on Orcas Island, Deer Harbor Marina with 110 slips for transient moorage; and on San Juan Island, Snug Harbor Resort Marina with over 50 boat spaces. Most have facilities for fuel and showers, and some have stores.

Derbies

In order to promote recreational salmon fishing in the islands, several derbies have been held in the Salish Sea in recent times. The Rosario Derby, which took place in December during the winter salmon season, began in the early 1980s. The Derby limited the number of entries to 100 boats and charged $125 per rod with a maximum of four rods per boat. The competition began with a shotgun start and ended with a $10,000 prize for the largest catch. In 1985, friends of Einar Nielsen established a derby in his name. Nielsen, Vice President and General Manager of Roche Harbor Resort and an enthusiastic sport fisherman, was found dead in his boat on top of a 50-pound salmon; apparently the struggle to land it gave him a fatal heart attack. Becky Barr continued the competition for several years and introduced the use of the proceeds for scholarships for local high school graduates. After her death, the derby became the Einar Nielsen & Becky Barr Memorial Fishing Classic, generally held in September at the peak of the coho season. At first, unlike many fishing competitions and derbies, the winners got to pick prizes donated by local businesses, and novices were encouraged to enter and learn from veterans, who gladly shared their knowledge of spots and methods. In the last 10 years cash prizes have been offered for first, second, and third place. In 2003, the Roche Harbor Salmon Classic—a derby with a 100-boat limit—was inaugurated, with a week-long fishing period during January or February.

After the salmon fishing season was moved from December and Rosario Resort came under new ownership, the Rosario Derby lapsed. In 2009 the season was opened in December again; under the leadership of Jimmie Lawson, president of the San Juan Islands Chapter of the Puget Sound Anglers Association, the Resurrection Derby ("resurrected" from the old Rosario Derby) was established in 2010. The San Juan Islands Chapter merged with the Fidalgo Chapter, and the Derby continued for several years under their joint sponsorship. The combined group subsequently wanted the contest based in Anacortes, which led in 2015 to two derbies: the Resurrection Derby in late January/early February and the Friday Harbor Salmon Classic in the first week of December. There are many other derbies held throughout the region, offering prizes for the largest fish caught; most are sponsored by local businesses as well as boat-making and boat-sales companies and fishing-gear outfits.

GOVERNMENT

National and State Fish Commissions

Vancouver Island and British Columbia, formed as the colony of British Columbia in 1866, did not enter the Canadian Confederation until 1871, so it was not until the 1872 *Fifth Annual Report* that the Department of Marine and Fisheries began to report on fishing in the region. In 1876, the *Fisheries Act* of 1868 was extended to British Columbia. The Act enabled the Crown to appoint Fisheries officials, authorized the Minister of Fisheries to manage the fisheries in general through regulation, specifically by issuing fishing licenses up to nine years in length. Officials also established regulations on methods, locations, and seasons of fishing; imposed fines for violations; and designated Fisheries officers, as justices of the peace, to enforce these regulations through fines and arrests. The Department of Fisheries was given the discretion to allow First Nations "to fish for their own use," a provision that would be used as a deterrent to Indigenous commercial fisheries. Due to reorganization and legislation, through the years the name of the department has changed, alternating between "Department of Marine and Fisheries" and just plain "Fisheries" (1884–1892, 1930–1969) and "Naval Services" (1914–1920), "Fisheries and Forestry" (1969–1971), "Environment" (1971–1976), and "Fisheries and Oceans" (1976–present). Under the latter, it is commonly known as "Fisheries and Oceans Canada."

The United States Commission on Fish and Fisheries was created in 1871 to investigate, promote, and preserve the fisheries of the United States of America, partly in response to the decline in the commercial fisheries on the East Coast. In 1903, it was reorganized as the United States Bureau of Fisheries under the newly created Department of Commerce and Labor; in 1940 it became part of the newly created Fish and Wildlife Service, under the Department of the Interior. The Commission's annual reports offer several insightful overviews of the Northwest fish industry, especially Richard Rathbun's "A Review of the Fisheries in the Contiguous Waters of the State of Washington and British Columbia" (1900); John N. Cobb's "Salmon Fisheries of the Pacific Coast" (1911); and George A. Rounsefell and George B. Kelez's *The Salmon and Salmon Fisheries of Swiftsure Bank, Puget Sound, and the Fraser River* (1938).

In 1890 Washington State Governor Elisha Ferry appointed the first State Fish Commissioner, James Crawford. A year later the Washington Legislature appropriated funds for a salmon hatchery, but it wasn't until 1895 that the first, on the Kalama River, was built. This action was in part due to the growing recognition that salmon populations were being overharvested. The first hatchery in the Puget Sound region was established in 1896, and by 1900 there were five in the region.

Regulation

In 1893 the Washington State Legislature passed an act "To Regulate and License the Catching of Salmon," which imposed restrictions on and required licenses for fixed gear only (i.e., pound nets, traps, or weirs). It restricted the mesh size, lead length, and spacing of fixed appliances and limited each licensee to three licenses, at $10 each. Four years later the Legislature repealed this act and replaced it with an act "Regulating the Catching of Salmon," which, while keeping the physical restrictions on fixed appliances, for the first time required a license for other types of fishing. Fees included: $25 for a purse seine; $5–$15 for a drag seine, depending on length; for gill nets, $1.00 for a set net and $2.50 for a drift net; and $25 for each "pound net, trap, or weir" in the Puget Sound area. These fees were modified by the 1899 act "Relating to Food Fishes," which imposed a tax of $1.00 for every 1,000 fish caught in the fish traps.

> We now know that for the past six or seven years we have over-fished our salmon.
>
> — Twenty-Eighth and Twenty-Ninth Annual Report of the State Fish Commissioner (1918)

In 1915 the Legislature passed a new game and game-fish code (the "1915 Fisheries Code") that provided for a chief game warden and a fish commissioner, both managed under Chief Game Warden L. H. Darwin of the Department of Fish and Game. As part of this code, license fees were modified: $100 for double-ended and $50 for single-ended traps on Puget Sound; purse seines remained at $25, but seines over 1,800 feet were prohibited; gill nets on Puget Sound were $5 plus one cent per foot for every foot over 600 feet of length (gill nets over 3,000 feet were prohibited) and set nets were $3.75; and beach seines were 3 cents per foot of length. The Code added the provision that "the owner or operator of the fish trap or pound net shall constantly maintain, during the weekly closed season, a watchman, whose duty, among other things, it shall be to cause such pound net or trap to be closed." Further, the law modified and detailed the catch tax by species for all means of catchment except gill-netters: $3.00 per 1,000 Chinook or steelhead; $1.50 per 1,000 sockeye; $1.00 per 1,000 coho or chum; and $0.50 per 1,000 pink. In 1919, the State Fish Commissioner observed that "the seemingly insignificant exemption from the catch tax of fish taken in gill nets and set nets permits fully seventy-five percent of the fish taken in the waters of the Columbia River to escape without the payment of any catch tax."

In 1921 the Legislature abolished the Fish Commission and replaced it with a Department of Fisheries, with a Division of Fisheries and a Division of Game and Game Fish, and established a State Fisheries Board. Six years later, largely at the behest of the fish trap owners and canners, the Board established regulations reducing the length and depth of purse seines, but there was such a large outcry that Governor Roland Hartley not only rescinded the action but requested, and received, the resignation of the whole Board. In 1932, by an initiative, the State separated food fish and game fish and created a Department of Fisheries (food fish) under an appointed director, and a Department of Game (game fish) under a six-member commission. The Legislature changed the latter to the Department of Wildlife, with a director appointed by the governor, in 1987. In 1994 the Department of Wildlife and Department of Fisheries were merged, creating the Washington Department of Fish and Wildlife, with a nine-member commission and a director appointed by the Commission.

Through all of these changes, Indigenous peoples struggled to maintain their treaty rights to fish. In 1894, faced with being forced out of their traditional fishing grounds around Point Roberts and Village Point, the Lummi Tribe petitioned the Bureau of Indian Affairs to call upon the U.S. District Attorney in Seattle to intervene on their behalf. After nothing was done, the Tribe sought the legal counsel of J. A. Kerr and W. B. McCord (attorneys who subsequently worked for the Pacific American Fisheries) to pressure the government to take the case to court; the resulting litigation was *The United States, et al. v. The Alaska Packers Association* in 1897. The presiding judge in the case, C. H. Hanford, who appeared to have an undisclosed monetary interest in the fish-canning business in the region, ruled against the Lummi on three grounds: the Treaty of Port Elliott gave the Lummi equal rights, not special fishing privileges such as permanent, protected locations; there was such an abundance of fish that the traps did not infringe on the Lummi's catch; and because the Lummi were selling fish to the APA, by curtailing the latter's business it would hurt the former's. The Lummi then asked the Bureau of Indian Affairs to appeal, and although the appeal reached the level of the United States Supreme Court, the United States Attorney General advised the Bureau to drop the case, and submitted a motion, which was granted, to do so on May 22, 1899. This would not be redressed for Indigenous peoples in Washington State until the 1970s.

The Washington State Legislature passed a bill mandating a 36-hour weekend closure of fish traps, but it was inconsistently enforced. On August 4, 1906, *The San Juan Islander* reported that "Henry Cayou, owner of Dot island fish trap, off Decatur island, was arrested Monday on complaint of Deputy Fish Commissioner Tarte for operating his trap on Sunday. He plead guilty and was fined $50 and cost by Justice Blair." Apparently, this legislation and others did little to slow the decline of fish stocks in the Salish Sea.

The attorneys and lobbyists retained by the cannery companies exerted a significant influence on legislation relating to fishing, at both the state and federal level. James Kerr and E. S. McCord, of the law firm of Kerr and McCord, began working for the Pacific American Fisheries in the late 1890s and were subsequently on annual retainer. In a testimony before the House Judiciary Committee on the impeachment of a federal judge in Seattle, Kerr noted that "nearly all of the statutes of this state [Washington], so far as they appertain to the fisheries business, were drafted either by Mr. Dorr [of Dorr and Hadley] or by our firm [Kerr and McCord]." Dorr and Hadley represented the Alaska Packers Association.

A precipitant for international regulation of the salmon fishing industry was the Hell's Gate blockage of the Fraser River in 1914, although action did not occur until the disastrous run of 1917. Because the affected salmon populations and industries fell within the jurisdiction of four entities—Canada and the Province of British Columbia and the United States and the State of Washington, the governments appointed a joint commission to investigate: the Hazen-Redfield Commission, jointly chaired by J. D. Hazen, Chief Justice of New Brunswick, and W. D. Redfield, U.S. Secretary of Commerce. After meetings with packers on both sides of the border in April of 1918, the next year the commission recommended a treaty that would establish an international commission to study the problem and establish regulations regarding the fishing season, gear, and catch. Although the Canadian Parliament ratified the treaty, the United States did not. This was due in part to the State of Washington, which objected to any "outside" regulations of the industry: as the Washington State Legislature declared in its 1911 session, "The State of Washington hereby affirms its title to all the public fisheries within its territorial limits, and insists that it has exclusive right, by virtue of its sovereignty, to keep, control and regulate all the fisheries within its borders without Federal interference." Specifically, PAF attorney E. S. McCord advocated for a 50% reduction in fishing without closing the season and protection of the rights of the State of Washington to regulate the fisheries. The result of this inaction delayed the two countries from addressing the situation internationally until the late 1930s.

In the late 1910s, halibut fishers and fish processors pressured the Canadian and United States governments to intervene to regulate the failing North Pacific halibut fishery. Although international negotiations collapsed in 1919, four years later the Convention for the Preservation of the Halibut Fishery of the North Pacific was signed and ratified by both countries, establishing the International Pacific Halibut Commission. The Convention was subsequently amended in 1953, 1976, and 1979, the latter being clarified by the North Pacific Halibut Act of 1982. With regulation of catch limits and prohibition of select gear, both the halibut population and catch rose until the 1970s, when it began to decline again due to more efficient fishing methods and greater number of boats. In the 1990s, "derby-style" fishing—where everyone competed for a season of a few days—was replaced with quota systems—where individual boats were awarded a percentage of the catch and the captain could decide when to fish. This has apparently led to a more healthy and sustainable halibut fishery. The International Pacific Halibut Commission is headquartered at the University of Washington in Seattle.

In 1924, the United States passed the White Act, which gave the Secretary of Commerce broad powers to regulate the time, place, and method of commercial fishing by establishing the conservation principle of an "escapement goal" (number of salmon that escape fisheries [i.e., are not harvested] and return to freshwater to spawn). The House of Representatives version of the bill went so far as to ban fish traps, but when it went to the

Senate the members of the Washington State delegation successfully blocked that provision from the final bill.

Voters in Washington State gained the right to initiative and referendum in 1912, and subsequently several fishing measures were proposed through initiatives. In 1924, Initiative 51 proposed the banning of both fish traps and purse seining; it failed to get the necessary number of signatures. Initiative 54, proposed four years later, also called for the ban of both types of fishing but it, too, failed to garner the minimum number of signatures required to place the Initiative on the ballot. Finally, in 1934, the Washington Fish Traps and Fishing Regulation Initiative, also known as Initiative 77, was passed by 65% of Washington State voters (in the region, San Juan County joined Whatcom County as two of the four counties in western Washington opposing the measure). (A contemporary countermeasure, Initiative 82, proposed new restrictions on net size, vessel length, and operating areas of purse seiners, but the backers failed to gather enough signatures to place the measure on the ballot.)

The initiatives prior to Initiative 77 had proposed limiting commercial fishing in general; it was an alliance between purse seiners, gillnetters, and sport fishermen that made the passage of Initiative 77 possible. The argument was made that the big companies' fish traps not only took the majority of the catch but, in particular, intercepted the salmon near the mouth of the rivers that they were returning to in order to spawn. (However, as Bert Huntoon of the PAF countered, in the previous four years "18 percent of the salmon have been caught in traps, 42½ percent with purse seines, 34½ with trolls, and 4 percent with gill nets.") Proponents formed the Salmon Conservation League of Washington—a coalition of the Washington State Sportsmen's Council, the Purse Seine Fishermen's Association, the Puget Sound Gill Netters' Association, and the Trolling Vessel Owners' Association—and lobbied for passage. Opponents, led by R. A. Welsh Jr. of the Bellingham Canning Company, formed the (rather lame sounding, in hindsight) Fishery Education Association.

The state law that resulted from Initiative 77 prohibited the use of fish traps for catching salmon within state waters, created special areas for trolling, and provided for salmon fishing seasons. Specifically, it made it "unlawful to construct, install, use, operate, or maintain, within any of the waters of the State of Washington, any pound net, fish trap, fish wheel, scow fish wheel, set net, weir, or any fixed appliance for the purpose of catching salmon, salmon trout, or steel head, or to take salmon, salmon trout, or steel head by any such means." The law also portioned Puget Sound into two areas, divided by a line that ran easterly from Angeles Point on the Olympic Peninsula to Penn Cove on the east side of Whidbey Island, then northerly to Sinclair Island, then northward along Lummi Island and to the mainland, enclosing Lummi Bay. To the east and south of this line, fishing was restricted to hook and line, except that mobile gear could be used from October 5 to November 20, excepting the weekend (4:00 p.m. Friday to 4:00 a.m. Sunday) closure. Although these area and seasonal restrictions seemed like a conservation measure, they in fact allowed purse seiners to catch sockeye and pink salmon in the Strait of Juan de Fuca and throughout the San Juan Islands. Then, in October and November, when the coho and chum salmon arrived in the "inner" Puget Sound area, they could purse seine them there. The sport fishers, mainly concerned with larger, "trophy" species such as Chinook—salmon that more readily take the hook—could catch them anywhere in region.

After the passage of I-77 into law, fish trap interests tried to oppose it through other legislation. Initiative 5, filed in late 1934, proposed to prohibit "the use of purse seiners and the owning, using or maintaining of any boat or other appliance in connection with their use in fishing for salmon." In 1935 the Legislature failed to pass this, and it was proposed for the general election of 1936, but the State Supreme Court struck the initiative from the ballot for failure of validation of the signatures. Several bills were introduced in the legislative session of 1937, including Senate Bill 29, which would have repealed Initiative 77 outright. The Bill was overwhelmingly defeated. The canneries gave up their opposition and shifted to gaining control of purse seiners for their fish supply. In 1933, it was estimated that the 686 licenses for fixed fishing appliances, together with all the gear, amounted to $2,272,372. The resulting shift in fishing methods and economics was major: in 1937, legal mobile gear included 1,111 gill nets, 213 purse seines, 395 troll units, and 49 reef nets.

In 1930, Canada and the United States came together again and proposed a Fraser River Convention to regulate fishing and mitigate environmental damage to salmon habitats, recommending the establishment of an International Pacific Salmon Fisheries Commission. It took the passage of Initiative 77 in 1934 to induce Washington State canning interests to lobby for the treaty, to a large extent because now canning companies could still operate fish traps in British Columbia but not Washington. (The pack of 1935, which was a bad fish year, clearly illustrated this: in contrast to 1934, when the number of U.S. cases was 340,787 compared to the Fraser River's 145,579, in 1935 the U.S. fell to 51,714 while Fraser River was 76,415.) The United States, largely driven by Washington State interests, added three understandings to the proposed treaty: prohibiting fishing gear (i.e., fish traps) banned by either Canadian or State law; imposing no regulations until two complete cycles of salmon breeding had been studied; and establishing a board to advise the international commission. The U.S. Senate ratified the treaty, with these understandings, in 1936, and Canada followed in 1937. The initial work of the International Pacific Salmon Fisheries Commission was primarily focused on the Fraser River sockeye salmon runs, addressing the Hell's Gate blockage and the Quesnel and Adams Rivers splash dams (temporary wooden dams used to raise the water level to float logs downstream to sawmills). Fish ladders and spillways were constructed at the former site and the two splash dams were demolished.

Washington State regulation of the commercial salmon fishing industry continued after World War II. In 1954, Washington State Initiative 192, "Regulation of Commercial Salmon Fishing," was proposed, defining districts and periods for commercial salmon fishing, establishing preserves, and prohibiting construction of certain kinds of gear or fixed appliances. Arguing that this initiative would favor large commercial companies over smaller businesses and that it would overturn standards developed by the Department of Fisheries, it was overwhelmingly defeated, 70% to 30%.

The "Washington Ban on Commercial Fishing of Steelhead Trout," Initiative 456, was placed on the ballot in 1985 and passed; it declared that natural resources should be managed by the State alone and petitioned the United States Congress to decommercialize steelhead trout. In 1995, Initiative 640 proposed rewriting fishing regulations to ensure certain rates of survival for non-targeted species, but it was defeated. The "Washington Restrictions on Commercial Fishing Initiative," I-695, of 1999, would have prohibited commercial net, troll, and trawl fishing in fresh- or marine waters within the State, except for tribal fishing conducted under valid treaties; it, too, was defeated, by 60%.

In 1973, 13 western Washington tribes brought suit against the State of Washington regarding their treaty rights to fish. In February 1974 federal district court Judge George Boldt decided that the wording of the treaties guaranteed to the tribes an allocation of salmon, which he set as 50%. The local reaction among non-Indigenous fishermen was one of outrage; at one point they prevented the Washington State Ferry *Kaleetan* from leaving the Friday Harbor landing by blocking its course with their gill net boats, and photos of protesting boats were featured in the *Seattle Times*. Jim Lawrence, whose wife Lisa Nash and family were registered as Swinomish tribal members and therefore entitled to their treaty rights' share, recounts how the Boldt Decision divided the fishing community of San Juan Island between "Cowboys and Indians" and relates how it was not safe to walk the same docks with belligerent white fishermen; they and their family lost many friends as a result.

> By dictionary definition and as intended as used in the Indian treaties and in this decision "in common with" means **sharing equally** the opportunity to take fish at "usual and accustomed grounds and stations"; therefore, non-treaty fisherman shall have the opportunity to take up to 50% of the harvestable number of fish that may be taken by all fishermen, and treaty right fishermen shall have the opportunity to take up to the same percentage of harvestable fish... However, fish taken for ceremonial and personal subsistence purposes shall not be counted in computing the 50% share of treaty right fishermen.
>
> — United States v. State of Washington, "Boldt Decision" 384 F. Supp. 312 (1974)

In the period from 1974 to 1978, the Boldt Decision was challenged in court 35 times. After lackadaisical enforcement by the State of Washington, in July of 1978 Judge Boldt stepped in and assumed jurisdiction over the fishery. Finally, in 1979, the United States Supreme Court reversed its 1976 decision not to hear an appeal and upheld the Boldt Decision, with some modifications such as including ceremonial and subsistence catches in the 50% allocation and reducing the tribal share if they did not use it. The State of Washington, which was charged with managing the resource, had to comply. The right to harvest from "usual and accustomed grounds" was upheld and extended to shellfish in 1994 by U.S. District Judge Edward Rafeedle.

In the 1970s, the focus of fishing regulation shifted back to the international realm. After the 1973 United Nations Conference on the Law of the Sea, resulting in setting the limit to national ocean resources at two-hundred-miles—largely in response to overfishing and territorial conflicts over fish resources—the U.S. Congress passed the Fish Conservation and Management (Magnuson-Stevens) Act of 1976, which established eight regional management councils under the National Marine Fisheries Service of the Department of Commerce. One of these was the Pacific Regional Management Council, which oversaw the Washington fishery. The Act has been amended significantly twice in recent years: the Sustainable Fisheries Act of 1996 and the Magnuson-Stevens Fishery Conservation and Management Reauthorization Act of 2006.

After cooperation faltered during the 1970s, in 1982 Canada and the United States negotiated the Pacific Salmon Treaty, which was ratified in 1985 and amended in 1999. It established a jointly run Pacific Salmon Commission, set quotas for Alaska and for Fraser River and Columbia River salmon, and committed the two countries to protecting and improving the spawning areas in rivers in those regions. The United States catch for sockeye and pink was reduced from 50% to between 24% and 33%, depending on predicted runs. In part this was due to United States interests in getting a larger share of other salmon species, especially Chinook and coho.

With the initial settlement of indigenously populated areas of what was to become British Columbia in the 1840s, the British government negotiated the "Douglas Treaties" with a half dozen Coast Salish groups on southern Vancouver Island. These treaties, in exchange for access to First Nations lands, guaranteed them the right to hunt, fish, and forage "as formerly," which clearly included traditional fishing methods, catches, and areas. In 1990 the Supreme Court of Canada found in *R. v. Sparrow* that where an Aboriginal group has a right to fish for "food, social, and ceremonial needs," it takes priority, after conservation, over other uses of the resource. The case was based on the arrest and charging of Ronald Edward Sparrow, a Musqueam who was fishing the Fraser River in accordance with what he claimed was his immemorial right. After being decided in favor of the Crown in the British Columbia Provincial County Courts, the case was ultimately brought to the Canadian Supreme Court in 1988. The 1990 decision resulted in what has been called the "Sparrow Test," which determines whether an action is consistent with Section 35 of the 1982 Constitution Act, which protects immemorial aboriginal rights. Although most of the First Nations groups affected by the decision have their traditional lands and uses on the west coast of Vancouver Island, there are some, such as the W̱SÁNEĆ (Saanich), that claim other areas in the Salish Sea.

In 2019, British Columbia adopted Bill 41, the Declaration on the Rights of Indigenous Peoples Act, harmonizing its laws with the United Nations Declaration on the Rights of Indigenous Peoples, which Canada had endorsed three years earlier. It has been argued that part of these rights is to fish in traditional use areas. The rights of Indigenous peoples to fish in their traditional use areas continues to be an evolving legal arena.

EDUCATION, RESEARCH, AND ADVOCACY

Coast Salish groups have a wealth of indigenous knowledge of the Salish Sea and its organisms. This knowledge includes awareness of the times and locations of fish runs, the habitats and feeding habits of fish and other seafood, and local current and tidal conditions. Families would return to their fishing spots in the San Juan Islands when they observed signs of the return of the salmon. This body of knowledge was passed from one generation to the next through traditional learning.

Euro Americans have a different approach to learning, based on scientific observation and learning. Various scientists accompanied both British and American explorations in the region and noted their observations on local marine species. James G. Swan, who settled in the Neah Bay area and described the Indigenous peoples of the area as well as their fishing in *The Northwest Coast, or, Three Year's Residence in Washington Territory* (1857), went on to write several scientific and economic reports on Washington fishes and fisheries, including the paper "On the Economic Value of the Giant Kelp and Other Seaweeds of the Northwest Coast of North America" (1893). The first scientific study of salmon was by Dr. George Suckley, who in 1858 read a paper on "Description of the Several Species of Salmonidae from the Northwest Coast of America" to the Lyceum of Natural History in New York, based on his work with Dr. J. G. Cooper on the survey of the Northern Pacific Railroad Route (*Explorations and Surveys to Ascertain the Most Practicable and Economical Route for a Railroad from the Mississippi River to the Pacific Ocean*). The full report on the zoology of the route was published by Congress in 1860. Suckley's findings, summarized in "On the North American Species of Salmon and Trout," were published after his death in the *Report of the Commissioner for 1872 and 1873* (U.S. Commission of Fish and Fisheries, 1874). At the same time, Dr. C. B. R. Kennerly was working with the United States

North West Boundary Commission and noting Indigenous peoples' names for salmon, in order to classify the various species. In 1888 the United States Fisheries Steamer *Albatross*, under the command of Captain Z. L. Tanner, began studies of the fish and fisheries of the region. Most of these scientific reports were published in the *Bulletin of the US Commission of Fish and Fisheries*, including those by Richard Rathbun (1892), J. W. Collins (1892), and William A. Wilcox (1894 and 1898), as well as in Rathbun's "A Review of the Fisheries in the Contiguous Waters of the State of Washington and British Columbia" (1899).

In 1910, Dr. John H. Cobb, editor of *Pacific Fisherman* and a field agent for the U.S. Bureau of Fisheries, wrote *The Salmon Fisheries of the Pacific Coast*, the most comprehensive scientific, economic, cultural, and historical work on the salmonids to date. Several revised editions were subsequently published under the title *Pacific Salmon Fisheries*. He also prepared a corresponding *Pacific Cod Fisheries* for the Bureau in 1915; it, too, went through several revised editions.

The establishment of a marine science institution in the San Juan Islands dates back to when Ed Warbass, one of the three founders of Friday Harbor, bought property on the harbor shore south of town. The University of Washington Friday Harbor Biology Station (now called the Marine Laboratories), under the guidance of Professor Trevor Kincaid of the Zoology Department, was established in 1904 on Warbass's property. In 1906, Warbass sold his property to Captain Andrew Newhall. After the Station moved to the temporarily closed cannery in Friday Harbor from 1906–1910, Newhall donated four acres of land, and a 20-by-75-foot, two-and-a-half-story structure housing the labs and lecture halls was built on concrete piers over the water. A year later, another building housing lecture spaces, administrative offices, and a dining hall was built up the slope; students there for the summer sessions slept in tents on wooden platforms. Locals referred to the campus as the "Bug Station." In 1924 the operations were moved to new facilities on the former Point Caution military reserve north of town. There, a campus of administrative offices, laboratories, and student housing grew over the years. The University of Washington owns and main-

University of Washington Friday Harbor Biology Station (courtesy of San Juan Historical Museum)

tains five marine preserves in the islands: Argyle Lagoon, Friday Harbor Laboratories, and False Bay Biological Preserves on San Juan Island, and the Cedar Rock and Fred and Marilyn Ellis Biological Preserves on Shaw Island.

As early as 1914 the Commissioner of the United States Bureau of Fisheries, Hugh McCormick Smith, urged the University of Washington to establish a school of fisheries. However, it was not until 1919 that the College of Fisheries, the first in the United States, was established, with John N. Cobb as its director. Under his tenure, the College's academic focus was on fishery technology, with courses on fishery products and cannery management. Cobb travelled throughout the Pacific Northwest documenting fisheries and canneries, which resulted in his 1919 publication *The Canning of Fish Products*. His photographs, catalogued and digitized in the Special Collections at the University of Washington, are an important source of information on the West Coast and Alaskan fisheries.

In 1919, the Association of Pacific Fisheries, the official organization of salmon canners on the West Coast, along with the

National Canners Association, established a branch laboratory in Seattle for research on salmon-canning issues.

After Cobb's death in 1930, the Department of Fisheries was formed in the College of Science, with William F. Thompson, a renowned fisheries biologist, as director. He revised the curriculum to emphasize basic science and fish biology. During World War II, it was reorganized as the School of Fisheries. After the war, the Fisheries Research Institute (FRI) was formed as a result of growing concern over dwindling Alaskan salmon resources. Originally in the University of Washington Graduate School, the FRI was moved to the newly re-established College of Fisheries in 1958.

Starting in the latter half of the twentieth century, several local organizations were formed to research, preserve, and protect the environment of the Salish Sea. In 1974, British Columbia passed an act that established the Islands Trust, a federation of local governments, which is responsible for "preserving and protecting the islands' unique amenities and environments." Two trustees are elected from each of the twelve local areas of the islands in the Canadian Salish Sea and two represent the Bowen

Steamer Violet Transporting UW Friday Harbor Labs Students (courtesy of San Juan Historical Museum)

Island Municipality. Part of the Trust's charge is to preserve and protect the islands' marine environment. In 1979, partly to help with the adoption and enforcement of the first San Juan County Comprehensive Plan, a group of local concerned citizens formed the Friends of the San Juans, which continues with the mission of "protecting and restoring the San Juan Islands and the Salish Sea for people and nature." The SeaDoc Society was founded in 2000 to conduct and sponsor scientific research in the Salish Sea. Its mission is "to ensure the health of marine wildlife and their ecosystems through science and education."

In the mid-1980s, with growing awareness of and concern about the environmental degradation of the Northwest Straits, the United States Congress authorized a study of the marine resources of the region, with possible incorporation in the Marine Sanctuary system. Regional representatives were skeptical of a federal, "top down" approach; with strong local opposition culminating in 1994, this process was abandoned in 1996. Senator Patty Murray and Representative Jack Metcalf then established a blue-ribbon committee, the Murray-Metcalf Commission, to study alternate ways of protecting and restoring marine resources in the region; as a result, Congress authorized the Northwest Straits Marine Resources Initiative in 1998. The Northwest Straits Commission provides funding, training, and support to seven marine-resources county-based committees in Northwest Washington: Clallam, Island, Jefferson, San Juan, Skagit, Snohomish, and Whatcom. In addition, the Northwest Straits Foundation was established as a non-profit to provide financial resources to the Initiative.

The San Juan County Marine Resources Committee (MRC) is a voluntary board of citizens established in 1996 by the Board of County Commissioners to advise the Board about issues that affect the marine environment of San Juan County. Its mission is to "protect and restore the marine waters, habitats and species of the Salish Sea to achieve ecosystem health and sustainable resource use." The Committee accomplishes its work through advice, funding, and supporting scientific research, and outreach. One of the first Committee projects was the establishment in the late 1990s of eight voluntary no-fish zones to protect rockfish; marine biologists, sport fishers, and conservationists are consulted on policy and projects. In 2004, the Board of County Commissioners, on the advice of the Committee, created the San Juan Marine Stewardship Area and asked the MRC to draft a management plan for the area. An Area Plan was adopted by the Commissioners in 2007 and implemented by focusing on six strategies: fostering a stewardship ethic in residents and visitors; reducing toxins entering the food web; managing activities to reduce harm to marine habitat and water quality; reducing the risk of large oil spills in our waters; recovering bottom fish species; and preserving marine access and views. Current projects include derelict vessel prevention; oil spill prevention; and efforts to create a plastic-free Salish Sea.

In 2007, the Washington State Legislature created the Puget Sound Partnership, an agency of state government, "to oversee the restoration of the environmental health of Puget Sound by 2020." The Partnership consists of a leadership council, an executive director, an ecosystem coordination board, and a Puget Sound science panel. The Partnership is responsible for coordinating, prioritizing, and monitoring the progress of recovery efforts implemented by a broad range of partner organizations: state and federal agencies, tribes, counties, cities, and private entities.

Among the multitude of research projects funded and directed by these groups and agencies, several are worth highlighting. The geology and seafloor bathymetry of the San Juan Islands is being mapped by the Center for Habitat Studies at Moss Landing Marine Laboratories in California in cooperation with the Tombolo Institute, the SeaDoc Society, Natural Resources Canada, and the Canadian Hydrographic Service. This survey has revealed previously unknown features of the ocean bottom in the islands, including extensive areas of sandy beds used by sand lance as well as possible new seismic fault lines. In partnership with the National Oceanic and Atmospheric Administration (NOAA) and the Northwest Straits Foundation, the Samish Indian Nation developed baseline data for bull kelp beds in the

Salish Sea, for the purposes of monitoring long-term trends in depletion and accretion. Using 2016 high-resolution aerial imagery, the team compared existing kelp beds with those described by a 2006 study by the Friends of the San Juans. This comparison indicated a 305-acre, or 36%, loss of the bull kelp canopy from 2006–2016. Loss varied from island to island, from a minimum of 6% to a maximum of 77% (the average was 49%). Some noteworthy examples include Stuart Island, which sustained a loss of 12.26 acres or 49%; Southern Lopez Island, with a loss of 83.33 acres or 37.5%; and southern San Juan Island, with a loss of 28.74 acres or 12.2%. In British Columbia, the SeaChange Marine Conservation Society has been working on the Salish Sea Nearshore Recovery Project, funded by Fisheries and Oceans Canada and the Pacific Salmon Foundation and in partnership with 34 entities, including industries and local and First Nations governments and agencies. The report on 2019–2020 field work mentions projects in four regions, including eelgrass surveys and restoration in Sechelt Inlet, Howe Sound, Burrard Inlet, and Vancouver's Stanley Park.

Three recent reports highlight the challenges faced by the current condition of the Salish Sea. In 1992 British Columbia Premier Mike Harcourt and Washington State Governor Booth Gardner signed an Environmental Cooperation Agreement, which established the British Columbia-Washington Environmental Cooperation Council and an international Marine Science Panel. Two years later the Panel issued *The Shared Waters of British Columbia and Washington: A Scientific Assessment of Current Status and Future Trends in Resource Abundance and Environmental Quality in the Strait of Juan de Fuca, Strait of Georgia, and Puget Sound* (Copping et al. *The Shared Waters Report* 1994). In May 2021 the Salish Sea Institute, part of Western Washington University, issued Kathryn L. Sobocinski's *State of the Salish Sea.*

> *The Salish Sea is compromised by the cumulative impacts of global climate change, regional urbanization and a growing population, and intensive human use and abuse across the ecosystem over the last two centuries.*
>
> — Dr. Kathryn Sobocinski, State of the Salish Sea Report (2021)

The basis of the report is the analysis of the Salish Sea as a complex ecosystem, "a biologically diverse inland sea that spans the international border, is surrounded by mountainous watersheds of spectacular beauty, and features a rich cultural history." The premise of the report is that by synthesizing the science and traditional cultural knowledge of the Salish Sea, we can better understand its interconnected and shared ecosystem and the threats facing its wellbeing.

In 2000, the Environmental Protection Agency (EPA) and Environment Canada (now Environment and Climate Change Canada) signed a Joint Statement of Cooperation to facilitate cross-border understanding, dialogue, and collaboration on issues affecting the Salish Sea. In July 2021 they produced the Health of the Salish Sea Report, using 10 indicators to identify areas of progress in environmental management and priorities for further action across the transboundary Salish Sea ecosystem. These include air quality, marine species at risk, Chinook salmon, Southern Resident killer whales, toxins in the food web, freshwater quality, marine water quality, stream flow, shellfish harvesting, and marine beaches. Except for shellfish harvesting, which they assess as improving, all others are rated as either neutral or declining, with particular concern for marine species at risk, Chinook salmon, Southern Resident killer whales, marine water quality, and stream flow.

In 2020 the Northwest Indian Fisheries Commission issued the *2020 State of Our Watersheds Report: A Report of the Treaty Tribes of Western Washington*. The report is divided into two parts: regional reports on the Pacific Coast and Puget Sound and Tribal Chapters, most of which are in the Salish Sea region. The emphasis is on watersheds and their importance to the health of the salmon, by documenting the environmental conditions and tracking trends in order to solve the loss and degradation of habitat by population growth, polluted stormwater runoff, climate change, and other significant factors. Chair of the Commission Lorraine Loomis, who recently passed away, noted:

> - *We must never forget the value of salmon to the spiritual, community and economic vitality of tribes and the ecology of the watersheds that sustain us all.*
> - *We must acknowledge that our salmon continue to decline because we are losing their habitat faster than it can be restored. We must reverse that trend. We must protect what sustains them.*
> - *Fisheries managers can't make more fish. Only hatcheries and healthy habitat can do that and both depend on good habitat for their survival.*
> - *We aren't managing salmon for today. We are managing them for future generations.*
>
> — Northwest Indian Fisheries Commission, *2020 State of Our Watersheds Report: A Report of the Treaty Tribes of Western Washington.*

Loomis emphasized the strategy for protecting and rebuilding salmon habitat expressed as *gwədzadad*, a Lushootseed word that means "Teachings of our Ancestors."

CURRENT REGULATIONS, CONDITIONS, AND ISSUES

Regulation

Washington's salmon and steelhead fisheries are managed cooperatively by the State of Washington and the treaty tribes in a unique government-to-government relationship. (This is a result of the 1974 Boldt Decision, which re-affirmed the Treaty Tribes' rights to harvest salmon and steelhead and established the Tribes as co-managers of Washington fisheries.) Each year, state and tribal representatives participate in two key public fish-management processes: the Pacific Fishery Management Council, which sets annual fisheries in federal waters from 3 to 200 miles off the coasts of Washington, Oregon, and California, and the North of Falcon process, which sets salmon fishing seasons for tribes and non-tribal members in inland waters such as Puget Sound, Willapa Bay, Grays Harbor, and state rivers.

Currently regulation of fishing and marine harvesting in the State of Washington is administered through the Department of Fish and Wildlife, which governs commercial, recreational, and tribal fishing and harvest. Most of the United States portion of the Salish Sea is within the Puget Sound Salmon Management and Catch Reporting Area 7; subareas include 7A (north to the international border and the Strait of Georgia); 7B (Bellingham region); 7C (Samish Bay); 7D (Sandy Point to Boundary Point); and 7E (East Sound). Recreational non-salmon fishing and crab, shrimp, and shellfish harvesting is regulated by region. Gear restrictions and size limits are fairly consistent from year to year; each year the State sets the area availability, season, and catch.

In Canada, commercial, recreational, and First Nations fishing is regulated by Fisheries and Oceans Canada. Commercial regulations involve licensing for various catches, including salmon and other finfish, and harvest of crustaceans, echinoderms, mollusks, and shellfish. Recreational ("sport fishing") regulations, which apply to gear, area, season, amount, and size, include fishing for both tidal and non–tidal waters salmon (Chinook and coho, which vary on amount and size, depending on hatchery or wild) and both tidal and non–tidal waters finfish (which mainly include ling cod and other rockfish, hatchery and wild trout, and white sturgeon), as well as harvest of crustaceans, echinoderms, mollusks, and shellfish. (For instance, daily limits include 75 clams; four or five Dungeness crab and red rock crab, depending on the area; 75 mussels; and six purple-hinged rock scallops and weather-vane scallops in the aggregate.) First Nation regulation involves the issuing of Aboriginal Communal Fishing Licenses, which apply to "harvest of fish for food, social or ceremonial (FSC) purposes." Mariculture in Canadian waters, which is administered jointly by Fisheries and Oceans Canada, Transport Canada, and the Province of British Columbia, is regulated through the issuance of aquaculture licenses.

Climate Change

The effect of climate change on fisheries in the Salish Sea is largely driven by three factors: rising sea levels, which change habitat; warming ocean temperatures, which affect populations of fish and other marine species; and acidification, which affects shell formation among mollusks and other organisms.

Sea level rise began around the beginning of the twentieth century; between 1900 and 2016, the world's oceans have risen about six to eight inches. It is predicted that the rate of sea level rise will increase, resulting in a possible rise of two to three feet by the end of the twenty-first century. The major portion of this is due to global warming caused by carbon emissions: higher temperatures melt glaciers and the ice sheets of Greenland and Antarctica, adding more freshwater to the sea. In addition, the increased heat of the water causes it to expand, and in some cases the removal of groundwater causes the level of the land to sink in relation to the level of the sea. The effects vary from place to place; in the Salish Sea region, ground masses are still rising due to glacio-isostatic rebound—the relief of the overburden of the

Pleistocene glaciers. In 2011, the Friends of the San Juans and scientists from the Coastal Geologic Services mapped predicted sea level rise in the San Juan Islands. Current low-lying areas would be most vulnerable, especially shores of sand and gravel—critical breeding grounds for forage fish—that could be "squeezed" by rising levels, causing marine habitats to change. The temptation of property owners is to protect their shorelines with "armoring" of concrete or stone embankments; however, armoring often exacerbates the process of erosion and makes shorelines less adaptable to change.

Global warming has also caused ocean temperatures to rise. According to the Intergovernmental Panel on Climate Change, oceans have absorbed 93% of the excess heat from greenhouse gas emissions since the 1970s. As a result, both surface—the upper 6–12 feet—and deeper sea temperatures have risen, and scientists predict that by 2100 the ocean temperature could increase by 1–4°C. This would cause changes in habitat, feeding, and breeding behavior of fish and other marine organisms. For example, Pacific Northwest salmon thrive in cold water, and temperatures exceeding 20°C can be lethal.

By taking in carbon dioxide from the atmosphere, global oceans have increased their pH, a trend called ocean acidification. The ocean is normally basic, or greater than seven on the pH scale; acidification has caused it to go toward neutral (not acidic, which is less than seven). The absorption of some 30%–40% of human-produced carbon dioxide leads to a chemical reaction in the seawater that results in an increase in hydrogen ions (H^+). This prevents sea creatures that form calcium carbonate shells or structures from doing so. Seasonal upwelling of waters with higher acidity threatens local seafood companies such as Taylor Shellfish Farms, with over 500 employed in operations and 11,000 acres in production at Samish Bay.

Piracy, Poaching, and Derelict Gear

Piracy and poachers of the maritime harvest has continued into the present. Both the Canadian Department of Fisheries and Oceans (Fisheries and Oceans Canada) and the Washington State Department of Fish and Wildlife have conducted operations to catch illegal fishers and seize illegal equipment. In late January/early February of 2021, Fisheries and Oceans Canada, in conjunction with the Canadian Coast Guard, seized 337 illegal commercial crab traps, including a 1.6 kilometer–long groundline with 21 traps attached, in Boundary Bay, which straddles the U.S.-Canada boundary. This is a higher number than in the past four years of such operations: 219 in 2017; 226 in 2018; 230 in 2019; and 136 in 2020. These large numbers from a relatively limited area indicate the severity of the problem.

One of the continuing hazards to marine life in the Salish Sea is the presence of derelict gear. Sometimes this takes the form of "ghost nets"—usually gill nets that were abandoned after becoming snagged on reefs and rocks on the sea bottom. These nets continue to capture and kill birds, fish, and marine mammals. In 2002, the Northwest Straits Initiative, a program authorized by Congress to protect and restore marine resources in the Northwest Straits, began the Derelict Fishing Gear Removal Project to locate and remove derelict fishing gear from Puget Sound. In cooperation with the Department of Fish and Wildlife and other federal and state agencies, and with funding from a $4.5-million American Recovery and Reinvestment Act grant, it developed removal guidelines, created a database of known derelict gear, established a phone-and-web-based reporting system, and began removing derelict fishing gear, primarily gill nets and crab pots. As of 2019, 5,809 nets had been recovered, at the cost of about $11 million. In a sample from 2002, of the 902 derelict nets recovered from Puget Sound and the U.S. portions of the Strait of Juan de Fuca, most (876) were gill nets, with a few purse seines (23), two trawl nets, and one aquaculture net. The majority of the gill nets were recovered from the San Juan Islands (499) and North Sound (which includes the area from the border to the north portion of Whidbey Island) (244). Most of these were taken from shallow waters; the harder and costlier task of recovering deepwater nets remains a major challenge. In 2019 the U.S. Army 569th Deep Divers helped to remove gear at depths of 150 feet in Haro Strait off the coast of San Juan Island. In addition, abandoned crab traps are plentiful; they, too, continue to capture crabs, leading to wasteful deaths. The National Oceanic and Atmospheric Administration estimated that there are 12,000 crab pots lost annually in Washington State; since 2002, the Northwest Straits Foundation has retrieved 3,600.

Finfish Net Pens

In the mid-1970s, business interests in both British Columbia and Washington State began to experiment with finfish net pen mariculture. In 1975, Aqua Sea Farms, funded by the Fisher Baking Company, was initiated off Lopez Island and managed by Nels Strandberg, a former science teacher at Lopez High School. Based upon the experience of sea farming in Norway, the operation received technical assistance from Dr. Earnest Brannon and others at the University of Washington. The operation was in Shoal Bay, at Anchor Jensen's Marina (now Spencer's Landing Marina). By 1981, they were processing and shipping 150,000 pan-sized coho. Installation of a new breakwater reduced water circulation, causing the fish to start dying, and the business, run at this time by Bob Ellis, was sold in 1983 and moved to Cypress Island; Icicle Seafood held the license until 2016. In the mid-1980s, Sea Farms of Norway proposed a 54-unit salmon pen in Griffin Bay, a controversial project that led to a moratorium on finfish net pen aquaculture in San Juan County. Despite efforts to reverse this with the application of stricter requirements for aquaculture in general at the State level, the moratorium remained in place until at least 1988. A new aquaculture permit was not granted until 1993, and then it was for Judd Cove Shellfish to raise oysters on Crescent Beach on Orcas Island.

Within the Canadian waters of the Salish Sea, finfish net pen aquaculture began in the early 1970s in protected British Columbia inlets such as Jervis and Sechelt. In the 1980s, when the industry shifted to raising Atlantic salmon, concerns arose among First Nations about competition with the market for wild salmon and among environmentalists about the negative impacts of disease and parasite transfer, escapement of Atlantic salmon, the use of pharmaceuticals such as growth hormones and antibiotics, and toxicants. The principal location of finfish net pens in the Canadian Salish Sea is in the Discovery Islands at the northern end of the Strait of Georgia, where there are currently 19 sites, most of them owned and run by Mowi ASA (formerly Marine Harvest), with a few run by Cermaq Canada and Grieg Seafood, all of which are based in Norway. By the mid-2010s the worth of finfish net pen aquaculture in British Columbia exceeded $500 million (Canadian), which is more than all the commercial salmon fishing in Alaska (which is the largest salmon fishery in the world).

Due to growing environmental concerns, Fisheries and Oceans Canada came under pressure to address open water finfish net pens, and at the end of 2020 Minister Bernadette Jordan announced that the remaining licenses were being renewed for only 18 more months, in essence setting a target of June 2022 as an end of finfish net pen aquaculture in the Canadian portion of the Salish Sea. Fisheries and Oceans Canada is working toward a transition to other forms of finfish aquaculture, such as land-based recirculating aquaculture systems.

In the late 1990s, several finfish net pens were established in the US portion of the Salish Sea by Cooke Aquaculture to raise Atlantic salmon. An early critic of finfish net pen aquaculture was Arthur Whiteley, former Professor Emeritus at the Department of Zoology, University of Washington, and member of the Marine Environmental Consortium. He wrote a letter in January 2002 to the Washington State Department of Ecology about the draft permit for open water net pens. In it he raised three areas of concern: "(1) the sediment impacts particularly affecting benthic ecosystems; (2) escapement of non-native Atlantic salmon; and (3) pathogens, disease and antibiotic use." Elaborating on the first, sediment impacts, he equated this form of mariculture to Concentrated Animal Feeding Operations (similar to terrestrial feed lots). The third concern—the transmission of antibiotics and diseases to the wild salmon stocks in the area—has been established by further scientific studies.

Whiteley's second concern, escapement, became a reality with the massive failure of the Cooke Aquaculture's finfish net pen near Cypress Island in August 2017, which sounded a wakeup call for many concerned about the health of wild salmon in the Salish Sea. The net pen was not only poorly maintained—the company had allowed buildup of over 110 tons of biofouling (mussels and other sea creatures on the nets)—but several of their cleaning machines had broken down. This event resulted in the release of 263,000 Atlantic salmon, the majority of the 305,000 fish—three million pounds—that were in the pens. Anglers caught some of the escaped Atlantic salmon in the region for months afterwards. The company was fined $332,000 by the State. Shortly after the event, the Wild Fish Conservancy filed suit against Cooke Aquaculture under the Clean Water Act; rather than defend themselves in court, the company agreed to settle for $2.75 million, which will go to the Rose Foundation to fund environmental projects to protect wild salmon and Southern Resident killer whales in the Salish Sea.

> *The economic, cultural, and recreational resources of these incredible waters will no longer be jeopardized by the negligent actions of this industry. We've invested so much in trying to recover our wild Pacific salmon populations, there is no sensible purpose for allowing non-native species into the Salish Sea. The day-to-day impact of invasive aquaculture—feces, disease, loose food pellets or lice—could have serious impacts. The state ban is a strong stance to ensure the protection of our marine environment and native salmon populations in the Salish Sea.*
>
> — Washington State Senator Kevin Ranker, March 23, 2018

As a result of this collapse and escapement, on March 22, 2018, Washington State Governor Jay Inslee signed a bill that would phase out non-native fish farming—including Atlantic salmon—by 2025. Cooke Aquaculture, whose aquatic lands leases expire in 2022, then sought, and was granted in January of 2021, permits to raise native, all-female, sterile steelhead trout in their four net pens located near Bainbridge Island and Deepwater Bay in La Conner. Recently the Wild Fish Conservancy sued the Company again under Section 505 of the Clean Water Act for endangering wild native salmon and steelhead, as well as related species such as the Southern Resident killer whales. The Conservancy is also seeking to buy the Company's leases in order to take over the four sites.

Southern Resident Killer Whales

Orcas or killer whales (*Orcinus orca*) are not only alpha marine mammal predators but also a keystone species in the Salish Sea. Orcas that are most commonly found in the Salish Sea are classified into two genetically distinct separate populations: Southern Resident killer whales and transient orcas or Bigg's killer whales. Southern Resident killer whales travel in three matrilineal groups, J pod, K pod, and L pod, and feed primarily on Chinook salmon from Southeast Alaska to central California. Southern Residents spend time, typically in the spring, summer, and fall, in the San Juan Islands and Salish Sea. Ironically, transient killer whales currently spend more time in the Salish Sea than the Southern Resident killer whales. Transients, which have a much looser social structure than resident killer whales and do not usually form large kinship groupings, travel in small groups and primarily eat seals, sea lions, and porpoises.

The fate of the Southern Residents is of paramount concern, as the health of that population is indicative of the overall health of the Salish Sea. In particular, there is deep concern about the falling population of Southern Resident killer whales, due to a "trifecta" of interrelated impacts: lack of prey due to the decline in salmon populations, particularly their preferred prey, Chinook salmon; vessel disturbances—the noise that interferes with the orcas' ability to communicate and hunt, the presence that disrupts foraging behavior, as well as ship strikes that can cause death; and pollution contaminants that are stored in their blubber. The lack of salmon can result in starvation, and this is compounded by the vessel impacts that cause the orcas to expend more energy hunting, all of which results in their fat stores being burned, releasing the bio-accumulated contaminants and causing additional impacts to their health. (The transient orcas found in the Salish Sea also have significant levels of contaminants in their blubber, but they are getting plenty to eat and their health isn't impacted from contaminant releases.) The transient orca populations are growing; the Southern Residents' population is not. Following a rapid, almost 20% decline in population from about 100 in the 1990s, Southern Resident killer whales were listed as threatened and endangered by Canada in 2003 and in the United States as an endangered species in 2005. Since then, the population has fallen to just 74.

In March 2018 Washington State Governor Jay Inslee established the Southern Resident Orca Task Force by executive order to examine and recommend solutions to these issues. The group, which was composed of representatives from diverse sectors of society as well as members of several tribes, who, as sovereign nations, chose to participate, met and submitted a *Year One Report* (November 2018) with 36 recommendations for orca recovery. It proposed four goals: "(1) increase Chinook abundance; (2) decrease disturbance of and risk to Southern Resident orcas from vessels and noise and increase their access to prey; (3) reduce the exposure of Southern Resident orcas and their prey to contaminants; and (4) ensure that funding, information and accountability mechanisms are in place to support effective implementation." In their second-year report, the Task Force assessed progress on implementing these recommendations, addressed emerging issues, and crafted new recommendations. These recommendations included: prey—increase hatchery production and reduce threats from the hydropower system (dam barriers) and pinnipeds and predatory fish; vessels—establish restrictions on speed and distance by whale-watch and other vessels (including a licensing system) and new standards for oil-barge tug escorts; and contaminants—prioritize chemicals of concern and fund prevention and cleanup. Two emergent systemic threats were identified: rapid human population growth, with its consequent development, and climate change, including ocean acidification. In 2021, Washington State implemented a commercial whale-watch licensing program, which restricts the commercial viewing of Southern Resident killer whales. Canada also has commercial whale watching regulations and both Canada and the U.S. have regulations pertaining to recreational boaters who are in the vicinity of whales. NOAA has recently (March 2021) issued *Species in the Spotlight Priority Actions 2021-2025* to address the threats to the Southern Resident killer whales. The key actions in this plan are to protect killer whales from harmful vessel impacts through enforcement, education, and evaluation; target conservation of critical prey; improve our knowledge of Southern Resident killer whale health to advance recovery and support emergency response; and raise awareness about the recovery needs of Southern Resident killer whales and inspire stewardship through outreach and education.

> *Once considerable migrations of Pacific salmon with diverse life histories brought marine-derived nutrients to watersheds. But the diminished runs of Pacific salmon, especially Chinook and coho salmon, are one example of reduced connectivity between the estuary and watersheds, in this case the connectivity of both adults migrating landward and juveniles migrating seaward.*
>
> — Dr. Kathryn Sobocinski,
> *State of the Salish Sea Report* (2021)

EPILOGUE

And It All Comes Back to Salmon

> *I have known my entire life that salmon were created to sustain all living things and that they serve as a measuring stick of our present and future physical and spiritual health.*
>
> — Billy Frank Jr., Chairman, Northwest Fisheries Commission, "Listen to the Salmon" (2006)

The decline in the populations of the five salmon species, particularly Chinook and coho, and steelhead trout since the late nineteenth century has been well documented. After the abandonment in the 1850s of the rich Sacramento River salmon fishery due to pollution, habitat loss, and overfishing, the industry moved north to the Columbia River, only to abandon that for the rich waters of the Salish Sea. Fishers then moved north again, to Alaska, "The Last Frontier," and out into deeper Pacific waters to catch the salmon before their return to their natal rivers and streams. What has become increasingly clear through this time period is the biophysical connectivity throughout the Salish Sea ecosystem and beyond, and particularly the central role that salmon play in that system. Salmon directly connect the vast estuary that is the Salish Sea with the watersheds that surround it.

In addition to the overharvesting of salmon by the commercial fishing industry, the destruction of their spawning and juvenile rearing grounds has threatened their survival. Beginning in the late 1880s, power companies began building dams on all of the major Northwest rivers that salmon traversed in order to reach spawning grounds. Under the New Deal's Public Works Administration, construction began on both the Bonneville and

Grand Coulee Dams in 1934. By 1937 there were 174 dams in the Columbia River drainage basin alone; many of these were constructed without adequate salmon ladders, the technology used to help fish bypass artificial river blockages. By 1942, the spawning grounds on the Columbia River had been reduced by 50%, according to the Oregon Director of Fish Culture, Hugh Mitchell. Grand Coulee Dam alone is estimated to have placed an impediment to one thousand miles of river, blocking one hundred thousand salmon and steelhead from upriver habitat.

> *Population growth drives urbanization and development, which in turn triggers structural changes to the landscape and seascape like habitat fragmentation, shoreline armoring, conversion of vegetated areas to impervious surfaces, and profound changes in watershed and wetland hydrology. These gradual but damaging trends also increase nutrient and contaminant loading to the estuarine waters and limit the scope and scale of local fisheries.*
>
> — Dr. Kathryn Sobocinski,
> *State of the Salish Sea Report* (2021)

But the loss of shoreline habitat for juvenile salmon and the forage fish that they feed on, particularly in the San Juan Islands, is equally, if not more, significant. In 2012, Eric Beamer and Kurt Fresh published a study that showed that a majority of the Chinook salmon genetic stocks from the surrounding Salish Sea watersheds spent some time as juveniles in the San Juan Islands. Most abundant were those from the Lower Fraser River, but significant populations came from the Nooksack/Samish, Skagit, Stillaguamish, and Snohomish Rivers, with smaller, but still significant stocks from the South Thompson River, East Vancouver Island (including the Cowichan River), and even West Vancouver Island. Modification and destruction of the shoreline habitat through eradication of vegetation and bunkering disrupt the environment for the juvenile salmon as well as egg-laying areas in the sand and gravel.

Although British Columbia and the states of Oregon and Washington had built hatcheries in the late nineteenth century, raised salmon did not help with salmon populations in the long run. British Columbia started an artificial hatching and planting of small fry as early as 1885 and stepped up production after the 1914 Fraser River Hell's Gate slide. Between 1919 and 1930 sockeye eggs from the lower Fraser and Skeena Rivers were transplanted to above the slide; by 1927, 2.25 billion fry had been raised and outplanted. But despite enhancing salmon stocks by 50 million fry annually for 40 years, stocks continued to decline. After studies by the Biological Board of Canada, it was determined that the hatchery program was ineffectual, and the government turned to enhancing spawning beds, building artificial spawning channels, controlling water flow, and constructing fishways.

On January 21, 2021, *The New York Times* published an article by Marie Fazio entitled "Northwest's Salmon Population May Be Running Out of Time," based largely on the *2020*

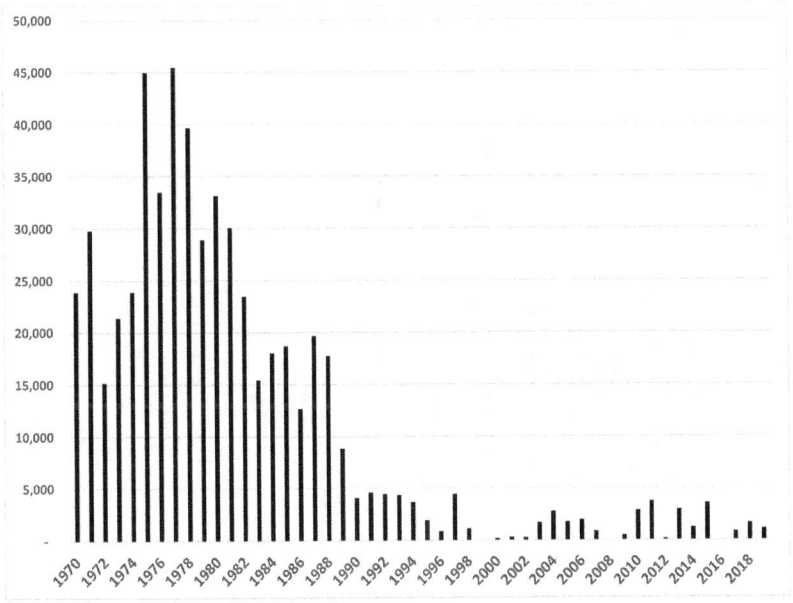

Chinook Salmon Catch (in numbers), San Juan Islands, 1970–2019

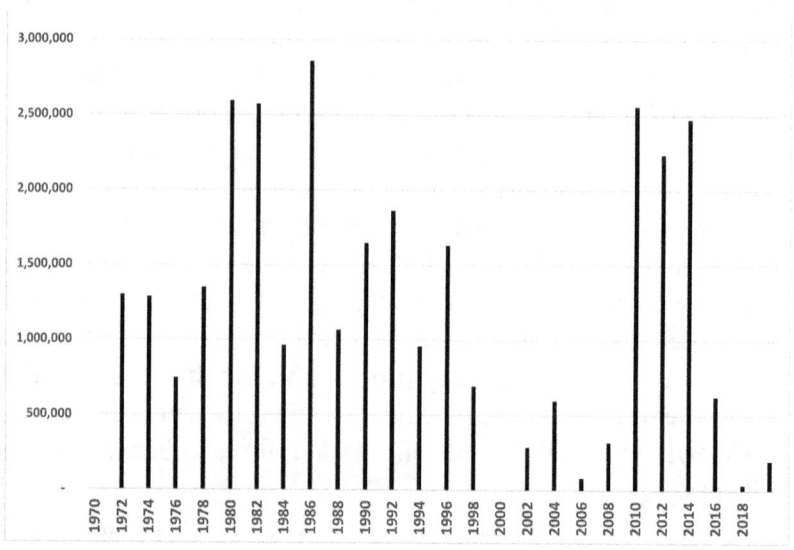

Pink Salmon Catch (in numbers), San Juan Islands, 1970–2019

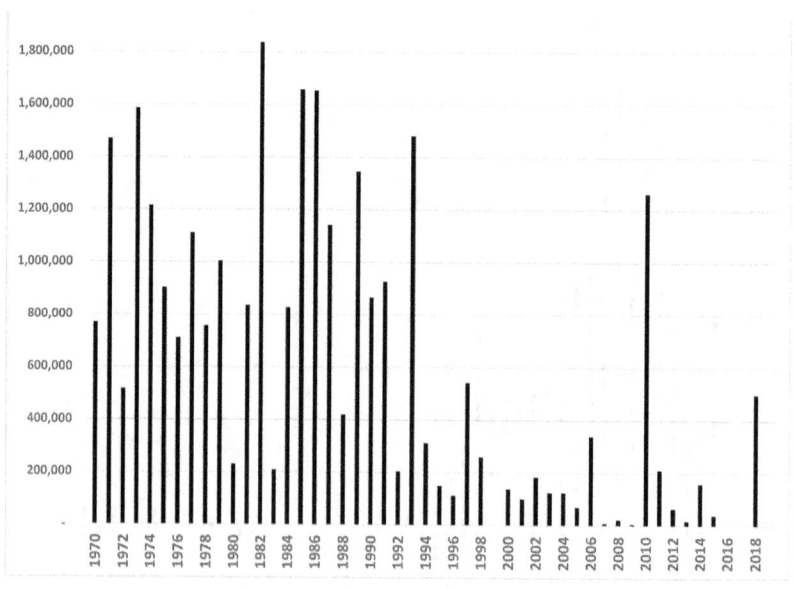

Sockeye Salmon Catch (in numbers), San Juan Islands, 1970–2019

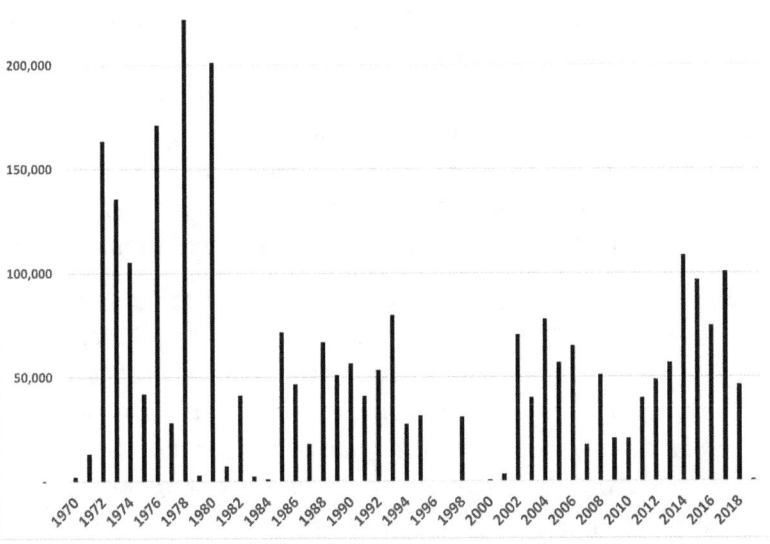

Chum Salmon Catch, (in numbers) San Juan Islands, 1970–2019

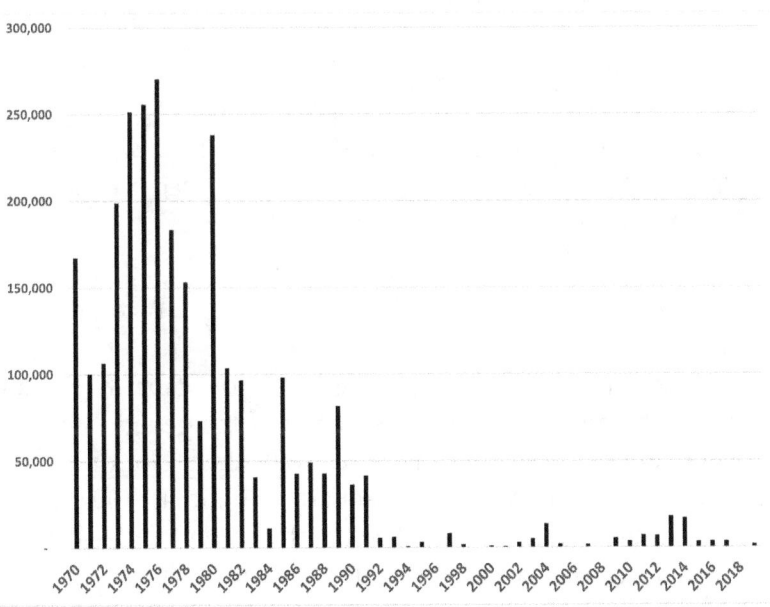

Coho Salmon Catch (in numbers), San Juan Islands, 1970–2019

State of Salmon in Watersheds report from the Washington State Governor's Salmon Recovery Office. After noting the good news that four endangered populations are either "making progress" toward or "approaching [the] goal" of population growth, the report details the bad news about the other 10 species that are either "not keeping pace" or "in crisis." It identifies four main historic factors—habitat, harvest, hydropower, and hatcheries—and adds two modern ones—climate change and predation.

> *Thirty years ago, the federal government determined Snake River sockeye were endangered, making it the first salmon population in the Pacific Northwest to be listed under the Endangered Species Act. Since then, 14 species have been listed in Washington. Determined to save this treasured icon, thousands of people across Washington State have worked tirelessly to increase salmon populations. Their efforts have slowed the decline of many populations and even brought some close to recovery.*
>
> *However, too many salmon remain on the brink of extinction. And time is running out. The climate is changing, rivers are warming, habitat is diminishing, and the natural systems that support salmon in the Pacific Northwest need help now more than ever.*
>
> — Washington State Governor's Salmon Recovery Office,
> Executive Summary, 2020 *State of Salmon in Watersheds*

The diminished ability of salmon to adapt to climate change is highlighted by a recent study of the genetic stock of sockeye salmon in the Skeena River watershed. Not only have sockeye returns dropped by three-quarters in the last 100 years—from 1.8 million in 1913 to 469,000 in the present day—the data seems to suggest that the populations of the 13 species studied that dropped the most were those with the largest body size, probably due to selective gillnetting.

A local project that works to address salmon survival and viability is Long Live the Kings. Founded in 1986, the group's first project was the transformation of a hatchery on the Wishkah River near Grays Harbor, which "focused on refining rearing techniques that mimicked nature, bolstering depressed wild Chinook and coho populations by supplementing them with hatchery-reared fish, and creating and restoring habitat." Jim Youngren had built the Glenwood Springs Hatchery on Orcas Island in 1978, using natural springs on his own land to create rearing ponds. He then established a Chinook run, isolated from spawning wild salmon. In 1986 Long Live the Kings assumed management of the facility, which continues to operate today. The Hatchery releases 750,000 juvenile Chinook salmon annually. More recently, Long Live the Kings has partnered with the Canadian Pacific Salmon Foundation on the Salish Sea Marine Survival Project, an international effort to determine why juvenile salmon and steelhead are dying—their survival rate has declined tenfold since the 1980s—in the Salish Sea, in contrast to coastal and Columbia River populations.

Of the three stream watersheds that the United States Boundary Survey team noted as bearing salmon stock in the 1850s, efforts to restore habitat for two of them are underway. On Orcas Island, the San Juan County Land Bank's Coho Preserve (Cascade Creek) was purchased with funds from the Salmon Recovery Funding Board. The stream there offers habitat for juvenile salmon and trout. In modern times, coho salmon were observed in Cascade Creek as early as the 1950s, and recently Jenny De Groot of Speckled Trout Consulting noted that female coho built redds—nests in the gravelly bottom for laying eggs—in November of 2019, and coho fry were seen in April of 2020. The Land Bank and the San Juan Preservation Trust also purchased land that included Zylstra Lake, which was built on False Bay Creek in the San Juan Valley watershed in the 1960s. The lower reaches of the creek were and can again be habitat for seagoing cutthroat trout and chum salmon, and the Zylstra Lake property may be used to establish year-round stream flow. The creek drains into False Bay, where the False Bay Biological

Preserve, purchased in 1974 and managed by the University of Washington's Marine Laboratories, covers 300 acres of tide lands and 23.3 acres of upland.

One of the more hopeful actions taken to restore the health of the Salish Sea ecosystem in recent history is the 2011 and 2014 removals of two dams on the Elwha River. The Elwha and Glines Canyon dams were built in the early 1900s as sources of hydroelectricity for Port Angeles and other nearby communities. In 1992, Congress passed the Elwha River Ecosystem and Fisheries Restoration Act, authorizing dam removal to restore the river ecosystem and the native fisheries dependent upon it. It took almost ten years for the first dam removal, but as a result the Elwha River has begun to flow freely again, releasing millions of cubic yards of sand and silt to the nearshore waters of the Strait of Juan de Fuca, resulting in the sedimentation of the estuary and expansion of the river-mouth delta. After being blocked for over a hundred years from their natal streams, salmon began returning just months after the removal of the dams, and now have access to over 70 miles of spawning beds in Olympic National Park. The fate of other dams, such as the Snake River Dams—the removal of which has been hotly contested for several years, remains uncertain.

But to honor the long history of Indigenous and Euro American fishers in the Salish Sea, we need to give the late Billy Frank Jr. the last word: "Listen to the salmon."

Acknowledgements

- Lovel Pratt: fellow crabber, helpmate, true friend and the love of my life
- Readers: Bill Engle, Morgan Frazier, Nancy McCoy, Bruce Robinson, Cal Ryan, Edrie Vinson, and Lynn Weber Roochvarg
- San Juan County Assessor's Office: John Kulseth and Chris Ledgerwood
- Friends of the San Juans and San Juan County Lodging Tax
- Lopez Island Historical Museum: Amy Hildebrand and Breton Carter
- Orcas Island Historical Museum: Brittney Maruska, Nancy Stillger, Edrie Vinson, and Terri Vinson
- San Juan Historical Museum: Kevin Loftus and Andy Zall
- Shaw Island Historical Museum: Cherie Christiansen
- San Juan Island Library
- Bob Guard, Mike Galligan, Shaun Hubbard, Robin Jacobson, Garreth Jeffers, Jay Julius, Geddes Martin, Doug McCutchen, Scott McCay, Mike O'Connell, Barbara Rosenkotter, Mike Vouri, Adam Whitridge, and Giles Zizou
- Bruce Conway, W. Bruce Conway, book design services
- Jill Twist, excellent editor—but all mistakes remain my own, despite her best efforts!

Mending Nets
(courtesy San Juan Historical Museum)

San Juan Islands Place Names

FISH AND OTHER SEA FOODS

PLANTS AND ALGAE

Eelgrass

In estuarine muddy or sandy areas, eelgrass beds thrive in the intertidal and nearshore environment. The predominant, native species is *Zostera marina*, whose rhizomes and roots hold the plants to the beds and whose blades, which can grow up to 3 feet in length, provide a rich environment for numerous species, including herring egg-laying as well as habitat for crabs and fishes. Eelgrass also helps dampen wave energy and trap sediments.

Kelp

Kelp beds are an especially important part of the Salish Sea ecosystem. The primary species is bull kelp (*Nereocystis luetkeana*), which has three parts: a holdfast, a root-like mass which anchors the plant to the shallow rocky bottom; the stipe, similar to a plant stem but hollow and filled with gas (including carbon monoxide), that connects the holdfast to a floating hollow bulb (up to 4 inches in diameter) attached to the fronds, and can grow up to 100 feet long; and the blade- or leaf-like fronds that can grow up to 10 feet in length and spread on the surface of the water to take up nutrients and photosynthesize. Bull kelp grows in one season, at an amazing rate of up to 5 inches a day; in the winter, they decay, the holdfast loosens, and the individual plants wash up on shores to provide shelter and habitat for several tideline species. Kelp "forests" can rise and fall with the tides and serve as habitat for fish and marine mammals such as otters, seals, and whales.

INVETERBRATES

MOLLUSKS

Bivalves

Mollusks include bivalves such as clams, cockles, mussels, oysters, and scallops, and gastropods such as limpets, snails, and whelks. Clam types included bent-nose (*Macoma nasuta*), butter or Washington (*Saxidomus giganteus* and *nuttallii*), geoduck (*Panopea generosa*), horse (*Tresus nuttallii* and *T. capax*), little-neck or steamer (*Leukoma staminea*), Pacific razor (*Siliqua petula*), sand (*Macoma secta*), and soft-shell (*Mya arenaria*). Most are located in the gravelly, muddy, or sandy intertidal and nearshore zones. Several mussels (*Mytilidae* Family) are native to the region; they cling to rocks and other submerged structures such as pilings in clusters by means of byssal threads. The blue mussel (*Mytilus trossulus*), which can reach 2 inches in length, is the most common species used in mariculture. The native Olympia oyster (*Ostrea lurida*), occupying shallow-water beds called "reefs," was probably once quite plentiful in the region. Both Pacific or Japanese (*Magallana gigas*) and Eastern (*Crassostrea virginica*) oysters were introduced for farming and have subsequently reproduced without cultivation. There are two types of scallops in the Salish Sea: pink (*Chlamys rubida*) and spiny (*C. hastata*). Both are about 2½ inches in diameter and are harvested in the subtidal zone by divers.

Chitons

Chitons are a form of mollusks that lack tentacles and eyes; their shells are divided into eight pieces. The largest species are the gumboot or giant Pacific (*Cryptochiton stelleri*), which at up to 12 inches is the world's largest, and mossy (*Mopalia muscosa*) and black (*Katarina tunicata*), both of which can reach 4 inches in length. Chitons, which adhere to rocks by means of a large, snakelike foot (which is the main edible part), can glide over surfaces to feed on algae and a film of diatoms and bacteria.

Gastropods

Other mollusks, usually found in the tidal zone, include abalone, cockles, limpets, snails, and whelks. Pinto abalone (*Haliotis kamtschatkana*), once common in the Salish Sea, are endangered because of overharvesting. The heart cockle (*Clinocardium nuttallii*), which is distinguished like all cockles by its ribs, inhabits the intertidal zone and deeper. Limpets (families *Lottidae* and *Acmaeidae*), whose shells are conical in shape, adhere to either individual rocks or rocky shorelines. Most are less than 2 inches in diameter, but when pried from their base offer a tidy bite of meat. There are two large (up to 5 inches long) snails in the region—the hairy triton (*Fusitriton oregonensis*) and moon snail (*Euspira lewisii*)—as well as several smaller (1 inch or less) periwinkles (family *Littorinidae*). Of the whelks, the wrinkled purple whelk or frilled dogwinkle (*Nucella lamellosa*), being the largest—reaching up to 2 inches—was the most commonly harvested.

ARTHROPODS

Barnacles

There are several species of barnacles in the Salish Sea, which can be found attached to rocks and other submerged substrates such as docks and pilings and even driftwood, kelp, and shells. The most common is the Acorn barnacle (*Balanus glandula*), which grows to ½ inch in diameter and the same in height.

Crabs

There are two main types of commercially harvested native crab: Dungeness (*Cancer magister*) and red rock (*C. productus*). Dungeness is the larger of the two—up to 10 inches across—with the average being 6-7 inches. It prefers sandy or muddy substrates and is usually associated with eelgrass beds, although it breeds and inhabits the subtidal zone. The red rock crab, which as its name implies is usually colored brick red, is smaller (up to 6 inches) and prefers rocky substrates. Indigenous peoples also harvested other crab species found in the intertidal zone of the seashore.

Shrimp

There are many species of native shrimp in the Salish Sea; the four most common commercially and recreationally harvested varieties are coonstripe (*Pandalus danae, P. hypsinotus, P goniurus*); pink; side-striped (*Pandalus dispar*), and spot (*Pandalus platyceros*). There are three species of coonstripe shrimp, all of which are harvested in the San Juan Islands. Dock (coonstripe) shrimp, with brownish bodies with brown lines and spots on the head and tail, may reach 5½ inches in length, excluding the antennae; they prefer areas of sand and gravel with swift tidal currents. Humpback (coonstripe) shrimp are a mottled reddish-brown in color, with some white patches on the lower head and tail; the largest of the three coonstripes, it may attain lengths of up to 7 inches, excluding the antennae. The humpy (coonstripe) shrimp, which is similar in appearance to the dock shrimp, except the stripes of the humpy are red to orange in color, is small, not exceeding 3 inches in length, excluding the antennae. The term pink shrimp applies to species: northern (*Pandalus eous*) and ocean (*P. jordani*). The northern pink shrimp is less than six inches long, smaller than the spot shrimp and the sidestripe shrimp; it can be distinguished from ocean pink shrimp by a small spine on the top of the third tail segment. Ocean (smooth) pink shrimp are almost identical in size and coloration to the northern (rough) pink shrimp, but the spine is absent from the third tail segment. The sidestripe shrimp (*Pandolopsis dispar*) is reddish orange in color with rows of white bars on its head and tail; it has long antennae, which are approximately 1.5 times the length of the body. Spot shrimp, deep pink to red in color with white stripes on the head and two pairs white spots on the tail end (hence the name), are the largest, reaching up to 9 inches in length, excluding the antennae. They are most commonly found in Hood Canal and the San Juan Islands.

Octopus

There are several types of octopus in the Salish Sea, but the most renowned is the giant Pacific octopus (*Enteroctopus dofleini*, formerly *Octopus apollyon*), or north Pacific giant octopus, which was also commonly known by the more ominous name of devil fish. The largest specimens can be up to 24 feet in arm spread, with a weight of up to 160 pounds. They have been found all the way from intertidal zone to as deep as 5,000 feet but prefer rocky areas where they can use caves or grottoes for their dens. Although Indigenous peoples hunted—usually by spearing—smaller individuals in tidal areas and the nearshore, there are several historical accounts of larger specimens washing ashore, being caught in nets, or captured in the water. It was not until the use of underwater breathing apparatus became popular that the larger individuals were encountered in deep waters.

ECHINODERMS

Sea Cucumbers

The California or giant red sea cucumbers (*Apostichopus californicus*), which is orange reddish in color, measures up to 20 inches in length (although it can expand to 3 feet when 'relaxed' in the water). Sea cucumbers are found in both shallow and deep waters. They inhabit both rocky and gravelly sea bottoms but avoid muddy or sandy areas. Sea cucumbers are collected for both the edible skin and the muscle, and the market is largely Asian.

Sea Urchins

Like sea cucumbers, sea urchins are found in both shallow and deep waters. There are three main species of sea urchin in the Salish Sea: green (*Strongylocentrotus drobachiensis*); purple (*S. purpuratus*); and red (*S. franciscanus*). Sea urchins consist of a flattened sphere skeleton, called a test, made of chalky plates, to which are attached spines, connected by ball joints. They range from subtidal zone to 300 feet deep, and like sea cucumbers, avoid areas of mud or sand; most are found in or near kelp beds. The red sea urchin is the largest, with a diameter of up to 7 inches and a spine length of 3 inches. The purple, with short, heavy spines, is the next largest, up to 6 inches in total diameter. The green urchin is smallest—up to 3½ inches total—and has finer spines. Sea urchins are harvested for their orange meat, a gourmet delicacy, particularly in Asian markets.

VERTEBRATES

FISH

Herring

Pacific herring (*Clupea pallasi*) used to be one of the most abundant fishes in the Salish Sea. They congregate in schools of thousands and are attacked by seagulls and other birds from above when a "ball" is forced towards the surface of the water by larger fish below.

I have often seen a shoal of herrings, when hotly pursued by the dogfish, dash into a little rock-bound nook, the water lashed into white spray by a thousand tails and fins, plied with all the power and energy the poor struggling fish could exert to escape the dreaded foe. A wall of rocks, right and left, ahead the shelving shingle—on they go, and hundreds lie high-and-dry, panting on the pebbles. It is just as well perhaps to die there, as to be torn, bitten, and eaten by the piratical cannibals that are waging the fearful havoc on the imprisoned shoal. The dogfish wound ten times as many as they eat, and, having satiated and gorged their greedy stomachs, swim lazily away, leaving the dead, dying, and disabled to the tender mercies of the sea-birds watching the battle, ever ready to pounce upon the unprotected, and end its miseries.

— John Keast Lord,
The Naturalist in Vancouver Island and British Columbia (1866)

Herring spawn in the early spring, usually in March or April. Because they can only lay their eggs on substrate and not in open waters, schools will migrate into shallow waters and the males will release thousands of sperm that form a milky cloud. The eggs laid by the females, around a millimeter in diameter, are very sticky, so that they adhere to eelgrass, seaweeds, and other objects—a fact that helped the Coast Salish harvest them by putting tree boughs in the water and then combing the roe off. The eggs hatch in 10 days' time, and the larvae, which primarily eat cephalopods, grow to 3 to 4 inches in length. They then go to the open ocean to mature for 3 years. Adult herring, which range in size from 4 to 8 inches in length, reach sexual maturity at about 7 1/2 inches, and they can grow to up to 12 inches or more.

Smelt

Four members of the smelt family are found in the Salish Sea: capelin (*Mallotus villosus*), surf (or silver) smelt (*Hypomesus pretiosus*), eulachon (or candlefish) (*Thaleichthys pacificus*), and the longfin smelt (*Spirinchus thaleichthys*). Most range in size up to eight inches, and feature narrow, silvery bodies with a dark stripe down the middle of the side of the body. Capelin and surf smelt spawn in salt water; capelin in September and October, surf smelt from June to September. Eulachon and longfin smelt are anadromous, migrating to fresh water to spawn; the eulachon from March to May, the long-finned smelt from October to December. Herring and smelt form a significant portion of the regional forage fish population.

Anchovy

The California or northern anchovy (*Engraulis mordax*), which ranges from British Columbia to Baja California, is the closest thing to the sardine in the Pacific Northwest (although the Pacific or California sardine's range extends to southeastern Alaska, it is not common in the Salish Sea) and historically fishers often called anchovies sardines. They are small—growing to about 7 inches—with long snouts that overhang a large mouth and are bluish green above and silvery below; adults have a faint silver stripe on the side. Anchovy spawn when two years old but don't live beyond four years or so; they spawn, in coves and bays, throughout the year, with peak activity from February to April, but unlike herring, they tend to stay away from the nearshore.

Halibut, Flounder, and Other Flatfish

There are several species of flatfish in the Salish Sea. As their name implies, they are flattened in shape and occupy the sea bottom, often disguised by spots or coloring that camouflages them on the seabed. Based on the side of the body where their eyes are located, these include two types of flounder: lefteye—speckled and Pacific sandabs—and righteye—Pacific halibut

(*Hippoglossus stenolepis*), arrowtooth (*Atheresthes stomas*) and starry (*Platichthys stellatus*) flounder, and several soles. Pacific halibut was the most common catch in the Salish Sea until overfishing led to new fishing grounds, first at Flattery Banks and then in Alaskan waters. Halibut can grow up to almost 9 feet long and weight up to 500 pounds.

Cod and Rockfish

Although several local fishes are called "cod," the term usually refers to greenlings and rockfish that inhabit the bottom of the tidal zone at the depth of 60 fathoms or more, in kelp beds and reefs. The most common is lingcod (*Ophiodon elongatus*), a greenling, which can attain the length of five feet. Other, smaller greenlings—kelp (*Hexagrammos decagrammus*), rock (*H. lagocephalus*), whitespotted (*H. decagrammus*)—were called "tommycod." Rockfish are generally named for their predominant color—brown, black, blue, copper, etc.—but are often lumped together by general color names: rockfish that are brown in color are called "rock cod"; in the past, darker species, such as black rockfish or black cod (*Sebastodes melanops*), were called "black bass," and reddish species, such as red rockfish (*S. rubberimus*), were sometimes called "red snapper." Pacific cod (*Gadus macrocephalus*) are also called "gray cod" because of their gray or brownish appearance; they can reach up to 6 feet in length and live to 20 years. Many of these are long-lived species and late to mature and reproduce, which have significant implications for fishing pressure.

Sturgeon

There are two types of sturgeon in the Salish Sea: green (*Acipenser medirostris*) and white (*A. transmontanus*). Both are anadromous like salmon: they spawn in fresh water and then go to the sea to mature, but unlike the salmonids they return to the sea every year and can reach huge sizes—whites can be up to 20 feet long and weigh up to 1,800 pounds, and greens to up to 7 feet and weigh up to 350 pounds. They are scavenging bottom feeders, usually in sandy or mud filled bays, and are not located in the San Juan Islands but near the rivers and streams in the periphery of the Salish Sea, such as near Boundary Bay and the mouth of the Fraser River.

Salmon

There are five principal species of Pacific salmon: Chinook; coho; sockeye; pink; and chum, plus a sixth, steelhead, that was once classified as a trout. All are alike in being anadromous: they hatch in fresh water, migrate to the sea as young fish, and then when mature return to their freshwater birthplace to spawn and then die (except for some steelhead). In addition to differing in size and characteristics of flesh, these salmon have different migration patterns, and therefore different fishing methods were used to catch them.

Chinook (*Onchorynchus tshawytscha*), which is also called "king", "spring," and "tyee," is the largest, weighing up to 135 pounds, but averaging 10-20. They have silver sides, black gums, and small black spots on their dark backs and both lobes of the tail. The spring-run population breeds February to April and spawns on gravelly beds in glacial rivers; fall-runs return to rivers July-November. Males mature in 2-5 years, females at 4-5. Adults spend 3-5 years in the salt water and are present in the region throughout most of the year, migrating along the coast lines. Some young (2-5-year-old) adult Chinook—called blackmouth salmon because of the black line around their mouths—migrate north to Canada and Alaska to mature, but a portion of these remain in the Salish Sea. Chinook are the most nearshore dependent of local salmon species.

Coho (*O. kisutch*), also known as "silver," are smaller than Chinook: up to 38 inches long and 30 pounds in weight, they average 30 inches long and 6-12 pounds. Coho also have silvery sides but white gums and no spots on the lower tail. Breeding males have a green head and back with bright red sides. Coho are in the Salish Sea year-round but most common in August and September.

Both Chinook and coho are prized as sport fish and can be caught by trolling with herring or similar bait.

Sockeye (*O. nerka*), or "red," lack distinctive spots but have a speckled greenish blue back and silvery sides. Breeding adults have bright scarlet bodies. They can reach up to 33 inches in length and weigh up to 15 pounds but average 25 inches and 5-8 pounds. Sockeye migrate through the islands to the Fraser River via standard routes—principally Haro and Rosario Straits—in June through October.

Pink (*O. gorbuscha*), "humpback" or "humpie," have metallic blue backs, silver sides, and large, oval spots on their backs and both lobes of the tail. Breeding males develop large humps on their olive-green backs (hence the nicknames), which blends into red on the sides. Adults average 4-6 pounds in weight but can reach 30 inches in length and 12 pounds. Pinks live two years before returning to spawn, so in every other (odd) year they migrate through the Salish Sea, in the summer.

Both sockeye and pinks do not feed during their migrations through the Salish Sea, and so were mainly taken through reef nets and (later) fish traps, purse seines, and gill nets—fishing gear that do not use bait or lures but entrap the fish.

Chum (*O. keta*), "keta," or "dog" salmon are speckled on the back and sides but lack black spots. Breeding adults are dark olive-green with brown and red splotchy vertical bars on the sides. Male breeding salmon develop large "teeth," resembling canine teeth, during spawning, which may explain their nickname. They average 25 inches in length and 10-15 pounds in weight but can reach 40 inches long and 33 pounds. Chum come later in the fall than the other species of salmon.

Steelhead or rainbow trout (*O. mykiss*, used to be *Salmo gairdneri*), has two main populations: one that remains in freshwater—rainbow trout—and steelhead, which are anadromous, or go to sea, like the other salmon species. Steelhead have a greenish back and silvery sides with black spots on the back, sides, tail, and dorsal fin. Breeding males have red on the cheeks and sides.

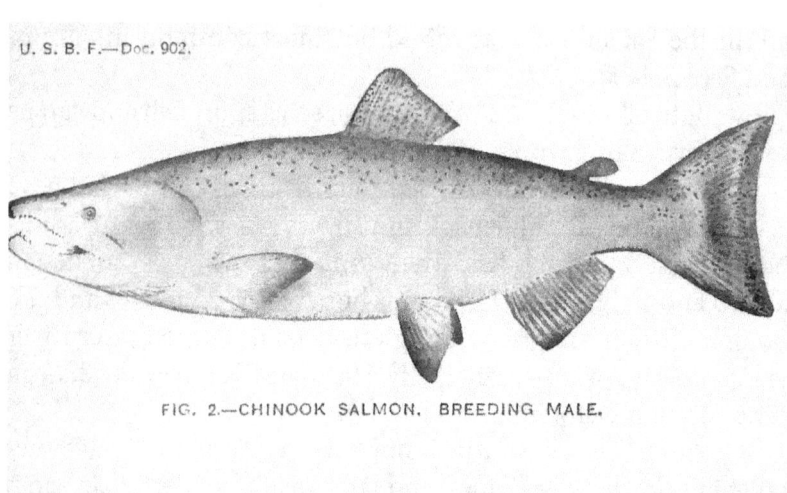

FIG. 2.—CHINOOK SALMON. BREEDING MALE.

FIG. 3.—SOCKEYE SALMON. ADULT MALE.

FIG. 4.—COHO SALMON. BREEDING MALE.

Species of Salmon

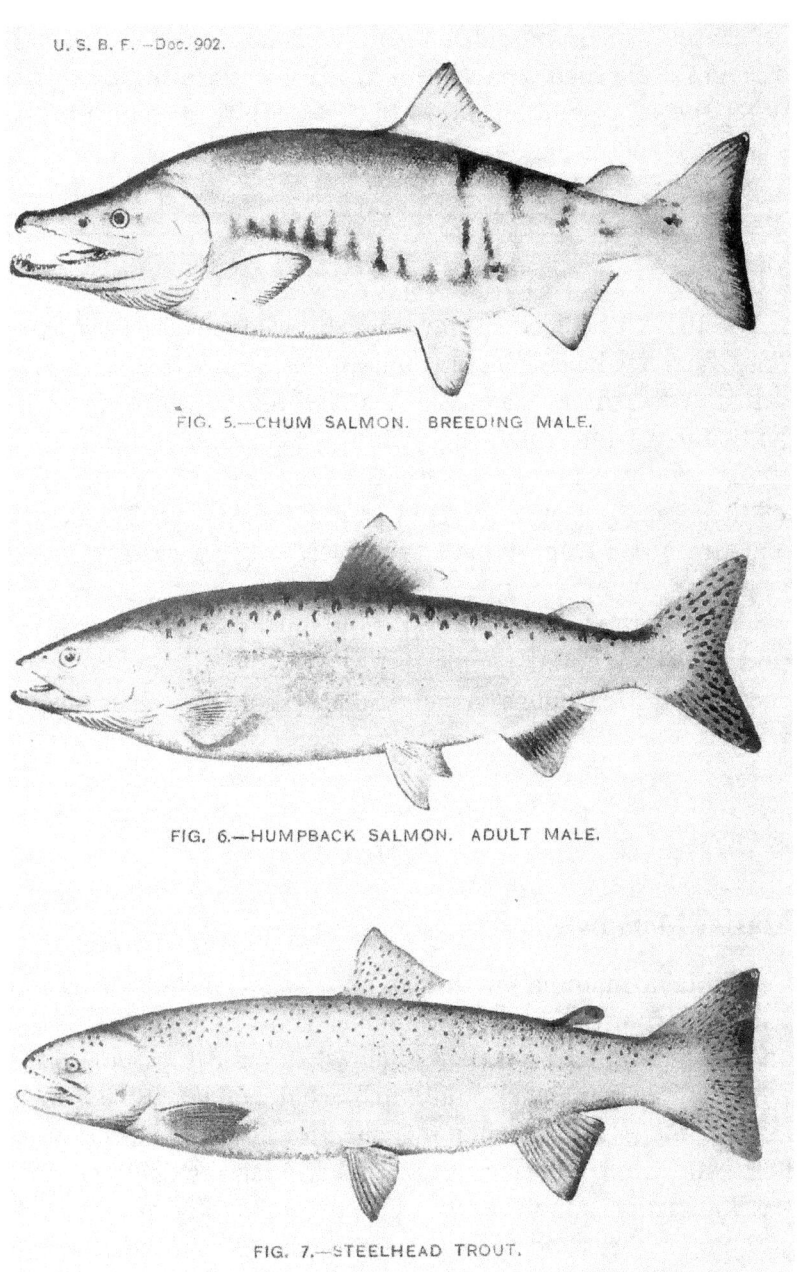

FIG. 5.—CHUM SALMON. BREEDING MALE.

FIG. 6.—HUMPBACK SALMON. ADULT MALE.

FIG. 7.—STEELHEAD TROUT.

John N. Cobb, *Pacific Salmon Fisheries* (1921)

They average 8-11 pounds but can reach up to 43 pounds, with a length of 45 inches. Steelhead have a life cycle similar to the other species of salmon except that some of them return to the sea after spawning and then return to spawn another year.

Dogfish

The North Pacific spiny dogfish (originally *Squalus acanthias*, but reevaluated as a separate species, *Squalus suckleyi*), also called a mud shark, is a coastal shark with a dark brown to grey body and a white belly. The "spiny" designation comes from a single, mildly venomous spine at the front of each of its two dorsal fins. It can get up to 5 feet in length but averages 2-4 feet for a mature adult. Dogfish have a relatively long lifespan—up to 80 years—and mature sexually late in life: females can reproduce when they are an average 35 years old; males 19. After fertilization, females retain the embryos for 18-22 months and the average litter is 22. Dogfish inhabit the nearshore as well as deeper waters.

MAMMALS

Marine Mammals

Maine mammals in the San Juan Islands include Dall's and harbor porpoise, harbor seals, Steller and California sea lions, and orca (Southern Resident killer whales and Bigg's or "transients"), gray, humpback, and minke whales. The Dall's porpoise (*Phocoenoides dalli*) is often mistaken for an orca because of its black and white coloring but is smaller in size, reaching only 7 feet in length. Harbor porpoises (*Phocoena phocoena*) are more common in the islands, of a grayish brown color, and reach about 6 feet in length.

Steller sea lions (*Eumetopias jubatus*) are massive, with the males reaching up to 2,500 pounds and 11 feet in length; females are 7 1/2 to 9 1/2 feet long and can weigh up to 800 pounds. California sea lions (*Zalophus californianus*) are noticeably smaller than Steller sea lions, with males reaching 9 feet and weighing around 800 pounds and females growing to 7 feet and up to 230 pounds. Both seal lion species can be seen hauled out on rocks along the coastline. Small and spotted gray in color and the most prolific of marine mammals in the San Juan Islands, harbor seals (*Phoca vitulina*), which can reach 6 feet in length, are often found hauled out on the rocky coastlines of the islands during the summer.

Orcas (*Orcinus orca*), which can reach 24-27 feet in length, are classified as two groups: up to 24 feet in length, Southern Resident killer whales, which, until recently, used to spend most (but not all) of the late spring, summer and early fall months (mid-May – October) in the San Juan Islands and feed mainly on Chinook salmon, and Bigg's or transients, up to 27 feet in length, which eat seals and other marine mammals. The gray (*Eschrichtius robustus*) (up to 45 feet), humpback (*Megaptera novaeangliae*) (up to 60 feet), and minke (*Balaenoptera acutorostrata*) (up to 30 feet) are all baleen whales; the latter is resident to the Salish Sea while the first two are regular visitors. In the past several decades, a group of about a dozen gray whales called the Sounders, which migrate from Mexico to British Columbia, have been observed from March into June feeding on ghost shrimp burrowed in the intertidal Snohomish River delta off Whidbey Island, which they gather by sucking up the upper layer of sediment on the sea bottom.

Reef Net Locations in the San Juan Islands

REEF NETS

Sources: Wayne Suttles, *Economic Life of the Coast Salish of Haro and Rosario Straits* (1951), Map 8 p. 154 and "Prehistoric and Early History Fisheries in the San Juan Archipelago" (1998), pp. 19-33 and Ralph Lillie, "Reefnet," IN Jackson, Wade, and Botsford, *The Fishermen and the Fisheries of the San Juan Islands*, pp.68-70. (* indicates modern legal location)

San Juan County

Battleship Island
    Battleship Island (*Battleship Island)

Decatur Island
    Decatur Head: 2 locations

Henry Island
    Open Bay (*Open Bay): off west side of bay

Johns Island
    Johns Island (*Johns Island): 2 locations

Lopez Island
    Flat Point (*Flat Point)
    Fisherman's Bay; 7 locations
    Shark Reef
    Iceberg Point (*Iceberg Point)
    Aleck Bay (*Aleck Bay): 3 locations
    Kellett Ledge

Orcas Island
    Point Doughty (*Orcas Island): 2 locations
    West Beach: 8 locations

San Juan Island
    Eagle Point: two sets of gear,
        one at flood and one at ebb tide
    Kanaka Bay: off headland southeast of the Bay
    Kanaka Bay: off west point of the bay
    Pile Point: off kelp bed
    Northwest of Pile Point: 2 locations
    Lime Kiln; off point north of lighthouse
    Andrews Bay (*Andrews Bay); north side of Low Island
    Mosquito Pass: 2 locations
    Mitchell Bay Reef (*Mitchell Reef)
    Smuggler's Cove (*Smuggler's Cove)

Shaw Island
    Neck Point (*Shaw Island #2)
    Lutz Bay: 5 locations
    Squaw Bay (*Shaw Island #1?): 9 locations

Stuart Island
    Reid Harbor (*Stuart Island #1): 2 locations
    Southeast Headland (*Stuart Island #2): 4 locations

Waldron Island
    Cowlitz Bay

Yellow Island
    Yellow Island

Outside of San Juan County

Birch Bay

Cherry Point *

Point Roberts *

Fidalgo Island

Lummi Island *

Pender Island (Canada)

Sinclair Island *

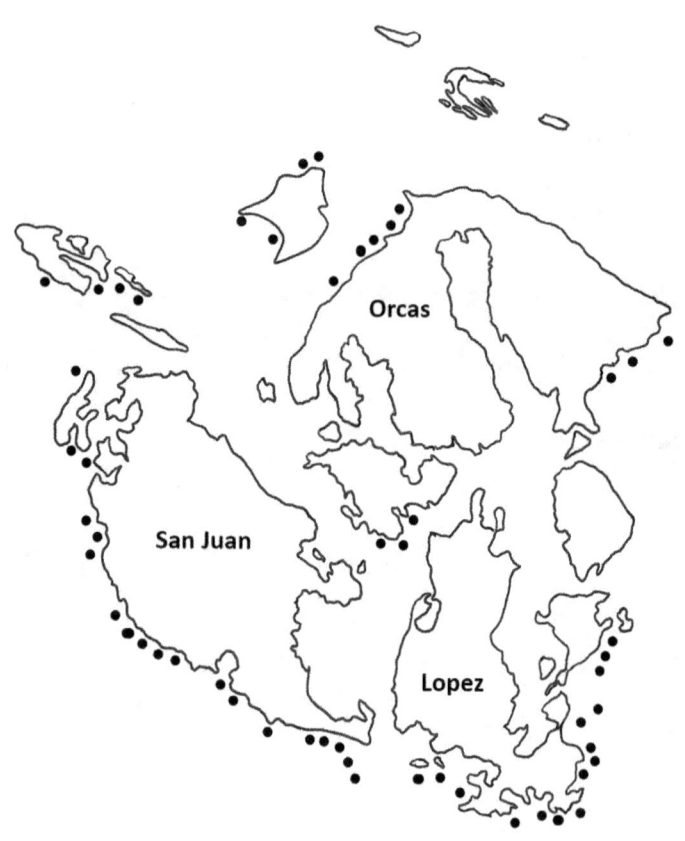

Fish Trap Locations in the San Juan Islands

FISH TRAPS

Decatur Island
    Between Decatur Island and Lopez Island
        Henry T. Cayou (Deer Harbor) 1909
    Dot Island
        Henry T. Cayou (Deer Harbor) 1909
        George & Barker Company (Blaine)

Henry Island
    Open Bay
        Shultz and Gross (Roche Harbor) 1898
        C. L. Christy and Christian Olsen-3 1904
        E A. Sims (Port Townsend) 1904, 1906
        Peter Graignic (Port Townsend) #369 1915

Johns Island
    Henry T. Cayou (Deer Harbor)

Lopez Island
    Aleck Bay
        Ernest Davis and John Troxell (Richardson)
        John Troxell (Richardson)
    Barlow Bay
        Hodgson & Graham (Richardson)
        Newton
    Hall Island
        John Troxell (Richardson)
    Huggins Bay
        John Troxell (Richardson)
    Iceberg Point
        D. Campbell #146 1915
    Kellet Ledge
        Henry T. Cayou (Deer Harbor) 1909

Long Island
    Henry T. Cayou (Deer Harbor) 1909
    Astoria Puget Sound Canning Company (Chuckanut) 1911-1912
Sperry's Lagoon
    Pacific American Fish Company (Anacortes) 1909
Watmough Bay
    Henry T. Cayou and J. P. Nelson 2 1901
    Watmough Fish Company 1902
Woody Island
    John Troxell (Richardson)

Orcas Island
East side
Northwest side
    Port Townsend Packing Company

San Juan Island
Andrews Bay (Brann's Bay)
    Shultz and Gross (Roche Harbor) 1905
    Peter Graignic (Port Townsend) #378 1915
Deadman Bay (Cowell's, Lime Kiln)
    Cornelius Coughlin (Friday Harbor) #806 1905
    Emmett Coughlin (Friday Harbor) #5719 1925
    Catherine Coughlin (Friday Harbor) #7662 1927
    Catherine Coughlin (Friday Harbor) #1744 1929
    H. B. Murray 1933
    Catherine Coughlin (Friday Harbor) #203 1934
Eagle Point (west of Eagle Cove)
    Ainsworth & Dunn (Seattle) #200 1901
    Ainsworth & Dunn (Seattle) #295 1901
    Alaska Packers Association #643 1901
    Fidalgo Island Canning Company
    Frazer Fish Company (Bellingham) 1905
    J. S. Woodin (Anacortes) #314 1905
    George C. Fisher & J. M. McCue (Bellingham) 1916

False Bay (South)
    Alexander and Bullock (1905)
    Henry Cayou (Deer Harbor) #6404 1918
Kanaka Bay
    Lester Turner (Seattle) #2044 1904-5
    Will A. Lowman (Anacortes) #2388 1905
    Salmon Bank Fish Company #104/105 1905
    J. C. Pringle (Port Townsend) 1906
    Coast Fish Company (Anacortes) #404 1908
    Henry Cayou (Deer Harbor) #4493 1923
    Will A. Lowman (Anacortes) #4263 1924
    American Floating Fish Trap Co. (Seattle) #4560 1925
    Henry Cayou (Deer Harbor) #6539 1928
    C. E. Alexander, J. F. Olinder, E. E. Murray #9031 1929
    Steele
Low Point, Griffin Bay
    J. K. McKenzie & Charles Tucker #1617 1917
Mitchell Bay
    Ed. A. Scribner (Roche Harbor) 1904
    Mitchell Bay Fish Company (Mitchell Bay) #408 1910, 1912, 1915
    Thomas Smith (Mitchell Bay) #412 1912
    Emerson Lightheart (Mitchell Bay) #5925 1919
    Friday Harbor Packing Company (Friday Harbor)
    Shultz and Gross (Roche Harbor)
Mosquito Pass
    Mosquito Pass (Bellingham) 1905
    Pacific American Fisheries (formerly Island Packing Company)
    Shultz and Gross (Roche Harbor)
Northeast Shore (?)
    Robert J. Smith & J. P. Brewster (Bellingham) 1905

Salmon Bank ("South San Juan")
- Alaska Packers Association #620 1899
- A. V. Reeves #1252 1899
- Alaska Packers Association #1788 1900
- Alaska Packers Association #620 1900
- Pacific American Fisheries #1244 1900
- Pacific American Fisheries #46/47/48/49 1900
- Pacific American Fisheries #2253 1900
- Sweeney #145 1900
- Ainsworth & Dunn (Seattle) #1548 1901
- Ainsworth & Dunn (Seattle) #1549 1901
- Lion Fishing Company (Bellingham) #2335 1903-5
- Dolphin Fishing Company (Bellingham) #1654 1904
- Lion Fishing Company (Bellingham) 1904-5
- Alexander & Bullock (Blaine) #47 1905
- Lion Fishing Company (Bellingham) #400 1905
- Lion Fishing Company (Bellingham) #488 1905
- Will A. Lowman (Anacortes) #220 1905
- Will A. Lowman (Anacortes) #220 1905
- Lummi Island Fishing Company (Anacortes) #606 1905
- Lummi Island Fishing Company (Anacortes) #1760 1905
- Mosquito Pass Fish Company (Bellingham) #2531 1905
- Mosquito Pass Fish Company (Bellingham) "Salmon Bank Trap No. 1" (1905-1933)
- J. C. Pringle (Port Townsend) #764 1906
- Shultz and Jakle #2635/2636 1911
- Edward Daugherty (Friday Harbor) #4119 1913

George Fisher (Bellingham) #3626 1914
Katherine Fisher (Bellingham) #152 1915
John Peterson (Friday Harbor) 1915
Cayou and Haroldson (Deer Harbor) #259 1916
Henry Cayou (Deer Harbor) #377 1916
San Juan Fishing and Packing #569 1916
Cypress Fish Company Anacortes #211 1917
Fisher & McCue (Bellingham) #2620 1917
Friday Harbor Packing (Friday Harbor) #5095 1917
John Troxell (Richardson) #3382 1917
Will A. Lowman (Anacortes) #776 1923
Henry Cayou (Deer Harbor) #752 1929
John Troxell (Richardson) #8883 1929
Salmon Bank Fish Company #5554/5555 1933
Shultz and Gross (Roche Harbor)
Anacortes Packing Company (Anacortes)

San Juan Island (?)
    S. A. Hall (Bellingham) #3640 1914
San Juan Pass (Cattle Point)
    Lion Fishing Company (Bellingham) #2335 1913
    Cascade Packing Company (Anacortes) #6715/6716 1917
    Nooksak Canning Company (Everett) #6015 1925
    William Griswold (Bellingham) #7925 1928
    B. W. Huntoon (PAF) #261 1934
    Seafood Investments #3351 1934
Smallpox Bay
    Eunice Troxell (Richardson) #315 1926, 1928, 1931

West/Southwest San Juan (?)
    Longhorn #2413 1905
    Mosquito Pass Fish Company (Bellingham) #2220 1905
    Cayou and Haroldson #4040 1912
    Emery Graham (Anacortes) #3982/3999/4065/4066/4067 1912
    Haro Fish Company (Bellingham) #465/466 1914
    Robert Flynn (Friday Harbor) #6888 1919
    Ashton Gross (Friday Harbor) #7310 1919
    S. B. Gross (Friday Harbor) #7311 1919
    San Juan Canning Company #501 1919
    Booth Fisheries (Seattle) #455 1921
    W. A. Clement (Friday Harbor) #1502 1921
    C. E. Alexander (Seattle) #9031 1929
    Astoria and Puget Sound Canning Company (Bellingham) #421 1929
    Henry Cayou (Deer Harbor) #6539 1929
    William Norton (Deer Harbor) #7462 1929
    Henry Cayou (Deer Harbor) #5476 1930
    Catherine Coughlin (Friday Harbor) #324 1932
    Frank Martinis (Anacortes) #9504 1933
    Mosquito Pass Fish Company (Bellingham) #4046 1933
    Salmon Bank Fish Company #4002/4003 1933
    A. J. Martini #6888 1934
Westcott Bay
    D. W. Wood #4894/4895 1926
    W. R. Morgan #4895 1928

Shaw Island
    South Side

Stuart Island
    Reid Harbor (outside)

Waldron Island
    Cowlitz Bay
    West Side
    Samuel Alsop
    Port Townsend Packing Company

Salting, Smoking, and Canning Operations in the San Juan Islands

SALTING, SMOKING, AND CANNING OPERATIONS

LOPEZ ISLAND

Richardson

Oceanic Canning Company (1895). The Oceanic Canning Company filed for articles for incorporation on October 23, 1895, with R. C. Kinleyside, J. A. Gould, and C. A. Phelps, proposing to build a cannery at Richardson. At first, Charles A. Phelps was the general manager; eventually, Thomas E. Ladner, with canneries at Ladner's Landing, B.C., became the general manager. Construction began in November of 1895 to prepare for the 1896 season. The buildings included a 40-by-100-foot net house, a 30-by-60-foot mess house, and a net wharf that measure 50-by-200 feet. Netting and twine was ordered from the American Net and Twine Company of Boston, six scows were built for the operations, and the steamer *San Juan*, Captain Hanson, was brought up from Seattle. The company was involved in a lawsuit contesting the construction of a fish trap at Salmon Bank; it was settled in 1896. The newspapers noted the sale of the company's pile driver and movement of their scows to Canada in 1898, it also reported that "three scows, three seine boats three purse seiners and some other fishing gear" were being brought from Canada for fishing near Lummi Island. It is not clear when this operation shut down.

Captain R. E. Davis (1900-?). In the early 1900s, Captain R. E. Davis salted barrels of the salmon that he had caught with fish traps; newspaper articles note his extensive production (440 barrels) at Richardson during August of 1901. It is not clear how many seasons this lasted.

Graham and Hodgson (1900-?). William Graham and N. P. Hodgson established a smoking operation at Richardson around the turn of the last century. It is not clear how many seasons this lasted.

Hidden Inlet Cannery (1913-1922). The Hidden Inlet Cannery, owned by a company of Englishmen and managed by J. C. Comeau, was built in the summer of 1913. The cannery itself, built on rock, was 30-by-150 feet, and ran two lines (although in 1914 the May 14th *San Juan Islander* noted that it would only operate one line that season). Apparently, it shut down in 1922, soon after the Hodgson-Graham Cannery burned down.

Hodgson-Graham (Salmon Bank) Cannery (1913-1922). The Hodgson-Graham Cannery, also called the Salmon Bank Cannery, was built in 1913 in time for the fishing season; Angus McGuire was the president. A two-line cannery with a capacity of 1400 cans a day, it was built on rock and had cement floors. The main building was 80-by-100 feet and a smaller one 40-by-66; there was also a boarding house for workers. In 1916, N. P. Hodgson sold both his store and the cannery to Ira Lundy. The cannery burned down in February 1922.

Fisherman Bay

Tuana Packing Company (1907-?). In 1907 S. M. Bugge, who had taken over the Island Packing Company, established the Tuana Packing Company on Lopez Island; there they packed clams from British Columbia Indians as well as from Port Townsend. (Bugge later established a clam cannery in Port Townsend.)

ORCAS ISLAND

Deer Harbor

Henry Cayou "Red" Cannery, The Orcas Island Canning Company, Deer Harbor Packing Company, and Orcas Packing Company (1914-1945). Around 1914 Henry Cayou built a facility on the west shore of Deer Harbor, called the "Red Cannery" to distinguish it from the "White Cannery" across the harbor. The cannery was first operated under the name of *The Orcas Island Canning Company*; later it became known as the *Deer Harbor Packing Company* and the *Orcas Packing Company*. A 1943 real estate contract lists, in addition to the cannery facility itself, an office, blacksmith shop, boiler room, superintendents building, a large rooming house, and a cook house. Laborers included Chinese, Filipinos, and Hawaiians. In the 1940s there were several liens upon the cannery for equipment and materials; eventually the mortgage company foreclosed on Joseph N. Dion and Sidney Blutreich, co-partners of Deer Harbor Packing Company, and the property, then owned by Sigmund Einstoss and the Orcas Packing Company, underwent a sheriff's sale again.

Northern Pacific Fisheries, George W. Hume Company "White Cannery," and Deer Harbor Fisheries Company (1917-1920s). Around 1917 William J. Norton and the *Northern Pacific Fisheries* built a cannery on the east shore of Deer Harbor for the *George W. Hume Company*, subsequently called the "White Cannery" to distinguish it from Henry Cayou's "Red Cannery." After Bloedel Donovan Lumber Mills placed a lien on lumber used in its construction, The *Deer Harbor Fisheries Company* was packing salmon at its cannery in 1919. A year after the Western Fisheries cannery at West Sound burned down in August 1920, they leased the Deer Harbor Fisheries cannery, which was then owned by the Yokohama Specie Bank. The cannery must have closed down and been demolished several years later.

Floating Cannery (1930-?). In 1930 William J. Norton established a floating cannery in Deer Harbor; it is not clear how long this lasted.

West Sound

Deer Harbor Packing Company, Northern Pacific Fisheries Company, and Western Fisheries (1910s-1920). The Tyee Fish Company, which incorporated in East Sound, Orcas Island, in 1912, operated fish traps on the west side of Orcas Island. In 1913 they contemplated erecting a cannery near Double Island in

West Sound. William J. Norton of Deer Harbor, one of their partners, bought property (located near Camp Four Winds) as well as water rights from them; these interests were sold in September 1913, to the *Deer Harbor Packing Company*. (Two years later, when the Deer Harbor Packing Company sold land to William Norton, H. W. Behnke was president and J. B. Playter was secretary.) In 1918 *Northern Pacific Fisheries Company* built a cannery on land purchased from William Norton and Henry Cayou at West Sound. *Western Fisheries* was operating this cannery when it burned down in August 1920; the next year, Western Fisheries leased the Deer Harbor Fisheries cannery.

SAN JUAN ISLAND

Hudson's Bay Company

Belle Vue Sheep Farm. Prior to the establishment of Belle Vue Sheep Farm, the Hudson's Bay Company sent over a crew to salt salmon obtained from local Indigenous fishers on the west side of San Juan Island. This operation continued throughout the 1850s, with up to 2,000 barrels of salted salmon per annum.

Friday Harbor

Island Packing Company (1894-1964). In 1894 the Island Packing Company established a cannery near the current ferry dock. It was absorbed by the Pacific American Fisheries Company and became the *Friday Harbor Packing Company* in 1899. At first, Chinese were imported seasonally to work the canning apparatus; later, Japanese laborers worked there with whites often women. Closed intermittently in the 1950s, it was used for canning peas and strawberries during late1950s and early 1960s; it closed permanently in 1964.

Island Packing Company (II) (1903-19??). In 1901 John Broder (1854-1917) established a creamery on the waterfront between Sweeney's warehouse and Brown's mill; two years later he sold a half interest to George Mead, and they built a cannery, as well as a new creamery, on the waterfront at the base of West Street for clams and fruit. In 1905, the *Island Packing Company* was re-organized as a joint stock company, with Broder as president, Mead as secretary, L. B. Carter as treasurer, and E. H. Nash as general manager. They built a large addition to accommodate a salmon canning plant and extended the wharf by 40 feet.

San Juan Canning Company (1912-1940s). In late 1912 the *Journal* noted that articles of incorporation had been filed for the San Juan Canning Company, whose officers were Joseph S. Groll, president and manager, John Haubner, vice president, and E. H. Nash, secretary and treasurer, to be located at "the old Brown sawmill site" (*Journal* December 19, 1912). Then, the *San Juan Islander* stated that Groll was in Seattle arranging for machinery and contracting for "oriental labor" for a new "San Juan Packing Company" (*San Juan Islander* December 27, 1912, p. 4), and in February of the following year the paper noted that it was being erected at the site of the old Brown Mill (*San Juan Islander* February 28, 1913, p. 1). Anticipating its imminent opening, the *Islander* described it as a two liner with a projected capacity of 1600 cases per day; the main floor space was 80-by-172 feet, with a smaller (30-by-110 feet) space used for office and store room (*San Juan Islander* May 16, 1913, p. 1). Later in the year (July 4th) the paper mentioned that the plant was up and running. In addition to salmon processing, beginning in the 1920s the cannery was used for peas. The cannery was torn down in the 1940s.

Mitchell Bay

Red Cross Fish Company (1899-1900). In 1899 the Red Cross Fish Company herring packing plant was established at Mitchell Bay on San Juan Island and Max Johnson, who had worked for years in fisheries off the coast of Norway, was hired as the manager. In addition to smoking the herring, packers also pickled them with salt in 50-gallon wooden barrels. On March 12, 1900, the packing and smoke house burned; although the company planned to rebuild, they never did so.

Argyle Spit

Jackson Cannery (1948; 1950-1970s). In 1948, John Jackson built a smokehouse for kippering and hand-packing salmon on what was known as Little Island, connected to Argyle Spit at low tide. Two years later, he built Jackson Cannery and improved the road to Little Island. The 40-50 workers were mostly women (at a 3-1 ration) and they did all of the hand packing and were paid per can. After slowing down due to competition from fresh frozen salmon, Jackson Cannery was sold to John Theodore in the late 1970s.

SHAW ISLAND

Blind Bay

Shaw Island Canning Company (1912-?). The Shaw Island Canning Company incorporated in April of 1912, for the "business of fishing and canning all sea animals and will also can fruits and vegetables." The incorporators were Willard and George W. Quimbly, A. Clark Percy, A. A. Blank and F. A. Wheaton, all of Bellingham. A cannery was constructed on Blind Bay and the next year (1913) packed 5,400 cases of salmon.

STUART ISLAND

Reid Bay

Bernhardt Mordhorst. (1880s). In the 1880s, Bernhardt Mordhorst and Frederick Hay, both originally from Schleswig-Holstein, Germany, operated a herring fishery at Reid Harbor on Stuart Island. They not only supplied fresh herring for bait to halibut schooners going north to Alaska, but also had a saltery on the harbor and a smoking house on a small cove just outside. Mordhorst continued his herring operations after his partner's death in 1887.

WALDRON ISLAND

Fishery Point

Graham Brothers (1890s). The Graham Brothers, Gus and Glese, salted and barreled herring on Waldron Island in the 1890s.

Edouard Graignic (1890s). Edouard Graignic, a Frenchman who moved to Waldron in the late 1870s, beach seined for herring. The whole family was involved in cleaning, smoking, and packing—20 to a box—the catch. Graignic sailed to Victoria to market the pack in his sloop, *City of Paris*.

Thomas Brothers & Company (1890s). The Thomas brothers, Ellery and Ashton, established a herring smokery on Fishery Point on Waldron Island in the 1890s. They built two 60-foot-long smokehouses and sent the packed fish by boat throughout the region.

COMPANIES

Alaska Packers Association (1891-1960s). The Alaska Packers Association (APA) was consolidated in 1891 from 31 canneries, mainly to control the salmon packing industry in Alaska. Henry Frederick Fortmann, owner of the Arctic Packing Company, one of the original member companies, served as APA president from its inception until 1922. In 1916, the APA merged with several principally Californian companies to become California Packing Corporation (CalPack), which was eventually reorganized as Del Monte.

Andrews Bay Fish Company (est. 1896). Incorporated in January of 1896 with a capitalization of $6,000 by P. S. Cook, William Shultz, Samuel Gross, Dr. I. Harrison, and E. Harrison, the Andrews Bay Fish Company had its headquarters at Roche Harbor. They bought property there from Ed Warbass to build wharves and possibly a cannery.

Bellingham Bay Fishing Company (est. 1895). The Bellingham Bay Fishing Company was one of five corporations (Lopez Island, Lummi Island, Orcas Island, and San Juan Fishing Companies) formed in 1895 by F. I. Lord (son-in-law of Thomas E. Ladner, a Fraser River canneryman who was involved in the Oceanic Canning Company at Richardson, Lopez Island), W. J. Goode, and H. A. Fairchild (a Whatcom lawyer) and designed to spread consolidated fish trap ownership among smaller corporations.

Chlopeck Fish Company. Founded by brothers Con (Conrad) and Ed (Edward), who would buy fresh salmon from the San Juans, ship them to their plant in Seattle, and then salt them. The company went into receivership in 1903, due to the "unsound mind" of the head of the firm, Ed Chlopeck.

Coast Fish Canning Company (est. 1907). Will A. Lowman incorporated the White Crest Canning Company in 1899. In 1907 he renamed the business the Coast Fish Company and sold it to Farwest Fisheries in 1936.

Cypress Island Packing Company (est. 1903). Cypress Island Packing Company, incorporated in 1903, built a cannery in Anacortes. It specialized in packing sardines, but also handled salmon, smelt, herring, crabs, and clams.

Davis and Myers Fish Company (est. 1900). Captain R. (Rowland) E. "Rollie" Davis salted and smoked salmon at Richardson, Lopez Island, in the 1890s. Around 1900 he went into partnership with George T. Myers ("of Seattle") and they ran several fish traps off the south end of Lopez Island.

Deep Sea Fish Company. The Deep Sea Fish Company owned three fish traps off Cherry Point.

Deer Harbor Fisheries Company (1917s-1920s). Around 1917, Northern Pacific Fisheries built a cannery at Deer Harbor; the Deer Harbor Fisheries Company was packing salmon there in 1919. In 1921, J. W. Parks, head of the Western Fisheries Company, leased the facility after their cannery in West Sound burned. At the time the company was owned by the Yokohama Species Bank.

Deer Harbor Packing Company (1910s-1920s). The Tyee Fish Company's interests were sold in September 1913, to the Deer Harbor Packing Company. In 1915, when there was a sale by the Deer Harbor Packing Company of land to William Norton, H. W. Behnke was president and J. B. Playter was Secretary. In 1944, Whitney & Company foreclosed on a mortgage with Joseph H. Dion and Sidney Blutreich, copartners of the Deer Harbor Packing Company, for the land as well as the tide lands, wharf, and buildings of the fish cannery.

Everett Fish Company (1910s). In 1911 the Everett Fish Company, which prior to that time had packed and shipped salmon, proposed a two-line cannery in Everett. The company was known for its mild curing.

Friday Harbor Packing Company (1894-1964). In 1894 the *Island Packing Company* established a cannery near the current ferry dock in Friday Harbor. It was absorbed by the Pacific American Fisheries Company and became the Friday Harbor Packing Company in 1899. Closed intermittently in the 1950s, it was used for canning peas and strawberries during late 1950s and early 1960s; it closed permanently in 1964.

George & Barker Company (est. 1895; Point Roberts cannery 1900-1929). In 1885 George H. George and W. H. Barker, who had been connected with various canneries, formed a partnership as George & Barker and purchased the Astoria cannery of the Port [Point] Adams Packing Co. Basing themselves in Blaine, they established a cannery at Point Roberts in 1900 and contracted for fish from San Juan Islands fish traps as well as owning several traps outright. In 1910 the company leased the Barlow's Bay, Fleming, and Lawson camp sites.

Great Northern Fish Company (1890s). The Great Northern Fish Company, of Seattle, operated a salmon saltery during the late 1890s at Mitchell Bay, San Juan Island, as well as Richardson, Lopez Island, shipping thousands of barrels of salt salmon to Seattle.

Haines Oyster Company (est. 1892). One of the oldest wholesale shellfish companies in the Pacific Northwest, the Haines Oyster Company was established in 1892 by William Bullock Haines. His son, H. (Henry) L. (Luther) Haines discovered shrimp in the San Juans in 1903 and trawled for them through the early 1900s.

Hidden Inlet Canning Company (1913-1922). The Hidden Inlet Cannery, owned by a company of Englishmen and managed by J. C. Comeau, was built in the summer of 1913. Apparently, it shut down in 1922, soon after the Hodgson-Graham Cannery burned down.

Hodgson-Graham (Salmon Bank) Cannery (1913-1922). The Hodgson-Graham Cannery, also called the *Salmon Bank Cannery*, was built in 1913 in time for the fishing season; Angus McGuire was the president. A two-line cannery with a capacity of 1400 cans a day, it was built on rock and had cement floors. The main building was 80-by-100 feet and a smaller one 40-by-66; there was also a boarding house for workers. In 1916, N. P. Hodgson sold both his store and the cannery to Ira Lundy. The cannery burned down in February 1922.

George W. Hume Company. George Hume, along with his brother William, began canning salmon on the Sacramento River in 1864; two years later, they moved to the Columbia River. George soon expanded operations to the Puget Sound region. The company established a fish cannery at Deer Harbor in the late 1910s.

Iceberg Point Fish Company (est. 1896). In 1896 R. "Rolly" E. Davis, C. A. Phelps, and A. H. Davis filed articles of incorporation with the San Juan County Auditor for the Iceberg Point Fish Company. With a capital stock of $6,000, the company intended to "construct traps, catch and can fish, ship fresh fish, and build and operate canning plants" (*The Islander* April 2, 1896). The newspaper subsequently reported on sales of fresh fish as well as traps off Iceberg Point.

Island Packing Company (1894-1964). In 1894 the Island Packing Company established a cannery near the current ferry dock in Friday Harbor. It was absorbed by the Pacific American Fisheries Company and became the *Friday Harbor Packing Company* in 1899. Closed intermittently in the 1950s, it was used for canning peas and strawberries during late1950s and early 1960s; it closed permanently in 1964.

Island Packing Company (II) (est. 1903). In 1903 John Broder sold a half interest in his Friday Harbor creamery to George Mead, and they built a cannery on the waterfront at the base of West Street for clams and fruit. In 1905, the Island Packing Company was re-organized as a joint stock company, with Broder as president, Mead as secretary, L. B. Carter as treasurer, and E. H. Nash as general manager.

Jackson Cannery (1948; 1950/1-1970s). In 1948, John C. Jackson built a smokehouse for kippering and hand-packing salmon on what was known as Little Island, connected to Argyle Spit at low tide. Two years later, he built Jackson Cannery and improved the road to Little Island. The 40-50 workers were mostly women (at a 3-1 ratio), and they did all of the hand packing and were paid per can. After slowing down due to competition from fresh frozen salmon, Jackson Cannery was sold to John Theodore in the late 1970s.

Lopez Island Fishing Company. See *Bellingham Bay Fishing Company*.

Lummi Island Fishing Company. See *Bellingham Bay Fishing Company*.

North American Fisheries Company (1899-1904). The North American Fisheries Company was formed by entrepreneur Roland Onffroy in 1899 and purchased several fish traps in the San Juan Islands. In early 1900 it contracted with the *Puget Sound Packing Company* to can fish from its traps. Two years later it built a cannery, web house, and a forty-foot square, three and a half story "China house" in Anacortes. Upon the failure of the Chicago commission house of Porter Bros., whose president was also the president of North American Fisheries, in 1903, the company went into receivership. A year later, when *Pacific American Fisheries* was acquired and reorganized, the operations of the *North American Fisheries Company*, along with those of the *Pacific Packing & Navigation Company*, were incorporated into the *Pacific American Fisheries*.

Northern Pacific Fisheries Company (1916-1918). In 1916, William J. Norton sold portions of land on the west shore of West Sound and granted right-of-way access as well as water rights for the purposes of building a cannery there. A year later Henry Cayou also sold some land. In 1917 an attorney for Bloedel Donavan Lumber Mills sued Norton and the Northern Pacific Fisheries Company for the cost of materials supplied for building a cannery there, and a year later they placed a lien on the property. It is not clear what happened to the company after this.

Oceanic Canning Company (est. 1895). R. C. Kinleyside, J. A. Gould, and Charles A. Phelps filed for articles for incorporation for the Oceanic Canning Company on October 23, 1895, proposing to build a cannery at Richardson, Lopez Island. Thomas E. Ladner and P. P. Rithet became trustees the following year. At first, Phelps was the general manager; eventually, Ladner, who owned canneries at Ladner's Landing, B.C., became the general manager.

The Orcas Island Canning Company (1914-?). Around 1914 Henry Cayou built a facility on the west shore of Deer Harbor, called the "Red Cannery" to distinguish it from the "White Cannery" across the harbor. The cannery was first operated under the name of *The Orcas Island Canning Company*; later it became known as the *Deer Harbor Packing Company* and the *Orcas Packing Company*.

Orcas Island Fishing Company. See *Bellingham Bay Fishing Company.*

Orcas Packing Company. See *Deer Harbor Packing Company* and *The Orcas Island Canning Company.*

Pacific American Fisheries (1899-1966). Pacific American Fisheries (PAF) was incorporated in 1899 and soon became the largest trust operating fish traps and canneries in Washington State. The PAF was formed to take over the bankrupt Franco-American North Pacific Canning Company, which had been established by the entrepreneur (and schemer) Roland Onffroy in 1898. The company was incorporated in New Jersey with a capital of $5,000,000. The officers consisting of a wholesale grocer, meatpacker, attorney, and several financiers, were all from Chicago; thus it became known as the "Chicago Syndicate." Pacific American Fisheries was reincorporated in Portland, Maine, on Christmas eve, 1904, with a capitalization of $1,500,000. In 1928, Pacific American Fisheries was reincorporated under the laws of Delaware as the Pacific American Company, a publicly held corporation with a capitalization of $7,500,000. A year later the name was changed to Pacific American Fisheries, Inc., and was only changed back in 1961, five years before its demise.

Pacific Packing & Navigation Company (1901-1904). In 1901, Roland Onffroy worked to establish an all-encompassing Alaskan and Pacific Northwest salmon trust. On July 19, the Pacific Packing and Navigation Company (PP&N) was incorporated in New Jersey with $25,000,000 from eastern capital and local Bellingham bank loans. Despite his extensive efforts, the new corporation was not able to get control of the *Alaska Packers Association* (APA), which continued to produce canned salmon, principally in Alaska but also in the Puget Sound region. In 1902, the APA inaugurated a "Salmon War," when they underpriced their lower-grade salmon (but not their higher-grade red salmon), eventually forcing the PP&N, as well as the Pacific American Fisheries into receivership.

Port Townsend Packing Company. In 1900 the Port Townsend Packing Company, J. O. Spencer (brother of Theodore W. Spencer of Blakely Island), stockholder, purchased five fish traps in the San Juan Islands owned by Captain Anderson, W. H. Brown, Hugh Eldridge, W. R. Moultray, and T. R. Kershaw, all of Whatcom County.

Puget Sound Fish Company (est. 1911). In 1911 *The San Juan Islander* noted that the "San Juan Fish Company and the Puget Sound Fish & Oyster Com. have consolidated under the name of the Puget Sound Fish Co."

Puget Sound Potash and Kelp Fertilizer Company (est. 1913). Founded at Port Stanley, Lopez Island, in 1913, the Puget Sound Potash and Kelp Fertilizer Company built a plant to manufacture three products: potash, used for gunpowder in World War I; kelp fertilizer; and iodine. It closed in the 1920s due to lack of business.

Red Cross Fish Company (est. 1899). In 1899 the Red Cross Fish Company herring packing plant was established at Mitchell Bay on San Juan Island and Max Johnson, who had worked for years in fisheries off the coast of Norway, was hired as the manager. In addition to smoking the herring, packers also pickled them with salt in 50-gallon wooden barrels. Often women, called "chokers," were the ones who prepared the herring by gutting them. On March 12, 1900, the packing and smoke house burned.

San Juan Canning Company (est. 1912). In late 1912 the *Journal* noted that articles of incorporation had been filed for the San Juan Canning Company, whose officers were Joseph S. Groll, president and manager, John Haubner, vice president, and E. H. Nash, secretary and treasurer, to be located at "the old Brown sawmill site" (*Journal* December 19, 1912). Then, *The San Juan Islander* stated that Groll was in Seattle arranging for machinery and contracting for "oriental labor" for a new "San Juan Packing Company," and in February of the following year it was being erected. By 1913, they were packing as many as 20,000 cases a year. The cannery was torn down in the 1940s.

San Juan Fishing Company. See *Bellingham Bay Fishing Company*.

San Juan Packing Company. See *San Juan Canning Company*.

Shultz and Gross (1896-1905). In 1896 Samuel Gross teamed up with William Shultz in the fish trap business; a year later they purchased tide lands near Mitchell Bay. In 1898 Shultz and Gross built a fish trap off the south end of Henry Island. After dissolving his partnership with Gross in 1905, Shultz worked with Captain George J. Willey operating the *Blaine Packing Company* (1906) and the *Crest Canning Company* in Anacortes (1907).

Shaw Island Canning Company (est. 1912). The Shaw Island Canning Company incorporated in April of 1912, for the "business of fishing and canning all sea animals and will also can fruits and vegetables." The incorporators were Willard and George W. Quimbly, A. Clark Percy, A. A. Blank and F. A. Wheaton, all of Bellingham.

Straights Fishing Company. Principally owned by Whatcom County interests, the Straights Fishing Company owned several fish trap locations in the San Juan Islands; these were acquired by the *Puget Sound Packing Company* in 1900.

Tuana Packing Company (est. 1907). In 1907 S. M. Bugge, who had taken over the *Island Packing Company*, established the Tuana Packing Company on Lopez Island; there they packed clams harvested by British Columbia Indigenous peoples as well as from Port Townsend. (Bugge later established a clam cannery in Port Townsend.)

Tyee Fish Company (est. 1912). In May of 1912, the Tyee Fish Company of East Sound, Orcas Island, was incorporated with $30,000 capital stock. The officers were M. L. Kimple, president, and C. O. Reed, secretary. They operated fish traps on the west side of Orcas, and, based on records of a 1913 lease from William J. Norton for water rights to their cannery, talked about building a cannery near Double Island in West Sound. The Tyee Fish Company's interests were sold in September 1913, to the *Deer Harbor Packing Company.*

Washington Fish & Oyster Company. In the 1950s, the Washington Fish & Oyster Company became a major player in the salmon industry in the Salish Sea. When the *Friday Harbor Canning Company* was having financial difficulties and stopped canning, Gerald Crosby, who had been directing tendering operations for the Cannery, recruited the fishing fleet, many of whom were from Gig Harbor, to provide the salmon to the Washington Fish & Oyster Company in Seattle.

Watmough Fish Company (est. 1902). In 1902, C. R. Hadley and H. C. Griffith, of Whatcom, together with J. P. Nelson, incorporated the Watmough Fish Company, with capitalization of $50,000. Hadley and Griffith purchased Henry T. Cayou's interest in the Nelson and Cayou fish traps at Watmough Bay, Lopez Island.

Western Fisheries. Western Fisheries built a cannery near Skagway, Alaska. In 1918, they built a cannery in West Sound, Orcas Island. It burned in 1922, so they leased the facilities of the *Deer Harbor Fisheries Cannery.*

White Crest Canning Company (est. 1899). Will A. Lowman built the White Crest Cannery at L Avenue and 4th Street in Anacortes in 1898, where they canned clams. Lowman incorporated the White Crest Canning Company a year later. In 1905 they started canning salmon. Lowman owned many pile drivers, purse seiners, fish traps, and tenders, including fish traps at Kanaka Bay and Salmon Bank, and utilized the Jensen brothers' boat *Venture*. In 1907 he renamed the business the *Coast Fish Company* and sold it to *Farwest Fisheries* in 1936.

Boat and Ship Builders in the San Juan Islands

BOAT AND SHIP BUILDERS

William and James Crook. Garrison Bay, San Juan Island. William Crook, and his son James, homesteaded the site of English Camp after its abandonment by the Royal Marines in 1874. Based on the evidence of half-hull models found at their place as well as William's background as a shipwright in England, they probably built several boats at Garrison Bay.

Dennison Brothers. Shaw Island. B. F. "Frank" Dennison and his brother George W. built several boats on Shaw Island, including the *Raven* (1902).

Fowler Brothers. Shaw Island. Frank Eugene "Gene" and Elihu Burritt "Bert" Fowler worked on several boats built on Shaw Island. Gene helped Del Hoffman build the sloop *Reliance* (1907). Bert built the fish tender *Alco* (1917) for Alaska Sanitary Packing Company of Seattle. (Del Hoffman also built the tug/fish tender *Bermuda* (1909) for E. B., Jr., B. E., and W. O Fowler.)

Del Hoffman. Hoffman Cove, Shaw Island. Del Hoffman built boats at his place on Shaw Island, including the tug/tender *Arthur G.* (1901); the sloop *Reliance* for A. Lauron for cod fishing in Alaska (1907); the tug/fish tender *Bermuda* for E.B., Jr., B.E., and W.O Fowler of Shaw Island (1909); and the fishing boat *Klatawa* for Will Jakle (1912).

Jensen's Shipyard. Friday Harbor, San Juan Island. Brothers Albert, Frank, Joseph "Joe", and Peter "Pete" Jensen, together with Joseph "Joe" Groll, established the Friday Harbor Lumber and Manufacturing Company on the waterfront at the base of West Street in 1904. In addition to milling and planing, they built ships there. In 1907, the stock of the company was sold to several local citizens; the Jensen brothers and Groll continued to hold some stock. In 1910, Albert Jensen left to establish Jensen's Shipyard on the south side of the Harbor which eventually became the Albert Jensen & Son Shipyard. One of the first boats he constructed was the *Nereid*, which served as a tender for the Friday Harbor Packing Company. Eventually Albert and his son Nourdine built 150 boats there. (Jensen's Shipyard continues in operation today under the ownership of the Port of Friday Harbor.)

Newhall. Cascade Bay, Orcas Island. In 1883, Edward P. Newhall purchased a water-driven sawmill at Stockade Bay near Olga on Orcas Island; upon determining that Cascade Lake would be a better source, he relocated to Cascade Bay four years later. Edward persuaded his brother Andrew to join him there, and Andrew engineered a dam, canal, and pipe system for the newly established Cascade Bay Lumber and Manufacturing Company. When business began to decline around 1902, Andrew secured a government mail contract and purchased the steamer *Buckeye* for the route. From the shipyard in Cascade Bay James A. Scribner of Friday Harbor built the steamer *S.S. Islander* (1904), as well as the launch *Sport*, and steam launch *Loretta* (1899). Andrew Newhall sold the property to Seattle shipbuilder Robert Moran in 1905.

Norman Shipyard. Mud Bay, Lopez Island. Michael (Mikael) Severin Norman and his son Arthur established a shipyard on the northeast shore of Mud Bay and built several boats there, among them *Uno* (1894) and the launch *Outlook* (1913, for John Franklin Troxell).

Reed & Cayou. Reed Harbor, Decatur Island. William "Bill" or "Will" H. F. and Joseph "Joe" Reed began building boats on Decatur Island in the 1890s. The name was changed from Reed Brothers to Reed & Cayou in 1903 when brother-in-law Henry T. Cayou joined them to build his first boat, the *Mary C.* (named after Cayou's wife Mary, a Reed). Also known as Reed's Shipyard, they built over 40 boats there, including *Buffalo*; *Fearless*; *Hillside 11*; and *Helen T.*

Schruder Yard. Otis, Mud Bay, Lopez Island. Originally located elsewhere on Lopez Island, in 1902 Peter (Peder) Schruder bought eleven and a half acres from P. E. Peterson at Otis, at the head of Mud Bay. He and son Louis "Louie" built a shipyard, as well as a sawmill, there, and over the next few years built fishing as well as other boats: *Alpha* (1901); *Hope* (1902); a sloop for W. J. Morgan of Ketchikan, Alaska (1904); *Nemesis* (1909); *Cilside* (1907); *U and I* (George T. Peterson, 1912); and a fishing boat for George W. Dennison (1912). Louie also worked at the Norman Shipyard.

James and Edward Scribner. Friday Harbor, San Juan Island. Father James A. and son Edward "Ed" A. Scribner came to San Juan Island around 1901, where both worked as shipwrights in addition to regular carpentry. James worked on the *Islander* for Andrew Newhall at the Cascade Bay Lumber Company, Orcas Island, and later at a workshop rented from Friday Harbor Packing Company, building among other vessels a pile driver for merchant N. E. Churchill. Ed built launches for Henry Bailer, S. M. Bugge, Peter Kirk, Ernest Rahorst, and Glen Tulloch.

Sebelin Brothers. Fisherman Bay, Lopez Island. Wilhelm "William" Christian and Christian "Chris" Sebelin ran a shipyard on the shores of Fisherman Bay in the early twentieth century. Prior to that, they built the *Dora* for themselves at MacKaye Harbor near Richardson in 1918 and purse seined in the 1920s and 1930s. During the 1940s, they were listed as oar makers and according to local lore had designed a machine for making oars.

Skansie Shipyard. Gig Harbor. The Skansie shipyard was founded by brothers Peter, Mitchell, Joe, and Andrew Skansie, who had immigrated from the island of Brac, Dalmatia (currently part of Croatia). In the early 1900s they began to modify purse seiners, which at the time were rowed by oar with a crew of eight men, to power boats, as well as increasing the length of the hull and adding cabins. Peter and Joe eventually returned to fishing, but Mitchell and Andrew continued the business, building much of the Gig Harbor Croatian purse seine fleet that fished the San Juan Islands, among other places.

R. C. and Bruce Willis. Olga, Orcas Island. R. C. Willis was listed as a shipwright in the 1900 federal census. Together with his son Bruce he built the ketch-rigged shrimp boat *Ailsa*, as well as several skiffs, in 1903 for the Haines Oyster Company.

FISHING BOATS AND SHIPS

Note: This is by no means a complete list of the ships and boats that have been used for fishing in the Salish Sea, but rather examples of more noteworthy vessels that have had prominent positions in local maritime history. For more complete lists, see Terry Jackson, John Wade, and Wally Botsford, *The Fishermen and the Fisheries of the San Juan Islands* (n.d.), John Wade and Terry Jackson, *The Link Between the Two Harbors* (n.d.), and "Purse Seiners of Anacortes" in Bret Lundsford, *Croatian Fishing Families of Anacortes* (2011), pp. 110-120. Another, online source is the Tacoma Public Library's *Ships & Shipping Index* https://cdm17061.contentdm.oclc.org/digital/collection/p17061coll11 Boats and ships are listed alphabetically in the following manner: **Name.** *Type, date built, dimensions (length, beam, draft, and gross tonnage [gt]/net tonnage [nt]), owner and/or captain, building history, and use history.*

Ailsa. Ketch-rigged Shrimp Boat, 1903. Built and owned by R. C. Willis and son Bruce of Olga, Orcas Island.

Alco. Fish Tender, 1917, 40' long, 11.8' beam, 5' draft. Built by E. B. "Bert" Fowler, Shaw Island, for Alaska Sanitary Packing Company of Seattle. Reported lost to fire, Juneau, Alaska in 1927.

Aloma. Fishing Boat/Tender, 1943, 47' long, 25 gt/17 nt. Built by Norman F. Mills at Jensen's Shipyard for himself. Used for dogfish dragging during World War II and later reef net servicing and tendering.

Alpha. Steamer, 1901, 53.9' long. Built by A. Marcusen and Peter and Louie Schruder, Mud Bay, Lopez Island.

Aniakchak. Fishing Boat, 1931, 43.4' long, 11.3' beam, 6' draft. Built by I. D. Nordyke at Friday Harbor for himself.

Arlee. Steam launch. Capt. H. H. Davis.

Arthur G. Tug/Tender, 1901, 34.5' long. Built by Del Hoffman, on Fisherman Bay, Lopez Island (commuting from Shaw Island) for J. S. Groll, Lopez Island.

Baldy. Fishing Boat, 1907, 55.2' long, 14.1' beam, 5.4' draft, 7 nt. Built by M. Norman, Richardson, Lopez Island.

Bermuda. Tug/Fish Tender, 1909, 47.15' long, 11.8' beam. Built by Del Hoffman, Shaw Island, for E. B., Jr., B. E., and W. O Fowler of Shaw Island.

Blakely. Fishing Boat, 1936, 41.9' long, 12.2' beam, 6.4' draft, 23 gt/15 nt. Built by R. S. Spencer for R. S. Spencer and E. D. Spencer at Thatcher, Blakely Island. In 1964 her home port was Los Angeles, CA.

Blue Sea. Fishing Boat, 1917, 42.3' long, 14' beam, 6.2' draft. Built by F. E. "Gene" Fowler of Shaw Island for San Juan Canning Company. Wrecked in Alaska in 1928.

Buddy. Fishing Boat, 1933, 40' long, 11.2' beam, 6' draft, 14 gt/9 nt. Built by Albert Jensen, Friday Harbor, for Chester Tift.

Caprice. Fishing Boat, gas schooner?, 1905, 50.4 long, 11.8' beam, 4.6' draft, 13.73 gt/9.34 nt. Built by Wm. H. F. Reed, Decatur Island for Fidalgo Island Canning Company.

Charlie Boy. Steel Hull Gillnetter, 1969, 32' long, 12 ton. Built by owner Pierre Franklin of Lopez Island, to be used at Bristol Bay.

City of Paris. Fishing Sloop, 1894. Owner/skipper Edouard Graignic of Waldron Island.

Commando (ex-*Trio*). Shrimp Boat (then converted to Tug for Cary-Davis), 1911, 52' long. 16.3' beam, 6.6' draft. Built by Wm. H. F. Reed, Decatur Island, for Walter Larson (1/3), Oscar Cammon (1/3), and Martin Cammon (1/3), all of Gertrude, WA.

Crescent. Steam Shrimper. Captain Blackman, Seattle Oyster & Fish Company.

Daring. Fishing Boat, 1925, 43.1' long, 10.3' beam, 5.5' draft, 15 gt/10.62 nt. Built by Wm. H. F. Reed & J. M. Reed on Decatur Island for Wm. H. F. Reed.

Deep Sea. Fish Tender/Tug, 70.6' long, 16' beam 6.5' draft, 52 gt/35 nt. Built by Albert Jensen, Friday Harbor. Lost at Anchorage, AK, in 1942.

Denny M. Fishing Boat, 1950, 39.6' long, 12.4' beam, 6.3' draft, 20 gt/13 nt. Built at Jensen's Shipyard, Friday Harbor, as a purse seiner for Ed Martel. Converted to a troller, and then used by Alfred Chevalier, his wife Adeline (Mordhorst) and son Barney for crab harvesting in Wrangell, Alaska; they died from exhaust fumes. The boat was recovered, restored, and turned back into a troller for Alaskan waters.

Dora. Purse Seiner, 1918, 38.5' long, 11.1' beam, 5' draft, 12.65 gt/10.69 nt. Built by Wilhelm Sebelin at McKay Harbor, Richardson, Lopez Island for Sebelin Bros.

Edna. Coal-fired Steam Tug, later converted to diesel. Built for Astoria Puget Sound Canning Company at Chuckanut.

Ella. Charles Williams, chartered by Henry T. Cayou. Fire in 1909.

Emma H. Fishing Boat, gas schooner, 1941, 39.4' long, 11.9' beam, 6.5' draft, 19 g./13 nt. Built by Albert Jensen at Friday Harbor for Sigvard Hansen of Ketchikan, AK.

Esther. Steam launch. Worked for Friday Harbor Packing Company.

Ethel M. Fishing Boat, 1955, 32.3' long, 11.1' beam, 5.1' draft. Built at Jensen's Shipyard for Kenneth Martin.

Evelyn. Fishing Boat, gasoline schooner, 1913, 39' long, 13' beam, 4.2' draft, 15 gt/10 nt. Built at Richardson, Lopez Island.

Falcon. Fish Tender?, 1918, 38.4' long, 9' beam, 4.4' draft. Built by E. B. Fowler on Shaw Island for Alaska Sanitary Packing of Seattle.

Fawn. Steam Fishing Boat, 1900, 37' long, 10.4' beam, 4.3' draft, 11 gt/7 nt. Launched April 12, 1900, by J. Jones and J. M. Reed at Decatur Island. Model by Wm. H. F. Reed. "Heading to Alaska." Captain Jones worked for White Crest Canning Company of Anacortes.

Fearless. Fish Tender, 1912, 80' long, 17.4' beam, 8' draft. Built by Wm. H. F. Reed on Decatur Island for Henry T. Cayou. Lost in Alaska in 1960.

Frolic. Troller, 1908, 36' long, 15 hp gas engine. Built in Bellingham, later converted to gillnetter, fished by Bill Mason and John C. Jackson in 1946-7.

G. Vasa. Steam Shrimper. Captain Bert Hale, Seattle Oyster & Fish Company.

Genius. Purse Seiner/Tender, 1920, 50 hp Frisco Standard gas engine. Built and skippered by Nick Skansi of Gig Harbor, tendering for the Friday Harbor Canning Company; skippered by son-in-law Gerald Crosby upon Nick's death in 1939.

Griffin. Steamer Tender/Tow, 1899, 46' long, 11.2' beam, 4.5' draft, 11 gt. Built by Benjamin and Albert Jensen, Friday Harbor. In 1900 Joseph, Albert, and Frank Jensen were working on it in southeastern Alaska for the Great Northern Fish Company; in that season they packed about 13,000 barrels of salt salmon. Name changed to *MacDowell*. Lost to fire.

Harvester King. Kelp Harvester, barge, 100 hp Fairbanks Morse semi diesel engine. Built on the mainland, the *Harvester King* was used to harvest kelp for the Puget Sound Potash and Kelp Fertilizer Company, which was founded in 1913 and built at Port Stanley in 1917. It had a 16-foot cutter bar, which could be raised or lowered depending on the cutting conditions; upon being cut the kelp was moved to a large open hopper amidships. After the plant closed in 1920, the *Harvester King* was used as a ferry on the Anacortes-Friday Harbor-Sidney BC run for one season in 1922. It was then rebuilt as a freight boat and renamed the *F. H. Marvin*.

Hector. Fish Tender, 1897, 41.7' long, 9' beam, 3' draft. Built by James Holden at Westcott Bay, San Juan Island for self. Worked for both William Shultz and Captain R. E. Davis. Sold by Holden in 1901 to George Fowler and Tom Wakefield of Shaw Island for "general jobbing work." Explosion/fire in 1913 but still recorded in 1915.

Helen B. Columbia River Model Gillnet Bowpicker. The *Helen B.*, along with the *Donna B.* and the *Redwing*, were used by the Croatian Bajovich family (John and his three sons John Jr., Martin, and Albert) of West Seattle, gillnetting the Salmon Bank in 1941-2 for the Friday Harbor Cannery.

Helen T. Fish Boat, 1912, 57' long, 15' beam, 21 nt, 50 hp Standard engine. Built by Wm. H. F. Reed at Decatur Island for Henry T. Cayou, for charter to George & Barker Company of Blaine.

Hermosa. Steam Tug. West Sound. Boiler by Reid Boiler Works; engine by B. B. Iron Works.

Home 2. Purse Seiner, 1916. 62' long; 40 hp Frisco Standard engine. Built at Blind Slough, Oregon; rebuilt in 1940s by Jack Bujacich, Sr., repowered with Cummins diesel engine. Bought in 1924 by John Ross, Jr., and his brothers Adam and Emmett of Gig Harbor; it fished the San Juans for years and served as a trainer for many future skippers.

Hope. Steam Tug, 1902. Built by Peter and Louie Schruder at Richardson, Lopez Island.

Hydah. Trawler, Tender, Research Vessel, 1942. Built as a trawler by Norman Blake in 1942, the *Hydah* was skippered by Cleve Vandersluys for daytime research work at the University of Washington Friday Harbor Laboratories and evenings and weekends servicing reef nets: laying anchors during pre-season, loading the fish and taking them to the Jackson cannery when the salmon were running, and then gathering the gear at the end of the season. The *Hydah* was also used in research for the Salmon Fisheries Commission, following salmon fry through the San Juans to the Pacific Ocean.

Industry. Whaling Scow-Schooner, four 250-gallon tanks. James Dawson and Abel Douglas, British Columbia Whaling Company.

Jefferson Davis. United States Revenue Cutter, Cushing Class Topsail Schooner, 90'. Completed in 1853 in Rhode Island and sailed around Cape Horn to Puget Sound. Used by members of the U. S. North West Boundary Survey for collecting, exploring, and surveying the San Juan Islands in 1859.

Kate. Whaling Schooner, 47-tons. James Dawson and Abel Douglas, British Columbia Whaling Company, whaled in the Saanich Inlet in the late 1860s.

Katy Thomas. Fishing Sloop, 1894, 38.1' long, 12' beam, 3.6' draft. Built by A. J. Hinckley on Waldron Island for Thomas Brothers of Waldron Island.

Kitty Rader. Fishing Boat, 1883, 34' long. Built by A. R. Rader, Shaw Island, for John Ross.

Klatawa. Tug/Tender, 1912, 50.2' long, 15.8' beam, 4.8' draft. Built by Del Hoffman, Shaw Island, for William Jakle, Friday Harbor, who worked for the Hidden Inlet Canning Company.

Laurel. Steam Tug, 1898?. Captain John Eden, Jesse Bird engineer, towing fish scows for Island Packing Company.

Lobo del Mar. Fish Tender, ketch-rigged schooner, c. 1980, 38' long, 4' draft, 12 nt. Designer, builder, owner Tom Chamberlin, of Lopez Island.

Lorna. Fishing Boat, 1960, 31.9 long, 11.5 beam, 5.8' draft. Built by Jensen's Shipyard, Friday Harbor, for Pacific American Fisheries, Bellingham.

Mary C. Steam Tug, 1903, 70.7' long, 18.3' beam, 8.8' draft, 93 gt/47 nt, 380 hp. Built by Reed and Cayou at Decatur Island—their first boat. Henry T. Cayou owner (named for his wife Mary Reed).

Mia. Shrimp Boat, steamer, 4 tons. Haines Oyster Company.

Michigan. Steam Fish Tender. Purchased by the Island Packing Company in 1894 for a fish tender. Tended Shultz and Gross fish traps. Partially destroyed by fire in 1896 and repaired.

Mida. Fishing Boat, 1971. Built at Jensen's Shipyard Friday Harbor for Ed Pinnow.

Monaghan. Freight/Fishing Boat, 1911, 56.2' long, 14' beam, 5.8' draft, 36 gt/25 nt. Built by Chas. H. Curry at Orcas, Orcas Island. Lost in 1963 at Ketchikan, AK.

Nereid. Steam Tender, 1911 72.7' long, 16.75' beam, 6.4' draft, 29 gt. Built by Jensen Brothers, sold to the Friday Harbor Packing Company.

Nokomis. Fishing Boat, gas schooner, 1908, 52.4' long, 11.2' beam. Designed by C. H. Clift, Jr., built by F. L. Clift on Shaw Island for C. H. Clift of Orcas Island and D. Campbell of Bellingham, WA.

Octoo. Shrimp Boat, steamer, 1908, 38' long, 11' beam. Built at Reed Shipyard on Decatur Island for Seattle Oyster and Fish Company.

Orlou. Shrimp Boat, steamer, sister to **Octoo**, 1909, 35' long, 11' beam, 3.8' draft. Built at the Reed Shipyard on Decatur Island for Seattle Oyster and Fish Company.

Outlook. Fishing Boat, 1900s, 36' long, gas powered. Built by Norman Shipyards for John Franklin Troxell.

Paradise. Fishing Boat, 1926, 59.2' long, 16.2' beam, 7.5' draft, 51 gt /34 nt. Built by J. M. Reed and Elmer Barger in Anacortes.

Patricia. Gillnetter (converted to a Troller), 1965. Built by Jensen's Shipyard, Friday Harbor, for J. G. Jones.

Peggy Sue. Fishing Boat, 1961, 39.2' long, 11.8' beam, 6.1' draft, 19 gt. Built on Lopez Island.

Raven. Steamer Tug, 1902. Built by Dennison Brothers, Shaw Island.

Ref. Tug, 50' long, 100 hp distillate engine. Used for towing piledrivers and scows for Will Lowman. Leith Wade was crewman, engineer, and then skipper.

Reliance. Sloop, 1907, 30.8' long, 10' beam, 4.5' draft, 7 nt. Built by Del Hoffman and Gene Fowler, Shaw Island, for Andrew Larson for cod fishing in Alaska.

Roche Harbor. Hauled Oceanic Canning Company pile driver to Barlow Bay.

Rover. Shrimp Boat, steamer, 4 tons. Haines Oyster Company.

Rustler. Schooner, 1883, 50' long, 16.6' beam, 5.8' draft. Built by J. N. Fry, East Sound, Orcas Island, for himself. Later sold to J. D. Warren for sealing in North. Wrecked Boxing Day 1887 at Nitnat; Capt. J. W. Dodd and crew saved.

Sally J. Gillnetter, 1920. Built for Bastian P. Jevick on the Duwamish River in Seattle; named for Jevick's younger sister. Fished off Iceberg Point for 50 years; sold in 1983 to James Bergdahl and used off Stuart Island in experimental nori seaweed farming.

Salmonero. Gasoline Launch. 55' long. Used by E. A. Sims, Port Townsend canneryman. She hit the reef off Discovery Island in July 1922.

San Juan. Steamer. Oceanic Canning Company.

Sea Bird. Deep Sea Troller, 1948, 34.2' long, 10.6' beam, 5.4' draft. Built at Albert Jensen Yard, San Juan Island, for Alfred & Barney Chevalier of Stuart Island.

Setrocana (*Anacortes spelled backwards*). Steamer. Bert Butts, captain; worked for the Porter Fish Company hauling supplies and piles drivers to fish traps.

Skiddoo. Fishing Boat, 1911, 32' long, 8' beam, 16 hp Standard engine. Built at the Reed Shipyard, Decatur Island; launched January 5, 1911. First powerboat for Henry Cayou. Lost to fire at Mitchell Bay in 1920s or 30s.

Sockeye. Sardine Seiner and Tender, 1928, 78' long, 18' beam, 150 hp direct reversible Eastern Standard diesel engine. Originally built as the *Carol Dean* as a sardine seiner, it was purchased by the Friday Harbor Canning Company and renamed the *Sockeye*. She served as a packer, with a 150,000 lb. capacity, skippered by Leith Wade among others. After being drafted as a Coast Guard Reserve vessel during World War II, she was refitted in the early 1950s to drag for bottom fish in northern British Columbia.

Standard. Gasoline Tug, 1909, 40' long, 9' beam, 3.5' draft, 30 hp Standard engine. Built by Reed Brothers, Decatur Island, for Henry T. Cayou. Hold lined with galvanized iron. Converted to "pleasure launch."

Strumpet. Troller, 1972, 32.9' long, 12.6' beam, 5.2' draft. Designed by Jay Benford, built by Jensen's Shipyard for Ernie Gann.

Tanya. Fishing Boat, 1927, 33.4' long, 9' beam, 4.4' draft. Built at Mud Bay, Lopez Island.

Triumph. Whaling Schooner, 1871, 40' long. Owner and captain Abel Douglas, whaling in the Gulf of Georgia.

U and I. Auxiliary Launch, 1912, 28' long, 8' beam, 7.5 hp Miamus engine. Built at L. P. Schruder boat yard, Lopez Island, for George T. Peterson for fishing at Cape Flattery.

Velvet. Crab Fishing Boat, 1952, 46.8' long, 14.1' beam, 8.1' draft, 37 gt. Built by Albert Jensen & Sons for E/N Peacock.

Venture. Steamer Tug/Cannery Tender, 1907, 70.5' long, 15.3' beam, 5.4' draft, 175 hp steam plant. Albert, Joseph, and Frank Jensen, owners; Albert sold his interest to his brothers in 1911. Hired by White Crest Canning Company of Anacortes for several fishing seasons, starting in 1908, and then the Coast Fish Company. In 1925 bought by Wagner Towing and repowered; purchased by Foss Launch & Tug in 1937 and renamed *Hildur Foss*. Intentionally sunk April 1, 1949.

Verdun. Fishing Boat, 1919, 33.9' long, 10' beam, 4' draft. Built by Frank Jensen, Friday Harbor, for Frank and Joseph Jensen (1/2 &1/2). First used trolling in southeast Alaska.

Veteran. Purse Seiner, 1926. Built by the Skansie Shipbuilding Company and owned by Peter Skansie, Gig Harbor. Fished Salmon Bank and other San Juan locations from the 1920s through the 1970s.

Vibes. Fishing Boat, 1934, 39' long, 10.6' beam, 5.3' draft, 14 gt/9 nt. Built by Alphonse Meyer of Oak Harbor on Decatur Island for Roy E. Erb (1/2) and N. G. Miller (1/2); value $4,500.

Vina. Fishing Boat, 1932, 29' long, 9' beam, 4' draft, 7.48 gt. Built by Victor Wesander of Port Stanley, Lopez Island, for himself.

Vita. Shrimp Boat, steamer, 4 tons. Haines Oyster Company.

Wadena. Fishing Boat, gas schooner, 1912, 50.4' long, 13.8' beam, 5' draft, 24 gt/16 nt, 30 hp. Built by Albert Jensen, Friday Harbor, for Straits Fish Company.

Wamega. Purse Seiner and Fish Tender, gas schooner, 1912, 57.8' long, 13.8' beam, 5' draft, 24 gt/16 nt. Built by Albert Jensen for Straits Fish Company. Captained by Frank and Esther Norland.

Wanderer. Fish Tender, originally a schooner, 1911, 43.5' long, 12' beam, 4.4' draft, 14 tons burden. Built by S. V. Blake of Port Stanley on Decatur Island, for self.

Waseca. Fishing Boat, gas schooner, 1912, 50.4' long, 13.8' beam, 5' draft, 24 gt. Built by Albert Jensen for Straits Fish Company.

Water Baby. Fishing Boat, 1940, 46' long, 11' beam, 6' draft. Built by Albert Jensen & Sons, Friday Harbor, for Clyde Welcome.

Wauneta. Fishing Boat, gas schooner, 1912, 50' long, 13.8' beam, 5' draft, 24 gt/16 nt. Built by Albert Jensen for Straits Fish Company.

Westland. Purse Seiner. Purchased by the Ross brothers (John, Sr., Adam, and Emmett) of Gig Harbor in 1928 for fishing in the San Juans; rebuilt from the guards up (with a new pilot house) in the 1940s by Jack Bujacich, Sr.

Wildfire. Fishing Boat, gasoline schooner, 1924, 34.2' long, 10' beam, 4' draft, 8 gt. Built on Guemes Island.

Windentide. Fishing Troller, 1953, 39' long, 10.8' beam, 5.8' draft, 14 gt/11 nt. Built by Chet North, Deer Harbor, for himself.

Zebeitka. Shrimp Trawler, steamer, 1900s, 10 tons. Captain H. L. Haines named her for his sister. Haines Oyster Company of Seattle. The boat was chartered in 1905 by the University of Washington Marine Station in Friday Harbor for transportation and dredging for marine plants and animals.

?? 1903. Gasoline Launch, 25'2" long, 5'3" beam, 4 hp gasoline engine. Built by Reed and Cayou, Decatur Island, for Henry T. Cayou. "The planks of the hull are all full length, vertical grain fir, fastened to strong oak ribs. The 'house,' with windows all around, in oak sash, is handsomely finished in oak and native maple. Eight miles per hour, 4 hp gasoline engine."

Numbered Boats. Boats with just numbers, unnamed, indicate that they belonged to a company, most often a fish trap or cannery operation. Several numbered dories—probably belonging to the Alaskan Packers Association—serviced the fish traps at South Beach on San Juan Island. There is a historical photo of some numbered two-masted boats, possibly for salmon fishing, moored at Friday Harbor.

FIshing Boats Rafted at Cannery, Friday Harbor
(courtesy San Juan Historcal Museum)

ISLAND FISHERS

Note: "Fishers" is used in a general sense: those involved in all aspects of fishing, including fish trap owners and cannery executives, labor contractors, lawyers and lawmakers, captains and engineers, etc. "Island" extends beyond those who only lived in the Salish Sea region in general and the San Juan Islands in particular to those whose business affected fishing in the islands.

John Broder (1854-1917). A native of Ireland, John Broder immigrated to the United States in 1880, homesteaded in California, and then joined the Klondike Gold Rush in 1900. A year later, he established a creamery and then a clam and fruit cannery in Friday Harbor, eventually partnering with *George Meade* in the cannery business. He died in 1917 in Bellingham.

S. (Samuel) M. (Mandrup) Bugge (1868-1939). S. M. Bugge was born in Norway and arrived in the United States in 1875, eventually moving to Port Townsend in the 1890s. In 1907 he took over the Island Packing Company in Friday Harbor and later organized and incorporated the Tuana Packing Company on Lopez. In the 1910s Bugge returned to the Olympic Peninsula, where he died.

Joseph "Joe" Elmer Cagey (1871-1942). Joe Cagey, who was Samish, reef netted at several sites off Iceberg Point, Lopez Island.

A. (Alexander) R. (Russel) Campbell (1852-1937). A. R. Campbell, born in Canada to Scots parents, worked as a civil engineer in Bellingham; he specialized as a surveyor of fish trap locations in the Salish Sea.

Henry T. (Thomas) Cayou (1869-1959). Henry T. Cayou was born in Deer Harbor, Orcas Island, to Louis Cayou and his second wife, *Mary Ann Sulwham* of the Mitchell Bay Band. After Louis' death, Mary Ann married the chief fisherman of the San Juan (Mitchell Bay) Tribe, *Pe-el (Harry Seawalton Sturgeon)*, and Henry claimed later in life that he learned how to fish from his stepfather starting at age nine. Cayou built the first fish trap in the San Juan Islands, off Eagle Point on San Juan, in 1888; eventually he owned dozens of traps. By the time of his death, he was thought to have caught five million salmon in his lifetime.

Edward "Ed" A. (Alfred) Chevalier (1874-1958). Ed Chevalier was born in Waterloo, Iowa, and moved with his family to western Washington, and then to San Juan Island in 1891 with his mother Caroline and brother Bert. There he met *Mary Smith*, daughter of *Robert Smith* and *Lucy Ontanna Jack*, and they were married on Pearl Island on January 4, 1896. He and Mary homesteaded half of Spieden Island. Ed learned how to reef net and fished from several locations, the prime one being at the mouth of Reid Harbor on Stuart Island. Ed and Mary's son Albert married *Bernhardt Mordhorst's* daughter Adaline, and their youngest daughter Caroline ("Toots") married *Norman Mills*; both families were involved in fishing with the extended Chevalier family, particularly the reef netting business.

Conrad "Con" (1872-1923) and **Edward "Ed" Chlopeck** (1863-1908). Con and Ed were co-owners of the Chlopeck Fish Company, with a wharf and fish processing plant at the foot of Wall Street in Seattle. They would make frequent trips to Friday Harbor to buy fresh fish—mainly spring salmon—from the fish trap companies.

John N. Cobb (1868-1930). John N. Cobb worked a field agent for the U.S. Bureau of Fisheries and as editor of Pacific Fisherman. In 1910 he wrote The Salmon Fisheries of the Pacific Coast, which went through several editions, as well as a companion Pacific Cod Fisheries (1915). In 1919 he was appointed director of the newly formed University of Washington College of Fisheries. Cobb travelled throughout the Pacific Northwest documenting fisheries and canneries, which resulted in his 1919 publication The Canning of Fish Products.

Herbert "Bert" Lester Coffin (1869-1830). Born in Harrington, ME, Bert Coffin came to Friday Harbor in the late 1890s and married Florence Hankinson. He worked at the Island Packing Company canning clams and his journals offer detailed descriptions of cannery life at the time.

F. (Frederick) J. (John) Comeau (1875-1951). F. J. Comeau, born in New Brunswick, Canada, came to Lopez Island from Vancouver, B.C., to manage the Hidden Inlet Cannery (1913) at Richardson. In the late 1910s he and his family moved to Seattle, where he was owner and president of another fish cannery.

Gerald James Crosby (1912-1996). Gerald Crosby, born in Sheridan, MT, began tendering for the Friday Harbor Canning Company as the skipper of the *Genius*, which had been left to his wife *Bernice* by her father, *Nick Skansi*, of Gig Harbor. He later owned the purse seiner *Sea Comber* and the tender *Verona* and many Friday Harbor fishers learned their profession on his boats or under his direction of operations for the Washington Fish & Oyster Company. He died in 1996 in Gig Harbor.

R. (Rowland) "Rolly" E. Davis (1861-1933). Rolly Davis came with his father James and stepmother Amelia to Lopez Island in 1869. He homesteaded on Decatur Island and fished traps off Decatur and Long Islands, Iceberg Point, and Kellet Ledge, Lopez Island, from 1898 to 1901. In the 1890s he had a partnership with *William Shultz*, which they dissolved at the beginning of 1899. In 1901 he was involved in salting and smoking salmon. Rolly Davis moved his operations to Alaska in 1912.

E. (Everett) B. (Brainard) "Ed" Deming (1860-1942). Ed Deming was born and grew up in St. Louis, MO. With the firm of Deming and Gould, a marketing company for canned salmon and other products, he helped arrange for the financing and purchase of Pacific American Fishing Company. Moving to Bellingham, Deming became Director of the company from 1900-1901 and then, after its reorganization, from 1904 until his death in 1942.

B. F. "Frank" Dennison (1869-1911). Frank Dennison was born in Island County, Washington. He married Fannie Lawson on San Juan Island in 1896 and served for many years as an assistant light keeper on Smith's Island and later as a lighthouse keeper in Alaska. He also had land on Shaw Island, where he and his brother George built several boats, including the *Raven* (1902).

Goon Dip (ca. 1862-1933). After meeting Pacific American Fisheries (PAF) manager *E. B. Deming* at the Alaska-Yukon-Pacific Exposition on China Day (September 13, 1909), Seattle businessman Goon Dip became the sole labor contractor for the PAF. At first, he supplied Chinese workers; later he contracted with Japanese canners.

Abel Douglas (1841-1908). Abel Douglas arrived in Victoria in 1868 and began whaling with the British Columbia Whaling Company. The next year Douglas went into partnership with James Strachan, and they moved their operation to the Gulf Islands, where they whaled through the 1870s.

Richard "Dick" Edwards (1868-1917). Dick Edwards, the son of *Sit-sa-lam-athhe (Captain Jack) Edward* and *Kich sau malh*, reef netted from several sites off Iceberg Point on Lopez Island that his father and uncle had fished.

Sigmund Einstoss (1878-1954). Sigmund Einstoss was born in Austria and grew up in New York City, working among other jobs as a bookkeeper in a fish company. In the 1930s he worked in Alaska, where he helped organize the Alaska Trollers Marketing Association. In the 1950s, he built a cannery in Alaska as well as investing in the Deer Harbor and Friday Harbor canneries; due in part to his managerial and financials issues, both closed. When he died in 1954, his estate sold these properties.

James M. Fleming (1847-1928). James Fleming was born in New South Wales, Australia and came to the United States with his family in 1851. By 1879 he was on San Juan Island, where he homesteaded near Kanaka Bay. For many years the Fleming "ranch" (or "Fleming's Beach") became the site of a seasonal tent city for fishers working Salmon Bank and the west coast of the island. He and his family provided fresh produce and milk for the fishers there.

Henry Frederick Fortmann (1856–1946). Born in San Francisco, Henry Frederick Fortmann, owner of the Artic Packing Company, became president of the Alaska Packing Association upon its formation in 1891, a position he held until 1922. He then served on the board of directors until his death in 1946.

Frank Eugene "Gene" Fowler (1872-1945), **George J. Fowler** (1875-1957), **W. O. (William Oscar) Fowler** (1879-1957) and **Elihu Burritt "Bert" Fowler** (1887-1934). The Fowler brothers of Shaw Island were involved in several fishing related activities in the Salish Sea. Gene, W. O., and Bert had Del Hoffman build a tug/tender, *Bermuda*, for them in 1909; Gene helped Hoffman build several boats; and Bert built several fishing vessels, including the fish tender *Alco* (1917) and the *Falcon* (1918). George, who married Hoffman's sister Sadie, was a captain for several local boats and ships.

Billy Frank, Jr. (1931-2014). A Nisqually tribal member, during the 1960s and 1970s Billy Frank, Jr. worked for fishing rights on the Nisqually River and inspired others to advocate for Tribal fishing rights, which culminated in the Boldt Decision. He served for over 30 years as the Chairman of the Northwest Indian Fisheries Commission.

Jack Giard (1941-). Jack Giard came to Lopez Island in 1950 and has been reef netting for over 40 years with his outfit Lopez 4-Way Reef Net off of Fisherman Bay, one of only three operations currently working in the islands. He has also been a member of the Pacific Salmon Fraser River Panel and the San Juan County Marine Resources Council as well as president of the Washington Reef Netter Owners Association.

J. (Joel) A. (Abdon) Gould (1851-1923). J. A. Gould came to Seattle from Iowa in the 1890s and co-founded, with F. W. Keen, the Island Packing Company in Friday Harbor in 1894. (A year earlier he had founded the San Juan County Bank.) Together with Keen he had interests in canneries in Alaska and several lumber operations in the region. Gould built a house overlooking the cannery, which he later left, along with management of the bank, to his son Gene.

Edouard Graignic (1849-1900). Born in France, Edouard Graignic jumped ship in Victoria, BC and homesteaded on Waldron Island, where he fished for herring and halibut as well as dog fish for oil. He died in 1900, leaving behind his Swinomish wife *Lena* and eight of their children.

Samuel H. (Harriman) Gross (1835-1907). Samuel H. Gross, born in Ellsworth, ME, moved to California in his 20s and then north to the Fraser River Gold Rush. He married Mitchell Bay *Jane "Jennie" Quinalt Satart* in 1862. In 1868 Gross filed for a homestead on San Juan Island and farmed, but eventually declared bankruptcy. Around 1897 he teamed up with *William Shultz* in the fish trap business and was very successful, making a considerable amount of money before his death in 1907.

H. (Henry) L. (Luther) Haines (1886-1936). H. L. Haines, with the Haines Oyster Company of Seattle, harvested shrimp in Hood Canal. After discovering them in Harney Channel near Orcas Island in 1903, he deployed several steamers to trawl for them there and in other locations in the San Juans. Haines moved with his family to Friday Harbor in 1905. He skippered the steamers *Zebeitka* (named after his sister) and *Alta*.

John W. Haubner (1881-1950). Born in Texas, Haubner assisted Edmund A. Smith with the 1903 invention of the Smith Butchering Machine, aka "Iron Chink." Upon Smith's death he worked as the foreman of the Smith Canning Machine Company, allegedly holding one of its patents. Around 1910 he and his newly wed Gudrun (Runie) Johnson moved to Friday Harbor, where, along with W.E. Purcell, he worked as foreman for the Friday Harbor Packing Company and later as Vice President of the San Juan Canning Company. He died in 1950.

L. (Louis) D. (David) Hix (1844-1931). L. D. Hix ran a pile driving operation in the late 1890s and drove many of the fish trap and wharf pilings in the San Juans. He married the divorced wife of Edwin A. Hoffman (father of *Del Hoffman*), Cynthia Jane Bish. Hicks Bay on Shaw Island is a corruption of his name.

Chun Ching Hock (1844-1927). Chun Ching Hock (also called Chin Chun Hock or Chin Ching Hock) was the first labor contractor for Chinese cannery workers in the San Juan Islands. Arriving in San Francisco when he was 16, Chun moved to Seattle and first worked for the Yesler Mill but soon established his own mercantile store, the Wa Chong Company. Chun provided laborers for both the Friday Harbor Packing Company and the Salmon Banks Cannery in Richardson, Lopez Island. He was paid in cash or with real estate for each cannery worker and in the early 1900s owned land on the north of Friday Harbor, which he eventually sold to *J. A. Gould*, cannery owner and founder of the San Juan County Bank.

Delbert "Del" Eugene Hoffman (1870-1915). Del Hoffman was born in Pennsylvania and came to the San Juan Islands in the 1890s. He married Kate Irene Gordon in 1891 on Orcas Island; they had nine children, one of whom, Delbert David Hoffman (1903-1992), farmed and did carpentry work on Shaw Island. From his place on Hoffman Cove on Shaw Island Del Hoffman built many fishing boats, including the tug/tender *Arthur G.* (1901); the sloop *Reliance* for A. Lauson (1907); the tug/fish tender *Bermuda* for E. B., Jr., B. E., and W. O. Fowler of Shaw Island (1909); and the fishing boat *Klatawa* for Will Jakle (1912).

John C. (Cogswell) Jackson (1911-2001). John Jackson was born in Sunnyside, WA, and came to Friday Harbor with his family in the 1920s. He established several enterprises, including a mink farm on Egg Lake Road and the San Juan Island Golf Course. When feeding salmon heads and tails from the Friday Harbor Cannery to his mink, Jackson decided to establish his own cannery. This began as a salting and smoking facility on what was known as Little Island, connected to Argyle Spit on San Juan Island at low tide; two years later, Jackson built a cannery there, which ran until he sold it in the 1970s.

Albert Jensen (1873-1958). Born in Iowa in 1873, Albert Jensen, together with his brothers *Frank, Joseph "Joe"*, and *Peter "Pete"*, along with Joseph "Joe" Groll, established the Friday Harbor Lumber and Manufacturing Company on the Friday Harbor waterfront in 1904. He established the Jensen Shipyard on the south side of Friday Harbor in 1910; together with his son *Nourdine* (1914-2009) he built over 150 ships and boats, including the *Nereid* and the *Venture*.

Bert "Spider" Jones (1887-1981). Bert Jones's first job was working at a fish cannery, but he soon realized he could make more money stealing salmon from the many fish traps in the Salish Sea. With his 42-foot boat named *Spider*, throughout the 1920s and 1930s Jones would visit traps at night, gather fish, and then sell it to the buyers the next day.

John (Johan) Meier Larsen Jorgensen (1865-1932). John Jorgensen was born in Tonnes, Norway, either a cousin of or one of the several Jorgensen brothers who in either 1881 or 1888 immigrated together to the United States but had to change their names because of visa issues. He married Hanna Regina and move to Richardson in 1905, where he was involved in shipbuilding with his brothers. They had two sons, John Franklin and Lars, who were also involved in boatbuilding.

Jeremiah "Jay" Julius W'tot lhem (1974-). Julius is a Lummi fisher and owner of two seafood markets on San Juan Island. A former Chairman of the Lummi Nation, he is founder and president of Se'Si'Le, a non-profit dedicated to bringing "people and organizations into a deeper and truer understanding of Indigenous histories and worldviews."

F. (Frederick) W. (Walter) Keen (1856-1929). Born in Nova Scotia, Canada, F. W. Keen immigrated to the United States in the 1870s and settled in Oregon, where he married Christena "Tenna" S. Smith. In 1894, together with *J. A. Gould*, he established the Island Packing Company. Keen and Gould also had joint interests in lumbering enterprises, and Keen is often listed as a "lumber man" or "capitalist" in the census.

John Kertula (1851-1916). John Kertula was born in Finland and made his way to Waldron Island, where he married *Louisa*, widow of Louis La Porte, in the 1890s. Apparently, he had an uncanny ability to locate good sites for fish traps and was active in the Waldron fishing industry.

Trevor Kincaid (1872-1970). Dr. Trevor Kincaid joined the biology department of the University of Washington in 1898 and retired in 1942. He established the Puget Sound Biological Station at Friday Harbor in 1904. Among other achievements, Kincaid was instrumental in the introduction of the Pacific oyster from Japan for farming operations in the Salish Sea.

R. (Robert) C. Kinleyside (1860-1937). R. C. Kinleyside was born in Ohio and came to Lopez Island in the 1890s, where he was one of the incorporators of the Oceanic Canning Company at Richardson in 1895. In 1897, both he and the Oceanic

Canning Company bought tidelands at Richardson. By 1900, he had moved to California, where he died in 1937.

Thomas E. (Ellis) Ladner (1836-1922). Thomas E. Ladner, together with his brother William, came to the Delta region of the Fraser River in 1868 and established Ladner's Landing. While William went into farming, Thomas established canneries; he, as well as his son-in-law F. I. Lord, was financially involved in San Juan Islands fish traps and the Oceanic Canning Company at Richardson, Lopez Island.

Jim Lawrence (1951-) and Lisa Nash (1959-). Jim first worked at the Jackson Cannery; later, Jim and Lisa gillnetted, under Lisa's Swinomish tribal affiliation after the Boldt Decision.

Harry Roland Lemaister (1884-1956). Harry Lemaister was born in Port Townsend to *John Lemaister* and *Maggie Brown*, the daughter of Lopez Island homesteader *Charles Brown* and *Conna (Mary Jane)*, of a Northern Tribe. (Several of Harry's siblings married into the *Cayou* family.) In addition to farming and cutting wood, Harry fished, both beach seining with horses and reef netting. He, along with T. J. Blake, Lloyd Weeks, and Harold Hammond, formed the Four Way reef net gear that is still used today off Fisherman Bay, Lopez Island.

Lorraine Loomis (1940-2021). Having worked in fish processing since 1970, Lorraine Loomis became fisheries manager of the Swinomish Indian Tribal Community soon after the Boldt Decision. She joined the Northwest Indian Fisheries Commission around 1980, serving as Vice Chair from 1995 until 2014, when she became Chair following the death of *Billy Frank Jr.* Loomis was the lead negotiator for the North of Falcon salmon fisheries planning process and involved in developing and implementing the U.S./Canada Pacific Salmon Treaty.

Beatrice "Betty" Annette Lowman (1914-2011). "Reef Net Betty" Lowman, the granddaughter of *Will Lowman*, was instrumental in publicizing the revival of reef net fishing in the Salish Sea in the 1930s.

W. (William) A. (Alvin) "Will" Lowman (1863-1943). Will Lowman was born in Indiana and came to Anacortes in 1893. There he built the White Crest Cannery at L Avenue and 4th Street in 1898, where they canned clams. Lowman incorporated the White Crest Canning Company a year later. In 1905 they started canning salmon. Lowman owned many pile drivers, purse seiners, fish traps, and tenders. In 1907 he renamed the business the Coast Fish Company and sold it to Farwest Fisheries in 1936.

George Mead (1840-1913). George Mead, of Seattle, went into business with *J. Broder* in 1903 canning clams at their facility on the Friday Harbor waterfront. In 1905 this firm was reorganized as the Island Packing Company, a joint stock company, with Broder as president, Mead as secretary, L. B. Carter as treasurer, and E. H. Nash as general manager; they doubled the capacity of the facility. Two years later Broder bought Mead and his son Walter's stock.

Norman Mills (1914-2008). Norman Mills was born at Roche Harbor on San Juan Island and married *Caroline "Toots" Chevalier* in 1937, thereby joined the extended fishing family of the Chevaliers. He helped the family reef net as well as fishing with his boat *Aloma*.

Bernhardt Mordhorst (1843-1936). Bernhardt Mordhorst was born in Schleswig-Holstein, Germany, and emigrated to the United States sometime in the 1860s. He made an application for a homestead on Reid Harbor on Stuart Island in 1876 and received the patent in 1883. There, together with his fellow German Frederick Hay (or Hayes), he ran a herring fish operation, including a saltery on his property and a smoking house on the cove outside the harbor. They would sell fresh herring to the halibut schooners that would stop by on their way to fish in Alaska. After his partner died in 1887, he married Katherine "Kate" Rosler and had six children.

Andrew Newhall (1844-1915). Persuaded by his brother Edward to join him on Orcas Island, Andrew helped establish the dam, canal, and piping for a water-driven sawmill for their Cascade Bay Lumber and Manufacturing Company. In 1904 he had shipwright *James A. Scribner* build the steamer *Islander* there, as well as some launches. After Newhall sold the company and land to Robert Moran, he moved to Friday Harbor, where he donated part of his land for the Puget Sound Biological Station campus.

Michael (Mikael or Mekal) Severin Norman (1856-1935) and **Arthur Norman** (1887-1963). Michael Norman was born in 1856 in Norway to Steffen and Malli (Molly) Jorgensen, one of several brothers who immigrated to the United States together but had to change their names because of visa issues. He came in either 1882 or 1887 with his wife Dorothea Ovidea and son Arthur. Michael Norman is listed in the 1900 census as residing on Lopez Island as a boatbuilder, and in later censuses as a shipyard bookkeeper and a boat carpenter. Together with his son Arthur he built boats at Mud Bay. Arthur also captained a tugboat. Michael died at Port Stanley, Lopez Island, in 1937. Arthur was married to Violet Vogt in 1931 at Mt. Vernon and died in 1963.

William "Bill" J. (John) Norton (1888-1970). William J. Norton was born in South Dakota and when young moved with his family to Deer Harbor. An entrepreneur, he was involved in the Tyee Fish Company of Eastsound, which operated fish traps on the west side of Orcas Island. Norton established a store in Deer Harbor and was involved in the construction of the Northern Pacific Fisheries cannery on the west shore of West Sound and the Red Cannery (Deer Harbor Fisheries Company) for the George W. Hume Company. In 1931 he built a floating cannery and sawmill in Deer Harbor. William J. Norton was elected and served as a San Juan County Commissioner.

Christian "Christ" Olsen (1855-1933). Christ Olsen, who was born in Norway, married *Mary Anne "Marion" Dick* of the Mitchell Bay Band. Christ, together with their son *Herman* (1909-1974), reef netted several of the sites associated with Marion's family, including Open Bay, Henry Island.

Pe-el (Harry Sewalton Sturgeon) (1843-1914). Pe-el, also known as Harry Seawhalton or Swalton or even Seawhaton Harry, was said by his stepson *Henry Cayou* to be "the chief fisherman of the San Juan (Mitchell Bay) Tribe." In 1903 he married *Mary Ann Sulwham*, the widow of Louis Cayou. Her son Henry claimed later in life that he learned how to fish from his stepfather starting at age nine.

Carl Angelo "Punk" Perovich (1942-2008). Born in Gig Harbor, Carl Perovich began working as a kid on the fish-buying barge of his grandfather, *Niels "Carl" Nielsen*, at Fish Creek, San Juan Island. Being small and short, he was nicknamed "Punk" and had a special bunk designed for him on his uncle Leonard Crosby's purse seiner *Emily Jane*. After growing up fishing the Salmon Bank with Peter Babich of Gig Harbor, he began fishing southeast Alaskan waters, including herring, salmon, black cod, and halibut, and then moved on to King crab.

Joseph "Joe" M. (Miller) Reed (1873-1935) and **William "Bill" or "Will" H. (Henry) F. (Foster) Reed** (1870-1935). Joe and Bill Reed were born on Decatur Island and began building boats there in the 1890s. Together with their brother-in-law *Henry Cayou* they established the Reed and Cayou Shipyard, beginning in 1903 with the boat *Mary C.*, named for their sister and Cayou's wife. Over the years they built over 40 boats and worked on hundreds.

John Samuel Ross, Sr. (1861-1926). Born to the Jadrošić family on Premuda, an island in the Adriatic Sea that is now part of Croatia, John married Johanna (Eva or Iva) and they came to the United States in 1887, changing their name to Ross and settling in Gig Harbor, where they raised a family of ten. During the fishing season, John Ross, together with his sons John Jr., Emmett, and Adam, purse seined off San Juan Island and camped on the beach below Peter Lawson's farm on Eagle Cove.

Thomas Welcome Roys (1816-1877). Whaling in the Strait of Georgia, BC in 1868, Captain Roys killed many humpbacks with a cannon-fired harpoon that he invented. He then formed the Victoria Whaling Adventures Company but moved his operations to the outer coast of Vancouver Island.

"Harry" (Ho-Hal-Tet Ite) Samish (xwuhl-xwhal-tun) (1834-1899). Harry Samish, also known as "Old Harry," was the leader of a village on the eastern end of Samish Island. He operated reef nets off Iceberg Point, Lopez Island.

Jack K. (Kokeji or Koheiji) Saoka (1888-1962). Born in Kagawa, Japan, Jack K. Saoka immigrated to the United States in 1907 and first came to San Juan Island in 1917 to work at the Island Packing Company; because of his language skill he eventually became a supervisor and even established a florist business with his wife Yuki in Friday Harbor. They were relocated to an internment camp on the mainland in 1942.

Peder "Peter" Schruder (1853-1925) and **Louis "Louie" Schruder** (1877-1931). Peter Schruder was born in 1853 in Norway, one of several brothers who immigrated in either 1881 or 1888 to the United States together but had to change their names because of visa issues. He arrived on Lopez Island around 1900 and together with his son Louie built boats at Mud Bay. Peter died in 1925. Louie married Ellen Blanch Hart and had nine children. He died at Port Stanley in 1931.

James A. Scribner (1840-1923) and **Edward "Ed" A. Scribner** (1865-1951). Born in Maine, James and his son Ed moved first to Michigan and then San Juan Island around 1891. In addition to regular carpentry, James worked as a shipwright, building the *Islander* (1904) for *Andrew Newhall* and a pile driver of *N. E. Churchill*, as well as several other boats. Ed built launches for Henry Bailer, S. M. Bugge, Peter Kirk, Ernest Rahorst, and Glen Tulloch; he was also an agent for Kennebec boat motors. Ed had a reef net at Smugglers Cove and used his cabin on Mitchell Bay for his boat and crew.

Wilhelm "William" or "Billy" Christian Sebelin (1879-1946), **Christian "Chris" Sebelin** (1883-1949), and **John Sebelin** (1888-1970). William Sebelin, along with his younger brother Chris, ran a shipyard on the shores of Fisherman Bay, Lopez Island. Both were born in Germany; Chris was naturalized in California in 1906 and William in San Juan County in 1917. By the 1920 census William and Chris are enumerated as fishermen, purse seining, on Lopez. In the 1940 census the brothers are listed as oar makers; according to local history they had a special machine for making oars in their shipyard. John Sebelin came with his older brothers William and Chris to Lopez to fish and work on repairing boats; however, unlike them, he did not stay on Lopez. In 1925 he married Erna Schmidt (Erna Miller?) at Port Angeles and farmed in Clallam County until his death in 1970.

She-Kla-Malt (Thomas) (1825-1900). She-Kla-Malt, of Lummi ancestry, married *Mary Yakship Sluckhachwa* (1828-1924), a S'Klallam woman. He claimed one of the few "Indian Homesteads" in the islands, on the northeast coast of San Juan Island, and reef netted at Stuart Island. Their daughter *Maggie Playwhilloot Tom* (1855-1943) married *Charles Mason Fitzhugh* (1855-1927) and moved to her father's place on San Juan Island, where Fitzhugh worked as a fisher with Maggie's S'Klallam relatives. Their daughter, *Pearl Little* (1913-1983) was a skilled reef netter, as was Mason Fitzhugh's half-brother *Tom Phillips* (1877-1950).

William Shultz (1861-1925). William Shultz was born on July 14, 1861, in Delphi, IN. In 1889 he moved to Tacoma, and a year later to Roche Harbor, where he started as bookkeeper and eventually became general manager, superintendent, and vice-president of the Tacoma and Roche Harbor Lime Company. After leaving in 1905, he went into the fishing and canning industry. He formed a partnership with *Samuel Gross* using fish traps, as well as working with Captain *George J. Willey* operating the Blaine Packing Company (1906) and the Crest Canning Company in Anacortes (1907). In 1909 he, along with Willey and *W. E. Persell*, formed the Friday Harbor Packing Company and the Mitchell Bay Fish Company. He died on April 19, 1925.

Nicholas "Nick" Skansi (1890-1939). Born in St. Martin on the island of Brac, Dalmatia (currently part of Croatia), Nick Skansi emigrated to the United States with his brother John in 1910. They ended up in Gig Harbor, along with their cousins *Peter, Mitchell, Joe,* and *Andrew*, and began purse seining, first with the *Hioma* and later the *Companion*, which was built at the Skansie Shipyard. Nick's daughter, *Bernice*, married *Gerald Crosby*, who took up skippering the tender *Genius* after Nick's death in 1939.

Petar "Peter" Skansie (ca.1870-?), **Andres "Andrew" Skansie** (1876-1950), **Mitchell "Michael" Skansie** (1879-1939), and **Josip (Joseph) "Joe" Skansie** (ca. 1881-1960). In the early 1900s, the Skansie brothers, who had immigrated from the island of Brac, Dalmatia (currently part of Croatia), began to modify purse seiners to power boats by installing gasoline engines, increasing the length of the hull, and adding cabins. Peter and Joe returned to fishing, but Mitchell and Andrew continued the business, building much of the Croatian Gig Harbor purse seine fleet that fished the San Juan Islands, among other places in the Salish Sea.

Edmund A. Smith (1870-1909). Edward A. Smith invented a fish cleaning machine called the "Iron Chink" in 1903. Smith died in an automobile accident on his way to the display of his invention at the 1909 Alaska-Yukon-Pacific Exposition in Seattle.

Ashton Wayman Thomas (1865-1927) and **Ellery Rudland Thomas** (1863-1950). Originally from New Brunswick, Canada, Ashton Thomas, together with his brother Ellery, established a herring smokery in the early 1890s on Waldron Island at Fishery Point, which he got as a cash entry homestead. He also served a term as County Sheriff and drew the attention of John Develin and *F. W. Keen* to establishing a cannery in Friday Harbor. Ashton Thomas moved to Anacortes in the late 1890s and ran unsuccessfully for State Fish Commissioner; later he was involved in a herring and sardine packing company in Alaska.

John "Johnny Tom" Thomas (1853-??). Johnny Tom, the son of *She-Kla-Malt Thomas* and *Mary Yakship Sluckhachwa*, was born at Mitchell Bay, San Juan Island. In 1879 he obtained a homestead at the entrance to Reid Harbor on Stuart Island, offshore of which was a prime location for reef netting.

John Franklin Troxell (1877-1952). John Troxell was born in Texas and moved with his family to Lopez Island when his father Frank homesteaded there in 1885. He got his first job as a helper on a pile-driving crew and then worked on building fish traps with *Ernest Davis* and his brothers *"Rolly"* and *Arthur*. John Troxell and Ernest Davis put in a fish trap at Aleck Bay and fished it for the years 1901 and 1902; they then sold it for $50,000 and split the proceeds. After the sale, John married Eunice Davis, Ernest's sister. The new owners of the trap could not find the pile holes, so Troxell was called back to manage the trap for several years (and eventually claimed it again in the 1910s). He continued working on fish traps, owning and working locations throughout the San Juan Islands, until they were banned in 1934.

Francis Seymour Charles Cleve Vandersluys (1915-2004). Cleve Vandersluys was born in Calgary, Canada; in 1956 he came to Friday Harbor, where he skippered the *Hydah* for daytime research work at the University of Washington Friday Harbor Laboratories. Evenings and weekends he worked servicing reef nets: laying anchors during pre-season, loading the fish and taking them to the Jackson Cannery when the salmon were running, and then gathering the gear at the end of the season. Vandersluys also participated in research for the Salmon Fisheries Commission, following salmon fry through the San Juans to the Pacific Ocean.

Willian Leith Wade (1901-1986). Leith Wade was born in Quebec but grew up on Guemes Island, opposite Anacortes. He started work as a piledriver for Will Lowman (White Crest Canning Company) and then as an engineer and eventually skipper of several boats, including the *Ref*, the *Killdeer*, and the *Sockeye*. He tendered purse seiners and then became superintendent of the Friday Harbor Canning Company. In the 1950s, he gillnetted and set up a piledriving company.

George J. (John) Willey (1869-1952). In 1908, George J. Willey, along with *William Shultz*, and *W. E. Persell*, incorporated the Friday Harbor Packing Company and leased the Island Packing Company cannery from Pacific American Fisheries. Upon William Shultz's death in 1925, Willey took over as principal owner and manager until his retirement in 1935. He died in Port Townsend in 1952.

R. (Richard) C. (Charles) Willis (1832-1908) and **Charles Bruce Willis** (1872-1951). R. C. Willis was born in Liverpool, England and emigrated to the United States in the 1880s, ending up at Olga on Orcas Island. Listed as a shipwright in the 1900 federal census, together with his son Bruce he built a shrimp boat for the Haines Oyster Company. Bruce fished privately and worked for several fish companies, including the Porter Fish Company at Prince of Wales Island, Alaska.

GLOSSARY

Note: This glossary is not typical in that the terms and their definitions are not arranged alphabetically; rather, they are grouped topically, with specific **terms**, in bold and italic, defined within broader topics.

Boat and Ship Construction. Indigenous peoples constructed boats—principally canoes—by hollowing out logs. With the advent of Europeans and Euro Americans, boat builders used milled boards for clinker-built or lapstake construction. Modern construction methods are fiberglass, aluminum, or cement.

> ***Dugout.*** Indigenous peoples hollowed out logs, usually cedar because of the ease with which it could be split and worked. The lines of the canoe were carved with the eventual widening of the hull in mind; this was done by heating stones in a fire and then placing them in water in the hull, which was sometimes covered, to steam and soften the wooden hull fibers. Thwarts were then placed to both widen the hull and raise the gunwale and stem lines. Several types of regional canoes added material for the upper portions of the prow and stern, so that carvers were able to use only half of a large log, and not have to be too picky about selecting core wood that was intact and not fungal and spongy.
>
> ***Clinker-built*** or ***Lapstrake.*** "Clinker-built" or "lapstrake" construction consists of long boards that were attached horizontally to a framework such that each course overlaps the one below; the spaces in between were caulked with ***oakum***—a loose fiber obtained from untwisting old rope—and sealed with pine tar.
>
> ***Modern construction.*** Modern boats and ships are constructed of fiberglass, aluminum, and cement.

Boat and Ship Descriptive Terms. Several terms are used to describe a boat or ship.

Directions. The directional terms of a vessel (boat or ship) are *fore* (the front or towards the front), *aft* (the rear or towards the rear), and *athwart* (on the sides). The front of the vessel is called the *bow*; the rear the *stern*; and the middle the *midships*.

Measurements. The measurements of a vessel are the *length* (from bow to stern, parallel to the waterline), *beam* (width at its widest point), and *draft*, *draught*, or *draw* (vertical distance between the waterline and the deepest point of the boat, or minimum amount of water required to float a vessel).

Capacity. The capacity of a vessel is expressed by weight either as *gross* (full, with the weight of the vessel itself) or *net* (only the cargo) *tonnage*.

Parts. Not all vessels have a *deck*—some are open structures—but when they do, they can contain a *hold*, or space for storage of *cargo*, and superstructures such as pilot houses, for steerage.

Boat and Ship Motive Power. Boats and ships are propelled by paddling or rowing; sailing; steam; or internal combustion (gasoline or diesel).

Paddles and Oars. Indigenous paddles were mostly lance-shaped, with a thin end at the base, although some were elliptic with a narrowing point. The order of the paddlers in the canoe reflected that of the household, with the matriarch as steerer in the stern and paddlers arrayed according to family rank ahead of her. Europeans and Euro Americans introduced the use of oars—long poles of wood with carved handles at one end and flat blades at the other. They were secured in place with *oarlocks* or *rowlocks*, which could be as simple as two upright pins in the gunwale or as fancy as metal formed in the shape of a stirrup or circle surrounding the shaft. In addition to the *oarsmen* sometimes there was a *helmsman* or *steersman* at the *tiller*.

- **Sails.** Sailing vessels use a combination of masts, booms, yards, and gaffs to spread *sails*—triangular or quadrilateral sheets of woven bark or fiber such as cotton or synthetics—to catch the wind. The general term *spar* refers to all of these members. A *mast* is a vertical structure in the fore-and-aft line of the vessel; sailing boats and ships have at least one mast and multiple masts are defined by their relation to the main mast (i.e., the foremast, aft mast, etc.). Attached to the mast are several spars used to extend the sails: a *boom*—a horizontal pole, usually attached at one end to the mast in order to swing freely; a *yard*—a long spar, supported at its center, to which the head of a sail is "bent" (attached), or a *gaff*—a spar rising aft from a mast to support the head of a quadrilateral fore-and-aft sail: formed with a permanently fixed spar, or as one secured to the mast by hoops and hoisted with the sail. The term *rigging* refers to the system of ropes and cables with which the sails and spars are secured.
- **Steam.** The first engine-driven vessels were steam powered: water was heated in boilers by means of wood or coal burned in a furnace and the resulting steam drove mechanisms that either drove a screw propellor or turned a side or rear wheel.
- **Internal combustion.** Gasoline engines began to be used in fishing boats in the early 1900s and as the century advanced the horsepower (measure of mechanical power) became greater. The most popular engines were the 40 and 50 hp Frisco Standard, built in San Francisco. Diesel, a higher density energy source and therefore more efficient in terms of fuel storage on a vessel, was introduced in the 1920s. The most common makes were Atlas or Washington, with some Cooper-Bessemers; horsepower ranged from 90 to 120, depending on the number of cylinders. An important advance was the direct reversible engine, which allowed for easier shifting from forward to reverse.

Boat and Ship Types. Boat and ship types range in size from small craft—canoes, dinghies, dories, long or whale boats, and gigs—to large sailing craft such as sloops, schooners, brigs, and barks.

Bark (or Barque). A sailing ship, typically with three masts, in which the foremast and mainmast are square-rigged, and the mizzenmast is rigged fore-and-aft.

Bateau. A thirty-foot long, double-ended, flat-bottomed rowboat modified from a York River Boat for use by the Hudson's Bay Company on the Columbia River.

Brig. A two-masted, square-rigged ship with an additional gaff sail on the mainmast.

Canoe. A narrow, keelless boat with pointed ends, propelled by a paddle or paddles.

Dinghy. A small, usually open, boat used as transportation from a ship, sometimes rigged with a mast and sails.

Dory. A flat-bottomed boat with high flaring sides, sharp bow, and deep V-shaped transom.

Launch. An open motorboat, although sometimes the forward part of the deck may be covered. Launches, usually gasoline powered because of the smaller size of the engine, were used by fishers to visit their fishing or packing sites.

Long or Whale Boat. A long narrow rowboat made with both ends sharp and raking, often steered with an oar, and used by whalers for hunting whales.

Scow. A flat-bottomed boat with sloping ends used as a barge.

Sloop. A small sailing boat with one mast.

Schooner. A sailing ship with two or more masts, typically with the foremast smaller than the mainmast, and having gaff-rigged lower masts.

Boat and Ship Uses. Boats and ships were built for several uses.

Barge. A flat-bottomed boat used for carrying freight and usually towed by another vessel.

Gill Netter. The earliest gill net boats were Columbia River Salmon Boats, 22-23-foot-long double-ended open boats which sometimes had aft decks added for the netting. Originally rowed, in the 1900s the boats increased in size and added cabins, power engines, and turntables. Eventually they adopted power drums.

Pile Driver. A floating structure with a tower that held a steam-driven mechanism for driving piles, towed to the site.

Purse Seiner. Early purse seiners used two boats: a skiff and a scow. The four- or six-oared skiff was flat bottomed with a turned-up stern, 7 feet in the beam and 25 feet in length, the latter 8 feet of which was decked for stowing the seine. The 20-foot long, 8-foot-wide scow had hand winches on each end. In the 1900s, a self-propelled boat was developed with a gasoline engine and aft deck for the seine, but skiffs were still used to set the purse. Later, horsepower increased to 45–75, and the length of the boats correspondingly grew to 45–55 feet. From 1910–1920, boat length increased to up to 68 feet long. Built with rounded sterns, these boats featured an elevated section where a movable platform (turntable), set on a pivot, had a long roller. The turntable swung around when hauling the net aboard, and the roller was powered, which assisted the crew in pulling the net aboard by hand.

Reef Net Boat. The Straits Salish used a modified version of their large fishing canoe for the two boats flanking a reef net; they were designed for stability, with a sheared-off stern where the watchman could stand and spot the salmon entering the net while the rest of the crew lay low in the hull. Modern reef net boats are clinker-built, but follow the general lines of the canoes, with the addition of metal frame watch towers and hand or power winches for hauling in the nets.

Tender. A tender is a tug-like vessel with a crew of 8-10 men that would take the catch from a fish trap or fishing boat, place it in scows or, later, large holds, and transport it to either canneries or fresh fish markets.

Trawler. Trawlers were built to haul a large trawl net behind them; because of the weight and drag of the trawl net, they were steamers 50-75 feet in length, which were more powerful than the common fishing steamers. The trawl was let out on the starboard side; after a period from half an hour to 3 hours, the net would be hauled in—at first, by hand; later, by hydraulic drum—over the rail and the catch dumped on the deck, sorted, and placed in the hold.

Troller. Indigenous peoples used regular fishing canoes for trolling, attaching the line to their hand or oar to give the bait or lure an animated look. When clinker-built rowboats were introduced, they were used in a similar fashion. Larger, purpose-built boats with gasoline engines could use multiple lines, employing long poles or outriggers to separate the lines and first hand and then power reals to bring in the catch.

Fishing Gear. *Gear* refers to the materials and methods used to catch fish: nets, weirs, hook and line, and impaling.

Nets. The three basic methods of using nets are: ***encirclement*** (beach and purse seining), ***entanglement*** (gillnetting), and ***entrapment*** (reef netting and fish trapping). **Beach Seining** is conducted with a long seine net; a dory with one end attached was rowed toward the beach from a larger boat, which pays out the seine against the current in a large semicircle. When it is fully paid out, the line attached to the other end is rowed ashore and hauled in with horses (or men) to capture the enclosed fish. **Purse Seining** is done with a large boat accompanied by a large skiff: the skiff lets out the net from the boat in a circle which ends up at the mother boat, hopefully enclosing a school of salmon. This 'purse' is then drawn closed, and the net drawn into the boat. **Gillnetting.** Gill nets are webbing with meshes that allow the fish's head to enter and get caught by its gills; the size of mesh varied according to the species of fish. The top of the net was kept at the water's surface with floats; the bottom was weighted. There are two types of gill nets: ***stationary***, which are anchored in place; and ***drift***, which are allowed to float loose. **Reef Netting** consists of forming an artificial reef such that the salmon, following the current, will be funneled into a net suspended between two boats and caught.

Fish Trapping is stationery and consists of webbing or part wire netting, held in place and position by driven piles. Fish traps consisted of four parts: the lead, heart, pot, and spiller. The ***lead***, a long straight line of wire netting covered pilings placed diagonally to the prevailing tidal flow, diverted the salmon in their migration and lead them into the ***heart***, a funnel that was ten feet on the outside and narrowed to the ***pot***, a large, tarred cotton web pen. From the pot the salmon were turned into the ***spiller***, a bag similar to but smaller than the pot.

Weirs. Barriers, called weirs and usually made of brush or stakes that have matting adding, block the passage of fish and divert them into a pot or some sort of trap.

Hook and Line. A traditional means of fishing all over the world is by means of a ***hook***, attached to a ***line***, and weighted down with a ***sinker***. This can be a ***hand line*** or by means of hand or powered reels on poles or rods (***rod-and-line***).

Impaling. Small fish were impaled by means of ***rakes***: crossbars with small, sharp prongs attached to long shafts that could be 'swept' like a broom. Fish were speared with one or multi-prongs attached to a ***shaft***. ***Pitchfork-like spears*** were constructed of a shaft with a crosspiece with prongs set in a row. A ***leister spear*** consists of two flared prongs with backwards-pointing barbs flanking a shorter barb. Some spears had barbed or pronged heads with ropes attached that would detach from the shaft after impaling the fish, so that the fish could be hauled in after it had been allowed to 'run' for a while.

Transferring Fish. Once caught, there are several ways fish can be transferred from the gear to storage.

Brailing involves using a small net to transfer fish from a fish trap or larger net to the hold of a vessel; the net can either be a small purse or a larger sheet brail.

Gaffing uses a large iron hook attached to a pole or handle to land large fish; this was also called a pew or pugh. (Because this often damaged the flesh of a fish, "unpughed" fish were sought after for the fresh fish market.) In transferring fish from a barge to the cannery, a *pic*, or tool with a wood handle and a sharp metal point like a curved nail, was used to pick up a fish under the gills and toss it.

Preserving fish. Fish that are not freshly consumed can be preserved by means of drying and smoking, pickling (salting), barreling, canning, and freezing.

Drying and smoking. Indigenous peoples dried fish on racks, often with the help of smoke, which would discourage flies and other vermin as well as dogs. Europeans and Euro Americans used two types of smoked salmon: mild and hard. The fish were taken out of the **pickling barrels** and soaked to remove as much as the salt as possible. They were then attached on the skin side to a "bacon hanger"—a framework of wires that had "six or more points bent at right angles to the frame, terminating at the top in a hook." Each of these was hung from a round stick in the smoker. When the smoker was fully loaded, a small fire of non-resinous wood was built underneath. The fire was then maintained so as to provide more smoke and less heat, so that the fish was cured with the smoke rather than cooked by the heat. "Mild" smoking lasted about 8-10 hours, "hard" two days with additional curing.

Pickling (Salting). Pickling, or salting, was an early method for preserving fish. Picklers would remove the head, tail, and viscera of the fish and, after soaking it in saltwater, pack it with salt in a barrel.

Barreling. Barreling was the standard shipping method for preserved food at the time. Standard barrel sizes derive from the British measurement system based on the ***tun***, which contained 210 Imperial gallons or 252 U.S. gallons. A butt is a half tun (130 U.S. gallons), a tercian or puncheon a third tun (84 U.S. gallons), a hogshead a quarter tun (63 U.S. gallons), a ***tierce*** a sixth tun (42 U.S. gallons), and a ***barrel*** an eighth tun (32 U.S. gallons). Many accounts of local fish salting operations mention shipments of empty barrels from nearby port cities, and local merchants advertised "fish barrels" in 200, 100, and 50-pound sizes for sale. However, the standard of most salting facilities packing their mild salmon was the ***tierce***, which weighed 300 pounds.

Canning. Canning became the principal method of preserving seafood during the last quarter of the nineteenth century. Prior to 1900, most of the process of canning was done by hand. Workers would arrive in early spring to start manufacturing cans, which were cut, shaped, and soldered together in a separate facility. Machines that produced the cans were invented in the early 1900s. The standard case of canned salmon—usually wooden boxes called ***shooks***—contained 48 one-pound cans and it took about 10-12 six-pound fish to fill a case.

Freezing. Freezing fish, a process introduced to the region in the 1890s, consists of three principal features: getting fish fresh; freezing them; and coating them with a thin glaze of ice. Each fish is covered with oiled paper or parchment, wrapped with heavy brown paper, and packed in boxes of 250 pounds each, which were placed onto the refrigerator cars and shipped.

Shoreline Structures. There are several terms for marine structures attached to the shoreline

Dock. A place to 'park' (dock) a boat or ship.

Jetty. A structure of wood or stone extended into the sea to influence the current or the tide, or to protect a harbor or beach.

Pier. Often synonymous with *dock*, a pier is sometimes interpreted as the walkway leading to the dock, or parking area, itself.

Quay. A stone or concrete structure along the shore on navigable water used for loading and unloading vessels.

Wharf. A landing place constructed from the shore out into the water, often to achieve enough depth allow for boats or ships to tie up and load or unload.

Dock or Moorage Construction. In constructing a dock or other moorage facility, there are several components.

Deck. A structure of horizontal wooden planks that forms a surface for a wharf.

Dolphin. Dolphins—a group of piles driven together and bound with braided rope girdles or steel belts—used as a mooring post.

Gabion. A cage or crib constructed of logs and containing rocks, used for constructing a wharf.

Pile. A long log or pole, driven into the bottom of the sea with a pile-driver.

RESOURCES

Note: Instead of footnotes, the following archives, publications, and websites are offered as suggested sources for those who wish to explore the basis of this work as well as pursue the subject further. This section begins with ***primary resources*** (genealogical data, such as censuses, museum holdings, archives, and newspapers); ***local histories***; and ***general histories of fishing***. After that, they follow the general outline of the book: ***physical features*** (geology, tides, and currents); ***natural history*** (ecosystem and seashore zones); ***Indigenous fisheries and mariculture; early history of the islands*** (Coast Salish, explorations, Hudson's Bay Company, and surveys); ***modern boats and vessels***; ***types of gear***; ***preservation*** (canning); and ***fishing histories*** (theses and dissertations, publications, surveys, and governmental). ***Governmental regulation***, state and provincial, regional, national, and international, is an important aspect of modern times. The penultimate portion is on ***environmental issues***, such as climate change; piracy, poaching, derelict gear; finfish net pens; and the status of Southern Resident Killer Whales. The final section is on the ***salmon conservation and restoration***. For websites, rather than always citing the URL, enough information is provided to be able to search its location on the internet. Because of the numerous citations of HistoryLink.org Online Encyclopedia of Washington, it will be referred to as "HistoryLink."

Primary Resources

Archives. I have used all four island museums—Lopez, Orcas, San Juan, and Shaw—for primary material on local fishing, including written material, photographs, objects, and oral histories. This is also true of regional museums, such as Anacortes and the Whatcom County museums. The Northwest Regional Branch of the Washington State Archives has invaluable resources, some of which are searchable online. The provincial archives at the Royal British Columbia Museum in Victoria are an important source of information, unfortunately largely inaccessible during the pandemic. For information on the island fishing families, I have mined online genealogy resources, principally Genealogy.com and FamilyTree.com, as well as cemetery databases, such as FindaGrave.com. Several sites of the Washington Rural Heritage project have photographs, original writings, images of objects, oral histories, and published works that pertain to island fishing, particularly: Lopez Island, Lummi Island (especially the Reef Net Fishing Collection), Orcas Island, and San Juan Island.

Local and regional newspapers. Numerous local and regional newspapers were published during the early part of the historic period covered in this book, primarily the *Islander* (1891-1898) and the *San Juan Islander* (1898-1914)—both searchable online at http://chroniclingamerica.loc.gov/lccn/sn88085190/issues. Other early Territorial regional newspapers can be found in Washington State's digital archives: http://www.digitalarchives.wa.gov/Home. Two special newspaper editions should be noted: *The San Juan Islands Illustrated Supplement to The San Juan Islander* (1901) and the July 19, 1908, "Islands of San Juan County, Washington" special edition of the *Everett Morning Tribune*. The *Friday Harbor Journal* (available at the San Juan Historical Museum) is also a wealth of information; in addition to historic data, there have been several articles in this newspaper in the last 50 years on the history of fishing in the islands. Some regional papers have relevant material on the fishing industry in the Salish Sea: for instance, both the *Northwest Enterprise* (1882-1886) and the *Anacortes American* (1890-present) covered Anacortes and Skagit County fisheries. Some relevant material was generated farther afield; for instance, the *Spokane Spokesman-Review* featured reportage on the salmon catch and processing.

Industry publications specializing in Northwest fishing include the *Pacific Fisherman Journal*, of which the years 1903-1911 are accessible through the University of Washington digital archives. The January 1904 (Volume 2, Number 1) edition is particularly instructive, containing articles by David Starr Jordan, "The Salmon of the Pacific," Chris H. Buschmann, "Trap

Fishing," Barton W. Evermann, "The United States Bureau of Fisheries," and T. E. P. Keegan, "Old and Modern Ways of Canning Salmon." *Pacific Fisherman Yearbook* was published from 1903-1967 and contains yearly statistics on cases packed as well as articles on topics such as canning, fishing gear and methods, and the state of the industry.

Local histories

Published sources. Local fishermen have compiled and published two volumes of reminiscences: Terry Jackson, John Wade, and Wally Botsford, *The Fishermen and the Fisheries of the San Juan Islands* (n.d.) and John Wade and Terry Jackson, *The Link Between the Two Harbors* (n.d.). Jacilee Wray has written an insightful study of *Salmon Bank: An Ethnographic Compilation* for the National Park Service in 2003. Mike Vouri, who has researched and written about the fishers and fisheries of the San Juan Islands, expanded on this in his entry in HistoryLink *Salmon Bank (San Juan Island)* Essay 20510 posted on 2/16/2018. Mike, together with Julia Vouri, also discussed fishing in the two volumes they prepared for *Images of America* (Charleston, S.C.: Arcadia Publishing): *Friday Harbor* (2009) and *San Juan Island* (2010). Two other volumes in the *Images of America* series, Susan Lehne Ferguson and the Lopez Historical Society and Museum, *Lopez Island* (2010) and Orcas Island Historical Society and Museum, *Orcas Island* (2006), describe fishing and fishers of these islands. Other local and regional histories that mention fishing include Charles Ludwig, "A Brief History of Waldron Island" (1959; manuscript on file, San Juan Island Public Library) and James Bergquist, *The History of Stuart Island* (privately published, 2012).

Oral histories: Oral histories often record vivid accounts by those who were "in the room" (or, in this case, "on board"). Local sources include: Anacortes Museum—particularly those about fish pirates; Lopez Island Historical Museum—several fishers, with a special one of Jack Giard; Orcas Island Historical Museum—several fishers; San Juan Historical Museum—several fishers and a diver. The Washington Rural Heritage Project, particularly the Lummi Island Reef Net Fishing Collection, includes many oral histories by island fishers.

Place names: An early source on place names of San Juan Island is Bryce Wood, *San Juan Island: Coastal Place Names and Cartographic Nomenclature* (Ann Arbor, MI: University Microfilms International for Washington State Historical Society, 1980); more recently, there is Richard M. Blumenthal, *Maritime Place Names: Inland Washington Waters* (Seattle: Inland Waters Pub. Co., 2012). The Samish Nation has developed a website devoted to *Coast Salish Place Names of the San Juan Islands*.

General Fishing Studies

General studies on fish and fishing provide a background and context for local history: Brian Fagan, *Fishing: How the Sea Fed Civilization* (New Haven and London: Yale University Pres, 2017); David Montgomery, *King of Fish: The Thousand Year Run of Salmon* (Westview Press, 2003); and Richard White, *The Organic Machine: The Remaking of the Columbia River* (New York: Hill and Wang, 1995).

Physical Features

General. For information on the physical basis of fishing in the islands, consult:
Richard Beamish and Gordon McFarlane, *The Sea Among Us: The Amazing Strait of Georgia* (Madeira Park, BC: Harbour Publishing, 2014); Audrey DeLella Benedict and Joseph K. Gaydos, *The Salish Sea: Jewel of the Pacific Northwest* (Seattle: Sasquatch Books, 2015); and Kathryn L. Sobocinski, *The State of the Salish Sea* (Salish Sea Institute, Western Washington University 2021), particularly Section 2.

Geology. Ned Brown's *Geology of the San Juan Islands* (Bellingham: Chuckanut Editions, 2014) is the latest of several attempts to describe the complex history of the islands' geology. Recent bathymetric studies have been published by the SeaDoc Society.

Tides and Currents. For a general study of tides, see Jonathan White, *Tides: The Science and Spirit of the Ocean* (Trinity University Press, 2015). Annual tide tables, usually available at local hardware or sport fishing stores, should be consulted for local tides, or go to the Tides and Currents page of the National Oceanic and Atmospheric Administration (NOAA) websitehttps://tidesandcurrents.noaa.gov/noaatidepredictions.html?id=9449880&legacy=1. In 1963 the Canadian Department of Oceans and Fisheries Hydrographic Service published a *Current Atlas of the Juan de Fuca Strait to/a Strait of Georgia*, which contains wonderful diagrams of the currents throughout the Salish Sea.

Natural History

Marine Wildlife. There are numerous general field guides to marine life in the Salish Sea. Check out: Eugene N. Kozloff, *Seashore Life of Puget Sound, the Strait of Georgia, and the San Juan Archipelago* (Seattle: University of Washington Press, 1973); Steve Yates, *Marine Wildlife of Puget Sound, the San Juans, and the Strait of Georgia* (Chester, CT: The Globe Pequot Press, 1988); and Andy Lamb and Bernard P. Hanby, *Marine Life of the Pacific Northwest* (Madeira Park, BC: Harbour Publishing, 2005).

Shellfish: For a history of *native (Olympia) oysters* in general, see E. N. Steele, *The Rise and Decline of the Olympia Oyster* (Elma, WA: Fulco Publication 1957); for British Columbia, see Brian Kingzett, *An almost forgotten history of Native Oysters on Vancouver Island* (March 12, 2014) (https://research.viu.ca/deep-bay-marine-field-station/history-olympia-oyster). For the Shoalwater (later Willapa Bay) oysters, see Virginia Story, "Shoalwater Bay oysters begin feeding San Francisco in 1851" HistoryLink Essay 7850 posted 7/12/2006; Cynthia Nims, "Oyster Farming in Washington, Part 1 HistoryLink Essay 21070 posted 8/11/2020; and Cynthia Nims, "The Bush Act, allowing for the sale of state tidelands for oyster farming, is approved on March 2, 1895," HistoryLink Essay 21087 posted 8/21/2020.

Fish: The latest and most comprehensive volume is Theodore Wells Pietsch and James Wilder Orr, *Fishes of the Salish*

Sea (Seattle; University of Washington Press, 2019). For specific species, see:

Pacific Herring: Washington State Herring Stock Status Reports for the years 2008, 2012, and 2016; R. Walter Williams, *The Fishery for Herring (*Clupea pallasii*) on Puget Sound*. Washington Department of Fish Research Papers 2(1957?):5-105; Iain McKechnie et al, "Archaeological data provide alternative hypotheses on Pacific herring (*Clupea pallasii*) distribution, abundance, and variability," *PNAS* published online February 18, 2014; and David B. Williams, "Ancient Harvests: A History of Salish Sea Herring," *Salish Sea Currents Magazine, Encyclopedia of Puget Sound* (July 19, 2019).

Halibut: Richard Rathbun documents the rise of the Flattery Bank halibut fishery in his "Summary of the Fishery Investigations Conducted in the North Pacific Ocean and Bering Strait from July 1, 1888, to July 1, 1892, by the U.S. Fish Commission Steamer Albatross," *Bulletin of the Bureau of Fisheries*, Washington, DC: United States Government Printing Office, pp.158-163. See also: Kit Oldham, "Schooner *Oscar and Hattie* arrived at the Port of Tacoma with 50,000 pounds of halibut..." HistoryLink essay 8745 posted 8/27/2008.

Dogfish: Thomas F. Gedosch, "A Note on the Dogfish Oil Industry of Washington Territory," *Pacific Northwest Quarterly* Vol. 59, No. 2 (April 1968), pp.100-102.

Salmon: George Suckley, "On the North American Species of Salmon and Trout," United States Commissioner of Fish and Fisheries, *Report of the Commission for 1872 and 1873* Appendix B (Washington, DC: Government Printing Office, 1874); the beginning of John N. Cobb, "Salmon Fisheries of the Pacific Coast," Bureau of Fisheries Document 751, *Report of the Commissioner of Fisheries for 1910* (Washington, DC: United States Government Printing Office, 1911) contains a detailed description of commercial salmon species; and Russel Barsh, "Use of Coast Salish Knowledge in Early Studies of Pacific Salmon Zoology, 1855-1860," paper presented to the Georgia Basin Puget Sound Research Conference, Vancouver, BC March 26-29, 2007.

Indigenous Fisheries and Mariculture

Salish canoes: J. W. Collins, "Dugout canoes of Washington" IN "The fishing vessels and boats of the Pacific Coast," *Bulletin of the United States Fish Commission* 10 (Washington, D.C.: Government Printing Office, 1892); T. T. Waterman and Geraldine Coffin, "Types of Canoes on Puget Sound," *Indian Notes and Monographs* (New York: Museum of the American Indian, 1920); Frederick Howay, "The First Use of the Sail by Indians of the Northwest Coast," *American Neptune*, 1 (4):374-380). 1941; George Durham, "Canoes from Cedar Logs: A Study of Early Types and Designs," *Pacific Northwest Quarterly* April 1955:33-39; Bill Durham, *Indian Canoes of the Northwest Coast* (Seattle: Copper Canoe Press 1960); Leslie Lincoln, *Coast Salish Canoes* (Seattle: Center for Wooden Boats, 1991), which contains measured drawings of several canoe types; and John Jennings, *The Canoe: A Living Tradition* (Toronto: Firefly Books, 2002). Theodore Winthrop, *Canoe and Saddle* (Portland, OR: Binfords and Mort, n.d.) offers a Euro American description of travelling in Salish canoes. Actual canoes can be seen at the Island County Museum in Coupeville as well as at the Burke Museum, Seattle. Discussion of the transition to clinker-built vessels, particularly reef net boats, can be found at Lummi Island Heritage, part of the Washington Rural Heritage.

Indigenous fishing. There are several detailed studies of Indigenous people's fishing in the Salish Sea during the historic period; the first place to start is the work of Wayne Suttles: *Economic Life of the Coast Salish of Haro and Rosario Straits* (PhD dissertation, University of Washington, 1951); "Post-Contact Culture Change Among the Lummi Indians of Northwest Washington," *British Columbia Historical Quarterly* 18, Nos.1-2:29-102; "Central Coast Salish" IN *Handbook of North American Indians, Northwest Coast*, v. 7 (Washington DC: Smithsonian Institution Press, 1990); and "Prehistoric and Early History Fisheries in the San Juan Archipelago," ms. prepared for the National Park Service, May 1998, on file, San Juan Island National Historical Park. Diamond Jenness's work with the Coast Salish of Vancouver Island, with specific sections on their fishing practices, has been edited and published by Barnett Richling, *The WSÁNEĆ and their Neighbors* (Rock's Mills Press, 2016). Bernhard J. Stern, *The Lummi Indians of Northwest Washington* (New York: Columbia University Press, 1934) also discussed fishing among other topics. Hilary Stewart has summarized many studies and reports in *Cedar* (Vancouver: Douglas and McIntyre, 1984) and *Indian Fishing: Early Methods on the Northwest Coast* (Douglas & McIntyre, 1995). Daniel L. Boxberger's *To Fish in Common: The Ethnohistory of Lummi Indian Salmon Fishing* (Lincoln: University of Nebraska Press, 1979) contains a wealth of information on Lummi history during the transition from traditional reef netting through the period of fish traps to the effects of the Boldt decision and its impact on modern fishing; Boxberger is particularly helpful in having done the 'heavy lifting' of compiling statistics on the number of licenses for various fishing gear during this period. See also: Charles W. Wilson, "Report on the Indian Tribes Inhabiting the Country in the Vicinity of the 49th Parallel of North Latitude," 1866 *Transactions of the Ethnological Society of London*, n.s.,4:275-332; Gordon W. Hewes, "Indian Fisheries Productivity in Pre-Contact Times in the Pacific Salmon Area," *Northwest Anthropological Research Notes* Vol. 7 No. 2, Fall 1973; and Patricia Ann Berringer, *Northwest Coast Traditional Salmon Fisheries Systems of Resource Utilization* (MA Thesis, University of British Columbia, 1982).

Indigenous Mariculture. Although long an Indigenous tradition and practice in the Pacific Northwest, evidence for *clam gardens* has only been emerging in the last two decades. Judith Williams's *Clam Gardens: Aboriginal Mariculture on Canada's West Coast*, Transmontanus 15 (Vancouver, BC: New Star Books Ltd., 2006) is one of the first general treatments. Other, more site-specific studies include: "1,000-year-old First Nations clam gardens unearthed near Sidney" (*Times Colonist* May 27, 2013) and John Goodman, "Clam gardens provide new perspective on Fist Nations history" (*North Shore News* July 15, 2016).

Reef Netting: A place to start is the "Reef Net Fishing Collection," Lummi Island Heritage (searchable online), which has an extensive collection of artifacts and documents, both primary and secondary sources. See also: Franz Boas, *Second General Report on the Indians of British Columbia. I The Lku'ṅgEn* 1890; J. A. Kerr, "The Siwash Reef Net," *Pacific Fisherman Year Book* 1916:60; John N. Cobb, "Pacific Salmon Fisheries," Bureau of Fisheries Document 1902 *Report of the Commissioner of Fisheries for 1921* (Washington, DC: United States Government Printing Office, 1930), "Reef Nets" pp. 84-85; George A. Rounsefell, "Reef Nets," *The Salmon and Salmon Fisheries of Swiftsure Bank, Puget Sound, and the Fraser River* (Bulletin of the Bureau of Fisheries No. 27, Washington, DC: United States Government Printing Office, 1938), pp. 713-4; Wayne Suttles: *Economic Life of the Coast Salish of Haro and Rosario Straits* (PhD dissertation, University of Washington, 1951); Norman Alexander Easton, *The Underwater Archaeology of Straits Salish Reef-netting* (Master's Thesis, Simon Fraser University 1985); N. Alexander Easton, "The Underwater Archaeology of Straits Salish Reef-netting," *The Midden* 17(1985)1:9-12; Charles David Moore, "Reef nets," pp. 179-183, *Salmon Fishing Boats of the North American Pacific Coast* (Master's Thesis, Texas A&M University, 1993); Jack Giard, "The Ancient Art of Reef Net Fishing," *San Juan Islands Almanac*, pp. 16-19; "Ralph Lillie Correspondence with Jerry Anderson about History of Reef Netting," (ca. 1995-2005) Lummi Island Heritage; "Appendix D: The W̱SÁNEĆ Reef Net Fisher as Described by STOLX̱EŁ," Justin Fritz, *The SWLSWÁLET of the W̱SANEĆ Nation: Narratives of a "Native (Re) Building Process* (BA Thesis, University of Victoria, 2012); and Russel Barsh, "Coast Salish Reef-net Fishery, Parts 1 and 2, HistoryLink Essays 21237 and 21238 posted 5/23/2021. For the revival of reef netting in the Lummi area, see "Reef Net Betty," *The Puget Sounder*, September 1938 and Beatrice Annette Lowman ("Reef Net Betty"), "Reef Nets Come Back in Puget Sound Salmon Fishery," *Pacific Fisherman* June 1939. The San Juan County Land Bank's The Spit Preserve on Fisherman Bay on Lopez Island has a sign describing reef netting as well as several old boats. As this is being written (September 2021), there is a gear set off Fisherman Bay, Lopez Island, and several off Lummi Island.

Coast Salish peoples celebrated various versions of the **First Salmon Ceremony.** Erna Gunther, in "An Analysis of the

First Salmon Ceremony," *American Anthropologist* 28:605-617 (1926), describes the ceremony as practiced from California to Alaska. Wayne Suttles in *Economic Life of the Coast Salish of Haro and Rosario Straits* (PhD dissertation, University of Washington, 1951), pp. 172-179, reviews more region-specific rites and Diamond Jenness (Barnett Richling [editor], *The W̱SÁNEĆ and their Neighbors* [Rock's Mills Press, 2016], pp. 19-22), describes the rituals as practiced by the Saanich.

European and Euro American Fisheries

Early records of European and Euro American encounters and trade with the Salish in the region are covered in the journals, notes, and reports of the North West Boundary Survey of the United States Boundary Commission, which are invaluable to an understanding of the islands at the cusp of the Pig War. These are summarized in the *Geographical Memoir of the Islands between the Continent and Vancouver's Island in the Vicinity of the Forty Ninth Parallel of North Latitude*. In particular, see "Appendix C: Report of George Gibbs, Geologist, of an Examination of San Juan Island and of the Cowitchin Archipelago and Channel"; "Appendix D: Report of Henry Custer, Assistant, of a Reconnaissance of San Juan Island, and the Saturna Group"; and "Appendix E: Report of Dr. C. B. R. Kennerly of a Reconnaissance of the Haro Archipelago." The (unedited, and therefore more opinionated) diaries and journals of Kennerly and Gibbs are also insightful: see Russel Lawrence Barsh, "Scientists dine with Major Haller at Port Townsend on March 1, 1859," HistoryLink Essay 11196 posted 3/1/2016. Notes on the early Hudson's Bay Company fisheries are contained in Hartwell Bowsfield (ed.); *Fort Victoria Letters 1846-1851* (Winnipeg: Hudson's Bay Record Society, 1979) and William John Macdonald, "Notes by a Pioneer", MS, Provincial Archives of British Columbia (Victoria), which contain material pertaining to salmon barreling on San Juan Island. *Duwamish et al vs. United States of America*, F-275 (Washington DC: US Court of Claims, 1927) contains testimony on Salish settlement and fishing in the islands and Richard Somerset Mackie's *Colonial Land, Indian Labor, and Company Capital: The Economy of Vancouver Island, 1849-1858* (MA thesis,

University of Victoria, 1984) and *Trading beyond the Mountains: The British Fur Trade on the Pacific 1793–1843* (Vancouver: University of British Columbia Press, 1997) provide the historical context of the period.

There are several **General fishing histories** of the region: Cicely Lyons, *Salmon: Our Heritage* (Vancouver: Mitchell Pres, 1969); Courtland Smith, *Salmon Fishers of the Columbia* (Corvallis: Oregon State University, 1979); Washington State Department of Fisheries, *Commercial Fisheries Handbook* (Olympia: Washington Department of Fisheries, 1947); and Joseph E. Forester and Anne D. Forester, *Fishing: British Columbia's Commercial Fishing History* (Saanichton, BC: Hancock House Publishers Ltd., 1975).

Ethnic Euro American fishers are described in Bret Lunsford, *Croatian Fishing Families of Anacortes* (Anacortes: Croatian American Club of Anacortes, 2011) and Sverre Arestad, "The Norwegians in the Pacific Coast Fisheries," *Pacific Northwest Quarterly* 34:1 (January 1943):3-17.

Specific accounts of local fishers and fishing can be found in Beryl Troxell Mason's *John Franklin Troxell, Fish Trap Man* (Lopez Island: Watmough Publishing, 1991); Terry Jackson, John Wade, and Wally Botsford's *The Fishermen and the Fisheries of the San Juan Islands* (n.d.) and John Wade and Terry Jackson, *The Link Between the Two Harbors* (n.d.). Jim Lawrence's memoir, *Callused Hands Hungry Heart* (2011) has some vivid recollections of working in the Jackson Cannery as well as gillnetting, particularly after the Boldt Decision. The local museums house several oral histories of fishers, such as Jack Giard. For accounts of a deviant method of "fishing"—piracy—there is an engaging interview with Bert "Spider" Jones in Ron Strickland's *River Pigs and Cayuses: Oral Histories from the Pacific Northwest* (San Francisco: Lexikos, 1984); several archives, such as those at the Anacortes Museum, have oral histories that identify fish pirates and describe fish piracy; and for a fuller economic and social context, see Chapter 5, "Pirates of the Salish Sea," in Lissa K. Wadewitz, *The Nature of Boundaries: Salmon, Boundaries, and Bandits of the Salish Sea* (Seattle: University of Washington Press, 2012).

Modern fishing boats. A review of Pacific Coast powered fishing boats can be found in the "Pacific Power Fishing Fleet," *Pacific Fisherman Yearbook*, 1915, pp. 21-34 as well as J. W. Collins, "The fishing vessels and boats of the Pacific Coast," *Bulletin of the United States Fish Commission* 10 (Washington, D.C.: Government Printing Office, 1892). Scholarly studies of nineteenth and twentieth century fishing vessels include: Howard Chapelle, *American Small Sailing Craft* (New York: Norton and Company, 1951), which has a chapter on Columbia River Salmon Boats; Charles David Moore, *Salmon Fishing Boats of the North American Pacific Coast* (Master's Thesis, Texas A&M University, 1993); Katie Chase "Skansie Shipbuilding Company of Gig Harbor," HistoryLink Essay 20171, posted 10/24/2016; James A. Cole, *Drawing on Our History; Fishing Vessels of the Pacific Northwest and Alaska* (Seattle: Documentary Media, 2013); and Gordon R. Newell (ed.), *The H. W. McCurdy Marine History of the Pacific Northwest, 1966-1976* (Seattle: Superior Publish Co, 1977). The Lopez Historical Museum features the *Sally J*, Bastion Jevick's gillnetter, as an outdoor exhibit.

Types of Gear. General descriptions of fishing gear can be found in these publications: William H. Dumont and Gustaf T. Sundstrom, "Commercial Fishing Gear of the United States," *Fish and Wildlife Circular* 109 (1961) and Robert J. Browning, *Fisheries of the North Pacific: History, Species & Processes* (Anchorage: Alaska Northwest Publishing Company, 1974). Specific gear include:

Gillnetting: "Gill Nets," Richard Rathbun, "A Review of the Fisheries in the Contiguous Waters of the State of Washington and British Columbia," IN *Report of the United States Commissioner of Fish and Fisheries for the Fiscal Year Ending June 30, 1899* (Washington, DC: United States Government Printing Office, 1900); "Gill Nets," John N. Cobb, "Pacific Salmon Fisheries," Bureau of Fisheries Document 902 *Report of the Commissioner of Fisheries for 1921* (Washington, DC: United States Government Printing Office, 1921); "Puget Sound: Localities Fished," George A. Rounsefell and George B. Kelez, *The Salmon and Salmon Fisheries of Swiftsure Bank, Puget Sound, and the Fraser River* (Bulletin of the Bureau of Fisheries No. 27, Washington, DC: United States Government Printing Office, 1938); Irene Martin, *Legacy and Testament: The Story of Columbia River Gillnetters* (Pullman, WA: Washington State University Press, 1994); and "Gill Nets," Robert J. Browning, *Fisheries of the North Pacific: History, Species & Processes* (Anchorage: Alaska Northwest Publishing Company, 1974), pp. 181-193.

Purse Seining: "Purse Seines," Richard Rathbun, "A Review of the Fisheries in the Contiguous Waters of the State of Washington and British Columbia," IN *Report of the United States Commissioner of Fish and Fisheries for the Fiscal Year Ending June 30, 1899* (Washington, DC: United States Government Printing Office, 1900); "Purse Seines," John N. Cobb, "Pacific Salmon Fisheries," Bureau of Fisheries Document 902 *Report of the Commissioner of Fisheries for 1921* (Washington, DC: United States Government Printing Office, 1921); George B. Kelez, "The Purse-Seine Fishery," IN George A. Rounsefell and George B. Kelez, *The Salmon and Salmon Fisheries of Swiftsure Bank, Puget Sound, and the Fraser River* (Bulletin of the Bureau of Fisheries No. 27, Washington, DC: United States Government Printing Office, 1938); "Purse Seines," Robert J. Browning, *Fisheries of the North Pacific: History, Species & Processes* (Anchorage: Alaska Northwest Publishing Company, 1974), pp 142-181, and John Wade, "Changes in Fishing Gear over the Years," IN John Wade and Terry Jackson, *The Link between the Two Harbors* (n.d.), pp.78-80. Just recently (September 9, 2021), I watched as a seiner set their purse on Salmon Bank off South Beach, San Juan Island.

Fish Traps: For studying fish traps, see the plans (surveys) of traps on file at the Northwest Regional State Archives, Bellingham; John Goekler, "The Fish Traps...An Island Heritage," *The Islands' Weekly*, February 6-13, 1996; and Beryl Troxell Mason's *John Franklin Troxell, Fish Trap Man* (Lopez Island: Watmough Publishing, 1991).

Trolling: "Trolling," John N. Cobb, "Pacific Salmon Fisheries," Bureau of Fisheries Document 1902 *Report of the Commissioner of Fisheries for 1921* (Washington, DC: United States Government Printing Office, 1930) pp. 86-89; "Trolling," Patricia Ann Berringer, *Northwest Coast Traditional Salmon Fisheries*

Systems of Resource Utilization (MA Thesis, University of British Columbia, 1982) pp. 22-27; and "The Troll Fishery," Robert J. Browning, *Fisheries of the North Pacific: History, Species & Processes* (Anchorage: Alaska Northwest Publishing Company, 1974), pp. 216-237.

Weirs: J. Tait Elder et al., "On the Role of Coastal Landscape Evolution in Detecting Fish Weirs: A Pacific Northwest Coast Example from Washington State," *The Journal of Island Coastal Archaeology*, published online March 14, 2014.

Trawling: "Trawls," Robert J. Browning, *Fisheries of the North Pacific: History, Species & Processes* (Anchorage: Alaska Northwest Publishing Company, 1974), pp. 193-216.

Longlines: "Longlines and their Use," Robert J. Browning, *Fisheries of the North Pacific: History, Species & Processes* (Anchorage: Alaska Northwest Publishing Company, 1974), pp. 237-248.

Pots: "Pot Gear and its Use," Robert J. Browning, *Fisheries of the North Pacific: History, Species & Processes* (Anchorage: Alaska Northwest Publishing Company, 1974), pp. 249-255.

Harvesting kelp: "From Seaweed to Gunpowder," *The Shopper* February 5, 1986.

Preservation

Canning and canneries: General studies on canning include: John N. Cobb, *The Canning of Fish Products* (Seattle: Miller Freeman, Publisher, 1919); Charles L. Cutting, *Fish Saving: A History of Fish Processing from Ancient to Modern Times* (London: Leonard Hill, 1955); N. D. Jarvis, "Curing and Canning of Fishery Products: A History," *Marine Fisheries Review* 50(4):180-185; and Kit Oldham, *The first salmon cannery on the Columbia River opens at Eagle Cliff, Wahkiakum County, in 1866*, HistoryLink Essay 8036 posted 12/20/2006. Specific studies include: August C. Radke, *Pacific American Fisheries, Inc.: History of a Washington State Salmon Packing Company, 1890-1966* (Jefferson, NC: McFarland and Company, 2002); David Wilma, *Automated salmon cleaning machine developed in Seattle in 1903* HistoryLink Essay 2109 posted 1/01/2000; Lynn Weber/Roochvarg, *Chinese Workers in the San Juan Islands* HistoryLink Essay 11197 posted 3/4/2016 and *Japanese Community in the San Juan Islands, 1880-1942* HistoryLink Essay 11198 posted 3/7/2016; and *Special Report on the Salmon Canning Industry of the State of Washington as Relating to the Employment of White Labor, Made by the State Commissioner of Labor, November, 1915* (Olympia: State Bureau of Labor, 1915).

Modern Mariculture

Most of the sources for modern mariculture in the Salish Sea are from with the company's websites (Westcott Bay Sea Farms, Judd Cove Shellfish, Sweetwater Shellfish [Jones Family Farm], and Buck Bay Shellfish Farm) or press reportage on the industry, particularly the (Lopez) *Island Record, Islands' Weekly,* and the *Journal of the San Juans*.

Commercial Fishing During the Modern Period

Charles O. Junge, Jr., "Commercial Salmon Fishing Intensity in Puget Sound, 1939-1955," *Fisheries Research Papers* 2, no. 2:48-51 (Washington State Department of Fisheries, 1959) and Hans D. Radtke, *Washington State Commercial Fishing Industry: Total Economic Contribution*, prepared for the Seattle Marine Business Coalition, 2011.

Recreational Fishing

Gerry Kristianson and Deane Strongitharm, "The Evolution of Recreational Salmon Fisheries in British Columbia," Report to the Pacific Fisheries Resource Conservation Council (June 2006) and Washington State Department of Fish and Wildlife, *Washington State Sport Catch Reports* (the most recent is for the 'year' 2018-2019).

Government Agencies

United States Fisheries. Various government agencies have issued reports on fishing in the region. In the United States, at the federal level, these include, in chronological order: J. W.

Collins, "Report on the fisheries of the Pacific coast of the United States," IN *United States Commission on Fish and Fisheries report for 1888* (Washington, DC: United States Government Printing Office, 1892); J. G. Swan, "Notes on the Fisheries and the Fishery Industries of Puget Sound," IN *Bulletin of the United States Fish Commission* (Washington, DC: United States Government Printing Office 1894); William A. Wilcox, "The Fisheries of the Pacific Coast," *Report of the Commissioner for the Year Ending June 30, 1893* (Washington, Dc: Government Printing Office, 1894); William A Wilcox, "Notes on the Fisheries of the Pacific Coast in 1895," *Report of the Commissioner for the Year Ending June 30, 1896* (Washington, Dc: Government Printing Office, 1898); Richard Rathbun, "A Review of the Fisheries in the Contiguous Waters of the State of Washington and British Columbia," IN *Report of the United States Commissioner of Fish and Fisheries for the Fiscal Year Ending June 30, 1899* (Washington, DC: United States Government Printing Office, 1900); John N. Cobb, "Salmon Fisheries of the Pacific Coast," Bureau of Fisheries Document 751, *Report of the Commissioner of Fisheries for 1910* (Washington, DC: United States Government Printing Office, 1911); John N. Cobb, "Pacific Salmon Fisheries," Bureau of Fisheries Document 1902 *Report of the Commissioner of Fisheries for 1921* (Washington, DC: United States Government Printing Office, 1930); and George A. Rounsefell and George B. Kelez, *The Salmon and Salmon Fisheries of Swiftsure Bank, Puget Sound, and the Fraser River* (Bulletin of the Bureau of Fisheries No. 27, Washington, DC: United States Government Printing Office, 1938).

 Canada Fisheries. Vancouver Island and British Columbia, formed as the colony of British Columbia in 1866, did not enter the Canadian Confederation until 1871, so it was not until the 1872 Fifth Annual Report that Department of Marine and Fisheries began to report on the region. In 1876, the *Fisheries Act of Canada* was extended to British Columbia. Recent and current publications are available online at the Fisheries and Oceans Canada (DFO) website.

Regulation

The reports of the Washington State Fisheries regulation were published in Olympia, WA, by the State Printer: Reports 1–31 (1890–1921) are *Annual Reports of the State Fish Commissioner*; Reports 32–35 (1922–1925) are *Annual Reports of the State Supervisor of Fisheries*; Reports 36–41 (1926–1931) are *Annual Reports of the State Department of Fisheries and Game, Division of Fisheries*; and Reports 42–88 (1932–1978) are *Annual Reports of the State Department of Fisheries*. A signal report is L. H. Darwin, *The Fisheries of the State of Washington* (Olympia, WA: Washington State Bureau of Statistics and Immigration, 1916).

Public Interest Studies by educational institutions and non-profits include: Manfred C. Vernon and James W. Scott, eds. *Fisheries in Puget Sound: Public Good and Private Interest*, Occasional Paper #9, Center for Pacific Northwest Studies, Western Washington State College 1977.

Washington State regulation of fishing: Dennis A. Austin, *State of Washington Legislative Laws Pertaining to Puget Sound Salmon Fisheries, 1889 through 1920* (Olympia, WA: Department of Fisheries, Management and Research Division, 1972).

Treaty Rights: Russel L. Barsh, *The Washington Fishing Rights Controversy: An Economic Critique* (Seattle: University of Washington Graduate School of Business Administration, 1977); Daniel L. Boxberger, "Handbook of Western Washington Indian Treaties: With Special Attention to Treaty Fishing Rights," *Contributions to Aquaculture and Fisheries, Occasional Paper 1* (Lummi Island, WA: Lummi College of Fisheries, 1979); Beatrice Annette Lowman, "Reef Nets Come Back in Puget Sound Fishery," *Pacific Fisherman* June, 1939: pp. 45-48; and Ann Nugent, *Lummi Elders Speak* (Lynden, WA: Lummi Indian Business Council and Lynden Tribune, 1982).

International regulation of fishing: W. A. Carrothers, *The Fishing Industry of British Columbia*, unpublished manuscript on file, Royal British Columbia Museum and Archives, Victoria, BC (1937); William F. Thompson, "Effect of the Obstruction at Hell's Gate on the Sockeye Salmon of the Fraser River," *International Pacific Fisheries Commission, Bulletin #1* (New Westminster, BC, 1945); John F. Roos, *Restoring Fraser River Salmon: A History of* the *International Pacific Salmon Commission, 1937-1985* (Vancouver: Pacific Salmon Commission, 1991); Kit Oldham, "Canada and the United States sign the Pacific Halibut Convention on March 2, 1923," HistoryLink Essay 9152 posted 9/10/2009; and Lissa K. Wadewitz, *The Nature of Borders: Salmon, Boundaries, and Bandits of the Salish Sea* (Seattle: University of Washington Press, 2012).

Environmental concerns
   Overviews: Dr. Kathryn Sobocinski, *State of the Salish Sea Report* (Bellingham: Salish Sea Institute, 2021), available online; United States Environmental Protection Agency and Environment and Climate Change Canada, *Health of the Salish Sea Report* (2021), available online at EPA website; and Jewell Praying Wolf James, "The Search for Integrity in the Conflict over Cherry Point Coal Export Terminal," Special Insert from the Lummi Nation, *Whatcom Watch* August 2, 2013.

   Climate change: Dr. Kathryn Sobocinski, *State of the Salish Sea Report* (Bellingham: Salish Sea Institute, 2021), and available online, and United States Environmental Protection Agency and Environment and Climate Change Canada, *Health of the Salish Sea Report* (2021), available online at EPA website.

   Piracy, Poaching, and Derelict Gear: reportage on piracy and poaching in the Salish Sea has been covered by both the regional American and Canadian Press. For ***ghost nets***, see Thomas P. Good et al, "Ghosts of the Salish Sea: Threats to Marine Birds in Puget Sound and the Northwest Straits from Derelict Fishing Gear" *Marine Ornithology* 37:67-76 (2009); Washington Department of Fish and Wildlife Derelict Fishing Gear Removal Project, under "Species & Habitats," "Habitat and recovery protection"; and "Executive Summary," *Southern Resident Orca Task Force* November 2019.

   Finfish Net Pens: reportage on local (Lopez Island) finfish net pens occurred in both the *Islands' Weekly* and the *Journal of the San Juans*. Other reports include Anna Dabrowski, Fall 2010 Marine Environment Research Apprentice, "Net Pen Salmon Farming in the San Juan Islands: an analysis of Shoal Bay, Lopez Island; Griffin Bay, San Juan Island; Deepwater Bay,

Cypress Island," on file, Friday Harbor Laboratories, University of Washington, and Arthur H. Whiteley, Professor Emeritus at the Department of Zoology, University of Washington, January 17, 2002 letter to Lori LeVander, Permit Manager, Washington State Department of Ecology. Current conditions are reported by Lynda Mapes, "Fish farm caused Atlantic salmon spill near San Juans" *Seattle Times* January 30, 2018 and regional American and Canadian newspapers as well as the Wild Fish Conservancy *http://wildfishconservancy.org/industrial-fish-farms-threaten-puget-sound-once-more*.

Southern Resident killer whales: There are many publications on Southern Resident killer whales, the latest being Lynda Mapes, *Orca: Shared Waters, Shared Home* (Seattle: Braided River, 2021). Reports on the current state of the Southern Residents include Washington State Governor Jay Inslee, Southern Resident Orca Task Force, *Year One Report* (November 2018) and *Year Two Report* (November 2019) and NOAA *Species in the Spotlight Priority Actions 2021-2025* (March 2021).

Salmon Preservation and Restoration

Washington State Governor's Salmon Recovery Office, *2020 State of Salmon*; Marie Fazio, "Northwest's Salmon Population May Be Running Out of Time," *The New York Times* January 21, 2021; Dr. Kathryn Sobocinski, *State of the Salish Sea Report* (Bellingham: Salish Sea Institute, 2021); Long Live the Kings website *https://lltk.org/*; San Juan County Land Bank website: Nature Notes: Coho Reserve, Orcas Island, WA *https://sjclandbank.org/nature-notes-cascade-creek-fish/*; and Lynda Mapes, *Elwha: A River Reborn* (Seattle: Mountaineers Books, 2013).

PHOTO AND ILLUSTRATION CREDITS

Lopez Island Historical Society

Reed Shipyard, Decatur Island: Boat Built 1903 for Henry Cayou (2002.001.00212)

Pile Driving a Fish Trap (1985.001.00227)

Tarring Webs for the Oceanic Canning Company (1985.001.314)

Diver Jumping off Scow to Set Fish Trap Webs (1985.001.00305)

Watchman on Fish Trap (1985.001.00238)

Purse Seiners at Anchor, Aleck Bay, Lopez Island (1985.001.00076)

Gillnetters Waiting Turn of the Tide (1985.001.00075)

Wa Chong Company Letter (2021.001.00009a)

Women Cannery Workers, Wander Inn, Richardson, Lopez Island (1985.001.00292)

Richardson Cannery from Woody Island (1985.001.00346)

Canneries at Richardson, Lopez Island (1985.001.00288)

Hodgson Graham Cannery, Richardson, Lopez Island (1985.001.00246)

Hidden Inlet Cannery with Fishing Boats (1985.001.00235)

Tent Camp for Fishers at Lovejoy Point, Richardson, Lopez Island (1985.001.00228)

Orcas Island Historical Museum

Buckhorn Lodge with Fishers and their Catch, Orcas Island, WA, August 1928

Brochure, Salmon Bright Lodge

San Juan Island Historical Museum

Reef Net Fishing in Mitchell Bay (805.1)

Purse Seining on Salmon Bank (767.52)

Coast Salish Fishermen Reef Netting off Stuart Island (767.141)

Modern Reef Netters off Stuart Island (767.153)

Purse Seiners, Kanaka Bay (767.74)

Purse Seiner Home 2 (764.53)

Kanaka Bay Boats and Houses (784.1)

Fishing Boats Rafted at the Friday Harbor Packing Company Cannery (764.165)

Graignic Family in the City of Paris (778.142)

Women Cannery Workers (767.142)

Cans in Cannery Warehouse (767.102)

Fish Can Label (767.144)

Fish on Cannery Floor, Iron Chink (767.162)

Cookers in Cannery (767.154)

Nereid and other Fishing Boats at Friday Harbor Packing Company (767.71)

Reef Netters Bringing Their Catch to Sell (767.18)

John Ross, Sr. Family Encampment at Eagle Point (767.99)

Steamer Violet Transporting UW FH Labs Students (764.24)

UW Friday Harbor Biology Station (765.16)

Camping Tents at Fleming Place (767.26a)

Mending Nets (767.78)

Fishing Boats Rafted at the Cannery (764.121)

Tacoma Public Library, Northwest Room

Men Brailing Salmon from Shultz and Gross Fish Trap into the *Michigan* (WIL (C)-005)

Loading Scows at Shultz and Gross Fish Trap (WIL (C)-014)

Salmon Fishing on Puget Sound—Hauling in the Net (CNC-11)

UC Davis and Moss Laboratories

Bathymetry of the San Juan Islands

Graphs and Maps

Graphs and Maps by Lovel and Boyd C. Pratt

INDEX

A

Alaska Packers Association, 61, 79, 180, 203, 222–223, 282, 284, 296, 302

Aleck Bay, 76, 78–79, 88, 277, 281, 340

Anacortes, 72, 76, 78, 89, 94–95, 129, 135, 137, 151, 159, 174, 182, 196–197, 202, 212, 218, 282–286, 297, 300, 304–305, 311, 314–315, 318, 320–321, 333, 337–338, 341, 352–354, 362

anchovy, 128–129, 268

Andrews Bay, 41, 61, 67, 75–76, 86–87, 104, 145, 278, 282, 296

Andrews Bay Fish Company, 296

Argyle Spit, 178, 294, 300, 331

B

barrel, 126, 142, 154, 203, 349–350

barreling, 154, 347–348, 361

beach seine, 122

beach seining, 87, 122, 332, 347

Belle Vue Sheep Farm, 54, 155, 198, 292

Bellingham Bay Fishing Company, 296, 300–301, 304

Blaine, 61, 74, 76, 137, 159, 202, 281, 284, 299, 304, 316, 337

Blind Bay, 135, 176, 294

boats, 19-26, 55-59, 306-323

    barque, 345

brig, 345

clinker-built, 55, 82, 342, 346–347, 358

dory, 87, 346, 347

dugout, 18, 55, 107, 341, 358

lapstrake, 55, 342

launch, 56–57, 109, 308, 312, 314, 319–321, 323, 345

schooner, 48, 114–115, 129–130, 133, 312, 314, 316–322, 345

scow, 55, 67–71, 88, 90, 92–93, 95, 136, 158, 226, 316, 345–346

sloop, 48, 56, 122, 295, 307, 309, 313, 317, 319, 330, 345

Boldt Decision, 61, 228–229, 241, 332, 359, 362

Broder, John, 173, 292, 300, 324

Buck Bay, 149, 366

Bugge, S. M., 141, 174, 290, 304, 324

Bush and Callow Acts, 143, 145

C

Cagey, Joe, 324

Campbell, A. R., 324

camps, 25, 38–39, 45, 60, 72, 95, 126, 193, 197, 199, 202

canning, 68, 75–76, 78–79, 108, 125, 128, 140, 146, 157–158, 160–162, 166–167, 169–170, 172–173, 176, 179–180, 182–183, 185–189, 191–192, 204, 222, 226–227, 234–235, 282, 285–286, 288–294, 296–299, 301–305, 312–315, 317, 319–321, 326, 331–333, 337, 340, 348–349, 352, 354, 365–366 canoes, 18–23, 25–26, 29–30, 37–38, 42, 55, 72, 82, 103, 107, 130, 199, 342, 344, 346, 358

    Nootkan, 19–21, 25, 103

    northern or Haida, 23

    Salish, 20

    shovel nose, 22

Cascade Creek, 257

Cayou, Henry T., 56, 74, 87, 146, 281–282, 305, 313–314, 316–317, 320, 323, 325-326

Chevalier, Ed, 85, 325

Chlopeck Fish Company, 157, 189, 296, 325

Chlopeck, Con and Ed, 325

Chun Ching Hock, 329

City of Paris, 122, 313

Clallam, 236, 337

clam garden, 28–29

clams, 17, 28, 45–47, 117, 140–141, 147, 150, 173–174, 196, 212, 242, 262, 290, 293, 297, 300, 304–305, 333

climate change, 239–240, 242–243, 250, 256, 352

Coast Fish Canning Company, 297

Coast Salish, 19, 22, 24, 27–30, 33–34, 41–43, 45, 55, 60, 102, 129, 134, 155, 196, 230, 232, 267, 277, 350, 353, 355–356, 358–359

Cobb, John N., 110–111, 154, 176, 189, 191, 220, 234, 273, 325, 357, 360, 363–365, 367

cod, 31, 42, 48, 52–53, 113–114, 132–133, 136, 233, 242, 269, 307, 319, 335

Coffin, Herbert "Bert" Lester, 326

Columbia River, 21, 50, 60, 87, 102–105, 111, 158, 186, 221, 230, 251–252, 257, 299, 315, 345, 355, 363–365

Columbia River Salmon Boat, 102

Comeau, F. J., 176, 326

crab, 30, 126, 137-8, 150, 174, 211–213, 241–242, 244–245, 261, 264, 297, 313, 321, 335

crab traps, 244–245

Croatian, 59, 94, 100, 105, 197, 203, 310–311, 315, 338, 362

Crook, James and William, 56, 307

Crosby, Gerald, 305, 315, 326, 338

Cypress Island Packing Company, 297

D

Davis and Myers Fish Company, 297

Davis, R. E., 155, 288–289, 315, 326

Deadman Bay, 282

Decatur Island, 17, 56–57, 75, 138, 146, 223, 277, 281, 308, 312–314, 316–318, 320–323, 326, 335

Deep Sea Fish Company, 65, 79, 297

Deer Harbor, 41, 74, 146, 170, 176, 178, 204, 214–215, 217, 281–283, 285–286, 288, 290–292, 297, 299, 301, 305, 322, 325, 334

Deer Harbor Fisheries Company, 291, 297, 334

Deer Harbor Packing Company, 288, 290–292, 297, 301, 305

Deming, Ed, 79, 184, 326-327

Dennsion Brothers, 307, 327

derbies, 217–218

derelict gear, 244, 352

devil fish, 151, 265

diving, 117, 151, 153

dogfish, 113–114, 126, 134, 136, 267, 274, 311, 357

Dot Island, 75, 223, 281

Douglas, Abel, 114, 316–317, 320, 327

Douglas, James, 51, 54

E

Eagle Point, 61, 278, 282, 325

Eastsound, 146, 214, 334

Edwards, Dick, 81, 327

eelgrass, 29, 238, 261, 264, 267

Einstos, Sigmund, 327-328

El Nino - Southern Oscillation, 7–8

Euro American, 21, 23–24, 32, 55, 60, 85, 122, 169, 196, 200, 358, 361–362

European, 48, 60, 125, 149, 191, 359

Everett Fish Company, 157, 298

F

Fairhaven, 75, 118, 141, 146, 159, 189, 191

False Bay, 201, 234, 257, 283

finfish net pens, 245–246, 352

fish trap, 41, 63, 65–67, 69–71, 73, 75–79, 87, 104, 145, 194, 197, 200, 204–205, 221, 223, 226, 280, 283, 289, 296, 304, 323–325, 329, 339, 346, 348, 362, 364

fish trapping, 35, 60, 347

Fisheries and Oceans Canada, 134, 209–210, 219, 238, 242–243, 245, 247

Fisherman Bay, 58, 86, 146, 290, 309, 312, 328, 332, 337, 360

Fishery Point, 124–125, 157, 295, 338

fishing lodges, 214

fishing villages, 198

Fitzhugh, Charles Mason, 337

Fleming, James, 201, 328

flounder, 114, 268–269

forage fish, 243, 252, 268

Fortmann, Henry Frederick, 180, 296, 328

Fowler, Bert, Gene, and George, 307, 315, 319, 328

Fraser River, 34, 37, 50, 53, 61, 75, 78, 118–120, 139, 170, 195–196, 220, 223, 227, 230, 252–253, 270–271, 296, 328–329, 332, 360, 364, 367

freezing, 189–192, 347, 350

fresh fish, 83, 86, 123, 157, 189–192, 299, 325, 346, 348

Friday Harbor Biology Station, 233–234

Friday Harbor Marine Laboratories, 233–234

Friday Harbor Packing Company, 56, 66, 76, 79, 108, 158, 170–172, 192, 200, 203, 283, 292, 298–299, 308–309, 314, 318, 329, 337, 340

G

George & Barker Company, 75, 201–202, 281, 299, 316

George W. Hume Company, 288, 291, 334

Giard, Jack, 86, 329, 354, 360, 362

gillnetting, 34, 35, 100-101, 102–107, 112, 178, 197, 210, 228, 315, 345, 362

Goon Dip, 168, 327

Gould, J. A., 166, 172, 181, 289, 301, 329, 331

Graignic, Edouard, 87, 122, 124, 135, 196, 288, 295, 313, 329

Great Northern Fish Company, 75, 155, 195, 298, 315

Griffin, Charles, 198

Gross, Samuel, 75–76, 145, 296, 304, 329, 337

H

Haines Oyster Company, 56, 137, 299, 310, 317, 319, 321–322, 329, 340

Haines, H. L., 137, 322, 329-330

halibut, 30, 42, 48–49, 53, 113–114, 124, 126, 129–133, 211–212, 224, 268–269, 295, 328, 333, 335, 357

Harvester King, 139, 315

Haubner, John W., 162-172, 330

Hell's Gate, 118–120, 223, 227, 253

Henry Island, 41, 61, 75, 82, 85–87, 145, 200, 277, 281, 304, 335

herring, 29, 31–34, 42, 87, 93, 107, 110–111, 122–129, 157, 261, 266–268, 271, 288, 293–295, 297, 303, 328, 333, 335, 338, 357

Hidden Inlet Canning Company, 298, 317

Hix, L. D., 330

Hodgson-Graham Cannery, 174, 290, 298

Hoffman, Del, 307, 317, 319, 330–331

Home II, 99, 316

hotels, 214

Hudson's Bay Company, 49–50, 53, 122, 155, 198, 206, 288, 292, 345, 352, 361

I

Iceberg Point, 40, 78, 82, 86–87, 118, 277, 281, 299, 319, 324, 326–327, 336

Iceberg Point Fish Company, 299

Initiative 77, 225–226

Iron Chink, 158, 162–163, 166, 177, 338

Island Packing Company, 140–141, 146, 157, 166, 168–169, 171, 173–174, 181–182, 189, 283, 290, 292–293, 297–300, 304, 317, 324, 328, 331, 333, 336, 340

J

Jackson Cannery, 169, 178, 294, 300, 316, 332, 339, 360

Jackson, John, 178, 294, 330

Jensen's Shipyard, 307–308, 311, 313–314, 317–318, 320

Jensen, Albert and Nourdine, 56, 207, 308, 312–315, 319, 321–322, 330

Johns Island, 277, 281

Jones, Bert "Spider," 331

Jorgensen, John, 331-332

Judd Cove, 147, 245, 366

Julius, Jay, 332

K

Kanaka Bay, 24, 88–89, 95, 102–103, 108, 200–203, 278, 283, 305, 327

Keen, F. W., 181, 328, 332, 338

Kellet Ledge, 74, 281, 326

kelp, 29–30, 33, 35, 37, 41, 46, 71, 107, 111, 126, 130, 132, 138–139, 200, 232, 238, 261, 263, 266, 269, 278, 303, 315, 365

Kennerly, C. B. R., 41, 49, 198–199, 233, 361

Kertula, John, 196, 332

Kincaid, Trevor, 145, 233, 332

Kinleyside, R. C., 146, 172, 289, 301, 332-333

L

Ladner, Thomas E. , 333

Lawrence, Jim, 162, 179, 228, 333, 362

Lawrence, Lisa Nash, 333

Lemaister, Harry, 87, 333

Little, Pearl, 337

lobster, 40, 138

Long Live the Kings, 257

Loomis, Lorraine, 240, 333

Lopez Island, 17, 40–41, 49, 55, 57, 66–69, 74, 76, 78, 82, 86–88, 103, 118, 137–138, 141, 143, 146–147, 149, 155, 167, 169–170, 172, 174–175, 189, 200–201, 204–206, 214, 217, 238, 245, 259, 277, 281, 289–290, 296–298, 300–301, 303–305, 308–309, 311–314, 316–318, 320–321, 324, 326–329, 331–332, 334, 336–337, 339, 353–355, 360, 362, 364

Lowman, Beatrice "Reef Net Betty," 85–86, 333-334

Lowman, Will, 319, 332-334, 340

Lummi, 19, 28–29, 32, 38, 45–46, 55, 60–62, 74, 78, 80, 85–86, 99, 159, 173, 193, 222, 226, 279, 284, 289, 296, 300, 351, 353, 356–358

M

Mackaye Harbor, 58, 188, 204

marinas, 214, 216–217

Mary C., 56, 309, 317, 335

Mead, George, 140, 173, 293, 300, 334

Michigan, 70, 188, 317

Mills, Norman, 84, 325, 334

Mitchell Bay, 43, 67, 74–76, 86, 102, 125–126, 129, 135, 155, 157, 193, 195, 197–198, 278, 283, 293, 298, 303–304, 320, 325, 329, 335–337, 339

Mitchell Bay Band, 74, 193, 325, 335

Mordhorst, Bernhardt, 124, 146, 288, 294, 325, 334-335

N

National Oceanic and Atmospheric Administration, 245, 356

Nereid, 56, 172, 318

Newhall, Andrew, 56, 233, 308–309, 335, 337

NOAA, 238, 250, 356

nori, 139, 319

Norman, Michael and Arthur, 57, 308–309, 335

Norman Shipyard, 308–309

North American Fisheries Company, 191, 300

North of Falcon, 241, 332

North Pacific Gyre Oscillation, 8

North West Boundary Survey, 316, 361

Northern Pacific Fisheries Company, 291–292, 301

Northwest Indian Fisheries Commission, 239–240, 332

Northwest Straits Commission, 236

Norton, William "Bill" J., 335

O

Oceanic Canning Company, 68, 146, 172, 288–289, 296, 301, 319, 331–332

octopus, 30, 42, 117, 151, 265

Olga, 56, 107, 135, 137, 308, 310–311, 340

Olsen, Christ and Herman, 356

Open Bay, 41, 61, 82, 85–87, 103, 145, 200, 277, 281, 335

Orcas Island, 17, 41, 56, 74, 78, 85–86, 104, 107, 132, 135, 140, 149, 199, 204, 206, 214–217, 245, 257, 259, 277, 282, 290–291, 296, 301, 304–305, 308–311, 318–319, 325, 329–330, 334, 340, 353–354

Orcas Island Canning Company, 290–291, 301

P

Pacific American Fisheries, 69, 75, 79, 118, 126, 157, 166, 171, 180–182, 184, 195, 203, 222–223, 283–284, 292, 298–300, 302, 317, 327, 340, 365

Pacific Decadal Oscillation, 7

Pacific Fishery Management Council, 241

Pacific Packing & Navigation Company, 300, 302

Pe-el, 74, 325, 336

Perovich, Carl, 336

Phillips, Tom, 338

pickling, 154–155, 348–349

pile driving, 66, 194, 329

Pile Point, 61, 197, 278

piracy, 72, 244, 352, 362

pirates, 72–73, 200, 354, 362–363

poaching, 117, 244, 352

Point Roberts, 60–62, 75, 81, 85, 100, 137, 159, 201, 222, 279, 299

Port Townsend Packing Company, 282, 287, 302

power block, 96, 100

public facilities, 193, 206

Puget Sound Fish Company, 303

Puget Sound Partnership, 237

Puget Sound Potash and Kelp Fertilizer Company, 138, 303, 315

purse seining, 59, 77, 88–89, 93–99, 101-101, 106, 112, 196–197, 200, 202, 210, 220, 225–226, 310, 337-338, 347, 364

R

recreational fishing, 208, 366

Red Cross Fish Company, 125, 157, 293, 303

Reed & Cayou, 308–309

Reed, Bill, 336

Reed, Joe, 308–309, 336

reef netting, 17, 19, 22, 25–26, 35, 37–38, 45, 55, 60-61, 80–86, 189, 195-6, 227, 271-7, 311, 316, 325, 328, 332–333, 336, 339, 346-347 353, 355, 358–360

Reid Bay, 294

resorts, 214, 216

Roche Harbor, 75–76, 145, 173, 198, 216–217, 281–283, 285, 296, 319, 333, 337

rockfish, 113, 132–134, 237, 242, 269

roe gathering, 32

Ross, John, 196, 198, 316–317, 336-337

Roys, Thomas Welcome, 337

S

Saanich, 35, 40, 44, 74, 102, 114, 193, 231, 317, 361

Salmon, 118-121, 251-257, 270-274

    Chinook, 34–35, 100, 104, 142, 154, 156, 189, 196, 209–210, 212, 221, 226, 230, 239, 242, 248–253, 257, 270–271, 275

    chum, 154, 189, 210, 212, 221, 226, 255, 257, 270–271

    coho, 34, 100, 104, 108–109, 111, 154, 189, 196, 209–210, 212, 217, 221, 226, 230, 242, 245, 250–251, 255, 257, 270–271

    pink, 34, 117–118, 136, 150, 210, 212, 221, 226, 254, 262, 264–265, 270–271

    sockeye, 61–62, 74, 76, 80, 82, 100, 118, 120–121, 154, 179, 183, 185, 187, 189, 192, 210, 212, 221, 226–227, 230, 253–254, 256, 270–271, 320, 340

    steelhead, 211–212, 221, 228, 241, 248, 251–252, 257, 270–271, 274

Salmon Bank, 49, 61, 63, 73, 79–80, 105, 107, 118, 167, 174, 180, 283–286, 288–290, 298, 305, 315, 321, 327, 335, 354, 364

salting, 51, 54, 126, 154–155, 157, 178, 189, 195, 288–289, 326, 330, 348–350

Samish, 44, 86, 103, 143–146, 158, 193, 212, 238, 241, 243, 252, 324, 336, 355

Samish, Harry, 337

San Juan Canning Company, 108, 173, 187, 286, 288, 293, 303–304, 312

San Juan County Marine Resources Committee, 236

Saoka, Jack, 168, 337

Schruder Yard, 309

Schruder, Louie and Peter, 58, 311, 316, 337

Scribner, Ed and James, 309, 337-338

sea cucumbers, 28, 117, 152–153, 265–266

sea lions, 71, 200, 248, 274–275

sea urchins, 28, 42, 45, 117, 151–153, 266

sealing, 43, 114, 319

Sebelin Brothers, 309

Sebelin, Chris and William, 309, 338

Semiahmoo, 31, 34–35, 159, 193

set lines, 132

Shaw Island, 56, 86, 135, 176, 234, 259, 278, 287–288, 294, 304, 307, 311–312, 314–315, 317–319, 327–330

Shaw Island Canning Company, 176, 288, 294, 304

She-Kle-Malt, 338

shellfish farming, 147

shellfish harvesting, 208, 239, 241

shoreline structures, 193, 204–205, 350

shrimp, 56, 136–137, 151, 212–213, 241, 264–265, 275, 299, 310–311, 313, 317–319, 321–322, 329, 340

Shultz & Gross, 76, 181–182

Shultz, William, 75–76, 145, 172, 304, 315, 326, 329, 338-340

Skansi, Nick, 315, 326, 339

Skansie Shipyard, 59, 310, 339

Skansie, Andrew, Joe, Michael, and Peter, 59, 310, 339

smelt, 32, 122, 129, 268, 297

Smith, Edmund A., 162, 339

Songhees, 102, 193, 198

Songish, 26, 44

Sooke, 142, 193

Southern Resident killer whales, 239, 247–250, 274–275, 352

Sparrow Test, 230

sport fishing, 107, 209–210

State Fish Commissioner, 97–98, 111, 121, 137–138, 220–221, 338

Straits Salish, 29, 51, 345, 358

Stuart Island, 35, 82, 84–86, 124, 126, 129, 135, 139, 146, 195, 198, 238, 278, 287, 294, 319, 325, 333, 339, 354

sturgeon, 30–31, 74, 211–212, 242, 269, 325, 335

Swinomish, 228, 328, 332

T

tender, 56, 60, 83, 95, 192, 267, 307–308, 311–318, 320–322, 326, 328, 330, 338, 346

Thomas, Ashton and Ellery, 123–125, 340

Thomas, John "Johnny Tom," 340

trawling, 113, 134, 136, 365

Treaties, 17, 61, 228-229

trolling, 41, 107–110, 112, 189, 191, 196, 199, 214, 225–226, 271, 321, 347, 365

Troxell, John, 76, 78, 340

Tuana Packing Company, 141, 174, 288, 290, 304, 324

Tyee Fish Company, 291, 297, 304–305, 334

U

U.S. Coast and Geodetic Survey, 204

U.S. Coast Survey, 48, 197

United States Commission on Fish and Fisheries, 38, 190, 219, 367

V

Vandersluys, Cleve, 340-341

W

Wa Chong Company, 166–167, 329

Wade, Leith, 319–320, 341

Waldron Island, 17, 122, 124–125, 129, 135, 137, 145, 157, 278, 287, 295, 313, 317, 328, 331, 338, 354

Warbass, Ed, 233

Washington Department of Fish and Wildlife, 152–153, 222

Washington Fish & Oyster Company, 305, 326

Watmough Bay, 282, 305

Watmough Fish Company, 74, 282, 305

West Sound, 29, 129, 146, 204, 214, 291–292, 297, 301, 305, 316, 334

Westcott Bay, 92, 147–148, 286, 315, 366

Western Fisheries, 288, 291–292, 297, 305

whaling, 21, 43, 114–116, 316–317, 320, 327, 336

White Crest Canning Company, 297, 305, 314, 321, 333, 341

Whiteley, Arthur, 246

Willey, George J., 76, 172, 304, 337, 341

Willis, R. C. and Bruce, 56, 116, 135, 137, 151, 310–311, 341

Z

Zebeitka, 135, 322

Zeigler, Edgar J., 201

www.ingramcontent.com/pod-product-compliance
Lightning Source LLC
Chambersburg PA
CBHW072145070526
44585CB00015B/1004